Progress in Pain Research and Management
Volume 19

The Child with Headache: Diagnosis and Treatment

Mission Statement of IASP Press®

The International Association for the Study of Pain (IASP) is a nonprofit, interdisciplinary organization devoted to understanding the mechanisms of pain and improving the care of patients with pain through research, education, and communication. The organization includes scientists and health care professionals dedicated to these goals. The IASP sponsors scientific meetings and publishes newsletters, technical bulletins, the journal *Pain,* and books.

The goal of IASP Press is to provide the IASP membership with timely, high-quality, attractive, low-cost publications relevant to the problem of pain. These publications are also intended to appeal to a wider audience of scientists and clinicians interested in the problem of pain.

Previous volumes in the series
Progress in Pain Research and Management

Pharmacological Approaches to the Treatment of Chronic Pain: New Concepts and Critical Issues, edited by Howard L. Fields and John C. Liebeskind

Proceedings of the 7th World Congress on Pain, edited by Gerald F. Gebhart, Donna L. Hammond, and Troels S. Jensen

Touch, Temperature, and Pain in Health and Disease: Mechanisms and Assessments, edited by Jörgen Boivie, Per Hansson, and Ulf Lindblom

Temporomandibular Disorders and Related Pain Conditions, edited by Barry J. Sessle, Patricia S. Bryant, and Raymond A. Dionne

Visceral Pain, edited by Gerald F. Gebhart

Reflex Sympathetic Dystrophy: A Reappraisal, edited by Wilfrid Jänig and Michael Stanton-Hicks

Pain Treatment Centers at a Crossroads: A Practical and Conceptual Reappraisal, edited by Mitchell J.M. Cohen and James N. Campbell

Proceedings of the 8th World Congress on Pain, edited by Troels S. Jensen, Judith A. Turner, and Zsuzsanna Wiesenfeld-Hallin

Molecular Neurobiology of Pain, edited by David Borsook

Measurement of Pain in Infants and Children, edited by G. Allen Finley and Patrick J. McGrath

Sickle Cell Pain, by Samir K. Ballas

Assessment and Treatment of Cancer Pain, edited by Richard Payne, Richard B. Patt, and C. Stratton Hill

Chronic and Recurrent Pain in Children and Adolescents, edited by Patrick J. McGrath and G. Allen Finley

Opioid Sensitivity of Chronic Noncancer Pain, edited by Eija Kalso, Henry J. McQuay, and Zsuzsanna Wiesenfeld-Hallin

Psychological Mechanisms of Pain and Analgesia, by Donald D. Price

Proceedings of the 9th World Congress on Pain, edited by Marshall Devor, Michael C. Rowbotham, and Zsuzsanna Wiesenfeld-Hallin

Sex, Gender, and Pain, edited by Roger B. Fillingim

Pain Imaging, edited by Kenneth L. Casey and M. Catherine Bushnell

Progress in Pain Research and Management
Volume 19

The Child with Headache: Diagnosis and Treatment

Editors

Patricia A. McGrath, PhD

*Pain Innovations Inc., and Department of Pediatrics,
Faculty of Medicine, University of Western Ontario,
London, Ontario, Canada*

Loretta M. Hillier, MA

*Pain Innovations Inc.,
London, Ontario, Canada*

IASP PRESS® • SEATTLE

Library of Congress Cataloging-in-Publication Data

The child with headache : diagnosis and treatment / editors, Patricia A. McGrath, Loretta M. Hillier.
     p. ; cm. -- (Progress in pain research and management ; v. 19)
  Includes bibliographical references and index.
  ISBN 0-931092-30-2 (alk. paper)
  1. Headache in children. I. McGrath, Patricia A. II. Hillier, Loretta M., 1959- III. Series.
  [DNLM: 1. Headache Disorders--diagnosis--Child. 2. Headache Disorders--therapy--Child. WL 342 C536 2000]
RJ496.H3 C48 2000
618.92'8491--dc21

00-047140

Published by:

IASP Press
International Association for the Study of Pain
909 NE 43rd St., Suite 306
Seattle, WA 98105 USA
Fax: 206-547-1703
www.halcyon.com/iasp
www.painbooks.org

Printed in the United States of America

Contents

List of Contributing Authors   vii
Preface   ix
Acknowledgments   xi

1. Headache in Children: The Nature of the Problem
    Patricia A. McGrath   1

2. Headache Measures for Children: A Practical Approach
    Patricia A. McGrath and Andrea L. Koster   29

3. Differential Diagnosis of Headaches in Children
    and Adolescents
    A. David Rothner   57

4. Recurrent Headache: Triggers, Causes, and Contributing Factors
    Patricia A. McGrath and Loretta M. Hillier   77

5. Drug Therapies for Childhood Headache
    Simon D. Levin   109

6. Nondrug Therapies for Childhood Headache
    Patricia A. McGrath, Diane Stewart, and Andrea L. Koster   129

7. Treating Recurrent Headache: An Effective Strategy
    for Primary Care Providers
    Patricia A. McGrath and Loretta M. Hillier   159

8. A Cognitive-Behavioral Program for Treating
    Recurrent Headache
    Loretta M. Hillier and Patricia A. McGrath   183

9. Chronic Daily Headache in Children and Adolescents
    E. Wayne Holden, Pamela Bachanas, Kris Kullgren,
    and Jack Gladstein   221

10. Understanding Children's Headache: Current Status and
    Future Challenges
    Patricia A. McGrath   243

Appendix 1   Children's Headache Interview   253

Appendix 2   Parent Intake Form   267

Appendix 3   Parent Information Sheet: Migraine
             and Tension-Type Headache   281

Index   283

Contributing Authors

Pamela Bachanas, PhD *Department of Psychiatry and Behavioral Sciences, Emory University School of Medicine, Atlanta, Georgia, USA*

Jack Gladstein, MD *Department of Pediatrics, University of Maryland School of Medicine, Baltimore, Maryland, USA*

Loretta M. Hillier, MA *Pain Innovations Inc., London, Ontario, Canada*

E. Wayne Holden, PhD *ORC Macro Inc., Atlanta, Georgia, USA*

Andrea L. Koster, MA *Department of Psychology, University of Western Ontario, London, Ontario, Canada*

Kris Kullgren, PhD *Department of Psychiatry and Behavioral Sciences, Emory University School of Medicine, Atlanta, Georgia, USA*

Simon D. Levin, MD, FRCP *Department of Pediatrics, Faculty of Medicine, University of Western Ontario, London, Ontario, Canada*

Patricia A. McGrath, PhD *Pain Innovations Inc., London, Ontario, Canada; and Department of Pediatrics, Faculty of Medicine, University of Western Ontario, London, Ontario, Canada*

A. David Rothner, MD *Section of Child Neurology, The Cleveland Clinic Foundation, Cleveland, Ohio, USA*

Diane Stewart, MA *Pain Innovations Inc., London, Ontario, Canada*

Preface

In the last two decades, unprecedented scientific and clinical attention has focused on the special pain problems of children. Extensive research has created better insights into how children perceive pain and how clinicians can alleviate their suffering. However, undertreated pain continues to be a major problem for many infants, children, and adolescents. A large gap still exists between what we know about controlling children's pain and how we practice clinically, and the control of postoperative pain, cancer pain, painful sickling crises, and chronic pain remains problematic for children in many centers. In addition, we have learned that some pains traditionally regarded as "benign pains" of childhood represent a significant health and disability problem affecting many otherwise healthy children and adolescents.

Recurrent headaches are a cause of suffering and disability for children, a source of continuing anxiety and frustration for parents, and often a treatment challenge for health care providers. This book describes how to assess and treat children with headache from a multidisciplinary perspective, in a manner consistent with the neural and psychological mechanisms that mediate pain. Our intention is to provide a comprehensive text on diagnosis and treatment from a combined scientific and clinical perspective. We have invited experts in pediatric neurology and headache management to contribute their expertise in differential diagnosis, abortive and prophylactic drug therapies, nonpharmacological therapies (both traditional and complementary), and the management of chronic daily headache.

The first chapters present a framework for understanding the nature of childhood headache, including the extent of the problem, the objective assessment of headache features, and the differential diagnosis of headache type. In Chapter 4, we describe the common causative and contributing factors for the most prevalent types of childhood headache. We then introduce an assessment interview to enable health care providers to recognize which factors are relevant for which children. Children's headaches may be similar in type, frequency, and intensity, but may have quite different causative factors. Knowledge of the relevant factors for a particular child is essential for selecting the most appropriate treatment. Chapters 5 and 6 describe the myriad of drug and nondrug therapies available to treat headaches, present evidence for their effectiveness in children, and when possible describe explicit guidelines and contraindications for their use.

Chapters 7–9 detail how to use these therapies to prevent headaches, reduce pain, and minimize disability. We emphasize a comprehensive approach with treatment focused both on managing discrete headache episodes and on modifying the factors that provoke, exacerbate, or maintain the recurring pattern of headache. In Chapter 7, we describe a brief intervention for children with recurrent headache that was designed for use by primary health care providers. We describe a more intensive therapist-assisted pain management program for children with complex headaches and associated disability in Chapter 8. The difficult challenge of treating chronic daily headache is described in Chapter 9. Chapter 10 concludes the volume by presenting the unique challenges we face as we integrate an evidence-based, child-centered approach more efficiently into clinical practice.

These chapters cumulatively provide the information essential for accurate diagnosis and treatment of childhood headache. Diagnostic information, consistent with the International Headache Classification System, is repeated only as necessary to clarify the authors' descriptions of a specific headache type. We hope that this text provides a practical framework for understanding and assessing the factors that can trigger headache episodes, intensify pain, and prolong disability. We offer readers a cohesive rationale for selecting the most appropriate therapies for a particular child, based on consideration of the relevant causative and contributing factors.

PATRICIA A. MCGRATH
LORETTA M. HILLIER

Acknowledgments

We would like to express our sincere appreciation to the children and adolescents whose experiences have enabled us to learn much about the diagnosis and treatment of headache. In answering numerous questions about their headaches and their lives, they helped us understand the nature of their pain and its causative or contributing factors. Their participation in descriptive studies, pilot treatment programs, and randomized clinical trials enabled us to refine and evaluate effective pain management programs. We use pseudonyms in presenting case material to protect the confidentiality of these children and their families.

We are indebted to many colleagues who during the past 15 years shared our efforts to develop evidence-based treatment programs for children with headache as part of the mission for the Paediatric Pain Program at the University of Western Ontario. In particular, we would like to thank Cheryl E. Seifert for her outstanding research and administrative assistance, Sandra Boniface for her dedicated treatment of children with head injury, and George G. Hinton and James E. Boone for their consistent support of our pain clinic and research endeavors. We are also indebted to the Ontario Ministry of Health, Health and Welfare Canada (through its National Health Research and Development Program), the National Institutes of Health, the Children's Hospital of Western Ontario Foundation, and ChildCan for their support of various research studies on pain and headache in children.

We would like to thank IASP Press, particularly Elizabeth Endres, Roberta Scholz, and Dale Schmidt, for their positive suggestions, patient encouragement, and hard work on our behalf. We are indebted to Editor-in-Chief Howard L. Fields for reviewing selected chapters and for his helpful suggestions on differential diagnosis and drug therapies.

Finally, we would like to thank our friends and families for their constant support, especially John, Dan, Donna, Brian, Michelle, and Kaylee.

PATRICIA A. MCGRATH
LORETTA M. HILLIER

The Child with Headache: Diagnosis and Treatment.
Progress in Pain Research and Management, Vol. 19,
edited by Patricia A. McGrath and Loretta M. Hillier,
IASP Press, Seattle, © 2001.

1

Headache in Children: The Nature of the Problem

Patricia A. McGrath

*Pain Innovations Inc., London, Ontario, Canada; and Department of
Pediatrics, Faculty of Medicine, University of Western Ontario,
London, Ontario, Canada*

Headache, particularly migraine and tension-type headache, is a major problem for many children and adolescents. Headache causes significant suffering and disability in children, creates anxiety and disruption for their families, and represents a substantial cost to parents and the health care system. Clinical reports and descriptive studies have documented the features and presenting symptoms, but many questions remain unanswered about the etiology and management of childhood headache. Much attention has focused on elucidating the genetic, familial, environmental, and child characteristics that may predispose certain children to develop debilitating headache. Numerous studies in several countries have evaluated children with and without headache to identify risk factors and the psychosocial consequences of headache, but they have often yielded contradictory results.

This chapter evaluates what we know, presume, and speculate about the most common types of childhood headache. The chapter begins by describing the features and accompanying symptoms of headache, presenting the rationale for revising the classification of migraine. Prevalence data for childhood headache are summarized by age, sex, and country to illustrate the magnitude of this pain problem. The chapter concludes by reviewing the recognized risk factors and the impact of headache for children and their families.

A CHILD'S EXPERIENCE OF HEADACHE

Like adults, most children—even very young children—experience an occasional headache. Bille (1962) conducted interviews with the parents of

9000 Swedish schoolchildren. By the age of seven, 40% of the children had already experienced headache; this proportion increased to 75% by the age of 15. In a recent Canadian survey of children's pain experiences, 85% of the 5–7-year-old children interviewed had experienced headache, while the proportion increased to 100% for the 14–16-year-old adolescents (McGrath et al. 2000). Moreover, many of these children (58%) reported having had a headache in the previous month. They typically described the headache as lasting a few hours and rated the mean pain intensity at 5.9 on a 0–10 Colored Analog Scale (CAS, described in Chapter 2). However, most children did not regard these occasional headaches as a significant problem in their lives.

In contrast, as many as 40% of children and adolescents report that recurrent headache is a major cause of suffering and disability. These recurring pains are not symptoms of an underlying disease that requires medical treatment; instead, the recurrent headache syndrome is the disorder. Children's headache episodes vary widely in frequency. Some children suffer daily attacks for a few weeks, but then have no headaches for several months. Other children develop headache on an almost regular weekly or monthly basis. For most children there seem to be no obvious precipitating factors, and the attacks follow no predictable temporal pattern.

Headache intensity and duration also vary. A recent survey found that children with recurrent headache had a mean of 9.5 headaches (range 0–30) within the previous month; they rated their pain intensity as 6.5 (range 3–10) on the CAS (McGrath et al. 2000). Children reported various headache durations, including 1–2 hours (18%), 2.5–4 hours (16%), 4.5–6 hours (15%), and a few days (13%). They reported various frequencies of headaches, including 1 per month (20%), 1–2 per week (28%), 3–6 per week (15%), and constantly (15%).

The descriptions of children's headaches in this study are consistent with the information we have obtained in our research and clinical program through pain diaries, pain logs, and clinical interviews (McGrath 1987, 1990) and with data obtained in other descriptive studies (Vahlquist and Hackzell 1949; Bille 1962; Holguin and Fenichel 1967; Prensky 1976; Apley et al. 1978; Barlow 1984; McGrath and Unruh 1987; Hockaday 1988a; Ross and Ross 1988; Rothner 1993; Lee and Olness 1997; Welborn 1997). Most children's headaches vary extensively in frequency, length, and intensity. In addition, headache-related disability varies widely, from minor disruptions to children's activities during the headache to complete incapacitation during the attack and prolonged withdrawal from social and physical activities.

Headache in children may be unilateral but is usually bilateral, even for migraine. Children typically localize pain to the frontal and temporal regions.

They describe the pain quality either as "throbbing" or "aching," or (for young children) as "pounding" or "pushing." In our experience, these qualitative descriptions correspond to the neurologist's diagnosis of migraine and tension-type headache, respectively. While strong pain is typically associated with migraine, children's pain ratings for all types of headache vary along a continuum from mild to intense. Similarly, while nausea and vomiting are typically associated with migraine, many children satisfy the diagnostic criteria for migraine but do not experience nausea with each attack.

Although children may develop headache shortly after an obviously stressful event, usually there are no apparent triggers or warning signs. Parents may associate a child's pallor, lethargy, or irritable behavior with an impending headache, but few children experience a visual aura or any consistent physical warning sign. During each episode most children appear especially sensitive to light and sound, commonly reporting that bright lights and loud sounds intensify their pain. Children's responses to headache (their pain expression, use of interventions, disability behavior, and emotional distress) vary extensively and are not consistently correlated with headache severity. Some children become extremely distressed and disabled by relatively mild headache, while others continue their normal activities despite strong pain.

Recurrent headache creates uncertainty in parents, who typically continue to search for a clear-cut etiology. They often focus their search on environmental stimuli, tentatively identifying certain foods, weather conditions, or physical activities as probable causes. Parents may respond inconsistently to children's headache complaints, providing excessive emotional and physical support during some headache attacks, but suggesting that children manage independently during others. Parents may also increase their children's disability when they allow them to stay home from school, encourage them to withdraw from potentially stressful sports or social situations, and relieve them from routine responsibilities.

For example, Dennis, a 13-year-old boy, had experienced occasional headaches for several years. He was referred to our clinic because his headaches had increased following a head injury during a hockey game. Dennis had been pushed into the boards and for a few minutes afterwards he was unable to move his neck or head. Although medical tests revealed no abnormal findings, his headaches subsequently increased in frequency, occurring daily during some periods. He had missed 16 days of school in the past year due to headache.

Dennis described his headache as "a tight band around my head," with aching pain spreading to the top of his neck. The headache usually lasted 2–3 hours, but some stronger attacks lasted for several hours. He felt nauseous and dizzy throughout each attack. The pain intensity was quite variable, ranging from 5 to 10 on the CAS. During a headache, Dennis either tried to maintain his schedule or rested; he believed that sleeping was most effective. He also used acetaminophen for his strongest headaches, but felt distressed for a few hours even if the pain decreased.

Dennis's mother described him as a perfectionist who was very organized and liked routines. Because he was extremely responsible, his parents depended more on him for assistance than on their two other children. Dennis's relationships with his siblings were typically argumentative, and he was often irritated and angry with his peers at school.

Although Dennis's increased headache frequency coincided with his head injury, the pain assessment indicated that the primary cause was situation-specific stress related to his athletic and academic performance. Although he enjoyed hockey, he felt pressured to advance to a more competitive league. He had longstanding school difficulties and was unable to cope with the added stress of competitive hockey. His disability behavior was gradually increasing as his stress decreased, when he withdrew from hockey and school during headaches. (Our assessment interview is described in Chapter 8.)

Dennis completed a brief pain management program (Chapter 8), with a combined educational and behavioral emphasis. The therapist helped him to understand how his perceived lack of control in many situations triggered his emotional distress and subsequently caused a headache. Specifically, he was unable to cope with the normal teasing comments of his classmates at school, with the inevitable "ups and downs" of his performance in hockey and the reality of losses in some games, and with the different levels of responsibility given to him and his brothers. Dennis learned some basic problem-solving skills to improve his interactions with his classmates, teammates, and family. Although he had improved his interpersonal coping strategies, Dennis would continue to need assistance from his parents to effectively resolve some stressful situations. As part of his program, he also learned to use a few active methods of pain control depending on the situation in which he developed a headache, rather than only "toughing it out" or sleeping. At a follow-up appointment 3 months later, Dennis said that he had not experienced a headache since completing his program.

This case illustrates how internal and environmental factors can merge to blur the etiologic picture. Although some families recognize that stress resulting from children's anxieties about their performance in school, sports, and social situations can trigger headache, parents and children often believe that the primary cause is physical. Their continued focus on a previous injury or environmental stimulus leads them to overlook the true causative factors. As a consequence, children's anxiety increases, their headache worsens, and their disability behaviors gradually intensify. Headache (if attributed to external causes) is often inadvertently rewarded when children are allowed to stay home from school. Secondary gains associated with stress reduction may prolong a headache, extend disability, or contribute to new attacks when children are stressed.

In our experience, parents do not always seek health care assistance for a child's first mild headache, often believing that it is a common childhood headache that will dissipate naturally. If headaches recur (particularly if they are strong), parents bring their children to family physicians or pediatricians for evaluation. When routine medical examinations fail to reveal an organic disorder, parents may remain apprehensive about the cause for the headache and seek more specialized diagnostic tests. The longer children continue to have headache, the more likely are additional internal and environmental factors to share a role in their etiology. Thus, the emphasis of pain assessment should shift from an exclusive focus on headache type to a broader focus on the child with headache and consideration of all relevant etiologic factors. However, the current classification of headache continues to emphasize only the sensory features of headache and should be complemented by a practical system to characterize the relevant child features. (Our recommendation for a broader assessment is described in Chapter 4.)

DIAGNOSTIC CLASSIFICATION OF CHILDHOOD HEADACHE

Although children can experience many types of headache, tension-type and migraine represent the major categories. Tension-type headaches cause a dull, diffuse, and persistent pain that may last for hours, days, months, or years. Migraine headaches create a throbbing, more localized pain accompanied by nausea, vomiting, and photophobia, usually lasting several hours. Common and classic migraines are differentiated by the timing of symptoms, by the vasoconstrictive or vasodilation phase, and by the occurrence of auras (generally visual auras, such as blurring, flickering changes in the visual field, and flashing lights). Most young children experience common migraines, which lack early focal neurological symptoms. These common migraines are not always accompanied by nausea and vomiting. Adolescents may suffer from classic migraines, which are preceded by visual auras and accompanied by nausea and vomiting. (See Chapter 3 for a detailed review of differential diagnosis.)

Investigators in early pediatric studies generally defined migraine based on criteria proposed by Vahlquist (1955), Bille (1962), Prensky and Sommer

(1979), or the 1962 Ad Hoc Committee on the Classification of Headache. Children must experience paroxysmal headaches separated by symptom-free intervals and accompanied by two to four of the following symptoms: unilateral pain, nausea and/or vomiting, visual aura in connection with head-ache, and family history of migraine. However, as described previously, childhood migraine is often bilateral, may not be accompanied by nausea and/or vomiting, and is not preceded by visual aura. Thus, in 1988 the International Headache Society (IHS) proposed a new set of criteria that should be more appropriate for pediatric migraine (shown in Table I; Head-ache Classification Committee of the International Headache Society 1988).

While the diagnostic criteria for migraine are sensitive for adults, they still require modification for children (Gladstein et al. 1993; Seshia et al. 1994; Gallai et al. 1995; Winner et al. 1995; Raieli et al. 1996; Seshia 1996; Wöber-Bingöl et al. 1996b). The duration, location, and accompanying symp-tom criteria should be modified to conform to children's experience of head-ache. Abu-Arefeh and Russell (1994) concluded that the IHS criteria were

Table I
International Headache Society diagnostic criteria for migraine without aura

---

A. At least five attacks fulfilling B–D
B. Headache attacks lasting 4–72 hours* (untreated or successfully treated)
C. Headache has at least two of the following characteristics:
    1. Unilateral location
    2. Pulsating quality
    3. Moderate or severe intensity (inhibits or prohibits daily activities)
    4. Aggravation by walking stairs or similar routine physical activity
D. During headache at least one of the following:
    1. Nausea and/or vomiting
    2. Photophobia and phonophobia
E. At least one of the following:
    1. History and physical and neurological examinations do not suggest one of the disorders listed in groups 5–11 (organic disorder)†
    2. History and/or physical and/or neurological examinations do suggest such disorder, but is ruled out by appropriate investigations
    3. Such disorder is present, but migraine attacks do not occur for the first time in close temporal relation to the disorder

---

Source: Headache Classification Committee of the International Headache Society (1988).
* In children below age 15, attacks may last 2–48 hours. If the patient falls asleep and wakes up without migraine, duration of attack is until time of awakening.
† Groups 5–11 represent headache associated with: (5) head trauma; (6) vascular disorders; (7) nonvascular intercranial disorder; (8) substances or their withdrawal; (9) noncephalic infection; (10) metabolic disorder; (11) disorder of the cranium, neck, eyes, ears, nose, sinuses, teeth, mouth, or other facial or cranial structures.

generally adequate for their study on 5–15-year-old children and adolescents, but that the minimum acceptable duration of headache should be reduced from 1 to 2 hours. In their study, 5% of children with severe headache fulfilled all the criteria for migraine diagnosis, except that their headaches lasted less than 2 hours. In addition to reduced duration, Wöber-Bingöl and colleagues (1996b) concluded from their study of 437 children and adolescents that the diagnosis of migraine in children should include severe headache associated with nausea, even if the criteria of location, quality, and aggravation by physical activities were not fulfilled.

Maytal and colleagues (1997) used clinical diagnosis by pediatric neurologists to evaluate the validity of the IHS criteria for diagnosing migraine without aura in 253 children and adolescents. The IHS criteria showed high specificity (92.4% of children without migraine were correctly classified), but poor sensitivity (only 27.3% of children with migraine were correctly classified). The authors applied alternative case definitions to determine whether they could increase sensitivity without sacrificing specificity, but were unable to develop criteria that accurately replicated clinical diagnosis. They concluded that the IHS criteria should be less restrictive for children (e.g., fewer attacks, and only one rather than two of the specified features), but that further work was required to delineate developmental differences in headache characteristics.

In an ongoing multicenter prospective study, Winner and colleagues (1997) improved the sensitivity of the IHS criteria for diagnosing migraine in children less than 12 years old. The authors reduced the required headache duration from 4–72 hours to 1–48 hours, included bifrontal and bitemporal as well as unilateral location of headache, and allowed photophobia and/or phonophobia as concomitant symptoms.

While revisions to the IHS criteria for duration, location, and concomitant symptoms have improved their sensitivity for diagnosing migraine in children, these modifications may still be insufficient for infants and very young children. The diagnosis of migraine in infants and young children is based on clinical examination, family history, and parental observation. Vahlquist and Hackzell (1949) initially suggested that pallor and intense vomiting might indicate migraine in infants. Esler and Woody (1990) recommended that the criteria for presenting symptoms should include irritability, head banging or holding, sleep disturbance, behavioral disturbance, abdominal pain, and pallor. Barlow (1994) suggested that the common migraine syndrome in children is the mature expression of a periodic syndrome that first manifests in infancy. The primary presenting symptoms in infants include episodic vomiting, pallor, and behavioral change, but many infants indicate signs of head pain by their gestures or verbal expressions.

The sensitivity and specificity of the IHS criteria for diagnosing tension-type headache in children (Table II) has not been examined as rigorously as the criteria for migraine, presumably because clinical practice has generally supported their utility. In their study on the IHS criteria, Wöber-Bingöl and colleagues (1996a) evaluated 156 children and adolescents diagnosed with tension-type headache. In general, they found that the IHS criteria for tension-type headache had high sensitivity, but less specificity. They found one age-related difference: bilateral location was more common in adolescents than in children.

The adoption of uniform diagnostic criteria for childhood headache is essential from both a research and clinical perspective. Despite much study, many questions remain unanswered about the etiology of headache, the risk and prognostic factors, and the most effective interventions. To address these questions, we must be able to accurately identify children with different types of headache and to communicate meaningful diagnostic information across diverse study populations. It is equally important to better characterize the salient features that differentiate different types of childhood headache to help clinicians match various treatments to individual children.

Table II
International Headache Society diagnostic criteria
for episodic tension-type headache

A. At least 10 previous headache episodes fulfilling criteria B–D listed below. Number of days with such headache <180/year (<15/month).

B. Headache lasting from 30 minutes to 7 days

C. At least two of the following pain characteristics:
   1. Pressing/tightening (nonpulsating) quality
   2. Mild or moderate intensity (may inhibit, but does not prohibit activities)
   3. Bilateral location
   4. No aggravation by walking stairs or similar routine physical activity

D. Both of the following:
   1. No nausea or vomiting (anorexia may occur)
   2. Photophobia and phonophobia are absent, or one but not the other is present

E. At least one of the following:
   1. History, physical and neurological examinations do not suggest one of the disorders listed in groups 5–11 (organic disorder)*
   2. History and/or physical and/or neurological examinations do suggest such disorder, but is ruled out by appropriate investigations
   3. Such disorder is present, but tension-type headache does not occur for the first time in close temporal relation to the disorder

---

Source: Headache Classification Committee of the International Headache Society (1988).
* See Table I for definition of groups 5–11.

PREVALENCE AND NATURAL HISTORY OF HEADACHE

Epidemiologic studies on childhood headache provide information about the number of children affected with headache within a particular sample, often according to age and sex. Many studies use a two-stage process to identify children with headache. In a preliminary screening stage, all children are asked whether they have experienced a headache ever, during the past year, or now—in accordance with the study prevalence estimate—lifetime, period, or point, respectively. In a follow-up diagnostic stage, the children who report that they have headaches are interviewed in depth about the nature of their headaches or are examined to determine whether they satisfy explicit diagnostic criteria.

Many studies have reported prevalence rates for headache from children sampled in a health care practice (clinic-based), from the regional school system, or from the general population (community-based). Estimates vary widely due to differences in the sampling methods used, the age and sex of the study population, the headache diagnostic criteria applied, the country of origin, and the presentation and analysis of data (McGrath 1999).

To provide accurate and comprehensive prevalence rates for this text, we reviewed all epidemiologic studies of childhood headache. The literature search (MEDLINE and PsychINFO databases for the period May 1984–May 2000) included the topics of headache, migraine, and head injury, cross-referenced to children and cross-referenced separately to three terms—epidemiology, prevalence, and survey. In addition, we manually searched the main textbooks on pain in children, as well as reference lists of all relevant papers to identify studies published prior to 1984.

We reviewed all studies to determine whether they had a well-defined purpose, an adequate sample size, an appropriate study design for identifying children with headache, precise diagnostic criteria, a sufficiently high response rate (>75%) to enable the investigators to achieve their stated study objective, appropriate statistical analysis, and valid interpretation of findings. Fourteen studies on migraine satisfied these criteria (summarized in Table III). Prevalence estimates for abdominal migraine vary from 2.4% to 4.1% (Mortimer et al. 1993; Abu-Arefeh and Russell 1995), while those for nonmigraine headache vary from 6.3% to 49% (Vahlquist 1955; Bille 1962; Sillanpää 1976, 1983a,b; Egermark-Eriksson 1982; Pothmann et al. 1994).

As shown in Table III, community-based surveys in Sweden, Denmark, Finland, the United States, Israel, Great Britain, and the United Arab Emirates have yielded widely varying prevalence rates for migraine (1.4–27%), with much higher rates for general headache. As expected, prevalence rates

Table III
Prevalence estimates for headache in children and adolescents

Pain Condition	Study Type	Disease Definition	Source of Sample	Prevalence Estimate	Age (years)	Prevalence (%) Female	Male	All	Reference
Migraine	CS	Vahlquist 1955	Sweden, community	Lifetime	10–12 / 16–19			4.5 / 7.4	Vahlquist 1955
Migraine	CS	Vahlquist 1955	Sweden, school	Lifetime	All	4.4	3.3	3.9	Bille 1962
					7	1.7	1.1	1.4	
					8	2.7	2.7	2.7	
					9	2.9	3.5	3.2	
					10	3.3	4.0	3.6	
					11	5.7	3.7	4.7	
					12	6.9	3.5	5.2	
					13	5.9	4.0	5.0	
					14	4.8	5.4	5.1	
					15	8.2	1.5	5.3	
Migraine	CS	Ad Hoc Committee 1962	Denmark, school	Point	7–9	2.8	3.1	2.9	Dalsgaard-Nielsen et al. 1970
					9–11	4.3	4.5	4.4	
					11–13	6.0	6.0	6.0	
					13–15	7.7	7.3	7.5	
					15–17	9.5	8.4	9.0	
Migraine	CS	Vahlquist 1955	Finland, school	Point	7			3.2	Sillanpää 1976
Migraine	CS	Vahlquist 1955	South Wales, community	Lifetime	10–20	6.2–22.1	3.3–15.5		Deubner 1977
Migraine	CS	Modified from Vahlquist 1955	Great Britain, school	Point	10–18	2.5	3.4		Sparks 1978
Headache Migraine	CS	Modified from Vahlquist 1955	Israel, community	Point*	15–65+ / 15–24	~10*	~5 *		Abramson et al. 1980
Migraine	CS	Vahlquist 1955	Finland, school	Period (1 yr)	13	14.5	8.1	11.3	Sillanpää 1983a

Headache	Design	Criteria	Setting	n	Prevalence	Age (yr)				Reference
Migraine	CS, LC	Vahlquist 1955	Finland, school	2921	Period (1 yr)	7	2.5	2.9	2.7	Sillanpää 1983b
						14	14.8	6.4	10.6	
Migraine	CS	Modified from IHS 1988	USA, population	10169	Point	12–29	7.4	3.0		Linet et al. 1989
				3161		12–17	6.6	3.8		
Migraine	CS	IHS 1988	Scotland, school	1754	Period (1 yr)	All	11.5	9.7	10.6	Abu-Arefeh and Russell 1994
						5	3.0	3.7	3.4	
						6	8.1	6.8	7.4	
						7	4.1	2.8	3.5	
						8	5.9	8.5	7.3	
						9	5.9	6.6	6.3	
						10	11.6	11.4	11.5	
						11	11.4	15.3	13.2	
						12	18.0	20.2	19.1	
						13	23.7	14.8	19.0	
						14	27.0	4.0	16.2	
						15	13.6	14.0	13.8	
Migraine	CS	IHS 1988	Germany, school	4835	Lifetime	8–9	14.6	9.1	12.0	Pothmann et al. 1994
						12–13	12.6	8.2	10.3	
						15–16	14.3	7.2	10.5	
Migraine and headache	CS, LC	IHS 1988	Finland, community	3580	Period (1 yr)	8–9			2.7	Metsä-honkala et al. 1997
									27.3	
Migraine and headache	CS	IHS 1988	United Arab Emirates	1159	Period (1 yr)	6–14			13.7	Bener et al. 2000
									36.9	

Abbreviations: CS = cross-sectional; IHS = Headache Classification Committee of the International Headache Society; LC = longitudinal cohort.
* Prevalence estimate for age group interpreted from data presented in histogram. (Adapted from McGrath 1999.)

vary depending on the type of estimate—lifetime, point, or prevalence, age and gender of the study population, and diagnostic criteria. Many studies have reported data on the age of onset. Migraine onset is reported typically at 7–12 years of age (Vahlquist 1955), 6.9 years (Michael and Williams 1952), 7.3 years (Burke and Peters 1956), and less than 9 years (Krupp and Friedman 1953). The prevalence increases with age (Bille 1962; Russell 1994). However, several reports document onset of migraine in infants and very young children (Vahlquist and Hackzell 1949; Michael and Williams 1952; Krupp and Friedman 1953; Holguin and Fenichel 1967; Congdon and Forsythe 1979; Elser and Woody 1990; Barlow 1994). Barlow (1994) extrapolated a 1–2% prevalence rate for migraine in children under 2 years of age from published data.

Although most studies report a higher prevalence rate for girls (Vahlquist 1955; Bille 1962; Dalsgaard-Nielsen et al. 1970; Deubner 1977; Linet et al. 1989), some studies have found higher rates in boys (Michael and Williams 1952; Burke and Peters 1956) or no gender differences (Sillanpää 1976). Reported gender differences in prevalence probably reflect age by gender interactions. Linet and colleagues reported that migraine prevalence decreased with age among males, but they found an age-related increase among females. Similarly, Abu-Arefeh and Russell (1994) found that migraine was more common in boys by a ratio of 1.14:1 for children aged 12 years or younger, but for children over 12 years old, migraine was more common in girls, with a ratio of 2:1. In addition, they found that significantly more girls than boys had migraine with aura. The general conclusion from many studies is that migraine prevalence increases with age and that after age 10–12, prevalence is higher for girls.

The usual course of migraine in children has not been established. Although no prospective study has yet traced the natural history of migraine from childhood through adult life, some follow-up studies indicate that a high proportion of children (27–60%) continue to experience headaches (Bille 1973; Apley et al. 1978; Jay and Tomasi 1981; Larsson and Melin 1986). Paradoxically, the natural history of childhood headache is complicated by a high spontaneous remission rate as well as a high persistence rate. Bille (1962) conducted a 6-year follow-up study on 205 children and found that 31% of children had improved and 51% were migraine free. At 10-year follow-up, 32% were improved and 41% were migraine free (Bille 1973). Other clinical reports cite improvement and remission rates as high as 70% depending on the age of the child and the time for follow-up evaluation (Vahlquist and Hackzell 1949; Hinrichs and Keith 1965; Congdon and Forsythe 1979; Prensky and Sommer 1979).

In a 7-year follow-up of 2291 7-year-old schoolchildren, Sillanpää (1983) obtained different remission rates depending on a child's age of onset. Migraine had remitted fully in 20% of the children with onset at 0–7 years of age. Hockaday (1978) reported remission of migraine in 35% of males and 21% of females after an interval of 8–25 years. However, age of onset was not correlated with remission. Also, many adults reported prolonged periods of remission, from 4 to 10 years. Bille (1981) reported that 60% of participants from his original sample of 73 children with "pronounced migraine" were still having migraine after 23 years, even though many had been headache free for several years.

In summary, much evidence indicates that migraine remits for many children, recurs for some, and persists for others. As Linet and Stewart (1987, p. 462) concluded: "It is commonly held that the incidence of new cases of migraine and the frequency of attacks in existing cases begins to decrease with age beginning in the fourth decade. However, data are not available to clarify whether in fact attacks decrease or remit, whether the characteristics of migraine actually undergo marked change, or whether the incidence rapidly declines in older age groups (Dalsgaard-Nielsen [et al.] 1970; Clarke and Waters 1974; Waters 1974)."

RISK FACTORS FOR HEADACHE

Almost all studies of childhood headache report some information on associated demographic and psychosocial factors in an effort to identify the risk factors that may predispose children to develop migraine. Subsequent investigations compare children with and without migraine (typically using age- and sometimes sex-matched groups) to evaluate whether children differ significantly on the suspected risk factors. While this approach has been used to study genetic, familial, environmental, and individual characteristics, its major limitation is that the children in the migraine group already have headache and the suspected risk factors may not have existed prior to the condition. Few investigators have studied a cohort of headache-free children over time to identify which of them develop headache and to characterize how they differ from those who do not. This latter approach should provide the best information about true risk factors.

HERITABILITY

A positive family history of headache, particularly maternally, has long been regarded a risk factor and was initially included in the diagnostic

criteria for migraine. Messinger and colleagues (1991) found that the prevalence of headache increased from 64% when neither parent had headache to
85% when one parent had headache to 98% when both parents had headache. Research on twins reared together and apart has attempted to disen-
tangle the differential impact of genetics, family environment, and individual experience. Recent studies on the role of genetic factors for adult
migraine concluded that the heritability for the migraine phenotype is approximately 50% (Harvald and Hauge 1956; Merikangas et al. 1994;
Honkasalo et al. 1995; Larsson et al. 1995; Ziegler et al. 1998). The magnitude of heritability is similar for men and women (Larsson et al. 1995), even
though migraine is more prevalent in women (Stewart et al. 1991).

Ziegler and colleagues (1998) conducted interviews with 394 individual
twins. Using the IHS classification they reported a migraine prevalence of
41.9%. They found no evidence for shared family environmental risk factors
(e.g., social class of those rearing twins, family diet) for the development of
migraine. In contrast, nonshared environmental factors (e.g., accidents, illnesses, or stressful life events) appeared to play an important etiologic role
in migraine. Approximately 50% of the total variance in development of
migraine was attributable to these idiosyncratic environmental experiences.

EARLY LIFE FACTORS

While multiple family and environmental factors have been suggested
as risk factors, only one study has examined their role in early life as predictors for childhood headache. Aromaa and colleagues (1998) conducted a
longitudinal case-control study in Finland. As part of a more comprehensive
study of 1443 families, the investigators recruited young families expecting
their first baby and followed them until the child was 6 years old. They
obtained prospective information about the mother's pregnancy and delivery, the child's health at birth and throughout infancy and during the 6-year
study period (noting neurological problems, ear infections, long-term diseases, enuresis, travel sickness, etc.), the parents' adjustment to raising children, any family history of headache, the child's headache history at 3 and 5
years of age, the child's mental development, and psychosocial factors and
lifestyle. At school entry, 204 (21.7%) of the 968 6-year-old children had
suffered from headache that sometimes disturbed their daily activities; 144
of these children (14.9% of the entire sample) had headache that had disturbed their daily activities within the previous 6 months. Boys and girls
were similarly affected.

The investigators compared early life factors obtained at each of four
time periods (prenatal, infancy, 3 years of age, and 5 years of age) for the

144 children with headache and for a cohort of headache-free children to determine which factors predicted headache at age six. Logistic multivariate regression analysis revealed multiple factors associated with children's headache, including frequent headache in the mother before pregnancy and proteinuria during her pregnancy. In children, strong predictors for headache at age six included a maternal assessment of poor health and feeding problems, nocturnal confusion seizures, suspected headache in the child or a family member at 3 years, difficulties in falling asleep at 3 years, presence of long-term disease, nocturnal enuresis, travel sickness or headache at 5 years, concentration difficulties, behavioral problems, and unusual tiredness at 5 years. Depression and sleeping difficulties at 3 years were the strongest predictors of later headache. In contrast, divorce of the parents, having a one-parent family, or repeatedly moving house were not predictive of headache, nor were other variables such as number of siblings before the child was five or hours of television watching.

These investigators have compiled an extensive and impressive prospective record of early life factors, but have not yet linked them to a specific headache type or pain problem (e.g., frequent, severe, or debilitating headache). Since the lifetime prevalence of headache is high and increases with age, the multiple factors identified in this study as predictive of childhood headache may not be true predictors. The same factors did not consistently predict headache development before school age and later in school. However, the investigators have a unique opportunity to apply explicit diagnostic criteria to children, prospectively monitor headache for a subset of children, and then repeat the logistic analyses to more accurately identify predictive factors according to headache type or the severity of the pain problem.

PSYCHOLOGICAL FACTORS

The role of psychological factors in the development of migraine and tension-type headache in children has long been questioned. In 1937, Wolff first reported that "delicate, shy, (but with) unusual stubbornness or inflexibility" were common childhood traits recalled by adults with migraine. Various personality types were subsequently noted in clinical reports and research studies. Krupp and Friedman (1953) described children with migraine as sensitive, thorough, eager for approval, and serious about their school responsibilities. Vahlquist (1955) described children with migraine as having characteristics of neurovegetative instability, overdue ambition, and perfectionism. In his comprehensive study on childhood headache, Bille (1962) described children with migraine as fearful, tense, sensitive, and easily frustrated. Such characterizations are still common in clinical practice. Letters of referral to our clinic still include descriptions such as "worrier," "perfectionist," "eager to please," "mature beyond her years," "overachiever," and "little adult."

Numerous studies have evaluated the psychological characteristics of children with headache. Early studies described the personality characteristics of children referred for treatment to specialty clinics, while later studies evaluated differences between these children and healthy children without headache, specifically addressing children's anxiety and depression and maternal depression.

Several studies report that children with migraine are more anxious than those without headache (Bille 1962; Prensky and Sommer 1979; Maratos and Wilkinson 1982; Andrasik et al. 1988; Larsson 1988; Carlsson et al. 1996; Martin-Herz et al. 1999). Andrasik et al. (1988) compared 32 children with migraine with 32 children without migraine, who were matched for age, sex, and socioeconomic status. Children completed a battery of standardized measures (depression, anxiety, personality, behavior, psychosomatic symptoms, social adjustment, reading achievement, and vocabulary). Children with migraine (8–12 years old) had higher scores on all scales measuring depression and somatic complaints, but did not have higher anxiety scores. In contrast, the adolescents had higher levels of trait anxiety, in addition to depression and somatic complaints.

Other studies have also revealed no difference in anxiety between children with and without headache (Cooper et al. 1987; Cunningham et al. 1987; Kowal and Pritchard 1990). Kowal and Pritchard (1990) compared 23 children who had experienced headache for at least a year, with approximately two attacks per month, with 23 healthy children recruited from the same school. They administered several measures (anxiety, depression, children's behaviors, children's life events, family environment, and headache symptomatology) to test four specific hypotheses about the relationship among mood, behavioral disturbance, achievement level, and headache. The headache and control groups did not differ on measures of anxiety and depression, but differed on measures of shyness and sensitivity, psychosomatic disorders, and other behavioral disturbances.

Cunningham and colleagues (1987) compared anxiety and depression among three groups of children—one with migraine, one with nonheadache pain, and a pain-free group of outpatients. Although the 20 children with migraine were more anxious than the pain-free controls, their anxiety was equivalent to that of children in the nonheadache pain control, suggesting that it related more to the existence of a pain problem than to headache per se. The only characteristic unique to the children with migraine was a higher frequency of somatic complaints.

Research on depression in children with migraine reveals a similarly inconclusive pattern, with several studies reporting higher depression for migraineurs (Cooper et al. 1987; Andrasik et al. 1988; Larsson 1988; Kaiser 1992; Martin-Herz et al. 1999) and other studies reporting no difference among groups (Cunningham et al. 1987; Kowal and Pritchard 1990). Some of the disparity in findings among studies of anxiety and depression may be due to the differences in age of sample, headache severity, and comparison groups. For example, Martin-Herz and colleagues (1999) compared 32 adolescents with few or no headaches with 31 adolescents with high headache rates, recruited from a student sample. Results from their nonclinical sample showed that students with more frequent headache endorsed more symptoms of anxiety, depression, somatization, and functional disability, which suggests that the psychological effect related more to headache severity than to headache occurrence.

Almost all the related studies have first identified children with headache and then evaluated anxiety and depression in the sample. Only one study first diagnosed children with anxiety or depressive disorders and then evaluated whether there were differences in headache prevalence according to diagnosis. Egger and colleagues (1998) examined the association between chronic headache and psychiatric disorders in a population-based sample of 1013 children aged 9–15 years. They found striking gender differences. Headache was significantly more prevalent in girls with depression or anxiety disorders than in girls without these disorders, but the same was not true for boys. However, headache was significantly more prevalent in boys with conduct disorder.

A few studies have investigated the relationship between a mother's emotional state and childhood headache, suggesting that maternal depression is associated with recurrent headache, although not specifically with migraine (Zuckerman et al. 1987; Merikangas et al. 1988; Mortimer et al. 1992). However, investigations of the psychological state of parents of children with headache have not been thorough enough to reach definitive conclusions.

Many studies reveal a higher rate of somatic complaints for children with headache. Our early studies on pain experiences suggested that children with headache seem preoccupied with somatic complaints and report more pains than do children without headache, as shown by the two pain diaries completed by children with headache in Figs. 1 and 2 (McGrath 1990). The pain diary in Fig. 3, completed by an 11-year-old girl without

Type of pain: ~~twisted~~ leg Face #: 4   Date: 22nd April 86
H 100   while wrestling
        with dog
|——————————————————————————|———|

Type of pain: Bad Headache Face #: 8   Date: 22nd April 86
G 112   from cheese
|————————————————————————————————————|——|

Type of pain: paper cut   Face #: 7   Date: 23rd April 86
E 27
|——————|———————————————————————————————————|

Type of pain: bad Headache Face #: 4   Date: 24 April 86
H 84
|—————————————————————|——————————————————————|

Type of pain: bad headache Face #: 4   Date: 25 April
H 94
|——————————————————————|—————————————————————|

Type of pain: Cramps   Face #: 3   Date: 25 April
F 71
|——————————————|——————————————————————————————|

Type of pain: Headache   Face #: 8   Date: 26 April
G 105
|—————————————————————————————|———————————————|

Type of pain: dropped pliers on Face #: 3   Date: 28 04 86
F 62   toe
|———————————————|—————————————————————————————|

Type of pain: back ache   Face #: 4   Date: 28 04 86
E 34
|————————|————————————————————————————————————|

Type of pain: Sun Stroke   Face #: 3   Date: 28 04 86
F 55
|———|———|

Type of pain: backache   Face #: 3   Date: 29 04 86
F 91
|——————————————————————————|———————————————————|

Type of pain: hit ankle on Face #: 8   Date: 29 04 86
G 80   dishwasher door
|——————————————————————————————————|——————————|

Type of pain: back ache   Face #: 3   Date: 29 04 86
F 116
|—————————————————————————————————|———————————|

Type of pain: headache   Face #: 7   Date: 4 05 86
E 63
|————————————————————|————————————————————————|

Type of pain: hit ankle   Face #: 8   Date: 5 05 86
G 51   on chair leg
|————————————————|————————————————————————————|

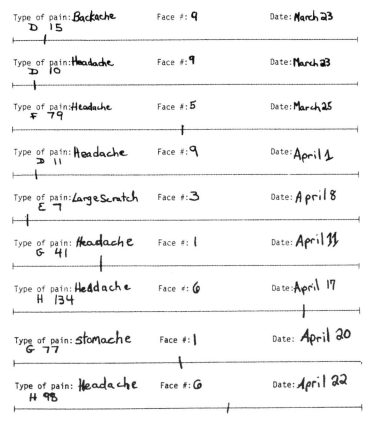

Type of pain: Backache   Face #: 9   Date: March 23
    D 15

Type of pain: Headache   Face #: 9   Date: March 23
    D 10

Type of pain: Headache   Face #: 5   Date: March 25
    F 79

Type of pain: Headache   Face #: 9   Date: April 1
    D 11

Type of pain: Large Scratch   Face #: 3   Date: April 8
    E 7

Type of pain: Headache   Face #: 1   Date: April 11
    G 41

Type of pain: Headache   Face #: 6   Date: April 17
    H 134

Type of pain: stomache   Face #: 1   Date: April 20
    G 77

Type of pain: Headache   Face #: 6   Date: April 22
    H 98

Fig. 2. The pain diary completed by a 14-year-old boy with recurrent headache, who rated the strength of his pain on a VAS and the unpleasantness on a FAS (diary is reprinted with permission from McGrath 1990).

headache, is typical of the pain experiences of healthy children. As shown, most of the pains listed are acute pains caused by injury or trauma associated with normal childhood activities, unlike the many aches listed in the diaries for children with headache. A subset of children with headache also report frequent abdominal pain or limb pain. Wyllie and Schlesinger (1933) coined the term "periodic disorder" to describe this long-recognized group of disorders. However, we do not know whether children with headache have been so affected by the repeated episodes that they become abnormally

---

← **Fig. 1.** The pain diary completed by an 11-year-old girl with recurrent headache, who rated the strength of her pain on a Visual Analogue Scale (VAS) and the unpleasantness on a Facial Affective Scale (FAS) (scales are described in Chapter 2; diary is reprinted with permission from McGrath 1990).

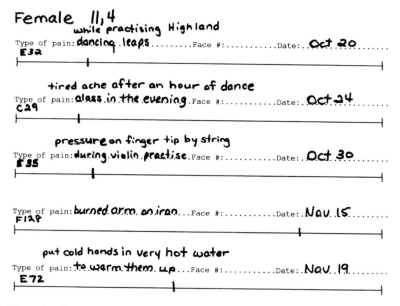

Fig. 3. The pain diary completed by an 11-year-old healthy girl, who rated the strength of her pain on a VAS and the unpleasantness on a FAS (reprinted with permission from McGrath 1990).

sensitive, or whether they may be predisposed to develop a variety of aches and pains.

We do know that many children with headache or migraine exhibit a high incidence of associated behavioral disturbances. Carlsson and colleagues (1996) compared psychosocial functioning in 113 Swedish schoolchildren (8–15 years old) with recurrent headaches and a group without headaches, matched by class year and sex. Overall, children with recurrent headache reported more stress and more psychological and somatic symptoms—specifically more pain in the stomach, back, and neck—than did the headache-free controls. Other reports suggest that children with migraine are more prone to cyclic vomiting, recurrent abdominal pain, motion sickness, limb pain, dizziness, frank vertigo, sleeping problems, bedwetting, and hyperactivity (Bille 1962; Koch and Melchior 1969; Prensky 1976; Del Bene 1982; Barabas et al. 1983; Carlsson et al. 1996).

In summary, research on psychological factors has evolved from an initial descriptive focus on the broad personality characteristics of children treated in specialty clinics to controlled trials using standardized measures to compare specific traits in children with and without headache. More recent studies include comparison groups of healthy children recruited from the community and children with other types of disease or pain. Such comparison groups should enable researchers to better differentiate factors specifically associated with headache from those associated with any long-term health problem. Regrettably, the findings of many studies are compromised by very small samples, multiple psychological measures, and limited power to evaluate statistically and clinically meaningful differences among groups.

Despite extensive interest and much research, many conclusions about the role of psychological factors are still tentative and speculative. What seems certain is that some children fit the stereotypic personality profile of "overachiever, conscientious, and perfectionist." However, we do not know how many. We also know that not all children with those traits develop headache. Similarly, there are subsets of children with headache who are anxious or depressed, or whose parents are anxious or depressed; again, we do not know how many. We have also learned that evidence of an associated factor is not evidence of causation. Instead, in some circumstances an associated factor is a consequence of pain and somatic concerns.

In essence, we have learned that there is no one link between psychological factors and headache in children. The links are many and complex, probably varying with age, sex, headache severity, and the manner in which children learn to resolve stressful situations within their family and lives.

ENVIRONMENTAL FACTORS

In the literature on childhood headache, the term "environmental factors" encompasses a broad array of weather conditions, light exposure, sound levels, family circumstances, food allergies, academic performance, physical exertion, menses, and mental stress. Each of these diverse factors has been evaluated in several studies. Parents or children complete questionnaires about which factors precipitate or exacerbate headache. Typically, parents endorse many and varied environmental factors, and investigators do not monitor prospectively whether these factors trigger or intensify headache.

In addition, few studies have concurrently evaluated the underlying child factors that might link apparently diverse environmental triggers. For example, data from our research program indicate that the failure to resolve normal childhood stressors associated with academic, social, and physical activities is a primary factor contributing to headache. The inability to resolve stress is the real headache trigger, not just the specific external stressor. Thus, we must interpret information on reported environmental factors within a broader perspective of what really is happening within a child's life. (Research on environmental factors has focused on their role as headache triggers, rather than as general risk factors; the results of these studies are described in Chapter 4.)

IMPACT OF HEADACHE

Although extensive efforts have been made to estimate the personal and economic impact of adult headache, only recently has similar attention focused on childhood headache. In our experience, the cost may be significant. Parents make repeated visits to primary care health providers, pediatricians, neurologists, complementary health specialists, and in some cases, the emergency room. Children are disabled during headache, miss school (so that often one parent misses work), and avoid or miss social and physical activities. Some families are hesitant to plan get-togethers and holidays for fear that children will be disabled by headache.

In 1962, Bille first reported high absence rates for children with headache, especially for girls. Subsequently, clinical reports have usually mentioned school absences, and recent studies are beginning to document broader disruptions to children's lives and their functional impairment (Sillanpää 1983a; Linet et al. 1989; Abu-Arefeh and Russell 1994; Holden et al. 1994; Carlsson et al. 1996; Lee and Olness 1997; Larsson 1998; Martin-Herz et al. 1999). In a series of studies, Langeveld and colleagues (1996, 1997, 1999) examined the impact of headache on quality of life for adolescents in Norway. In comparison to healthy control participants, adolescents with headache reported poorer functioning and less satisfaction with their life and health.

While some studies have reported the proportion of children who have consulted a specialist, there has been no rigorous evaluation of health care use according to the type of provider(s) and number of repeat visits. However, investigators have recently begun to examine such factors. In a follow-up study of Finnish children with migraine, Metsähonkala and colleagues (1997) reported that the children who had consulted a doctor within the previous 4 years had more nausea and missed more school than did those who had not consulted a doctor. Presumably, the factors that influence medical consultation and health care use in general vary among countries, depending on access to health care providers and associated costs for parents.

We know that headache causes significant suffering and disability for children and major disruption to their families. However, we lack comprehensive data about the full personal and financial impact of headache for children and their families and about the costs to the health care system.

SUMMARY

Migraine and tension-type headaches are a major problem for children and adolescents. Headache prevalence differs in some societies (or at some time periods) according to children's age and sex. Many children experience headache before the age of five, but the average age of onset in most studies is approximately 7 years. Migraine prevalence increases during the school years. More young boys (under 10) report headache than girls, whereas the trend seems to reverse as children mature. More adolescent girls suffer from headache than boys. For the vast majority of children, there seem to be no obvious precipitating factors and no predictable pattern of headache onset. Furthermore, there are no clear predictors for how long children will continue to have headaches. Some children will be afflicted for a few years, while others will suffer headaches throughout their adult lives. While we do not yet know the full impact of recurrent headache for children and their families, clinical studies have demonstrated significant levels of personal suffering, disability behaviors, and health care costs.

Almost all studies of childhood headache have described information on associated child characteristics in an effort to identify the risk factors that may predispose children to develop headache. These studies have evaluated a diverse array of environmental, family, and psychological features as potential distinguishing factors between children with and without headache. The results of many comparison studies are suggestive, rather than conclusive. Such studies show that some factors are associated with childhood headache, but cannot distinguish which factors are causes and which are consequences.

However, converging lines of evidence from these varied and sometimes contradictory studies provide some definitive information. A positive family history (especially maternal) predisposes children to develop headache, and situation-specific stress (related to family, school, or athletic activities) is a common trigger for headache attacks. However, the relevant feature underlying different stressors is probably children's inability to fully resolve the stressful situation, rather than simply exposure to the stress. Also, emotional distress (such as anxiety or depression) in children or their parents is an associated factor for some children with headache, but not for others.

Thus, despite extensive research, the roles of personality characteristics, anxiety, depression, and stress are not clear-cut. The relationships are complex, probably varying with age, sex, headache severity, and the manner in which children learn to identify and resolve stressful situations. Longitudinal studies that follow a heterogeneous cohort of children to see which of them develop headache have the most promise for providing definitive information about risk factors and causes.

REFERENCES

Abramson JH, Hopp C, Epstein LM. Migraine and non-migrainous headaches: a community survey in Jerusalem. *J Epidemiol Community Health* 1980; 34:188–193.

Abu-Arefeh I, Russell G. Prevalence of headache and migraine in schoolchildren. *BMJ* 1994; 309:765–769.

Abu-Arefeh I, Russell G. Prevalence and clinical features of abdominal migraine compared with those of migraine headaches. *Arch Dis Child* 1995; 72:413–417.

Ad Hoc Committee on Classification of Headache. Classification of headache. *JAMA* 1962; 179(9):127–128.

Andrasik F, Kabela E, Quinn S, et al. Psychological functioning of children who have recurrent migraine. *Pain* 1988; 34:43–52.

Apley J, MacKeith R, Meadow R. *The Child and His Symptoms: A Comprehensive Approach.* Oxford: Blackwell Scientific, 1978.

Aromaa M, Sillanpää ML, Rautava P, Helenius H. Childhood headache at school entry: a controlled clinical study. *Neurology* 1998; 50:1729–1736.

Barabas G, Ferrari M, Matthews WS. Childhood migraine and somnambulism. *Neurology* 1983; 33:948–949.

Barlow CF. *Clinics in Developmental Medicine,* Headaches and Migraine in Childhood, Vol. 91. Philadelphia: J.B. Lippincott, 1984.

Barlow CF. Migraine in the infant and toddler. *J Child Neurol* 1994; 9:92–94.

Bener A, Uduman SA, Qassimi EM, et al. Genetic and environmental factors associated with migraine in schoolchildren. *Headache* 2000; 40:152–157.

Bille B. Migraine in school children: a study of the incidence, and short-term prognosis, and a clinical, psychological and encephalographic comparison between children with migraine and matched controls. *Acta Paediatr Suppl* 1962; 51:1–151.

Bille B. The prognosis of migraine in schoolchildren. *Acta Paediatr Suppl* 1973; 236:38.

Bille B. Migraine in childhood and its prognosis. *Cephalalgia* 1981; 1:71–75.

Burke EC, Peters GA. Migraine in childhood. *AMA J Dis Child* 1956; 92:330–336.

Carlsson J, Larsson B, Mark A. Psychosocial functioning in schoolchildren with recurrent headaches. *Headache* 1996; 36:77–82.

Clarke GJR, Waters WE. Headache and migraine in a London general practice. In: Waters WE (Ed). *The Epidemiology of Migraine.* Bracknell, Berks: Boehringer Ingelheim, 1974.

Congdon PJ, Forsythe WI. Migraine in childhood: a study of 300 children. *Dev Med Child Neurol* 1979; 21:209–216.

Cooper PJ, Bawden HN, Camfield PR, Camfield CS. Anxiety and life events in childhood migraine. *Pediatrics* 1987; 79:999–1004.

Cunningham SJ, McGrath PJ, Ferguson HB, et al. Personality and behavioural characteristics in pediatric migraine. *Headache* 1987; 27(1):16–20.

Dalsgaard-Nielsen T, Engberg-Pedersen H, Holm HE. Clinical and statistical investigations of the epidemiology of migraine: an investigation of the onset age and its relation to sex, adrenarche, menarche and the menstrual cycle in migraine patients, and of the menarche age, sex distribution and frequency of migraine. *Dan Med Bull* 1970; 17:138–148.

Del Bene E. Multiple aspects of headache risk in children. *Adv Neurol* 1982; 33:187–198.

Deubner DC. An epidemiologic study of migraine and headache in 10–20 year olds. *Headache* 1977; 17:173–180.

Egermark-Eriksson I. Prevalence of headache in Swedish schoolchildren. *Acta Paediatr Scand* 1982; 71:135–140.

Egger HL, Angold A, Costello EJ. Headaches and psychopathology in children and adolescents. *J Am Acad Child Adolesc Psychiatry* 1998; 37:951–958.

Elser JM, Woody RC. Migraine headache in the infant and young child. *Headache* 1990; 30:366–368.

Gallai V, Sarchielli P, Carboni F, et al. Applicability of the 1988 IHS criteria to headache patients under the age of 18 years attending 21 Italian headache clinics. Juvenile Headache Collaborative Study Group. *Headache* 1995; 35:146–153.

Gladstein J, Holden EW, Peralta L, Raven M. Diagnoses and symptom patterns in children presenting to a pediatric headache clinic. *Headache* 1993; 33:497–500.

Harvald B, Hauge M. A catamnestic investigation of Danish twins. *Dan Med Bull* 1956; 3:150–158.

Headache Classification Committee of the International Headache Society. Classification and diagnostic criteria for headache disorders, cranial neuralgias and facial pain. *Cephalalgia Suppl* 1988; 8:44–45.

Hinrichs W, Keith H. Migraine in childhood: follow-up report. *Mayo Clin Proc* 1965; 40:593–596.

Hockaday JM. Late outcome of childhood onset migraine and factors affecting outcome, with particular reference to early and late EEG findings. In: Greene R (Ed). *Headaches*. New York: Raven Press, 1978, pp 41–48.

Hockaday JM. *Migraine in Childhood*. London: Butterworth & Co. Ltd, 1988a.

Hockaday JM. Definitions, clinical features, and diagnosis of childhood migraine. In: Hockaday JM (Ed). *Migraine in Childhood*. Cambridge: Butterworth & Co. Ltd., 1988b, pp 5–24.

Holden EW, Gladstein J, Trulsen M, Wall B. Chronic daily headache in children and adolescents. *Headache* 1994; 34:508–514.

Holguin J, Fenichel G. Migraine. *Pediatrics* 1967; 70:290–297.

Honkasalo ML, Kaprio J, Winter T, et al. Migraine and concomitant symptoms among 8167 adult twin pairs. *Headache* 1995; 35:70–78.

Jay GW, Tomasi LG. Pediatric headaches: a one year retrospective analysis. *Headache* 1981; 21:5–9.

Kaiser RS. Depression in adolescent headache patients. *Headache* 1992; 32:340–344.

Koch C, Melchior JC. Headache in childhood: a five year material from a pediatric university clinic. *Dan Med Bull* 1969; 16:109–144.

Kowal A, Pritchard D. Psychological characteristics of children who suffer from headache: a research note. *J Child Psychol Psychiatr* 1990; 31(4):637–649.

Krupp GR, Friedman AP. Migraine in children. *AMA J Dis Child* 1953; 85:146–150.

Langeveld JH, Koot HM, Loonen MC, Hazebroek-Kampschreur AA, Passchier J. A quality of life instrument for adolescents with chronic headache. *Cephalalgia* 1996; 16:183–196.

Langeveld JH, Koot HM, Passchier J. Headache intensity and quality of life in adolescents. How are changes in headache intensity in adolescents related to changes in experienced quality of life? *Headache* 1997; 37:37–42.

Langeveld JH, Koot HM, Passchier J. Do experienced stress and trait negative affectivity moderate the relationship between headache and quality of life in adolescents? *J Pediatr Psychol* 1999; 24:1–11.

Larsson B. The role of psychological, health-behaviour and medical factors in adolescent headache. *Dev Med Child Neurol* 1988; 30:616–625.

Larsson B, Melin L. Chronic headaches in adolescents: treatment in a school setting with relaxation training as compared with information-contact and self-registration. *Pain* 1986; 25:325–336.

Larsson B, Bille B, Pedersen NL. Genetic influence in headaches: a Swedish twin study. *Headache* 1995; 35:513–519.

Lee LH, Olness KN. Clinical and demographic characteristics of migraine in urban children. *Headache* 1997; 37:269–276.

Linet MS, Stewart WF. The epidemiology of migraine headache. In: Blau JN (Ed). *Migraine: Clinical and Research Aspects*. Baltimore: Johns Hopkins University Press, 1987, pp 451–477.

Linet MS, Stewart WF, Celentano DD, Ziegler D, Sprecher M. An epidemiologic study of headache among adolescents and young adults. *JAMA* 1989; 261:2211–2216.

Maratos J, Wilkinson M. Migraine in children: a medical and psychiatric study. *Cephalalgia* 1982; 2:179–187.

Martin-Herz SP, Smith MS, McMahon RJ. Psychosocial factors associated with headache in junior high school students. *J Pediatr Psychol* 1999; 24:13–23.

Maytal J, Young M, Shechter A, Lipton RB. Pediatric migraine and the International Headache Society (IHS) criteria. *Neurology* 1997; 48:607.

McGrath PA. The management of chronic pain in children. In: Burrows GD, Elton D, Stanley GV (Eds). *Handbook of Chronic Pain Management*. Amsterdam: Elsevier, 1987, pp 205–216.

McGrath PA. *Pain in Children: Nature, Assessment and Treatment*. New York: Guilford Publications, 1990.

McGrath PA. Chronic pain in children. In: Crombie IK, Croft PR, Linton SJ, LeResche L, Von Korff M (Eds). *Epidemiology of Pain*. Seattle: IASP Press, 1999, pp 81–101.

McGrath PA, Speechley KN, Seifert CE, et al. A survey of children's acute, recurrent, and chronic pain: validation of the Pain Experience Interview. *Pain* 2000; 1:1–15.

McGrath PJ, Unruh A. *Pain in Children and Adolescents*. Amsterdam: Elsevier, 1987.

Merikangas KR, Risch NJ, Merikangas JR, Weissman MM, Kidd KK. Migraine and depression: association and familial transmission. *J Psychiatr Res* 1988; 22:119–129.

Merikangas KR, Tierney C, Martin N, Heath AC, Risch N. Genetics of migraine in the Australian Twin Registry. In: Rose CF (Ed). *New Advances in Headache Research*. London: Smith-Gordon, 1994, pp 27–28.

Messinger HB, Spierings EL, Vincent AJ. Overlap of migraine and tension-type headache in the International Headache Society classification. *Cephalalgia* 1991; 11:233–237.

Metsähonkala L, Sillanpää M, Tuominen J. Use of health care services in childhood migraine. *Headache* 1996; 36:423–428.

Metsähonkala L, Sillanpää M, Tuominen J. Outcome of early school-age migraine. *Cephalalgia* 1997; 17:662–665.

Michael MI, Williams JM. Migraine in children. *Pediatrics* 1952; 41:18–24.

Mortimer MJ, Kay J, Jaron A, Good PA. Does a history of maternal migraine or depression predispose children to headache and stomach-ache? *Headache* 1992; 32:353–355.

Mortimer MJ, Kay J, Jaron A. Clinical epidemiology of childhood abdominal migraine in an urban general practice. *Dev Med Child Neurol* 1993; 35:243–248.

Pothmann R, Frankenberg SV, Müller B, Sartory G, Hellmeier W. Epidemiology of headache in children and adolescents: evidence of high prevalence of migraine among girls under 10. *Int J Behav Med* 1994; 1(1):76–89.

Prensky AL. Migraine and migrainous variants in pediatric patients. *Pediatr Clin North Am* 1976; 23:461–471.

Prensky AL, Sommer D. Diagnosis and treatment of migraine in children. *Neurology* 1979; 29:506–510.

Raieli V, Raimondo D, Gangitano M, et al. The IHS classification criteria for migraine headaches in adolescents need minor modifications. *Headache* 1996; 36:362–366.

Ross DM, Ross SA. *Childhood Pain: Current Issues, Research, and Management*. Baltimore: Urban & Schwarzenberg, 1988.

Rothner AD. Diagnosis and management of headaches in children and adolescents. In: Schechter NL, Berde CB, Yaster M (Eds). *Pain in Infants, Children and Adolescents*. Baltimore: Williams & Wilkins, 1993, pp 547–554.

Seshia SS. Specificity of IHS criteria in childhood headache. *Headache* 1996; 36:295–299.

Seshia SS, Wolstein JR, Adams C, Booth FA, Reggin JD. International headache society criteria and childhood headache. *Dev Med Child Neurol* 1994; 36:419–428.

Sillanpää M. Prevalence of migraine and other headache in Finnish children starting school. *Headache* 1976; 16:288–290.

Sillanpää M. Changes in the prevalence of migraine and other headaches during the first seven school years. *Headache* 1983a; 23:15–19.

Sillanpää M. Prevalence of headache in prepuberty. *Headache* 1983b; 23:10–14.

Sparks JP. The incidence of migraine in schoolchildren: a survey by the Medical Officers of Schools Association. *Practitioner* 1978; 221:407–411.

Stewart WF, Linet MS, Celentano DD, Van Natta M, Ziegler D. Age- and sex-specific incidence rates of migraine with and without visual aura. *Am J Epidemiol* 1991; 134:1111–1120.

Vahlquist B. Migraine in children. *Int Arch Allergy* 1955; 7:348–355.

Vahlquist B, Hackzell G. Migraine of early onset: a study of thirty one cases in which the disease first appeared between one and four years of age. *Acta Paediatr (Uppsala)* 1949; 38:622–636.

Waters WE. The Pontypridd headache survey. *Headache* 1974; 14:81–90.

Welborn CA. Pediatric migraine. *Emerg Med Clin North Am* 1997; 15:625–636.

Winner P, Martinez W, Mate L, Bello L. Classification of pediatric migraine: proposed revisions to the IHS criteria. *Headache* 1995; 35:407–410.

Winner P, Wasiewski W, Gladstein J, Linder S. Multicenter prospective evaluation of proposed pediatric migraine revisions to the IHS criteria. Pediatric Committee of the American Association for the Society of Headache. *Headache* 1997; 37:545–548.

Wöber-Bingöl C, Wöber C, Karwautz A, et al. Tension-type headache in different age groups at two headache centers. *Pain* 1996a; 67:53–58.

Wöber-Bingöl C, Wöber C, Wagner-Ennsgraber C, et al. IHS criteria for migraine and tension-type headache in children and adolescents. *Headache* 1996b; 36:231–238.

Wolff H. Personality features and reactions of subjects with migraines. *Arch Neurol Psychiatr* 1937; 37:895–921.

Wyllie WG, Schlesinger B. The periodic group of disorders in childhood. *Br J Child Dis* 1933; 31:1–20.

Ziegler DK, Hur YM, Bouchard TJ Jr, Hassanein RS, Barter R. Migraine in twins raised together and apart. *Headache* 1998; 38:417–422.

Zuckerman B, Stevenson J, Bailey V. Stomachaches and headaches in a community sample of preschool children. *Pediatrics* 1987; 79:677–682.

Correspondence to: Patricia A. McGrath, PhD, Pain Innovations, Inc., 38 Hampton Crescent, London, Ontario, Canada N6H 2N8. Fax: 519-471-8529; email: pamcgrat@julian.uwo.ca. Effective 1 July 2001: Department of Anesthesiology, School of Medicine, University of Utah, Salt Lake City, UT 84108, USA.

The Child with Headache: Diagnosis and Treatment.
Progress in Pain Research and Management, Vol. 19,
edited by Patricia A. McGrath and Loretta M. Hillier,
IASP Press, Seattle, © 2001.

2

Headache Measures for Children: A Practical Approach

Patricia A. McGrath[a,b] and Andrea L. Koster[c]

aPain Innovations, Inc., London, Ontario, Canada; bDepartment of Pediatrics, Faculty of Medicine, and cDepartment of Psychology, University of Western Ontario, London, Ontario, Canada

Pain assessment is an integral component of treating children with headaches. We need a reliable measure of headache activity and an understanding of the factors that cause or exacerbate headaches. Pain assessment is a dynamic process that begins with a diagnostic examination and culminates with a clinical decision that the child's headaches have improved sufficiently. Although the key aspects of assessment are the same throughout a treatment program, the assessment tools differ depending on the treatment phase—diagnosis, routine clinical monitoring of treatment efficacy, and evaluation at discharge to define whether a child has achieved the treatment objectives. In this chapter, we recommend a practical approach for assessing headache activity at each of these phases. We describe the assessment issues, developmental considerations, and psychometric properties important for selecting a headache measure in children. We conclude with suggestions for how to incorporate this information into a cost-effective approach for assessing headache activity and objectively evaluating treatment effectiveness. (Chapter 8 describes the procedure for evaluating and monitoring causative situational factors in simple recurrent headaches.)

PAIN ASSESSMENT IN CHILDREN

Increasing demand for evidence-based practice dictates that health care providers adopt clear guidelines for determining when treatments are effective and for identifying children for whom they are most effective. Clinicians need pain measures that are convenient to administer and whose resulting scores provide meaningful information about children's pain experiences. An extensive array of pain measures have been developed and validated for use with infants, children, and adolescents. (For comprehensive reviews of pain measures for infants and children, see Beyer and Wells 1989; Finley and McGrath 1998; RCN Institute 1999; McGrath and Gillespie, in press.) Children's pain measures are classified as physiological, behavioral, and psychological, depending on what is monitored—physical parameters, such as heart or respiration rate; distress behaviors, such as crying or facial expression; or children's own descriptions of what they are experiencing. Both physiological and behavioral measures provide indirect estimates of pain because the presence or strength of pain is inferred solely from the type and magnitude of responses to a noxious stimulus. In contrast, psychological measures can provide direct estimates for many different dimensions of pain (intensity, quality, affect, duration, and frequency), and offer valuable information on the impact of pain.

The criteria for an accurate pain measure for children are similar to those required for any measuring instrument. A pain measure must be valid, in that it unequivocally measures a specific dimension of a child's pain so that changes in pain ratings reflect meaningful differences in a child's pain experience. The measure must be reliable, in that it provides consistent and trustworthy pain ratings regardless of the time of testing, the clinical setting, or who is administering the measure. The measure must be relatively free from bias, in that children should be able to use it similarly, regardless of differences in how they may wish to please adults. The pain measure should be practical and versatile for assessing different types of pain and for use in diverse clinical settings.

BEHAVIORAL PAIN SCALES

Most behavioral pain measures are checklists of the different distress behaviors that children exhibit when they experience a certain type of pain. The rationale is that an objective evaluation of children's pain behaviors should provide an accurate estimate of the strength of their pain experiences. In developing behavioral pain scales, trained health care providers first observe several children when they are in pain and document any behaviors that seem to be caused by the pain. They then list the common pain behaviors on an itemized checklist. Parents complete such pain scales by checking off which of the listed behaviors they see when their children have a headache. On many scales, parents also rate the intensity of these behaviors. The intensity scores for each of the observed behaviors are summed to produce a composite pain score. Most behavioral pain scales were developed and validated to assess acute procedural or postoperative pain in otherwise healthy children (McGrath 1998; McGrath and Gillespie, in press).

However, behavioral measures are also valuable tools with which to assess pain severity, disability level, and medication use for children with headaches. Behavioral measures are flexible instruments that can monitor the most relevant behaviors for a particular child and document the effects of therapy. Parents and children can record children's reactions to headaches, the length and extent of any disability, and children's compliance with treatment recommendations. Moreover, clinicians can monitor children's school attendance, physical activity, peer activities, and use of pain control strategies using simple behavioral records (as described for our treatment program in Chapter 8). While these records do not provide a specific pain score, they provide the prospective information about children's headaches, pain management, and headache-related disability needed for a comprehensive treatment program.

Behavioral scales provide information that complements a child's description of his or her pain. Unless it is impossible to obtain information from children directly, clinicians should not rely exclusively on behavioral measures to determine headache intensity. Behavioral pain scores do not always correlate with children's own pain ratings (Beyer et al. 1990). Some children with headaches may experience pain but still continue their normal activities. Other children may be very disabled by their headaches, regardless of their intensity. Thus, it is important to interpret children's pain behaviors within a broader context.

PHYSIOLOGICAL PAIN SCALES

Physiological parameters that have been monitored in children as potential measures of acute pain include heart rate, respiration rate, blood pressure, palmar sweating, cortisol and cortisone levels, oxygen levels, vagal tone, and endorphin concentrations (Ross and Ross 1988; McGrath 1990; Sweet and McGrath 1998). Although physiological responses can provide valuable information about a child's distress state, more research is required to develop a sensitive system for interpreting how these parameters reflect the quality or intensity of children's headaches. At present, physiological parameters do not constitute valid clinical pain measures for children.

PSYCHOLOGICAL PAIN MEASURES

Psychological pain measures include a broad spectrum of projective techniques, interviews, questionnaires, qualitative descriptive scales, and quantitative rating scales designed to capture the subjective experience of pain (Champion et al. 1998; McGrath and Gillespie, in press). Projective techniques allow children to express their feelings about pain through their drawings, choice of colors, and interpretation of pictures or cartoons. As shown in Fig. 1, children can use drawings to depict the quality and intensity of their headache, as well as their emotional distress and heightened sensitivity. Projective methods generally complement children's direct ratings of their headache experience, and are very useful with young children or children who are unable to express their feelings verbally. Interviews, questionnaires, and intensity rating scales provide the most comprehensive information about children's pain, but they are necessarily limited to children with appropriate cognitive ability and communication skills. The common rating scales used for children's headaches are described below under "Pain Intensity Scales."

DEVELOPMENTAL ISSUES

Health care providers must consider the age and cognitive ability of a child when selecting a pain measure (Marcon and Labbé 1990). Children's understanding and descriptions of pain naturally depend on their age, cognitive level, and previous pain experience. Children begin to understand pain through their own hurting experiences; they learn to describe the different characteristics of their pains (intensity, quality, duration, and location) in the same way that they learn specific words to describe different sounds, tastes, smells, and colors. Most children can communicate meaningful information about their pain. Gradually they develop an increasing ability to describe specific pain features—the quality (aching, burning, pounding, or sharp), intensity (mild to severe), duration (a few seconds to years), frequency, location (from a diffuse location on the surface of the skin to a more precise internal localization), and unpleasantness (mild annoyance to an intolerable discomfort). Children's understanding of pain and the language that they use to describe pain come from the words and expressions used by their families and peers and from characters depicted in books, videos, and movies. (See McGrath and Unruh 1987; Ross and Ross 1988; McGrath 1990; Peterson et al. 1991; Gaffney 1993; Johnston 1993 for a more extensive review of developmental factors in children's pain.)

Fig. 1. Top: A child's drawing of a headache depicts a burning and pounding quality. Bottom: Eleven-year-old Adam captioned this drawing as follows: "It feels like I'm in a marching band, and my head is the drum."

As children mature, their understanding of pain changes from a primarily physical awareness to a more abstract understanding comprising both physical and psychological components (Gaffney and Dunne 1986, 1987; Gaffney 1988; Harbeck and Peterson 1992). In our clinic young children (4–6 years old) with extensive pain experience seem more mature cognitively than children of the same age with less pain experience. The children with greater pain experience can describe the characteristics of their headaches more fully and can use more sophisticated rating scales. Children's level of cognitive development determines how they are able to understand pain and may be more indicative of their perception, expression, and behavioral responses to pain than their chronological age may be. The recognition that children's concepts of pain follow a consistent developmental pattern provides a framework not only for evaluating their understanding of pain, but also for selecting pain measures that are appropriate for various ages and stages of cognitive development.

It is essential to communicate with children about pain using their own terminology. Most toddlers (approximately 2 years of age) can communicate the presence of pain, using words learned from their parents to describe the sensations they feel when they hurt themselves. They use concrete analogies to describe their perceptions. Gradually children learn to differentiate and describe three basic levels of pain intensity—"a little," "some or medium," and "a lot." By the age of five, most children can differentiate a wider range of pain intensities, and many can use simple quantitative scales to rate their pain intensity. Blanchard and colleagues (1981) indicate that a concrete-operational developmental level (approximately 8 years of age) must be reached before children can successfully master many pain intensity scales. For younger children, pictorial analogue scales (Johnson et al. 1990) or concrete physical scales such as poker chips (Hester 1979) may be more appropriate pain measures.

PAIN RATINGS—WHAT DO THE NUMBERS MEAN?

Children can use many analogue, facial, and verbal rating scales to rate the strength and quality of their pains (for review, see Champion et al. 1998; McGrath and Gillespie, in press). Children choose a level on the scale that best matches the strength of their own pain (i.e., a level on a number or thermometer scale, a number of objects, a mark on a visual analogue scale, a face from a series of faces varying in emotional expression, or a particular word from adjective lists). These scales are easy to administer, requiring only a few seconds once children understand how to use them. Many of these scales yield pain scores on a scale of 0–10.

However, the resulting pain scores from the different rating scales are not necessarily equivalent. Thus, it is important to know what the pain scores mean on different scales. Some scales simply use numbers to represent different pain intensity levels (e.g., no pain equals 0, mild pain equals 1, moderate pain equals 2, and strong pain equals 3). The numbers are often interpreted as if they represent absolute and accurate amounts of pain. But unless an investigator studies the relationship between a child's pain level and the numbers he or she uses to rate it—the psychometric properties—we only know that larger numbers mean stronger pain, and we do not know *how much* stronger. As a result, when evaluating treatment effects, we cannot assume that one child's report that a treatment lessened a headache from a score of 2 to 1 (moderate to mild) is equivalent to a reduction from 3 to 2 (strong to moderate) for another child. Similarly, when a child rates a headache as a 3, the pain level may not really be three times the strength of the pain he or she rates as a 1. Nevertheless, most pain scores are interpreted as if they represent numbers on equal interval or ratio scales.

The four types of measurement scales (nominal, as in the numbers designating players on a sports team; ordinal, as in the rank-ordering of children according to height; interval, as in the Fahrenheit temperature scale; and ratio, as in a yardstick) refer to four different relationships between the properties of an event or perception (e.g., pain intensity) and the number or metric system. Ratio scales have all the properties of the three other scales; they represent a set position or order between numbers, they show the magnitude of the difference between numbers, and the numbers reflect true ratios of magnitude. Each scale has a certain number of permissible mathematical calculations, so it is important to understand which type of scale one is using when measuring a child's pain or evaluating analgesic efficacy. Conclusions about how much more intense one type of pain is compared to another or how much pain is reduced are valid only when using true ratio scales (Price 1999).

PAIN INTENSITY SCALES

A recent review of pain intensity measures for children described more than 40 scales appropriate for clinical use, each with some evidence of validity and reliability (McGrath and Gillespie, in press). Several measures show promise for children with headaches, although only a few analogue, facial, and interview scales have ever been used for recurrent headaches. Table I lists these measures, the type of pain used to initially develop the scale, the scale methodology, the pain characteristics measured, the scale

Table I
Pain measures for children and adolescents

Name of Pain Measure (Reference)	Pain Type	Method	Pain Characteristic	Scale Type; Pain Score	Comments
Visual Analogue Scale (VAS) (Abu-Saad 1984; McGrath et al. 1985)	Acute, recurrent, and chronic pain	Analogue scale, vertical with endpoints designated as "no pain" or "strongest pain" (100 and 150 cm)	Intensity, affect, and emotions caused by pain	Quantitative; ratio scale properties; pain score 0–100	For children aged 5 yr and older
Colored Analogue Scale (CAS) (McGrath et al. 1996, 1999)	Acute trauma; postoperative, recurrent, and chronic pain	Analogue scale, varying in length, hue, and area	Intensity	Quantitative; ratio scale properties; pain score 0–10	For children aged 5 yr and older; psychometric properties demonstrated; versatility demonstrated for clinical and home use
Pain Ladder (Hester and Foster 1990)	Acute pain	Analogue scale, depicted as ladder	Intensity	Quantitative; may be ordinal or interval scale; pain score 0–10	For children aged 5–13 yr
Tactile Scale (TaS) (Westerling 1999)	Postoperative pain	Object scale: nine red balls increasing in size	Intensity and nausea	Quantitative; may be ordinal or interval scale; pain score 0–9	For children who are visually impaired
Multiple Size Poker Chip Tool (MSPCT) (St. Laurent-Gagnon et al. 1999)	Procedural pain (immunization)	Object scale: four poker chips varying in size (2–3.8 cm)	Intensity	Quantitative; interval scale; pain score 0–4	For children aged 4–6 yr

Measure	Type of pain	Format	Dimension	Scale/score	Notes
Facial Affective Scale (McGrath et al. 1985, 1999; McGrath 1990)	Acute, recurrent, and chronic pain	Discrete pictorial scale: nine faces varying in emotional expression	Affect	Interval scale; pain score 0–0.97	Intended to measure affective dimension of pain for children ages 5 yr and older; numerical values for faces were determined by children's own ratings, not by adults
FACES Pain Scale (Bieri et al. 1990; Goodenough et al. 1997)	Hypothetical levels, procedural pain	Discrete pictorial scale: seven adult faces varying in emotional expression	Intensity, affect	Interval scale; pain score 0–7	For children and adolescents aged 3–15 yr; initially developed to measure pain intensity; subsequently studied as measure of pain affect
Faces Pain Rating Scale (Wong and Baker 1988)	Procedural pain	Discrete pictorial scale: six faces varying in emotional expression	Intensity	May be ordinal or interval scale; pain score 0–6	For children and adolescents aged 3–18 yr; Instructions link each face to a different amount of hurt
Adolescent Pediatric Pain Tool (APPT) (Savedra et al. 1989; Tesler et al. 1991; Sinkin-Feldman et al. 1997)	Postoperative pain	Questionnaire with body outline, analogue scale, and adjective pain descriptor scale	Pain location, intensity, and quality	Descriptive information on multiple aspects, with some pain features scored on interval and ratio scales	For children and adolescents aged 8–17 yr
Children's Comprehensive Pain Questionnaire (CCPQ) (McGrath 1990)	Recurrent pain syndromes; chronic pain	Semi-structured interview with VAS, rating scales, and word descriptors	Sensory, affective, and evaluative dimensions; situational factors that intensify pain	Descriptive information on multiple aspects, with some pain features scored on interval and ratio scales	For children and adolescents aged 5–19 yr

type, and type of pain score obtained. At present, no one scale is appropriate
for all children and for all situations in which they experience pain. However, visual and colored analogue scales are ideal for most children over
five. In addition to possessing excellent psychometric properties, these scales
are versatile for use with acute, recurrent, and chronic pain and provide a
convenient and flexible pain assessment tool for use in hospital and at home.

Many analogue scales are variants of the traditional Visual Analogue
Scale (VAS)—a black 100-mm line with endpoints designated as "no pain"
and "strongest pain imaginable." Subjects mark the line to show their pain
level; the length of the line between the left endpoint (no pain) and their
mark represents the strength of their pain. These scales, used both for adults
and children, were developed to demonstrate how changes in perception
(e.g., of brightness, loudness, or pain) correspond with changes in physical
stimuli (e.g., light intensity, sound level, or noxious stimulation) (Teghtsoonian 1980; McGrath et al. 1985). Children over five are generally able to
use these scales to produce valid and reliable ratings of their pain intensity
(Abu-Saad 1984; McGrath 1990). The Colored Analogue Scale (CAS) is the
pain intensity scale that we generally use for children over five. In addition to
its psychometric properties (McGrath et al. 1996) and construct validity
(McGrath et al. 1999), the scale is convenient to administer, easy for children to understand, adaptable to many clinical settings, and useful for helping parents to monitor children's pain at home.

The Facial Affective Scale (FAS) was designed to capture the affective
dimension of pain. Preliminary studies showed that children aged 5–8 had
difficulty using the same analogue scale (e.g., a simple VAS with the endpoints changed to reflect pain intensity or pain affect) to measure different
dimensions of pain. The FAS presents an artist's sketch of nine faces representing different levels of distress and joy. The numbers representing affect
were determined in a previous study where children rated the expression
depicted by each face and assigned a number to determine its affective
value (McGrath et al. 1985; McGrath 1990). Children use the FAS to rate
how much a headache bothers them, as shown in Fig. 2.

Although children provide essential information about their pain in their
own words, specific verbal scales of pain intensity are not widely used.
However, we use verbal scales as part of headache assessment, using adjectives that children have used in our clinical program to describe their pain
(shown in Tables III and IV). Accruing data from studies on acute and
recurrent pain demonstrate their validity. Our verbal intensity scale is similar to the revised Word Graphic Rating Scale (WGRS), a component of the
Adolescent Pediatric Pain Tool (Tesler et al. 1991). In the WGRS, the terms
"no pain," "little pain," "medium pain," "large pain," and "worst possible

pain" are spaced at approximately equal intervals along a 0–100-mm line. Although subsequent research has shown that children do not rate the words at equal intervals, their use of the scale to measure their pain is still valid because children use the words as anchor points in marking the line (similar to an analogue scale), rather than simply circling the words.

HEADACHE INTERVIEWS, DIARIES, AND LOGS

Variations of the pain intensity scales and behavioral methods described above are used in almost all clinical studies on children's headaches, either in a clinical interview or in forms that children complete at home during treatment. In most studies, investigators use data obtained in studies of acute pain to infer the validity, reliability, and psychometric properties of such scales for assessing headaches. Rather than replicating previous studies on the properties of these scales, investigators have focused their attention on how best to use them to obtain accurate information, weighing the benefits of prospective monitoring versus retrospective recall, of the use of parent versus child informants, and of daily versus hourly documentation.

Clinical trials typically include a pain diary or pain log on which children record the intensity, frequency, and length of their headaches. These logs enable health care providers to monitor headache activity, disability behavior, and children's independent pain management (as shown in Fig. 2). Pain diaries can provide valid information about the frequency and intensity of children's headaches (Richardson et al. 1983; Labbé et al. 1985). Prospective records of headache activity generally provide more substantive and accurate information on specific headache features than does retrospective recall in a clinical interview. In initial interviews with 53 children and their parents, Andrasik et al. (1985) obtained estimates of the number of headaches per month, typical headache duration, and mean peak intensity. Children then completed daily headache diaries for a 4-week period to monitor these features. During the interview children had overestimated the prospective data on each headache feature.

We have also noted general disparities in headache frequency, pain intensity, and headache duration between responses in our initial interview with children (and parents) and our subsequent prospective monitoring of headache activity. However, we have not noted a consistent pattern of overestimation of headaches at the interview. Instead, we noted both under- and overestimations, with some children initially reporting only the most severe headaches and not mentioning all the headaches that they experienced. The less disabling, but often more frequent headaches were detected only through

Name: _____ Session: _____

COMPLETE A SEPARATE SHEET FOR EACH HEADACHE THAT YOU HAVE FROM NOW UNTIL YOUR NEXT TREATMENT SESSION.

1. Day _____ Date _____ When (what time) did it start? _____

2. Did the headache start slowly and get stronger?   Yes   No   Or, did it start suddenly at a strong level?   Yes   No

3. What were you doing when you started to get the pain? _____

4. How were you feeling emotionally? _____

5. At its strongest, how much did it hurt? (Use the red pain scale.) Pain Scale Number _____

6. At its strongest, how much did it bother you? (Draw a circle around the best words.)

        not at all   a little   between a little and a lot   a lot   very much

7. Which face shows me how how you felt deep when you had this headache? (Use the face scale.)

8. What methods did you use to stop the headache? When (what times) did you do this? How much did it help? (Note: If you took medicine, please list what you took and how much.)

   What I tried   Time   How much did it help?

   _____   _____   not at all   a little   a lot   it took it away
   _____   _____   not at all   a little   a lot   it took it away
   _____   _____   not at all   a little   a lot   it took it away
   _____   _____   not at all   a little   a lot   it took it away

9. When/what time did the headache end? _____

10. Did the headache end gradually?   Yes   No   Or, did it end suddenly?   Yes   No

11. What did you do then? _____

12. What do you think caused this headache? _____

13. What was the worst part of this headache for you? _____

Fig 2. A headache log used in our pain program. Children complete the form for each headache, and the therapist reviews the information with them at their next session.

prospective monitoring. The potential discrepancies between information obtained in the interview and diaries led us to revise our interview to better capture data on all headaches that children may develop. In addition, we ask children to describe their headache features based on their most recent headache episode rather than on a general impression, and we encourage parents and children to describe the usual pattern of headaches as well as the current pattern, which might be different. (Our interview questions are described in the next section; some are listed in Tables III–IV.)

While parents and children's headache ratings generally match, their descriptions of some features may vary. Andrasik and colleagues (1985) reported high levels of agreement between parents and children for headache intensity, but not for headache frequency. The initial discrepancy between parents' and children's ratings lessened throughout the treatment phase as parents and children focused more objectively on headache symptoms. During an interview, it is difficult to determine children's true headache frequency. Few children develop a specific number of headaches each week. Instead, frequency often varies according to the time period (usually according to school semesters rather than to seasons).

As noted in a sample of clinical trials, most studies monitor headache frequency, duration, and pain intensity (shown in Table II). But investigators use different methods to obtain this information and they evaluate headaches at different time periods, so that it is difficult to compare results across studies. Also, many of the pain intensity scales are confounded in that the different pain levels are defined according to headache disability (e.g., 0 = no headache; 1 = very mild headache; 2 = mild headache; 3 = moderate headache [pain is noticeably present]; 4 = severe headache [difficult to concentrate]; 5 = extremely intense headache [incapacitated]; Labbé and Williamson 1984; Labbé et al. 1985). When using these scales, children may report more about the impact of the headache in terms of its interruption to their lives than about its intensity level. While disability and pain levels may correlate for many children, they are distinct pain features and should be measured separately.

Headache activity, defined as a "headache index" or "headache sum," is usually a composite of headache intensity, frequency, and length or disability. This measure is often selected as the primary outcome in clinical trials for statistical comparison before and after treatment. However, it is not a uniform measure across studies because investigators use different methods to combine data on various headache characteristics. It is difficult to precisely compare treatment results across trials because investigators usually only report their unique composite headache index value; they do not report

Table II
Sample of headache measures used in clinical trials for children

Clinical Trial	Sample Size (Age)	Headache Characteristics	Measures	Measurement Period	Primary Outcome	Comments
Autogenic feedback (Labbé and Williamson 1984)	N = 28 (7–16 yr)	Frequency Duration Pain intensity Peak intensity	Q: How often? Q: How long? 6-point scale Weekly average	4 times/day	Headache index	Confounded intensity and disability scale
Multicomponent therapy (Allen and McKeen 1991)	N = 21 (7–12 yr)	Duration Frequency Pain intensity Medication Disability Situational factors EMG activity, skin temperature	Q: How long? Q: How often? 11-point scale Q: Type and quantity Q: School or activities missed Parent interview Physiological measures	4 times/day	Headache index	
Cognitive-behavioral therapy (Griffiths and Martin 1996)	N = 51 (10–12 yr)	Pain intensity Medication Affect/mood	6-point scale Q: Type, time, and quantity Standardized questionnaires	4 times/day	Headache index	Confounded intensity and disability scale
Relaxation training (Larsson and Carlsson 1996)	N = 26 (10–15 yr)	Frequency Pain intensity	Q: How long? 6-point scale	4 times/day	Headache sum	Confounded intensity and disability scale
Acupuncture (Pintov et al. 1997)	N = 22 (7–15 yr)	Duration Frequency Pain intensity	Q: How long? Q: How often? Visual analogue scale	Once/week	Frequency and intensity	Specific reduction specified

specific values for frequency, intensity, and other variables before and after treatment.

Three formal headache questionnaires for children were designed to capture headache characteristics, accompanying symptoms, precipitating factors, and interventions used. The Children's Headache Questionnaire consists of 35 headache descriptors, such as "awake with headache," "car or motion sickness," and "use prescription medication" (Labbé et al. 1985). Children and parents rate the occurrence of these descriptors on a 0–5 scale (5 = occurs without exception). Initial reliability and validity data was obtained for 28 children (aged 7–16 years).

The Children's Headache Assessment Scale is a parent report questionnaire to evaluate 44 factors that may precipitate or maintain headaches, such as emotional stress, physical conditions, social consequences, and coping responses (Budd and Kedesdy 1989). Parents rate the occurrence of these factors on a 0–6 scale (6 = always) based on their child's headaches during the previous 2 months. Initial reliability and validity data were obtained for 92 parents of children with headaches (aged 6–16 years) from an English-speaking American sample (Budd et al. 1994). Further evidence of the validity and reliability of this scale comes from a study of 160 parents of children (aged 6–16 years) from a Dutch-speaking Belgian sample (Bijttebier and Vertommen 1999).

The Children's Headache Interview is a semi-structured clinical interview that was revised from a more general recurrent and chronic pain questionnaire, the Childhood Comprehensive Pain Questionnaire (McGrath 1990). The interview includes questions about headache characteristics, situational factors that can cause or exacerbate headaches, children's and their family's responses to headaches, and potential sources of stress for children. A trained therapist conducts the interview with a child, while parents complete a brief pain history. (The Children's Headache Interview is included in Appendix 1.) Initial validation and evidence of reliability were derived from a study to evaluate the efficacy of a cognitive-behavioral pain management program for children with recurrent headaches (McGrath et al. 1993).

RECOMMENDATIONS FOR ASSESSING HEADACHE CHARACTERISTICS

Self-report measures represent the gold standard in pediatric pain measurement because they are the only direct source for obtaining information about a child's full pain experience. Both quantitative and qualitative assessment tools are needed for children with recurrent or chronic headaches to evaluate headache characteristics and to determine treatment effectiveness. These tools can be practically incorporated into a clinical interview and treatment program.

Syndrome duration, headache location, frequency, length, pain quality, pain severity, the nature and extent of accompanying physical symptoms, and disability level are all useful measures for evaluating children's headaches in clinical practice. Each should be assessed as part of the initial clinical examination. When possible, both the accompanying parent and the child should describe the child's headache characteristics, even though their responses may vary slightly. (In our clinical practice and in our research studies, we have found variability between parents and children in their reports of some headache characteristics, especially frequency. We have not found a consistent pattern in that parents or children over- or under-report symptoms. Instead, individuals simply differ with respect to which headache characteristics are most salient to them.)

Our recommended measures for headache frequency, headache length, pain intensity, pain affect, accompanying symptoms, and disability are based both on our clinical experience and on the results of our research studies. In our practice, we wish to be able to compare and contrast the efficacy of different therapies with children. Thus, we consistently obtain this information at pain assessment and record it on a database. With improved computer technology, an evidence-based practice model is becoming more feasible for private facilities. Information on headache characteristics is important for clinical records, and documentation on specific therapies is essential for billing. We periodically evaluate and refine our procedures on the basis of information learned from the children referred, as well as from published studies.

CLINICAL INTERVIEW

Our initial assessment begins with a structured interview, in which we ask parents and children a set of standard questions in a similar manner. This format ensures that we will obtain the same headache information from all children. We include open-ended questions, e.g., "Show me exactly where the pain is" and "What does it feel like?" as well as standardized questions of the type shown in Tables III–VI. Because our clinic is an integrated treatment and research program, we typically use both question formats for each headache characteristic. The first captures a child's unique response, and the second captures a response that can be more easily compared across different children. However, either question format would be adequate in clinical practice.

Table III
Children's Headache Interview: questions about frequency

How often do you get headaches now?
So you usually have them ...
    Hardly ever
    About once or twice in the last month
    About once or twice a week
    Several times a week (about 3–5 times)
    Every day
    Other (specify)
Do you always have headaches this often?
How do they change? What is the least number of headaches
    you get each week and what is the most?
Sometimes people get headaches more often at certain times
    of the year, week, day, or even during certain activities.
    Do you ever get headaches more often at these times?
    Winter, spring, fall or summer
    Mondays to Fridays or on weekends
    Mornings, afternoons, or at night
    When you are doing certain things, like sports
    At school or at home

SYNDROME DURATION

Syndrome duration should be determined at the initial consultation. Treatment efficacy (both drug and nondrug) may vary as a function of syndrome duration—possibly because different mechanisms may be involved when children have suffered headaches for many years. Parents are asked: "About how long has 'Mary' had headaches? Do you remember the first headache she had? Can you tell me about it? When did the headaches become a real problem ... and why?" Some parents clearly recall their child's first headache. If so, the circumstances may indicate whether stress was a possible cause. When children have had headaches for several years, the family may not initially have regarded them as a significant problem. It is important to learn what has happened to change the situation, such as the development of more severe or more disabling headaches.

HEADACHE LOCATION

The specific location of a child's headache should be noted at consultation and monitored throughout treatment. Children more accurately describe their headache features when they remember a specific headache than when they think about all their headaches. Children should be asked to remember their last headache and then point to the affected areas on their own head, with the location confirmed on an outline (Fig. 3). Follow-up questions are:

Table IV

Children's Headache Interview: questions about pain intensity

I'm going to read some words that describe how strong pain can be. I'd like
you to listen to them and pick out the one that best describes how strong your
headache was.

(~7 years and younger)	(~8 years and older)
a. A little bit	a. Slight
b. A little	b. Mild
c. Medium	c. Moderate
d. A lot	d. Strong
e. A real lot	e. Intense

Now I'd like you to use our pain scale to show me how much it hurts. (For the
Colored Analogue Scale: This scale is like a ruler. The bottom, where it is
small and there is hardly any color at all, means no pain at all. The top,
where it is large, very red, and a long way from the bottom, means the most
pain. I want you to slide the marker up the scale to show me how much
your headache hurts.)

Headache pain sometimes changes in strength after it starts. Does your
headache start low and get stronger or does it start strong?

Are all your headaches this strong?

If not, can you show me on the pain scale how strong they usually are?

"Was the pain on one side or both sides?" and if the child has not clearly
indicated whether the pain was uni- or bilateral, "Did the pain stay in the
same place for the whole headache? So, it did/did not spread out or change
places. Where did it spread or change to … and when? Are all your headaches in the same place?"

HEADACHE FREQUENCY

Headache frequency should be noted at consultation. This measure is
essential for establishing a baseline level of headache activity and is the
foundation for deciding whether a treatment has been effective. In our initial interview, we ask parents and children separately about headache frequency; questions for children are listed in Table III. Parents complete a
brief headache history on an intake form during or prior to their child's
appointment (Appendix 2). Our intention is to obtain a baseline measure of
headache frequency and to understand the child's perception of how often
he or she gets headaches. If we ask parents all pertinent questions in front of
the child, the child's answers could be influenced by the parents' responses.

Given that headache patterns vary, we try to capture information about
both the current and usual frequency of children's headaches. In some instances, parents seek treatment only when the headaches are at a peak

frequency, so that their reports of current frequency overestimate the usual number of headaches. Children's headaches may lessen regardless of the treatment they receive, simply because the frequency is returning to a previous and lower level. This effect, a regression toward the mean, complicates the interpretation of the results of many clinical trials. In order to minimize this effect in clinical practice, clinicians should note both the current frequency and the usual frequency at the initial interview. Children should then monitor headache frequency on a daily basis.

As part of the treatment program, children and parents independently keep a prospective record of headaches by using a monthly calendar sheet to mark headache-free days (Fig. 4) and by using pain logs to record more detailed information about headaches (Fig. 2). When children report a high headache frequency, typically associated with high disability, we ask that they emphasize headache-free days. The prospective records of headache frequency are the standard against which we evaluate treatment efficacy.

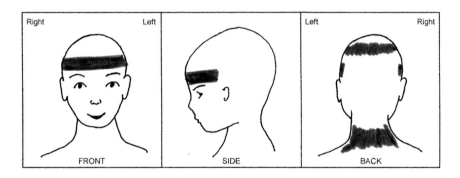

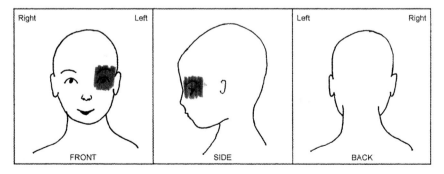

Fig. 3. A section from the Children's Headache Interview filled out by a 9-year-old boy (top) and a 15-year-old boy (bottom). Children mark the location of their headache on the outline or confirm the therapist's marks.

HEADACHE DURATION

Like headache frequency, headache length can vary widely—from 15-minute episodes to almost constant pain. However, individual children tend to have headaches of similar duration. Children report the length more accurately when asked to recall a specific headache. In our initial interview, we ask children to remember their last headache and describe what happened so that we know they are remembering a specific episode. We then ask, "How long did it last?" We confirm the length from a list of possible responses: "So it was a few minutes, about half an hour, 1 to 2 hours, 2½ to 4 hours, 4½ to 6 hours, all day (all waking hours), or other (specify)." As part of their treatment program, children monitor headache length prospectively, as shown in Fig. 2.

When children report an unusually short (e.g., a few seconds) or long (e.g., constant) headache, we ask additional questions to determine whether children are exaggerating a pain complaint in the absence of a headache. For short headaches, we note whether children just feel a brief sensation that is not really painful but prevents them from continuing activities. For long headaches, we determine exactly when children notice the headache each day (e.g., when they first wake up and open their eyes, after they brush their

Put a sticker down every day that you DO NOT have a headache. Fill out a headache log when you have a headache.

Fig. 4. A pain calendar for prospectively monitoring headache attacks. This calendar illustrates the record for an 8-year-old boy who used colored stickers to mark the days when he did not have a headache.

teeth, or at breakfast) and when it ends (e.g., after school, after dinner, or just before they go to sleep). Some children with long headaches are diagnosed with chronic daily headache, while others are diagnosed with a disability problem (see Chapters 7 and 9).

PAIN INTENSITY

In our initial interview, we ask children to think about their last headache and remember how strong the pain felt that day. "How much did it hurt?" We confirm the strength rating using both a word scale and an analogue pain scale, as shown by the questions in Table IV and Fig. 2. (The CAS is shown in Fig. 5.) In describing the strength of their headaches, children often indicate that they have two distinct types—brief, mild, nondisabling headaches and longer, stronger, disabling headaches. If so, we note the frequency of both types. Children then monitor pain intensity prospectively as part of their treatment program.

PAIN AFFECT

In our initial interview, we ask children to think about their last headache and remember how they were feeling when they had the headache that day. We are interested in evaluating pain affect to help us explore the cause and understand the impact of the headaches. Our clinical data suggest that children with underlying psychological distress often report conflicting intensity and affect values—strong pain intensity with neutral or even positive affect, or mild pain with very high negative affect, for example: "It's really strong and it's almost always there but I just deal with it," or "It's a 3 but it really bothers me and I can't do anything because of the headache." In contrast, children whose headaches are caused primarily by situational factors usually rate pain intensity and affect more consistently.

We inquire about the emotional impact of the headaches for children, telling them: "I'm going to read some of the words people feel when they have headaches and I wonder if any of these words describe how you felt— sad, annoyed, miserable, upset, angry, frightened, worried, or anxious?" We then show children the FAS (Fig. 6) and ask them to: "Choose the face that looks like how you feel when you have your headache. Choose the face that looks like how you feel *deep down inside,* not just how you look on the outside." Children then monitor pain affect prospectively as part of their treatment program.

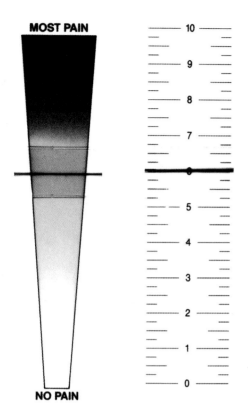

Fig. 5. The Colored Analogue Scale for measuring pain intensity. Children slide the marker along the scale to the level that matches the strength of their headache, and then turn the scale over to record the corresponding number.

PAIN QUALITY

After discussing pain intensity in the initial interview, we ask children to describe the quality of their pain sensation: "We've talked a lot about how much it hurt, but it's also important to know what your headache felt like. Some pains are sharp, like needles, and some are dull, like a pushing feeling. What did your headache feel like?" We then ask: "Do any of these words describe how your pain felt—sharp, dull, aching, pounding, cold, hot, burning, stinging, throbbing, tingling, or cutting?" The list includes common responses, such as pounding, and atypical responses, such as cold or tingling, to help us identify children who may have unusual symptoms or who may exaggerate symptoms.

ACCOMPANYING SYMPTOMS

Once children have remembered what the headache felt like, we ask them to think about other things they might have felt when they had that headache (Table V). The symptom checklist includes common features of

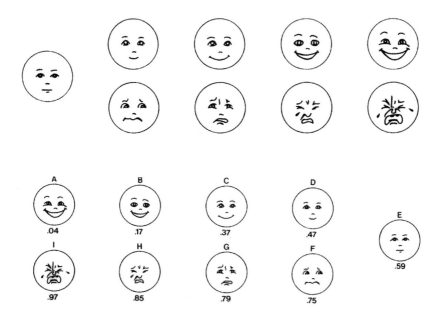

Fig. 6. The Facial Affective Scale for measuring pain affect. Children choose the face that best matches how they feel during a headache, and then turn the scale over to record the corresponding letter for the face and its affective value.

headache, such as light sensitivity, and atypical features, such as sweaty hands, to help us identify children who may have unusual symptoms or who may exaggerate symptoms. We then ask: "Did you have a warning signal that your headache was going to start? Sometimes people have a visual aura; that means they see things in their eyes just before they get a headache. Did that happen? What was it like? Do you ever have any warning signals that your headaches will start? What are they?"

Young children who have seen many specialists for the management of their headaches may inadvertently endorse various symptoms that they do not regularly experience during their headaches. It is essential to confirm that they can accurately describe the accompanying symptoms and to estimate how often they experience them. Our clinical impression is that children are not exaggerating, but that they gradually believe they always have the symptoms because parents report all signs and symptoms (regardless of how infrequent) at a consultation visit and because children have been asked so often about these aspects that they think they are part of the headache problem. As an example, a parent responded "yes" when the neurologist asked whether her son had double vision when he had headaches. The neurologist then confirmed with the boy, "So you see double when you have a headache?" The boy agreed. The neurologist then wrote "CAT" on a sheet

Table V
Children's Headache Interview: accompanying symptoms checklist

Now I'd like to ask you other things you might have felt when you
  had this headache. Did you:
  1. Have aches in your arms or legs?
  2. Have aches in your neck or shoulders?
  3. Feel dizzy?
  4. Feel that light bothered your eyes?
  5. See bright lights, dots, flashes out of the corner of your eyes?
  6. Feel that sound bothered you?
  7. Feel really tired?
  8. Feel sick to your stomach?
  9. Throw up?
  10. Have a sore throat?
  11. Feel hot and sweaty?
  12. Feel your heart beat really fast?
  13. Have sweaty hands?
Do these same things happen every time you have a headache?

of paper and asked "Can you show me what would you see when you had a headache?" The boy wrote "CCAATT," confirming that he thought he had double vision but had no idea what double vision really was.

HEADACHE DISABILITY

The disability children experience from their headaches should be noted at consultation and monitored throughout treatment. Disability management is an important component of pain management. During the initial interview, it is possible to obtain a global assessment of a child's disability—either proportional or excessive—in comparison to headache severity. Children who have had headaches for a long time are at risk for developing more disability behaviors when they try to avoid supposed pain triggers or when they benefit from reduced stress or increased attention during headaches. The initial questions we ask children are listed in Table VI.

Disability is usually assessed in children by noting the number of school days missed, the number of hours resting or sleeping during headaches, and the number of sporting or social activities missed. These overt behaviors can be easily documented, but they do not fully represent the nature and extent of a child's headache disability. More subtle signs of disability are revealed as children are followed more closely in a treatment program. These include a progressive shift in a child's recreational activities, perhaps moving from peer to solitary activities or from active team sports to passive hobbies, and changes in what they do at school. They may still attend school, but may have obtained permission to rest at their desk or to opt out of certain classes.

Table VI
Children's Headache Interview: disability questions

Now I'd like to ask you about the effects or impact of these
  headaches on your life. What is hard about having
  headaches?

Do your headaches often interfere with what you are doing?

Have they ever prevented you from:
  1. Playing sports?
  2. Doing homework?
  3. Going to parties or movies?
  4. Doing household chores?
  5. Playing or socializing with friends?
  6. Watching TV?
  7. Playing computer games?

Have your headaches ever prevented you from attending
  school?

If so, how many days have you missed this week … this
  month … this year?

TREATMENT EVALUATION

The evaluation of all therapies for children's headaches is based on a "before and after" comparison of headache activity. *Headache activity,* a common outcome measure in many clinical studies, refers to a composite index of frequency, intensity, and disability. Unfortunately, there is no generally recognized format for how each of these components is assessed; thus, headache activity is not a specific and uniform measure of a child's headaches across different studies. In clinical practice, each component individually could be a meaningful index of headache improvement. In many instances, concurrent positive changes are noted in frequency, intensity, and disability. However, children may experience a more profound change in one component than in another. For example, treatment may significantly lessen the number of headaches a child has, but the intensity may be the same when a headache does occur. Sometimes treatment may lessen headache intensity and accompanying disability, but the frequency of attacks may be unchanged. Thus, treatment evaluation should be based on a consideration of each component and its relevance for a particular child.

SUMMARY

Pain assessment is an integral component of diagnosis and treatment for children with recurrent headaches. Extensive research throughout the past decade has validated many behavioral and self-report scales as pain measures for children. Behavioral scales must be used when children are unable to communicate directly about their pain experience; these scales provide only an indirect estimate of pain intensity, but can provide direct measures of pain-related disability. When children can describe their headaches, they should be asked to use age-appropriate self-report measures.

Several self-report tools can be easily incorporated into a semi-structured clinical interview to enable health care providers to objectively document children's headaches—location, frequency, length, pain intensity, pain quality, disability level, and accompanying symptoms. Children's records of these headache characteristics in simple pain logs and diaries can provide an accurate baseline for determining treatment efficacy.

Ordinary clinical care is a form of research, because health care providers are determining the causes for children's headaches, selecting an intervention from various alternatives, evaluating the effectiveness of the intervention and any side effects, and adjusting the treatment as required to maintain a proper balance between effectiveness and side effects. All health care professionals constantly evaluate the effectiveness of their treatments, even if they do not detail their evaluations in a consistent manner for all children. Future decisions about patient care are guided by previous treatment results. The increasing trend toward evidence-based health care requires that clinicians simply keep more objective and more consistent records as part of ordinary clinical care. We now have the knowledge to evaluate children's headaches with practical, time- and cost-effective methods. The benefits will be a vastly improved understanding of the causes of children's headaches and an enhanced ability to select the best treatment for each child.

REFERENCES

Abu-Saad H. Assessing children's responses to pain. *Pain* 1984; 19:163–171.
Allen KD, McKeen LR. Home-based multicomponent treatment of pediatric migraine. *Headache* 1991; 31:467–472.
Andrasik F, Burke EJ, Attanasio V, Rosenblum EL. Child, parent, and physician reports of a child's headache pain: relationships prior to and following treatment. *Headache* 1985; 25:421–425.
Beyer JE, Wells N. The assessment of pain in children. *Pediatr Clin North Am* 1989; 36:837–854.
Beyer JE, McGrath PJ, Berde CB. Discordance between self-report and behavioral pain measures in children aged 3–7 years after surgery. *J Pain Symptom Manage* 1990; 5(6):350–356.
Bieri D, Reeve RA, Champion GD, Addicoat L, Ziegler JB. The Faces Pain Scale for the self-assessment of the severity of pain experienced by children: development, initial validation, and preliminary investigation for ratio scale properties. *Pain* 1990; 41:139–150.
Bijttebier P, Vertommen H. Antecedents, concomitants, and consequences of pediatric headache: confirmatory construct validation of two parent-report scales. *J Behav Med* 1999; 22:437–456.
Blanchard EB, Andrasik F, Neff DF, Jurish SE, O'Keefe DM. Social validation of the headache diary. *Behav Ther* 1981; 12:711–715.

Budd KS, Kedesdy JH. Investigation of environmental factors in pediatric headache. *Headache* 1989; 29:569–573.

Budd KS, Workman DE, Lemsky CM, Quick DM. The children's headache assessment scale (CHAS): factor structure and psychometric properties. *J Behav Med* 1994; 17:159–179.

Champion GD, Goodenough B, von Baeyer CL, Thomas W. Measurement of pain by self-report. In: Finley GA, McGrath PJ (Eds). *Measurement of Pain in Infants and Children,* Progress in Pain Research and Management, Vol. 10. Seattle: IASP Press, 1998, pp 123–160.

Finley GA, McGrath PJ (Eds). *Measurement of Pain in Infants and Children,* Progress in Pain Research and Management, Vol. 10. Seattle: IASP Press, 1998.

Gaffney A. How children describe pain: a study of words and analogies used by 5–14 year-olds. In: Dubner R, Gebhart GF, Bond MR (Eds). *Pain Research and Clinical Management,* Vol. 3. Amsterdam: Elsevier, 1988, pp 341–347.

Gaffney A. Cognitive developmental aspects of pain in school-age children. In: Schechter NL, Berde CB, Yaster M (Eds). *Pain in Infants, Children, and Adolescents.* Baltimore: Williams & Wilkins, 1993, pp 75–85.

Gaffney A, Dunne EA. Developmental aspects of children's definitions of pain. *Pain* 1986; 26:105–117.

Gaffney A, Dunne EA. Children's understanding of the causality of pain. *Pain* 1987; 29:91–104.

Goodenough B, Addicoat L, Champion GD, et al. Pain in 4- to 6-year-old children receiving intramuscular injections: a comparison of the Faces Pain Scale with other self-report and behavioral measures. *Clin J Pain* 1997; 13:60–73.

Griffiths JD, Martin PR. Clinical-versus home-based treatment formats for children with chronic headache. *Br J Health Psychol* 1996; 1:151–166.

Harbeck C, Peterson L. Elephants dancing in my head: a developmental approach to children's concepts of specific pains. *Child Dev* 1992; 63:138–149.

Hester NK. The preoperational child's reaction to immunization. *Nurs Res* 1979; 28:250–255.

Hester NO, Foster R, Kristensen K. Measurement of Pain in children: generalizability and validity of the pain ladder and the poker chip tool. In: Tyler DC, Krane EJ (Eds). *Pediatric Pain,* Advances in Pain Research and Therapy, Vol. 15. New York: Raven Press, 1990, pp 79–84.

Johnson RS, Lichstein KL, Hoelscher TJ. Child migraine: behavioral assessment and treatment. In: Morgan SB, Okwumabua TM (Eds). *Child and Adolescent Disorders: Developmental and Health Psychology Perspective.* Hillsdale: Lawrence Erlbaum Associates, 1990, pp 241–266.

Johnston C. Development of psychological responses to pain in infants and toddlers. In: Schechter NL, Berde CB, Yaster M (Eds). *Pain in Infants, Children and Adolescents.* Baltimore: Williams & Wilkins, 1993, pp 65–74.

Labbé EE, Williamson DA. Treatment of childhood migraine using autogenic feedback training. *J Consult Clin Psychol* 1984; 52:968–976.

Labbé EE, Williamson DA, Southard DR. Reliability and validity of children's reports of migraine headache symptoms. *J Psychopathol Behav Assess* 1985; 7:375–383.

Larsson B, Carlsson J. A School-based, nurse-administered relaxation training for children with chronic tension-type headache. *J Pediatr Psychol* 1996; 21:603–614.

Marcon RA, Labbé EE. Assessment and treatment of children's headaches from a developmental perspective. *Headache* 1990; 30:586–592.

McGrath PA. *Pain in Children: Nature, Assessment and Treatment.* New York: Guilford Publications, 1990.

McGrath PA, Gillespie J. Pain assessment in infants and children. In: Turk DC, Melzack R (Eds). *Handbook of Pain Assessment.* New York: Guilford Press, in press.

McGrath PA, deVeber LL, Hearn MT. Multidimensional pain assessment in children. In: Fields HL, Dubner R, Cervero F (Eds). *Proceedings of the Fourth World Congress on Pain,* Advances in Pain Research and Therapy, Vol. 9. New York: Raven Press, 1985, pp 387–393.

McGrath PA, Hinton GG, Boone JE. Management of recurrent headaches in children. *Abstracts: 7th World Congress on Pain.* Seattle: IASP, 1993, p 151.

McGrath PA, Seifert CE, Speechley KN, et al. A new analogue scale for assessing children's pain: an initial validation study. *Pain* 1996; 64:435–443.

McGrath PA, Girvan DP, Hillier LM, Seifert CE. Post-operative pain in children: can parents integrate assessment and management? *Abstracts: 9th World Congress on Pain.* Seattle: IASP Press, 1999, p 201.

McGrath PJ. Behavioral measures of pain. In: Finley GA, McGrath PJ (Eds). *Measurement of Pain in Infants and Children,* Progress in Pain Research and Management, Vol. 10. Seattle: IASP Press, 1998, pp 83–102.

McGrath PJ, Unruh A. *Pain in Children and Adolescents.* Amsterdam: Elsevier, 1987.

Peterson L, Harbeck C, Farmer J, Zink M. Developmental contributions to the assessment of children's pain: conceptual and methodological implications. In: Bush JP, Harkins SW (Eds). *Children in Pain: Clinical and Research Issues from a Developmental Perspective.* New York: Springer-Verlag, 1991, pp 33–58.

Pintov S, Lahat E, Alstein M, Vogel Z, Barg J. Acupuncture and the opioid system: implications in management of migraine. *Pediatr Neurol* 1997; 17:129–133.

Price DD. *Psychological Mechanisms of Pain and Analgesia,* Progress in Pain Research and Management, Vol. 15. Seattle: IASP Press, 1999.

RCN Institute. *Clinical Guideline for the Recognition and Assessment of Acute Pain in Children: Recommendations.* London: RCN Publishing, 1999.

Richardson GM, McGrath PJ, Cunningham SJ, Humphreys P. Validity of the headache diary for children. *Headache* 1983; 23:184–187.

Ross DM, Ross SA. *Childhood Pain: Current Issues, Research, and Management.* Baltimore: Urban & Schwarzenberg, 1988.

Savedra MC, Tesler MD, Holzemer WL, Wilkie DJ, Ward JA. Pain location: validity and reliability of body outline markings by hospitalized children and adolescents. *Res Nurs Health* 1989; 12:307–314.

Sinkin-Feldman L, Tesler M, Savedra M. Word placement on the Word-Graphic Rating Scale by pediatric patients. *Pediatr Nurs* 1997; 23:31–34.

St. Laurent-Gagnon T, Bernard-Bonnin AC, Villeneuve E. Pain evaluation in preschool children and by their parents. *Acta Paediatr* 1999; 88:422–427.

Sweet SD, McGrath PJ. Physiological measures of pain. In: Finley GA, McGrath PJ (Eds). *Measurement of Pain in Infants and Children,* Progress in Pain Research and Management, Vol. 10. Seattle: IASP Press, 1998, pp 59–81.

Teghtsoonian M. Children's scales of length and loudness: a developmental application of cross-modal matching. *J Exp Child Psychol* 1980; 30:290–307.

Tesler MD, Savedra MC, Holzemer WL, et al. The Word-Graphic Rating Scale as a measure of children's and adolescents' pain intensity. *Res Nurs Health* 1991; 14:361–371.

Westerling D. Postoperative recovery evaluated with a new, tactile scale (TaS) in children undergoing ophthalmic surgery. *Pain* 1999; 83:297–301.

Wong DL, Baker CM. Pain in children: comparison of assessment scales. *Pediatr Nurs* 1988; 14:9–17.

Correspondence to: Patricia A. McGrath, PhD, Pain Innovations Inc., 38 Hampton Crescent, London, Ontario, Canada N6H 2N8. Tel: 519-495-8287; Fax: 519-471-8529; email: pamcgrat@julian.uwo.ca. Effective 1 July 2001: Department of Anesthesiology, School of Medicine, University of Utah, Salt Lake City, UT 84108, USA.

The Child with Headache: Diagnosis and Treatment.
Progress in Pain Research and Management, Vol. 19,
edited by Patricia A. McGrath and Loretta M. Hillier,
IASP Press, Seattle, © 2001.

3

Differential Diagnosis of Headaches in Children and Adolescents

A. David Rothner

*Section of Child Neurology, The Cleveland Clinic Foundation,
Cleveland, Ohio, USA*

Headache is a common disorder in children and adolescents that causes discomfort and may lead to absence from school and work. Most headaches in children and adolescents are not associated with organic disease. Physicians must consider both physical and psychological factors in determining a diagnosis and selecting therapy. A thorough history, coupled with a complete physical and neurological examination and, if needed, selected laboratory tests, will aid in arriving at the correct diagnosis. Treatment is most effective when the specific headache type and its etiology can be determined. This chapter reviews the common types of headache seen in pediatric practice and provides a systematic approach to diagnosis and treatment.

HISTORICAL ASPECTS AND EPIDEMIOLOGY

Hippocrates described migraine 25 centuries ago; Galen coined the term *hemicrania* 600 years later. William Henry Day, British pediatrician and author of *Essays on Diseases in Children* (1873), recognized that nonorganic, nonvascular headaches were the most common type of headache in children and stated: "Headaches in the young are for the most part due to bad arrangements in their lives." In a landmark epidemiologic study, Bille (1962) reported on the frequency of headache in 9000 schoolchildren. Three books and two journals have focused on pediatric headache and are useful references (Friedman and Harms 1967; Barlow 1984; Hockaday 1988; Rothner 1995b; Smith 1995).

Bille (1962) studied the entire school-age population of Uppsala, Sweden between the ages of 7 and 15. He noted that by age seven, 2.5% of children had frequent tension headache, 1.4% had migraine, and 35% had infrequent headache of other varieties. By age 15, 15.5% had frequent tension headache, 5.3% had migraine, and 54% had infrequent headache of other types. Bille concluded that the frequency of migraine is higher in prepubertal males than in prepubertal females, but that after puberty, the frequency of migraine is higher in females. The frequency of mixed headache and/or tension headache is lowest in children under age seven, increases between the ages of 7 and 12, and is highest between the ages of 12 and 18. The overall prevalence of headache increases in the period from preschool to adolescence. Overall, headache prevalence by age seven is 37–51% and at ages 7–15, 57–82% (Mortimer et al. 1992; Lipton 1997).

Lipton (1997) has thoroughly reviewed the classification and epidemiology of headache in children, discussing methodological issues, case definitions, incidence, prevalence, relationship to socioeconomic status, and prognosis, addressing the question of increasing prevalence.

CLASSIFICATION

In 1988, the International Headache Society (IHS) published guidelines for headache classification (Headache Classification Committee 1988). However, the IHS diagnostic criteria (reviewed in Chapter 1) are neither specific nor sensitive to headache in children. A revised set of IHS criteria for migraine headache in children has been proposed (Winner et al. 1997). The definition of tension headache in children and adolescents is currently being revised (Gladstein and Holden 1996).

In addition, headache can be classified by plotting the temporal pattern of the headache against its severity (Rothner 1978). This classification identifies five patterns: acute, acute recurrent (migraine), chronic progressive (organic), chronic nonprogressive (tension), and mixed (migraine and tension) (Figs. 1, 2).

An *acute headache* is a single event with no previous history of headache. Most such headaches are associated with febrile illnesses. If the headache is associated with neurological symptoms or signs, an organic process should be suspected. The differential diagnosis of an acute headache involves consideration of a wide variety of disorders (Table I). *Acute recurrent headaches* are usually migrainous. If the same headache has occurred, resolved, and reoccurred several times, migraine is most likely. These headaches are painful, but not life-threatening. If migraine headaches are associated with neurological symptoms or signs, organic etiologies must be considered. *Chronic progressive headaches* worsen in frequency and severity

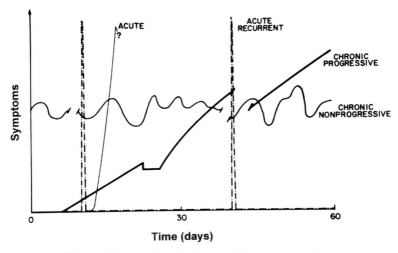

Fig. 1. Types of headache according to temporal patterns.

over time. They are often accompanied by symptoms of increased intracranial pressure and neurological signs. An organic process is most likely
(Table II). *Chronic nonprogressive headaches,* commonly known as *tension-type headaches* or *muscle contraction headaches,* occur frequently or
daily. The episodic variety occurs less than 15 days per month and the
chronic variety occurs more than 15 days per month. These headaches are
not associated with symptoms of increased intracranial pressure or progressive neurological disease, and are not life-threatening. The general and neurological examinations are normal, and laboratory studies are negative. Psychological factors are frequently important.

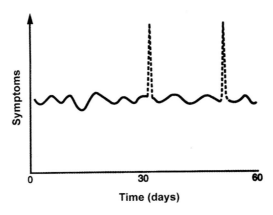

Fig. 2. The mixed headache syndrome (chronic nonprogressive and acute recurrent).

Table I
Causes of acute headache

Acute Generalized	Acute Localized
Systemic infection	Sinusitis
CNS infection	Otitis
Toxins: lead, CO_2	Ocular abnormality
Post-seizure	Dental disease
Electrolyte imbalance	Trauma
Hypertension	Occipital neuralgia
Hypoglycemia	Temporomandibular
Postlumbar puncture	Joint dysfunction
Trauma	
Vascular thrombosis	
Hemorrhage	
Exertion	

The *mixed headache syndrome* is a combination of acute recurrent headaches (migraines) superimposed on a pattern of daily or almost daily chronic nonprogressive (tension) headaches. The syndrome is not life-threatening, although the pain may be disabling. Psychological factors are important.

PATHOPHYSIOLOGY

Both extracranial and intracranial structures may be sensitive to pain. Pain from extracranial and intracranial structures from the front half of the skull are mediated via the fifth cranial nerve. Pain from the occipital half of the skull is mediated via the upper cervical nerves. Inflammation, irritation, displacement, traction, dilatation, or invasion of any of these pain-sensitive structures will cause pain. Perception of pain is modified by psychological factors, ethnic factors, age, and previous experience with pain (McGrath 1990). Pain intensity should *not* be taken as an absolute indicator of severity.

The pathogenesis of migraine is unknown. The neurovascular hypothesis, based on biochemical studies and measurement of neurotransmitters

Table II
Causes of chronic progressive headache

Tumor
Pseudotumor
Subdural hematoma
Hydrocephalus
CNS infection
Chiari malformation

Table III
Headache questionnaire

1. Do you have one type or two types of headache?
2. When did the headache begin?
3. How did the headache begin?
4. How often does the headache occur?
5. Are the headaches intermittent, constant, or progressive?
6. Do the headaches occur at any special time or under special circumstances?
7. Are the headaches related to specific foods, medications, or activities?
8. Are there warning symptoms before the headache?
9. Where is the pain located?
10. What is the quality of the pain (sharp, dull, pounding)?
11. How severe is the headache (on a scale of 1–10)?
12. Are there associated symptoms?
13. How long does the headache last?
14. What do you do during the headache?
15. What makes the headache better? Worse?
16. Do symptoms continue in between the headaches?
17. Are you being treated for any other problem?
18. Do you take medication regularly or intermittently?
19. Does anyone else in your family have headaches? What kind?
20. What do you think is causing your headache?

and regional cerebral blood flow, considers migraine to be an inherited sensitivity of the trigeminal vascular system (Moskowitz 1991). Cortical, thalamic, or hypothalamic mechanisms initiate the attack secondary to internal or external stimuli in a genetically predisposed individual. The impulses spread to the cranial vasculature to produce a cascade of neurogenic inflammation and secondary vascular reactivity. Released vasoactive neuropeptides activate endothelial cells, mast cells, and platelets, which then increase extracellular amines, peptides, and other metabolites. This process results in sterile inflammation and causes pain that is transmitted centrally via the trigeminal nerve.

Improved understanding of serotonin (5-HT) and its relationship to headache has resulted in improved treatment for both acute and chronic headaches (Peroutka 1990). The 5-HT receptors are implicated in constriction of cerebral blood vessels. Abortive agents, including dihydroergotamine and sumatriptan, have potent activity at 5-HT_{1D} receptor sites. Several potent 5-HT antagonists are effective prophylactic agents for migraine, including methysergide, cyproheptadine, amitriptyline, and verapamil. Improved understanding of the physiology and chemistry of migraine will enable researchers to synthesize new drugs to treat migraine (Solomon 1995).

EVALUATION AND LABORATORY TESTS

Headache evaluation is the key to treatment (Rothner 1995c). A thorough history is necessary to differentiate the various headache types and their etiologies. The history begins with details of early childhood development, school function, previous medical problems, previous medications for both headache and other disorders, and drug and alcohol use. The patient and his or her parents should be asked about anxiety, stress, and depression, which could be associated with recurrent headache. The family history should include family members with migraine or tension headaches or psychological problems. A second set of questions deals with the headache itself; a suggested format is provided in Table III. A third set of questions should deal with symptoms of increased intracranial pressure or progressive neurological disease, including ataxia, lethargy, seizures, visual disturbances, focal weakness, personality change, and loss of abilities.

Chronic pain affects eating, sleeping, playing, and school function. Emotional and personality considerations are of great importance in the older child and adolescent. Headache may cause or be the result of school failure and absenteeism. Headache is often provoked by stress related to peers, family, and school. Depression and anxiety frequently coexist with headache (Kowal and Pritchard 1990). The interaction between the child and the parents during the interview should be noted because it may reflect problems not discussed. With adolescents, a private interview is necessary.

Patients with migraine or tension headache have no symptoms of increased intracranial pressure or progressive disease. If headaches have increased dramatically in severity or if they are severe enough to awaken the child, potentially serious etiologies should be considered. The physician should conduct a general physical examination, paying careful attention to the vital signs, including blood pressure and temperature. The skin should be examined for neurocutaneous abnormalities such as those seen in neurofibromatosis. In most children and adolescents with tension and/or migraine headaches, the general examination is normal.

A neurological examination should be conducted to investigate signs of trauma and/or nuchal rigidity. The circumference of the head, condition of the optic fundi (looking for abnormalities such as hemorrhages and papilledema), eye movements, muscle strength, reflexes, and coordination should be recorded. Any abnormality on the neurological examination requires further study, as children and adolescents with tension and migraine headaches should have normal neurological examinations.

The choice of laboratory tests rests upon the differential diagnosis (Rothner 1995c). "Routine" laboratory tests are not helpful. If the patient is critically ill or if the history suggests increased intracranial pressure or a progressive neurological disease, testing is necessary. The electroencephalogram (EEG) is of limited value in the evaluation of headache. Nonspecific abnormalities are found in normal children, and 9% of children with migraine will have benign focal epileptiform discharges (BFED) without any evidence of epilepsy (Kinast et al. 1982). However, if the patient has had loss or alteration of consciousness, or exhibits abnormal movements, an EEG may be useful. Evoked potentials and brain electrical activity maps have not proven to be of value in evaluating headaches.

The diagnosis of structural central nervous system (CNS) disorders has been aided by computed tomography (CT) and magnetic resonance imaging (MRI). Both are rapid and accurate methods of evaluating the intracranial contents. They easily identify congenital malformations, cranial infections, trauma, neoplasms, and degenerative, neurocutaneous, and vascular disorders. An MRI scan may demonstrate lesions not visible on CT, including sinus pathology and disorders of the craniospinal region. In patients with migraine or tension headache with no neurological symptoms and a normal neurological examination, imaging is not required (Maytal et al. 1995).

Psychological evaluation is useful in individuals with chronic, recurrent, or disabling headache unresponsive to treatment (Rothner and Jensen 1995). Many parents consciously or unconsciously promote the continuation of the pain syndrome. A psychologist is an essential part of the team working to resolve the patient's difficulties; the patient and his or her parents should be reassured that the pain is genuine and that the goal of assessment is to investigate factors that might be worsening or maintaining the pain.

SPECIFIC HEADACHE SYNDROMES

ACUTE GENERALIZED HEADACHE

In a study of 37 children seen in the pediatrician's office for headache (Kandt and Levine 1987), 30% had infections such as pharyngitis and otitis, and infectious disorders were important in 22 patients. Children with a family history of migraine were more likely to have headache, and sleep disorders were more common in headache patients than in a general group of pediatric patients. Further studies of this nature are warranted.

If an acute headache is associated with neurological symptoms or signs, an organic disorder should be suspected and referral to a pediatric neurologist is indicated. Headache represents anywhere from 1% to 4% of patients seen in pediatric emergency rooms, and 3–17% of these patients have serious medical conditions (Rothner 1998).

MIGRAINE HEADACHE

Migraine is a recurrent headache, characterized by episodic, periodic, and paroxysmal attacks of pain separated by pain-free intervals. Associated symptoms include pallor, anorexia, abdominal pain, nausea, vomiting, phonophobia, photophobia, and a desire to sleep.

The incidence of migraine with aura in males is 6.6/1000 and peaks at 5–6 years of age. The incidence of migraine without aura in males is 10/1000 and peaks at 10–11 years. The incidence of migraine with aura in females is 14/1000 and peaks at 12–13 years. The incidence of migraine without aura in females is 18/1000 and peaks at 14–17 years (Stewart et al. 1991). Winner and colleagues (1997) and others have suggested that the IHS criteria (Headache Classification Committee 1988) require modification, since migraine in children is usually bilateral and shorter in duration.

Migraine headaches in children and adolescents *never* occur daily (Rothner 1986). They are frequently bitemporal or bifrontal. Children tend to have one to four attacks per month. Their headaches tend to start after school and last less than 2 hours; they are relieved by sleep and analgesics. In adolescents, the frequency of migraine with aura seems to increase slightly, as does that of unilateral headache. The frequency of attacks increases, and attacks can occur in the morning. Attacks also last longer and are more difficult to relieve. In later adolescence, migraine may be superimposed on daily or almost-daily tension headache, the *mixed headache syndrome.*

Migraine attacks may be precipitated by triggers, but their role in children's migraine has not been well documented. Diet, anxiety, stress, school, fatigue, excessive sleep, lack of sleep, minor head injury, exercise, menses, travel, illness, odors, medications (e.g., birth control pills), and hunger are possible factors. Specific foods containing vasoactive substances have been implicated, including bacon, ham, and salami (containing nitrites), aged cheese and red wine (containing tyramine), oriental food (containing monosodium glutamate), and chocolate (containing phenylethylamine) (Peatfield et al. 1984).

Most children and adolescents with migraine are not likely to show clinically significant levels of depression, although those with migraine appear to have more depressive symptoms than do their peers without headaches (Martin and Smith 1995). Early investigations suggested that recurrent pediatric headache was associated with increased levels of anxiety, but more recent work has not supported this relationship (Cooper et al. 1987).

Migraine is a familial disorder; 50–90% of children with migraine have a first- or second-degree relative with this disorder. It is not clear whether migraine is an autosomal dominant or a multifactorial condition (Joutel et al. 1993).

Pediatric migraine has been correlated with an increased incidence of car sickness, sleep disturbances, syncope, mitral valve prolapse, and Tourette's syndrome. These relationships require additional investigation.

Migraine with aura occurs in 15% of patients with migraine. A visual aura, including brightly colored lights, moving lights, scotomata, and fortification spectra, precedes the headache by 15–30 minutes. Other symptoms such as dysphasia, dysesthesia, hemiplegia, and speech disturbance may also briefly occur. Headache is contralateral to the aura and is described as severe and throbbing. It is followed by anorexia, abdominal pain, nausea, and vomiting. Children with this type of headache appear pale, avoid light and noise, and seek sleep as it may relieve their pain.

Common migraine occurs in 70% of children and adolescents. A visual aura is not present, but an autonomic aura may occur prior to the headache, with symptoms including pallor, irritability, lethargy, and personality change. The parents frequently describe their children as being quiet or grouchy, appearing pale and glassy-eyed, and having rings under their eyes. The headache that follows is usually bilateral and throbbing, and is associated with abdominal pain, anorexia, nausea, vomiting, photophobia, and phonophobia. Children seek out a dark, quiet place and attempt to sleep. The usual episodes last 1–6 hours and occur one to three times per month. There is considerable variability in the frequency, severity, and duration of attacks.

Complex migraine is characterized by paroxysmal headache and transient neurological abnormalities. Most attacks resolve spontaneously without sequelae. It is important to differentiate complex migraine from more serious conditions such as seizures or a vascular occlusion. An MRI scan, coupled with magnetic resonance angiography (MRA) of both the cervical and intracranial vessels, helps to differentiate migraine from more serious conditions. If the migraine is associated with neurological abnormalities, albeit transient, referral to a pediatric neurologist is indicated.

Hemiplegic migraine is the association of recurrent hemiparesis (muscular weakness or partial paralysis on one side of the body) and headache. The familial form is inherited as an autosomal dominant condition. The hemiparesis may precede, accompany, or follow the headache. Other etiologies include thromboembolism, arteriovenous malformation, moyamoya syndrome (a vascular abnormality), mitochondrial disorders, and tumors. Oral contraceptives may increase the frequency of this disorder. It may also be precipitated by mild head trauma. The hemiparesis usually resolves within 24 hours. An MRI and MRA should be obtained.

Ophthalmoplegic migraine is the association of a headache and a complete or incomplete third nerve palsy on the same side. The headache may precede, accompany, or follow the neurological deficit. The pain is behind the eye. Examination reveals a unilateral dilated pupil and lateral deviation of the eye. The patient may have ptosis and diplopia. An MRI and MRA are needed to differentiate this disorder from an aneurysm. The third nerve palsy may last for weeks; steroids may shorten its duration.

Basilar artery migraine is defined as recurrent attacks of occipital headache and neurological symptoms referable to the cerebellum, brainstem, and occipital cortex. Patients may present with visual symptoms, sensory symptoms, dizziness, vertigo, ataxia, dysarthria, or quadriparesis and loss of consciousness. Nausea and vomiting are frequent. Symptoms usually clear within 24 hours. Epilepsy, vascular disease, and demyelinating disease should be excluded. EEG, MRI, and MRA may be needed.

Confusional migraine mimics a toxic encephalopathy. It most commonly occurs in adolescents. The headache is followed by confusion and an expressive or receptive aphasia. Concussion, viral encephalitis, and drug abuse should be excluded. Toxicology screening, EEG, imaging studies, and lumbar puncture may be indicated. The episodes last 6–12 hours and may be precipitated by mild head trauma. Data concerning treatment for this syndrome are not available.

Migraine variants are episodic, recurrent, and transient neurological events in a known migraine patient, in a patient who will develop migraine later, or in a patient who has a family history of migraine. Headache is not necessarily prominent.

Paroxysmal vertigo occurs between the ages of 2 and 6 years. The episodes are sudden, brief, and consist of inability to maintain equilibrium. There is *no* loss of consciousness. Nystagmus may be present. Symptoms last only a few minutes. These patients often develop migraine in later years.

Paroxysmal torticollis is rare. It consists of recurrent episodes of head tilt, headache, nausea, and vomiting in infants and young children. The episodes last hours to days. The outcome and treatment of this disorder are not known.

Cyclic vomiting consists of recurrent episodes of unexplained abdominal pain, nausea, and vomiting, which may lead to dehydration. Headache may not be present. The episodes may occur monthly and last 24–48 hours. Structural gastrointestinal abnormalities and metabolic disorders should be excluded. Attempts have been made to prevent recurrent episodes using prophylactic migraine therapy.

Alice-in-Wonderland syndrome includes visual illusions and spatial distortions associated with migraine headache. Children with this rare disorder describe micropsia, macropsia, and other distortions of perception. Some investigators consider these brief visual symptoms to be part of the aura. This type of visual-perceptual abnormality has also been reported with infectious mononucleosis, complex partial seizures, benign occipital epilepsy, drug ingestion, and psychiatric disorders.

Migraine sine hemicrania. Patients exhibiting ophthalmological manifestations of migraine such as monocular scotomas, blindness, or homonymous hemianopia *without* headache are referred to as having *migraine sine hemicrania.* The disorder appears to be more common in females and during adolescence.

Epilepsy equivalent. Epilepsy and migraine are both common disorders and may coexist in a single patient. The association of episodic headache, nausea, and vomiting, and an abnormal EEG has been termed an *epilepsy equivalent.* These episodes are most often migraine with an abnormal EEG. Epileptiform EEGs occur in 9% of migraine patients (Kinast et al. 1982). If the patient has altered consciousness or convulsive movements, the diagnosis may indeed be epilepsy. In such cases, administration of anticonvulsants is appropriate (Marks and Ehrenberg 1993).

MANAGEMENT OF MIGRAINE

Management of migraine must be based on the patient's age, the frequency and severity of attacks, the presence of an aura, the patient's reliability and attitude toward medication, and the presence of psychological factors. Once assured that there is no serious underlying problem, many patients with infrequent episodes appear to have fewer and less distressing attacks. Both pharmacological and nonpharmacological methods are used to treat migraine (Wasiewski and Rothner 1999). Treatment begins with patient education, removal of triggers, and normalization of lifestyle.

Pharmacological therapy. Pharmacological therapy of migraine can be divided into (a) suppression of pain, nausea, and vomiting; (b) attempts to abort the impending attack; and (c) prevention of future attacks (Igarashi et al. 1992; Wasiewski and Rothner 1999). Detailed information on drug therapies, including dosages, is presented in Chapter 5; this section on pharmacological therapy is included to summarize the treatments I have found most useful in my practice.

Symptoms can be suppressed by pain medication such as acetaminophen or nonsteroidal anti-inflammatory agents (NSAIDs), singly or in combination. Nausea and vomiting can be relieved by antiemetics. Mild sedatives are helpful to promote sleep. Only infrequently do patients require narcotic analgesics or medications containing barbiturates. Medication given at the onset of an attack is more effective. My preference is to begin with ibuprofen at the recommended dosage in association with an antihistamine, and if the patient has severe vomiting, an antiemetic. The patient should rest in a dark, quiet room and apply a cold compress to his or her forehead. If after 2 hours the patient remains in considerable pain, acetaminophen should be given at the recommended dosage. I rarely find it necessary to add barbiturates or narcotic analgesics to this combination.

If the above analgesic or combination of analgesics, antiemetics, and sedatives is unsuccessful in treating the acute migraine attack, abortive medications can be considered. Abortive medications include the oral, nasal, rectal, and parenteral ergotamines; the combination of isometheptene mucate, dichloralphenazone, and acetaminophen (Midrin; Carnrick); NSAIDs; and the various triptans. While all of these medications are used in adolescents, none of them have been specifically approved by the U.S. Food and Drug Administration (FDA) for the treatment of migraine in children or adolescents. I rarely use ergot preparations in children or adolescents as they may indeed increase nausea and vomiting. I find Midrin a useful medication as it contains a vasoconstrictor, an anxiolytic, and an analgesic. In children under 12 weighing between 30 and 50 kg, I begin with one capsule initially, followed by one an hour later if symptoms persist, followed by another one an hour later if symptoms persist (a total of three capsules). In a patient over the age of 12 or weighing more than 50 kg, I use two capsules at the onset, one an hour later, one an hour later, and one an hour later if symptoms persist (a total of five capsules). The patient should lie down in a dark, quiet room and use a cold compress. If Midrin does not work, the triptans should be tried. They have been tested in pediatric and adolescent patients. The oral dosage of sumatriptan (Imitrex; Glaxo Wellcome) is 25 mg for patients weighing between 30 and 50 kg and between the ages of 8 to 12, and 50 mg for those weighing more than 50 kg or over the age of 12. The patient may repeat the dosage 2 hours later if no relief is obtained. The maximum dosage is 50 mg for the younger child and 100 mg for the older child. Sumatriptan (Imitrex) nasal spray is available in 5- and 20-mg dosages. If the patient does not respond to these measures, consideration can be given to the parenteral use of dihydroergotamine.

Preventive medication should be considered in children or adolescents who have frequent migraine attacks (more than three attacks or 4 days of disability/month) and in whom symptomatic and abortive medication has not been effective. Prophylaxis should be considered in children and adolescents who are missing excessive school or work. If effective, such medications should be used for 4–6 months and then weaned. If a specific agent does not work, it should be discontinued after 6–10 weeks and another medication tried. Medications used in preventing migraine include cyproheptadine, propranolol, amitriptyline, calcium channel blockers, NSAIDs, and antiepileptic medications (see Table IV of Chapter 5 for suggested doses). The FDA has not approved any of these medications for the prevention of migraine in children or adolescents. When used as a migraine prophylactic, propranolol may cause or aggravate depression, and cyproheptadine may cause fatigue and weight gain. The calcium channel blockers may cause constipation, and the NSAIDs may cause gastric distress. Amitriptyline has been associated with drowsiness and prolongation of the Q-T interval on an ECG recording.

Nonpharmacological therapy focuses on the avoidance of trigger factors, a regular diet, normal sleep patterns, discontinuation of inappropriate and overused analgesics, relief of stress, and the use of counseling, relaxation therapy, and biofeedback (McGrath and Reid 1995; Rothner and Jensen 1995). Foods containing monosodium glutamate, nitrites, and tyramine should be restricted. Caffeine and alcohol consumption should be eliminated. Medications that may precipitate or aggravate migraine, including vasodilators, bronchodilators, oral contraceptives, and stimulants should be discontinued when possible. Biofeedback, relaxation training, and stress management have been useful in children and adolescents with migraine. Chapter 6 covers nondrug therapies in detail.

MIGRAINE PROGNOSIS

Most children and adolescents with migraine respond to treatment. "Refractory" migraine may be due to an incorrect diagnosis, i.e., misdiagnosing migraine in a patient with mixed headache syndrome or daily muscle contraction headache, or may result from treatment with inappropriate medications. Patient and family education enhances the treatment program, and written material and audiovisual aids are useful adjuncts.

In a 20-year follow-up study of schoolchildren, Bille (1981) found that 23% of those who had suffered migraines as children were migraine-free before the age of 25, boys significantly more often than girls. At the age of 50, more than half the migraine group still had migraine attacks. The author suggested that 30% of childhood migraineurs will go into remission, 30% will continue having migraine on a regular basis, and 40% will go in and out of migraine for varying periods of time (Bille 1981).

Matthews and colleagues (1987) suggested that vascular headache of childhood may evolve into a daily headache syndrome of adults, called "transformed migraine." Prospective long-term studies are needed to confirm this hypothesis.

CHRONIC PROGRESSIVE HEADACHE

Headache that worsens in frequency and severity over time and that is associated with symptoms of increased intracranial pressure or an abnormal neurological examination may be caused by an intracranial abnormality (Table II). Neuroimaging is almost always necessary (Cohen 1995). The headache in pseudotumor cerebri can be intermittent or constant (Corbett 1983). Papilledema is usually present. The blind spot may enlarge, and the visual fields may be constricted. This syndrome is common in older children and adolescent females. The disorder may be idiopathic or secondary to medical conditions, including menstrual irregularity, obesity, withdrawal of steroid therapy, hypervitaminosis A, or use of medications, including out-dated tetracycline. An MRI scan is usually normal. The lumbar puncture shows an elevated opening pressure of between 250 and 600 mL of water. Treatment may include weight loss, discontinuation of certain medications, repeated lumbar punctures, diuretics, and steroids. The patients should be closely followed for changes in visual field or visual acuity. If vision is progressively impaired, lumbar peritoneal shunting or optic sheath decompression should be considered. Patients with this disorder should be referred to a pediatric neurologist for ongoing management.

TENSION-TYPE HEADACHE
(CHRONIC NONPROGRESSIVE HEADACHE)

Other names for chronic nonprogressive headache include tension-type headache, chronic daily headache, muscle contraction headache, and psychogenic headache. These headaches are common in adolescents (Rothner and Jensen 1995; Gladstein and Holden 1996). Bille (1962) states that they are three times more common than migraine by age 15. Features of the syndrome are distinct from those of migraine. The pathogenesis of this disorder is not clear, but depression, stress, anxiety, and somatic preoccupation are thought to play major roles. The disorder may occur alone or in association with migraine ("mixed headache syndrome").

The clinical features of tension-type headache in adolescents have not been well defined, but symptoms are similar to those in adults. Most patients are female. The headache is frontal or holocephalic and pressure- or band-like. Associated tenderness in the occipital and cervical regions may be present. The pain may be present for the entire day or a portion of the day, or may come and go throughout the day. The pain is moderate when compared to migraine. Many adolescents with tension-type headaches continue their usual activities. A few seem mildly bothered by light or noise and develop mild nausea. Some use over-the-counter medications in excess; others have stopped taking such medications, as they were not helpful. Many are able to identify aggravating factors, including fatigue due to erratic sleep patterns and stressful situations at home or school. Patients often feel that their headaches aggravate their fatigue, impair their concentration, and cause irritability and anxiety. Many patients are temporarily aided by resting. These headaches rarely awaken patients from sleep. Exercise can worsen the headaches, but weather and food do not seem to be contributing factors. Many patients are unable to recognize their "stress" until they undergo psychological evaluation and counseling. Many are honor students and have excessive absences from school. Inadvertently, many parents perpetuate their children's headaches by providing secondary gain in the form of increased attention and relief from responsibilities.

Tension-type headaches are not preceded by an aura and are bilateral. Patients describe the pain vaguely. Associated symptoms are mild and may include blurred vision, nausea, fatigue, dizziness, and syncope. No symptoms of increased intracranial pressure or progressive neurological disease are noted. Most patients have no underlying medical condition. A minority have co-existing chronic fatigue, fibromyalgia, or recurrent abdominal pain. Laboratory studies and neuroimaging are negative.

If the patient has daily or constant headache for longer than 8 weeks, has no symptoms of increased intracranial pressure, a normal general physical examination, and a normal neurological examination, an organic etiology is unlikely. A psychological interview is essential to the diagnosis.

Patients with chronic headache pain frequently show various associated psychological and behavioral symptoms (Cooper et al. 1987; Kowal and Pritchard 1990; Martin and Smith 1995; Rothner and Jensen 1995). Both the psychological factors and learned behavioral patterns serve to maintain the symptoms.

Depression, anxiety, and stress have been studied in patients with tension-type headaches. What is considered stressful by one individual may seem trivial to another. Factors considered precipitants in children and adolescents include genetic predisposition; major negative life changes, including parental divorce, moving, and death of a close friend or relative; perceived lack of achievement; fear of failure; and somatic preoccupation. Many of our patients are overachievers, superior students who are active in extracurricular activities, but despite doing well in school, they are not attending regularly. Some of our patients have had previous multiple somatic symptoms, including abdominal pain and limb pain. Pain models may be present in their family.

In our clinic, the psychological evaluation includes standardized testing and structured interviews with the child and parents (Rothner and Jensen 1995). *It is essential that the family view the psychologist as part of the team needed to resolve the patient's difficulties.*

The episodic tension-type headache does not present a serious problem unless it becomes frequent or continuous and results in altered function. The *occasional* use of over-the-counter analgesics (including acetaminophen and ibuprofen, either separately or combined) is usually sufficient, along with rest in a dark room with an ice pack and the avoidance of stressful situations. Daily or frequent use of aspirin, caffeine- or barbiturate-containing compounds, and narcotic analgesics should be avoided. If gastric irritation occurs, NSAIDs should be discontinued. Patients who have used excessive over-the-counter analgesics, narcotics, barbiturates, tranquilizers, sedatives, and caffeine-containing compounds must discontinue their use (Symons 1998).

Psychological intervention may be useful. Williamson and colleagues (1993) have reviewed the pediatric headache literature in this area. In patients with frequent or daily headache, daily tricyclic antidepressant medication may be quite useful when combined with psychological interventions (Schulman and Silberstein 1992). The efficacy of these medications in improving tension-type headache in adults without depression has been well studied. Tricyclics seem more beneficial than selective serotonin reuptake inhibitors. Since many adolescents are sensitive to medication, gradual introduction of amitriptyline, beginning with a 5-mg dose at bedtime, is useful. Every 2–3 weeks, the dose is increased by 10 mg, and the pain is often diminished with doses between 30 and 60 mg per day. If significant depression coexists, child psychiatry consultation is needed. Amitriptyline may cause sedation, dry mouth, and postural hypotension. If higher dosages are used or syncope occurs, an ECG is indicated. If the dosage is built up slowly, side effects can be minimized. If sedation is a problem, protriptyline given three times a day may be helpful. Beta-blockers can induce or aggravate depression.

Caution should be exercised to avoid daily use of NSAIDs or acetaminophen, as these medications can perpetuate headache pain (Symons 1998). Patients with sensitive or tender muscles may benefit from physical therapy and daily exercises. Trigger point injections have not been well studied in adolescents.

Data are lacking on the outcome of these therapies and the long-term prognosis in pediatric patients. Since the pathogenesis of this disorder is not well understood, and because stress, anxiety, and depression seem to play a role, I recommend combining psychological and conservative medical interventions. Patients must attend school regularly. Whether early recognition of this syndrome, coupled with appropriate therapies, will decrease the prevalence of tension-type headache in adults remains to be determined.

MIXED HEADACHE SYNDROME

Pediatric and adolescent patients may also have mixed headache syndrome, which is migraine superimposed on tension-type headache. This combination is not uncommon and requires a combined psychological and pharmacological approach.

OTHER HEADACHES

Cluster headaches are rare in children and uncommon in adolescents. They consist of severe unilateral pain lasting 30–45 minutes behind or around the eye. Ptosis, miosis, conjunctival injection, nasal congestion, and rhinorrhea coexist. Attacks occur several times a day and frequently awaken the patient at night. Episodes occur over several weeks or months and then disappear for months to years. Treatment may include steroids, methysergide, ergotamine, oxygen, and lithium (Maytal and Lipton 1992).

Temporomandibular joint dysfunction presents with unilateral or bilateral pain just below the ear, which is aggravated by chewing. Patients describe clicking and locking of their jaw. The incidence is unknown in the pediatric population. Patients have tenderness over their jaw and limitation of mouth opening. The syndrome is seen with arthritis or after an injury, but it is more commonly associated with muscle spasm and fatigue in patients with "stress," malocclusion, bruxism, teeth clenching, and excessive gum chewing. A combination of muscle relaxants, anti-inflammatory drugs, and counseling is beneficial. Major dental surgery and costly therapeutic programs are usually unnecessary.

Occipital neuralgia is unilateral or bilateral pain in the posterior part of the head starting at the upper neck or base of the skull. The pain is aggravated by movement or hyperextension of the head. This problem is seen in athletes and in individuals involved in flexion-extension automobile accidents. Physical examination is either normal or may show cervical tenderness, limitation of motion, and decreased sensation over the C2 dermatome. MRI of the cervicocranial junction is indicated to rule out a congenital anomaly or other pathological process. Treatments include a soft cervical collar, analgesics, muscle relaxants, local injections, and physical therapy. Only rarely is surgery needed. The prognosis is quite good (Dugan et al. 1962).

Other. Four headache syndromes, infrequently seen in pediatric and adolescent medicine, are specifically responsive to indomethacin. These are *exertional headaches,* which are precipitated by sports; *cyclic migraine,* in which the patient exhibits cycles of migraine headache daily for several weeks followed by 3–4 months without headache; *chronic paroxysmal hemicrania (CPH),* a disorder of women characterized by daily multiple unilateral attacks of pain lasting 5–30 minutes; and *hemicrania continua,* characterized by unilateral steady nonparoxysmal hemicrania localized to the frontal part of the head, not associated with nausea and vomiting, and occurring predominantly in women. Indomethacin can be dramatically helpful in these patients, but it must be carefully monitored (Rothner 1995a).

SUMMARY

Headache is common in children and adolescents. A thorough history and examination, a neurological evaluation with charting of the temporal pattern of the headache, and an evaluation of psychosocial factors will ensure a correct diagnosis. Laboratory testing is unnecessary in most instances, and should be tailored to the specific headache syndrome. Psychological factors may be important in all forms of headache and should be evaluated in each case. A comprehensive approach that includes both medical and psychological interventions will usually result in improvement.

REFERENCES

Barlow CF. *Headaches and Migraine in Childhood.* Philadelphia: Blackwell Scientific, 1984.

Bille BS. Migraine in school children. *Acta Paediatr Scand* 1962; 51(Suppl 136):1–151.

Bille B. Migraine in children and its prognosis. *Cephalgia* 1981; 1:71–75.

Cohen BH. Headaches as a symptom of neurological disease. *Semin Pediatr Neurol* 1995; 2:144–150.

Cooper PJ, Bawden HN, Camfield PR, et al. Anxiety and life events in childhood migraine. *Pediatrics* 1987; 79:999–1004.

Corbett JJ. Problems in the diagnosis and treatment of pseudotumor cerebri. *Can J Neurol Sci* 1983; 10:221–229.

Day WH. *Essays on Diseases of Children.* London: J & A Churchill, 1873.

Dugan MC, Locke S, Gallagher JR. Occipital neuralgia in adolescents. *N Engl J Med* 1962; 267:1166–1170.

Friedman AP, Harms E. *Headaches in Children.* Springfield, IL: Thomas, 1967.

Gladstein J, Holden EW. Chronic daily headaches in children and adolescents: a two year prospective study. *Headache* 1996; 36(6):349–351.

Headache Classification Committee of the International Headache Society. Classification and diagnostic criteria for headache disorders, cranial neuralgias, and facial pain. *Cephalalgia* 1988; 8(Suppl 7):1–96.

Hockaday JM (Ed). *Migraine in Childhood.* London: Butterworths, 1988.

Igarashi M, May WN, Golden GS. Pharmacologic treatment of childhood migraine. *J Pediatr* 1992; 120:653–657.

Joutel A, Bousser MG, Biousse V, et al. A gene for familial hemiplegic migraine maps to chromosome 19. *Nat Genet* 1993; 5:40–45.

Kandt R, Levine R. Headache and acute illness in children. *J Child Neurol* 1987; 2:22–27.

Kinast M, Lueders H, Rothner AD, Erenberg G. Benign focal epileptiform discharges in childhood migraine (BFEDC). *Neurology* 1982; 32:1309–1311.

Kowal A, Pritchard D. Psychological characteristics of children who suffer from headache. *J Child Psychol Psychiatry* 1990; 31:637–649.

Linder S. Subcutaneous sumatriptan in the clinical setting: the first 50 consecutive patients with acute migraine in a pediatric neurology office practice. *Headache* 1996; 36:419–422.

Lipton RB. Diagnosis and epidemiology of pediatric migraine. *Curr Opin Neurol* 1997; 10(3):231–236.

Marks DA, Ehrenberg BL. Migraine-related seizures in adults with epilepsy, with EEG correlation. *Neurology* 1993; 43:2476–2483.

Martin SE, Smith MS. Psychosocial factors in recurrent pediatric headache. *Pediatr Ann* 1995; 24(9):469–474.

Mathew NT, Reuveni U, Perez F. Transformed or evolutive migraine. *Headache* 1987; 27:102–106.

Maytal J, Lipton RB, Salomon S, et al. Childhood onset cluster headache. *Headache* 1992; 32:275–279.

Maytal J, Bienkowski RS, Patel M, Eviatar L. The value of brain imaging in children with headaches. *Pediatrics* 1995; 96(3):413–416.

McGrath PA. *Pain in Children: Nature, Assessment, and Treatment.* New York: Guilford, 1990.

McGrath PJ, Reid GJ. Behavioral treatment of pediatric headache. *Pediatr Ann* 1995; 24(9):486–491.

Mortimer MJ, Kay J, Jaron A. Epidemiology of headache and childhood migraine in an urban general practice using Ad Hoc, Vahlquist and IHS criteria. *Dev Med Child Neurol* 1992; A34:1095–1101.

Moskowitz M. The visceral organ brain: implications for the pathophysiology of vascular head pain. *Neurology* 1991; 41:182–186.

Peatfield RC, Glover V, Littlewood JT, et al. The prevalence of diet induced migraine. *Cephalgia* 1984; 4:179–183.

Peroutka S. Developments in 5-hydroxytryptamine receptor pharmacology in migraine. *Neurol Clin* 1990; 8:829–839.

Rothner AD. Headaches in children: a review. *Headache* 1978; 18:169.

Rothner AD. The migraine syndrome in children and adolescents (review). *Pediatr Neurol* 1986; 2:121–126.

Rothner AD. Miscellaneous headache syndromes in children and adolescents. *Semin Pediatr Neurol* 1995a; 2(2):159–164.

Rothner AD (Ed). Headache in children and adolescents. *Semin Pediatr Neurol* 1995b; 2(2):101–177.

Rothner AD. The evaluation of headaches in children and adolescents. *Semin Pediatr Neurol* 1995c; 2(2):109–118.

Rothner AD. Headache emergencies: evaluation, differential diagnosis and treatment. In: Bernard L, Maria MD (Eds). *Current Management In Child Neurology.* Hamilton, Ontario: B.C. Dicker Inc., 1998, pp 331–335.

Rothner AD, Jensen VK. Chronic nonprogressive headaches in children and adolescents. *Semin Pediatr Neurol* 1995; 2(2):151–158.

Schulman EA, Silberstein SD. Symptomatic and prophylactic treatment of migraine and tension-type headache. *Neurology* 1992; 42(Suppl 2):16–21.

Smith MSE (Ed). Headaches. *Pediatr Ann* 1995; 24(9):446–491.

Solomon GD. The pharmacology of medications used in treating migraine. *Semin Pediatr Neurol* 1995; 2(2):165–177.

Stewart WF, Linet MS, Celentano DD, et al. Age and sex-specific incidence rates of migraine with and without visual aura. *Am J Epidemiol* 1991; 134:1111–1120.

Symons DNK. Twelve cases of analgesic headache. *Arch Dis Child* 1998; 78:555–556.

Wasiewski WW, Rothner AD. Pediatric migraine headache: diagnosis, evaluation and management. *Neurologist* 1999; 5:122–134.

Williamson DA, Baker JD, Cubic BA. Advances in pediatric headache research. *Adv Clin Child Psychol* 1993; 15:275–304.

Winner P, Wasiewski W, Gladstein J, Linder S. Multicenter prospective evaluation of proposed pediatric migraine revisions to the IHS criteria. *Headache* 1997; 37:545–548.

Correspondence to: A. David Rothner, MD, The Cleveland Foundation, S-71, 9500 Euclid Avenue, Cleveland, OH 44195, USA. Tel: 216-444-5514; Fax: 216-445-9139.

The Child with Headache: Diagnosis and Treatment.
Progress in Pain Research and Management, Vol. 19,
edited by Patricia A. McGrath and Loretta M. Hillier,
IASP Press, Seattle, © 2001.

4

Recurrent Headache: Triggers, Causes, and Contributing Factors

Patricia A. McGrath[a,b] and Loretta M. Hillier[a]

[a]*Pain Innovations Inc., London, Ontario, Canada;* [b]*Department of Pediatrics,
Faculty of Medicine, University of Western Ontario,
London, Ontario, Canada*

Although recurrent migraine and tension-type headache are distinguished primarily on the basis of their presumed vascular and muscular origins, respectively, the understanding of headache pathophysiology remains complex. Multiple factors are relevant in the etiology of recurrent headache in children. While hereditary factors may predispose certain children to develop headache, other factors trigger headache attacks, increase pain, prolong disability, or maintain the cycle of repeated attacks. Our research indicates that several cognitive, behavioral, and emotional factors share a key etiological role in this pain syndrome. Typically, several factors are evident for all children with recurrent headache, but the extent to which they represent a trigger, the primary underlying cause, or a secondary contributing factor varies for individual children.

Thus, to adequately treat children with recurrent migraine and tension-type headache, we must ascertain which factors are relevant for which children, rather than simply determining which headache features satisfy which differential diagnostic criteria. Treatment emphasis should shift accordingly from an exclusively headache-centered focus to a more child-centered focus. In this chapter, we describe a child-centered framework for understanding and treating recurrent headache based on the relevant triggers, causes, and contributing factors.

HEADACHE TRIGGERS

Headache triggers are the specific environmental, physical, emotional, and psychological stimuli thought to provoke headache attacks. Frequently reported triggers for children and adolescents include high humidity, hot weather, bright sunlight, loud noise, many different foods, school, strenuous physical activity, fatigue, car travel, menses, mental stress, and worry. These varied triggers were first documented in descriptive studies on childhood migraine in which parents described the circumstances associated with a child's headache onset, reporting any suspected triggers (Vahlquist and Hackzell 1949; Bille 1962; Rigg 1975; Brown 1977; Rothner 1978; Fenichel 1981; Shinnar and D'Souza 1982; Barlow 1984; Hoelscher and Lichstein 1984).

Eventually, a more systematic approach was adopted to obtain data on suspected headache triggers. Comprehensive lists of all the frequently reported triggers were compiled from descriptive studies and included as questionnaires in several clinical and epidemiologic studies. Parents (or children) considered all possible triggers, indicating which ones provoked or exacerbated the child's headache attacks. These studies yielded much valuable information on the prevalence of different headache triggers across large samples of children in different countries. However, questionnaire-derived data reveal only which stimuli parents believe cause headache, and not necessarily the stimuli that truly provoke attacks. Investigators typically do not monitor children's exposure to "presumed" triggers to prove whether or not they cause headache.

ENVIRONMENTAL AND PHYSICAL TRIGGERS

Questionnaire studies reveal an extensive array of environmental triggers for children's headache such as soda/pop, chocolate, eggs, nuts, cheese, milk, wheat products, heat, high humidity, physical activity, bright lights, loud noise, schoolwork, and computer use (Dalton and Dalton 1979; Leviton et al. 1984; Labbé et al. 1985; Budd and Kedesdy 1989; Budd et al. 1994; Lee and Olness 1997; Bijttebier and Vertommen 1999; Bener et al. 2000). Parents typically report multiple triggers for their child, with some parents claiming that many triggers can independently cause headache and others indicating that several triggers in association are to blame. However, despite a widely held belief in their causative role, there is almost no scientific evidence that certain weather conditions, physical activities, or foods trigger headache attacks in children. In fact, even the role of hormonally mediated factors in headache onset is largely limited to self-report. We were unable to locate any studies in which girls prospectively monitored headache activity in order to demonstrate an association between headache and menarche or phase of the menstrual cycle.

Children's exposure to different food triggers has been monitored in several dietary intervention studies (Forsythe and Redmond 1974; Congdon and Forsythe 1979; Egger et al. 1983, 1985; MacDonald et al. 1989). Suspected food triggers are removed in a prescribed sequence from children's diets and then gradually reintroduced. Alternatively, children are randomized to receive either the trigger food or a placebo. The results of these studies fail to confirm that foods are independent headache triggers for children. Children do not consistently have fewer headache attacks on restricted diets, and do not have more attacks when the suspected foods are reintroduced. (The efficacy of dietary interventions for childhood headache is reviewed in Chapter 6.)

No other studies provide explicit data on children's exposure to environmental headache triggers. Instead, relevant data are mentioned in an almost anecdotal manner within publications that describe the results of various clinical trials for childhood headache. In these studies, children often monitor the circumstances associated with their headache onset in daily diaries. These prospective records have not revealed any specific environmental triggers for headache attacks that are independent of other, more relevant causes.

For example, bright sunlight, hot humid weather, low or rapidly dropping barometric pressure, noisy, crowded events, and "too much running" (in various sports) are the environmental triggers most frequently reported by parents and children in our clinic. As part of our treatment program, we prospectively monitor children's activities to evaluate the situations in which they develop headache. To date, we have been unable to document any weather condition, physical activity, or food that was truly an independent headache trigger for even one child. Instead, we have consistently identified other, more salient causes (e.g., stress, as described later in this chapter) underlying the apparently diverse environmental triggers. We also have documented that children can develop "learned environmental triggers" as a result of their parents' beliefs and their own anxiety.

LEARNED TRIGGERS

Learned triggers are neutral environmental stimuli that eventually can provoke a headache attack—but only because children are anxious about them. When parents realize that their child is prone to recurrent headache attacks, they usually search the child's immediate environment for the cause(s). Most parents already know that certain weather conditions and foods can trigger adult headache, so at first they conclude that similar triggers are responsible for their child's headache. However, as children develop headache in many different situations (i.e., without the suspected weather or food triggers), parents continue to scrutinize the physical circumstances associated with headache onset and tentatively identify other environmental stimuli as additional triggers.

Some parents, convinced that these environmental stimuli are the only causes, unduly emphasize their importance. Children are encouraged to try to avoid these potential headache triggers. When they cannot avoid them, they approach them with such apprehension, fear, and anxiety that they develop a headache from their emotional reactions. The resulting headache convinces them and their parents that the suspected environmental stimuli are true headache triggers. Some children will gradually become conditioned to become anxious when confronted by these stimuli, and so eventually the stimuli will trigger headache attacks.

The longer children endure the apparently unpredictable headache attacks and the more their parents search for environmental causes, the greater is the risk that such children will develop learned triggers. Susceptible children continue to attribute their headache attacks only to external stimuli, not to their anxiety, so that new headache triggers will develop and be reinforced (Joffe et al. 1983; Andrasik et al. 1986; McGrath 1990). In our clinic, we have noted many circumstances in which children develop learned headache triggers, including the school bus, sunny days, gym class, stale classroom air, various foods, horror movies, not wearing sunglasses, and not wearing a hat. To distinguish between learned triggers and real causes, it is necessary to monitor prospectively what is happening in children's lives and how they are reacting to external events, as shown in the following case study.

Case study: learned triggers and causative factors. Julia, a 13-year-old girl, had experienced migraine headache for 3 years. She had 2–4 attacks each month, with some attacks preceded by a "rainbow of lights." She then had strong pain that was localized around her right eye. She vomited soon after headache onset and the pain lessened slightly, but the headache and some abdominal pain continued for approximately 12 hours. Julia had tried some medications (acetaminophen and an anticonvulsant) for pain relief, but she believed that sleep and rest were more effective. She was very disabled by her recurrent headache, often missing 3–4 days of school during each attack. Throughout her recovery period, her mother comforted her and massaged her feet and body.

Julia had a positive family history of headache and pain. She had both maternal and paternal female relatives who suffered from frequent headaches and/or abdominal pains. Julia's mother had abdominal pains as an adolescent and still suffered from frequent migraine headaches triggered by certain weather conditions and dairy products. Julia and her mother had identified several triggers for Julia's headache attacks, including low-pressure weather conditions, school dances, concerts, and several foods (particularly eggs). Julia once had a severe migraine after eating eggs; since then, she reported that she always got a headache after she ate eggs. Her apparent sensitivity to eggs became the focus of much family attention, particularly when they went to restaurants and needed to check all the ingredients in Julia's order.

Julia's pain assessment revealed more relevant causes for her headache than the environmental triggers she and her mother had identified. (Our pain assessment procedure is described in Chapter 8.) Julia felt awkward and uncomfortable with her peers in social situations. She became very anxious about any planned gatherings, but did not express her feelings and often developed a headache shortly beforehand that prevented her from attending the event. Her family's strong belief that headaches were caused only by environmental triggers prevented them from recognizing and addressing other possible internal causes. In fact, her mother's certainty that physical stimuli triggered headache led Julia to become excessively concerned about them. She therefore tried to avoid all these suspected triggers and when she encountered them, she often developed a headache. However, the primary trigger was probably her increased anxiety about the situation, not the specific foods she ate or the noise level at a party. In addition, Julia's positive family history created an environment that encouraged disability and prevented independent pain management. Mother and daughter shared a common experience as headache "sufferers."

A therapist provided feedback to Julia and her mother about the factors we believed were the real causes for her headache attacks. She recommended that Julia complete a pain management program. In order to lessen her headache attacks, Julia needed to resolve the stressors that were truly responsible for triggering her headaches. To decrease headache-related disability, she also needed to use more active and independent pain control strategies during headache attacks. (Our cognitive-behavioral program is described in Chapter 8.)

At the start of her program, Julia strongly disagreed with many of our conclusions—especially that her anticipatory anxiety, rather than a physical stimulus, was the primary headache trigger. With the therapist's assistance,

Julia gradually realized that she had unknowingly eaten eggs at times without getting a headache. She also recognized that she was very concerned about her appearance and popularity with peers. Over six pain management sessions, she learned how to lessen her anxiety so that she could enjoy social activities with her peers. The therapist also taught Julia to use biofeedback and relaxation techniques to control her pain and encouraged both her and her mother to support one another as headache controllers, rather than sufferers. At the end of this program, Julia was having two tension-type headaches per month that lasted only 3 hours. She had minimal disability during and after each headache. At her two follow-up visits (at 3 months and 2 years), Julia was completely headache free.

EMOTIONAL AND PSYCHOLOGICAL TRIGGERS

Parents and children commonly cite worries about school, anxiety about sports performance, frustration with siblings and peers, and stress associated with daily life as specific triggers for children's headache attacks (Vahlquist 1955; Bille 1962; Brown 1977; Hockaday 1982; Maratos and Wilkinson 1982; Barlow 1984; Budd et al. 1984; Leviton et al. 1984; Passchier and Orlebeke 1985; Cooper et al. 1987; McGrath 1987, 1990; Budd and Kedesdy 1989; Lewis et al. 1996; Lee and Olness 1997; Metsahonkala et al. 1998; Bijttebier and Vertommen 1999; Langeveld et al. 1999; Bener et al. 2000). Strong evidence shows that emotional and psychological factors—unlike parent-reported environmental triggers—do cause headache attacks. Prospective monitoring of children's daily activities and their feelings about these activities confirms that children's emotional reactions, especially anxiety, can provoke headache.

Clinical trials in which investigators evaluate headache activity within the broader perspective of what is really happening within a child's life often reveal the presence of stress and anxiety (Waranch and Keenan 1985; Richter et al. 1986; P.J. McGrath et al. 1988; Larsson et al. 1990; P.A. McGrath et al. 1993; Osterhaus et al. 1993; Griffiths and Martin 1996). Schoolwork, strenuous activity during sports, loud music at a party, and high humidity do not trigger headache attacks. Instead, children's anxiety is the common factor underlying these apparently diverse situations—anxiety about whether they will complete assigned schoolwork to their standards, whether they will perform well on the team, and whether they will have fun and feel accepted at a party.

Children with headache often report more stress than do children without headache (Passchier and Orlebeke 1985; Andrasik et al. 1988; Larsson 1988). However, they are not necessarily more anxious than children without headache (Cooper et al. 1987; Cunningham et al. 1987; Kowal and Pritchard 1990). Similarly, they do not necessarily encounter more frequent or difficult life stressors than do children without headache (Cooper et al. 1987). Some children with headache may simply respond to normal stress-inducing situations (involving school, sports, peers, and family) with poor coping strategies. Their inability to adequately deal with the situation (e.g., teasing about their appearance by classmates, pressure to perform from a coach) progressively adds to their underlying anxiety about school, social gatherings, and sports. Anxiety builds until a headache develops, which temporarily removes them from these potentially stressful situations. Since headache attacks occur in diverse physical environments, parents may not recognize the underlying link of unresolved stress.

The importance of situation-specific stress as a major headache trigger is confirmed by the results of clinical trials on cognitive-behavioral therapies. When children learn how to recognize stressful situations and lessen their anxiety, their headache attacks decrease (Andrasik et al. 1985; P.J. McGrath et al. 1988; Labbé and Ward 1990; Larsson et al. 1990; P.A. McGrath et al. 1993; Osterhaus et al. 1993). However, there is no simple and direct relationship between children's anxiety and headache onset. The etiology of recurrent migraine and tension-type headache is complex. The accruing results of our research and clinical program indicate that multiple, but different, factors may be relevant for the start of headache, for the onset of specific attacks, and for the maintenance of recurrent headache syndrome. Below we present a model for recurrent headache that provides a framework for assessing the relevant causative and contributing factors for children.

RECURRENT HEADACHE—A MULTIFACTORIAL ETIOLOGY

Our understanding of the multifactorial etiology of recurrent headache originated from data accrued in our pediatric pain program, as well as from the results of studies reviewed in preceding chapters. In 1983 we opened a pain clinic as an integral component of our research program in pediatric pain. Almost immediately we were inundated with referrals for children with various types of headache. At that time, despite advances in understanding the plasticity and complexity of pain processing, children's pain had only been studied from the traditional disease model (wherein pain was simply and directly proportional to the nature and extent of tissue damage). Little information was available about children's pain experiences from a multidimensional perspective, particularly the factors that could modify children's headache.

Thus, when we began to treat children with headache, we also began to systematically document their pain features, identify possible risk factors and triggers, and assess the contextual or situational factors that had been shown to modify pain in adult and animal studies (e.g., expectation, relevance of pain, and control). (See Price [1999] for a comprehensive review of studies demonstrating how contextual factors affect pain perception in humans and modify nociceptive mechanisms in animals.) Our first research objective was to document the factors relevant for maintaining recurrent headache, so that we could develop effective treatment programs for children.

Since 1983, we have continued to concurrently study and treat children with recurrent headache. Subsequent research objectives have been to condense our lengthy assessment procedures so that they could be used more easily in regular clinical practice (rather than restricted for use in specialty clinics), to rigorously evaluate various treatment regimens, and to better match headache treatment to the individual child by determining at consultation which children would benefit from which therapy. Although every study we conducted and each child we treated in our program has contributed to our knowledge base, the results of two studies have been crucial in shaping our theoretical and empirical model for recurrent headache in children.

DESCRIPTIVE STUDY—CHILD CHARACTERISTICS AND SITUATIONAL FACTORS

Our first descriptive study evaluated the child characteristics and situational factors that might contribute to the onset or maintenance of recurrent headache. Pain assessments were conducted for 200 children aged 5–17 years who had been diagnosed with recurrent migraine or tension-type headache (McGrath 1987). The assessment included independent structured interviews with children and their parents, completion of standardized personality, anxiety, and depression inventories for children, and prospective monitoring of headache attacks for 1 month. The interview provided information about children's headache history, their behavior during attacks, parents' criteria for evaluating the presence and severity of their children's headache, the type and effectiveness of interventions used, and the parents' headache and pain history. (This interview was the original version of the Children's Headache Interview, included in Appendix 1.)

We analyzed children's and parents' responses on all assessment measures and observed some strikingly similar profiles for children regardless of their age, sex, or whether they experienced migraine or tension-type headache. The only differences in pain profiles by diagnosis were for headache characteristics—location, quality, intensity, length, and frequency—which is not surprising, given that these features are used in the diagnostic classification. Several situational factors were present for all children, but the extent to which they contributed to headache onset or pain severity seemed to vary.

Children shared a similar history with respect to medical consultation, diagnosis, and headache management. Parents did not always seek treatment when their children first began to experience occasional headache. However, parents become very worried as their child developed more frequent or intense headache. They then consulted their family physicians and often a pediatrician or neurologist, who reassured them that their child did not have a tumor or other medical problem. These clinicians informed families that children had migraine and/or tension-type headache and often recommended that parents administer analgesics during attacks as needed, but usually did not explain how parents could identify and manage any causative factors. As headache persisted, families become increasingly anxious. They questioned whether physicians had failed to diagnose the real problem and feared that their children, especially girls, would continue to suffer headache throughout their lives.

Moreover, the lack of concrete information on how to deal with the causes rather than treating the symptoms created several pain management problems. Children lacked independent strategies for reducing pain during attacks, often relying exclusively on rest and sleep or parental intervention. There was usually no set plan for managing headache attacks. Some busy parents responded very inconsistently, so that their children gradually exaggerated their pain complaints or developed new symptoms to capture their parents' attention. Some parents inadvertently prolonged headache-related disability when they allowed children to stay at home instead of attending school, encouraged them to withdraw from potentially stressful sports or social situations, and relieved them of their routine household responsibilities. These secondary gains prolonged headache episodes or contributed to the development of new attacks when children were stressed.

Many parents believed that headache attacks were provoked only by environmental stimuli; they often denied that stress was a possible trigger. Some parents did not understand that stress could lead to headache and other somatic complaints. However, we found that stress was a common trigger. Many children seemed to respond to normal stressful situations (e.g., school, sports, and peers) with poor coping strategies. Their inability to truly resolve the stress added progressively to their anxiety. Their anxiety increased until a headache developed, which temporarily removed them from the source of stress. Since headache attacks occurred in different physical environments, parents often did not recognize the underlying link of unresolved stress.

Most of the children did not have serious emotional problems. Approximately 50% were described as anxious by parents or by themselves, while 75% had very high expectations for achievement (scholastic, familial, and sports). Hypochondriasis, depression, or anxiety was noted for approximately 50% of the adolescents, as reflected by significant elevations on subscales of the Basic Personality Inventory (Jackson 1976). Only 10% of children and adolescents presented with headache due to serious psychological depression.

About 25% of children had drastically reduced their physical activities to prevent headache, despite no clear evidence that physical exertion triggered headache attacks. Another 25% participated in an extremely high level of competitive sports; in fact, they were often very stressed by the competitiveness, so that they derived little enjoyment from their participation. Children who were in these minimal or excessive sports categories often could not describe any time periods when they felt mentally or physically relaxed.

In summary, the results of this descriptive study indicated that several situational factors were present for children with recurrent migraine and tension-type headache. These included cognitive factors—parents' and children's understanding and beliefs; behavioral factors—parents' and children's actions during headache attacks and their wider behavioral responses to potential headache triggers; and emotional factors—parents' and children's anxiety, fears, and frustrations about the headache problem. A combination of these factors contributed to headache etiology, pain, and disability. However, after interpreting the assessment measures and prospectively monitoring headache activity, we concluded that the importance of these factors varied among children. In our clinical opinion, the same factor could be a primary cause for some children, but only a secondary contributing factor for others. Consequently, a headache management program should address each set of factors, but should be flexible enough to meet the unique needs of a child and family.

RANDOMIZED CLINICAL TRIAL—MODIFYING CAUSATIVE AND CONTRIBUTING FACTORS

The 200 children who had participated in the descriptive study were subsequently followed for treatment in the pain clinic. Since the findings from the descriptive study suggested that headache treatment should be targeted at contributing cognitive, behavioral, and emotional factors, we used the assessment results for each child as the basis for an individualized treatment program. A therapist used a cognitive-behavioral approach to modify each factor that had been identified. She determined the most appropriate tools for each child, such as biofeedback for children who needed concrete examples of how their feelings could produce observable physiological changes, a practical problem-solving component for children who did not effectively resolve stressful situations, and behavioral contracts to encourage children to follow a consistent plan during headache attacks. We documented the specific therapeutic tools used for each child and the number of sessions needed to modify the causative factors. (Nondrug therapies, including biofeedback, are described in Chapter 6.)

Almost all children who enrolled in this exploratory clinical trial experienced a significant decrease in pain intensity and headache attacks within eight treatment sessions. This high success rate confirmed our clinical judgment that the factors identified in children's pain assessment had been critical in maintaining their recurrent headache. However, we needed to ensure that these positive results were due primarily to the treatment program and not to unknown intervening factors. Therefore, we designed a randomized controlled trial to objectively evaluate the efficacy of a cognitive-behavioral program for recurrent headache. We used the data on headache frequency and pain intensity from the descriptive study to calculate the sample size to ensure that treatment evaluation would not be confounded by differences due to age, sex, headache frequency, pain severity, headache length, and syndrome duration.

After a comprehensive pain assessment, 293 children (147 girls, 146 boys), ranging in age from 4.6 to 17.5 years (mean age 11.1 years) with migraine or tension-type headache were randomly assigned to one of three conditions: the cognitive-behavioral program, a feedback intervention (to control for the effects of information about recurrent headache), and a 4-month waiting-list control (to control for spontaneous remission of headache). In the feedback intervention, a therapist met with parents 1 month after the pain assessment to provide general information about the features of recurrent headache, recommendations for pain management, and information about common causative and contributing factors. (The feedback intervention is described in more detail in Chapter 7, as the foundation for our basic educational intervention for children with recurrent headache.)

Children in the cognitive-behavioral condition received the same general feedback information after their pain assessment, but then participated in six additional treatment sessions, held once every two weeks. Therapists followed a structured protocol for each 1-hour session, wherein they assisted children and parents to recognize the true triggers and underlying causes, to consistently use some nondrug pain control strategies during head-ache attacks, to learn how to recognize and lessen physiological stress with biofeedback-assisted relaxation exercises, and to identify and resolve any relevant stress related to school, sports, or family. The protocol included a practical behavioral management component to decrease any maladaptive pain or disability behaviors. The therapists progressively covered all com-ponents throughout the program, but in a flexible manner so that they could vary the emphasis within a session according to children's unique needs (e.g., more assistance in identifying a stressful situation that preceded a headache attack, more help in using a relaxation tape). (The structured pro-tocol and program hand-outs for this trial are described in detail in McGrath 1990; the revised protocol is described in Chapter 8.)

Four months after their initial pain assessment, children were reassessed by a research assistant who did not know which treatment they had received. The children who received the cognitive-behavioral program had signifi-cantly fewer and milder headache attacks in comparison to children in the other treatment groups (McGrath et al. 1993). Moreover, the children's re-sponses during the post-treatment interview indicated that many of the fac-tors we had originally identified as causes or contributing factors were no longer present. After treatment, children and parents were able to identify relevant triggers (usually stress), and did not report multiple environmental triggers. They provided examples of how they resolved stressful situations, and they tried to follow a consistent headache management plan. These results confirmed our clinical judgment that several cognitive, behavioral, and emotional factors combine to cause recurrent migraine and tension-type headache. While several factors are evident for all children with recurrent headache, the extent to which they represent a trigger, primary underlying cause, or secondary contributing factor varies for individual children and their families.

A MODEL OF RECURRENT HEADACHE

The results of these descriptive and intervention studies are consistent with our increasing appreciation of the plasticity and complexity of children's pain. We know that a child's pain is not simply and directly related either to the extent of their physical injuries or to the severity of their disease. Tissue damage initiates a sequence of neural events that may lead to pain, but many factors can intervene to alter the sequence of nociceptive transmission and thereby modify a child's pain perception (McGrath 1990). Although the causal relationship between an injury and a consequent pain seems direct and obvious, what children understand, what they do, and how they feel all affect their pain.

It is essential to recognize and evaluate the mediating impact of these factors in order to relieve any type of pain that children experience. Differences in situational factors may account for why the same tissue damage can evoke pains that vary in intensity, and may partially explain why proven analgesics can vary in effectiveness for different children and for the same child at different times. The results of our studies indicate that certain cognitive, behavioral, and emotional factors may have a causative rather than a mediating role in recurrent headache.

As an example, Fig. 1 depicts a typical sequence of events during a child's early headache attacks. Children must cope with a stressful situation, usually involving routine circumstances that all children encounter with their families, peers, school activities, or sports. Unable to comfortably control the situation, they become increasingly anxious about it. Their anxiety provokes a headache attack. Their headache-related pain and distress removes them from the situation, temporarily distancing them from the source of stress. But if parents fail to recognize the source of stress or are unable to help children to cope with the situation, then children will continue to experience anxiety in similar situations and be prone to additional attacks.

However, as headache attacks persist, a different set of factors emerges for all children with migraine and tension-type headache, regardless of their explicit diagnosis or the circumstances surrounding their first attacks. We have documented headache characteristics, causative and contributing factors, and treatment outcome for every child referred to our clinic. Our clinical

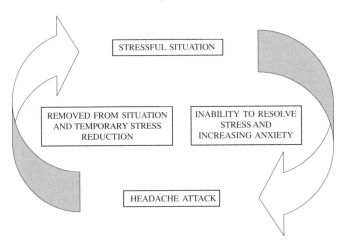

Fig. 1. A model depicting the impact of unresolved stress in provoking a headache attack.

group, typically the director (P.A. McGrath), two therapists, and a variable number of trainees, met weekly to review the pain assessment results for all children (including both children enrolled in specific research protocols and children referred to the clinic for treatment). Our guiding principle was to reach a conclusion (even a very preliminary one for some children) about the probable causes for headache from the information obtained through interviews and pain logs. We then confirmed or corrected our conclusions as we monitored children throughout their treatment program. We progressively refined a list of causative and contributing factors for children with headache. These data, combined with the results of studies described in this volume, shaped the theoretical and empirical base for our understanding of the multifactorial etiology of recurrent headache, as illustrated in Fig. 2.

This model for recurrent headache provides a framework for assessing the relevant causative factors for children, based on our knowledge of the plasticity and complexity of children's pain. Some factors are relatively stable for a child, such as age, gender, cognitive level, previous pain experience, family learning, and cultural background (shown in the open box in the figure). These child characteristics shape how children generally interpret and experience the various sensations caused by tissue damage. In contrast, the cognitive, behavioral, and emotional factors (shown in the shaded boxes) are not stable. They represent a unique interaction between the child and the situation in which the pain is experienced (Ross and Ross 1988; McGrath 1990). These situational factors can vary dynamically, depending on the specific circumstances in which children experience headache attacks. Some of these factors can eventually trigger headache attacks, while others can intensify pain and distress, prolong headache-related disability, or maintain the cycle of repeated headache. While they may be unable to change the more stable child characteristics, parents and health care providers can dramatically improve children's headache by modifying situational factors.

COGNITIVE FACTORS

Parents' understanding of the cause of headache, possible treatments, and long-term prognosis guides their behaviors toward children and shapes children's emotional responses to the pain problem. Parents often hold inaccurate beliefs about headache etiology, effective drug and nondrug therapies, and the role of environmental versus stress triggers. The common cognitive factors we have documented are listed in Table I. Children typically share their parents' erroneous beliefs and expectations. In addition, some children have unrealistic expectations for achievement or set unattainable goals.

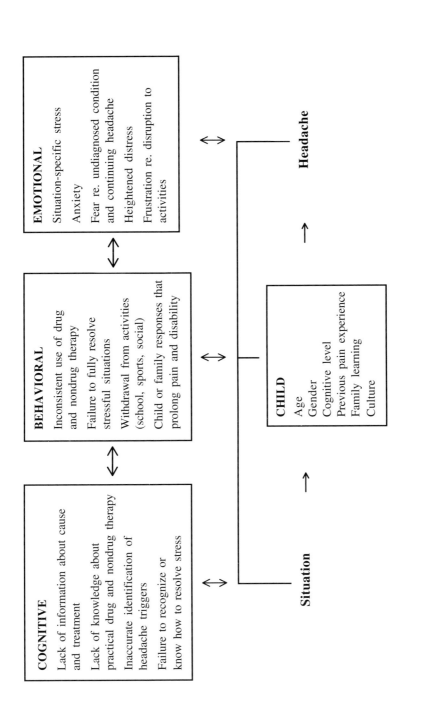

Fig. 2. A model of the factors that cause recurrent headache in children.

Table I
Cognitive factors for children with recurrent headache

Beliefs about Headache Etiology
Belief in a single, as yet undiagnosed, cause
Inaccurate understanding of the primary and secondary causes
Belief in "presumed" environmental triggers
Expectation of headache and related disability continuing for years
Beliefs about Pain Control
Poor knowledge about using and evaluating drug therapies
Little knowledge of effective nondrug therapies
Belief that children should rest and sleep during all attacks
Reliance on a particular, but ineffective, method
Belief that no treatment will be effective
Beliefs about the Role of Stress
Limited understanding that stress can cause headache
Little knowledge about the situations that are continuing stressors for children
Little understanding of the impact of children's high expectations for achievement

Beliefs about headache etiology. Unlike acute pain, migraine and tension-type headaches are not correlating symptoms of an injury or disease. Nevertheless, parents usually try to understand recurrent headache from an acute pain perspective, where pain is due to a single cause and can be relieved by a single treatment. They do not understand that headache attacks, unlike most pains that their children have already experienced, may have several interrelated causes. Parents expect that they will eventually find one treatment that will immediately stop the recurrent attacks. Thus, they may reject potentially effective treatments after only one attempt, even though the treatment would address some of the causes and might help to lessen headache severity over time. This lack of understanding about the multifactorial etiology of headache leads some parents to continue to search for specific environmental triggers that children could avoid to prevent future headache attacks. Their children are then at risk for developing various learned headache triggers, as described previously.

Parents' expectations about how their children will feel during headache attacks have a profound impact on the children, intensifying their distress, anxiety, and pain. Many parents expect that children will be nauseous or disabled for a certain time period whenever they have a headache, regardless of the medication they use. Some parents expect that children will continue to experience headache throughout their lives. Mothers who experience migraine headache themselves often inform us that their daughters will suffer from the same type of headache as they mature. When they believe that hereditary factors are primarily responsible for the development of headache, they unintentionally communicate to their daughters that they have no control in changing the future course of continuing pain and disability.

Beliefs about pain control. Parents' beliefs about how to manage pain during headache attacks directly influence how they respond when their children develop a headache. Most parents lack a clear rationale for how to select effective drug and nondrug therapies and how to use them appropriately, so that children's headache pain is often undertreated. Although analgesics can effectively lessen pain and shorten a headache, many parents do not administer medication to children as needed. Some parents are concerned that young children may become dependent or even addicted to "painkillers," and most parents are genuinely confused about what medication to use and when to administer it. Although they may have used over-the-counter (OTC) analgesics appropriately and confidently to control acute pain for their children, parents frequently are uncertain what to use when their children experience repeated headache attacks. Some parents are apprehensive about long-term medication use in children, particularly when package labeling on many products cautions against their use in children under 16 years old. Consequently, these parents may administer less than a therapeutic dose or may administer doses too infrequently to relieve their children's headache.

In contrast, a few parents always administer the correct OTC dose at headache onset as a precaution against increasing pain, even though the mild pain may not have intensified or nondrug methods might have relieved the headache. Occasionally, parents may rely on a potent medication such as acetaminophen with codeine if a child needed it once to control an atypically severe headache attack. Children may develop a false reliance on this (or any) medication so that they become very distressed if parents hesitate to administer it when they first complain about pain. If parents decide to wait and see whether children need it—without carefully explaining that other effective pain control methods might be more appropriate for this headache—children become so upset and anxious that their pain intensifies. Frustrated parents often give in and eventually administer the medication to calm the child. Afterwards, they administer the product (typically a specific brand name) consistently at headache onset. Surprisingly, parents and children may rely on certain products (or nondrug methods) for pain control even though they are only intermittently effective. We have noted many instances in which children believe that they must always use cold compresses, take decongestants, rest or sleep, or have a massage when they have a headache, even though they acknowledge that those treatments do not always lessen their headache.

Almost all parents have used some nondrug methods with children during their headache attacks. However, as is the case for drug therapies, most parents do not know which methods to use or how to use them appropriately. For example, some parents may use distraction as a first step in pain control, even though their child's headache was strong at onset and they should have administered medication. Children learn quickly that distraction is not effective, although it may have been effective for a mild headache. Parents may try various methods in a seemingly haphazard manner, so that children learn that there is no predictable plan for selecting methods based on pain severity or on their scheduled activities. Children may become increasingly doubtful about the possible effectiveness of such methods.

Parents' attitudes and beliefs about nondrug therapies exert a powerful influence on children. Some parents, especially those whose own headache attacks are relieved only by potent medication, doubt the efficacy of any nondrug therapy. Even if they attempt to show their children these techniques, they often communicate their own negative attitude. Parents' negative expectations will counteract any potential benefits. Other parents may select only passive nondrug methods that increase children's dependency and lack of control. Parents may not know how to assist children to use active and independent pain coping strategies that they could incorporate into their regular activities. These methods could improve children's control, lessen pain, and minimize any maladaptive disability behaviors.

Many parents and children believe that no treatment will fully relieve headache attacks, but that some passive pain control methods (such as withdrawing from activities and sleeping) allow children to be comfortable until the headache runs its course. Children gradually learn that they must suffer through attacks, even though several effective treatment options are available. They may gradually equate each attack with a predictable time course of disability.

Beliefs about the role of stress. While parents generally acknowledge the role of stress in provoking some types of adult headache, they often have difficulty in accepting that stress is a relevant factor for their children. They may equate stress with major life events such as marital discord, unemployment, moving house, illness, or a death in the family. Parents do not understand that these events are not the typical sources of stress for children with recurrent headache. Instead, the primary source is continuing stress associated with normal childhood activities—school, sports, and social relationships. Children with headache are unable to fully resolve the stress they experience. Either they cannot recognize their true feelings or their feelings have been minimized because they seem trivial from their parents' adult perspective.

Some parents describe their children as effortlessly achieving excellent grades, excelling in sports, and having many good friends. Often parents are confident that their children do not feel pressured to maintain success in all aspects of their lives. However, closer monitoring reveals that their children are feeling pressured; typically their schoolwork has become more difficult, sports have become more competitive, or social demands have changed. These changes are usually gradual, so that parents may not have noticed their progressive impact.

As described in Chapter 1 on risk factors for headache, some children with headache fit the stereotypic personality profile of "overachiever, conscientious, and perfectionist." These children generally have extremely high expectations for themselves and set unrealistically high goals for achievement. They openly worry about their performance so that parents may more easily recognize that these children are stressed. However, most children who experience achievement-related stress are not overtly anxious and worried. They simply believe that they should always do well. They reveal their anxiety more subtly, in that some aspect of their performance usually disappoints them. Parents may be pleased by their performance and dismiss these seemingly unimportant concerns. Yet, children's continual minor dissatisfaction indicates that they are experiencing persistent stress. They measure their self-worth primarily by their performance scores—grades in school, ranking in sports, or popularity with friends. These children are often unable to differentiate between doing their best and being the best in all their activities. Since it is impossible to always excel, they are constantly stressed by the risk of some type of failure.

BEHAVIORAL FACTORS

Parents' and children's beliefs guide what they do to relieve pain during headache attacks and shape their broader efforts to resolve the cause of headache. Various behaviors are critical for the development of recurrent headache, as listed in Table II. Typically, a child presents several of these behaviors, with all contributing equally to the pain syndrome. Parents' uncertainty about how to control pain can lead them to respond to children's headache complaints in a manner that inadvertently increases children's distress, pain, and disability. Moreover, when parents seek additional diagnostic tests, attribute headaches solely to environmental triggers, and fail to identify and resolve relevant stress triggers, their behaviors directly maintain the cycle of repeated headache attacks.

Child and parent behaviors during headache attacks. As noted above in the section "Beliefs about Pain Control," most parents lack a clear rationale

Table II
Behavioral factors for children with recurrent headache

Child and Parent Behaviors during Headache Attacks
Inconsistent parental responses
Ineffective use of analgesic drugs and independent nondrug therapies
Withdrawing children from school, sports, or social activities
Relieving children from routine family responsibilities
Parental responses that reinforce illness and disability
Parental modeling of pain behaviors
Parent Behaviors in Response to Repeated Headache Attacks
Primary focus on additional medical consultations and diagnostic investigations
Persistent search for environmental triggers
Failure to resolve continuing sources of stress

for how to select and use drug and nondrug therapies to control children's headache. As a result, they do not use potentially effective therapies in an appropriate or consistent manner. When children's headache pain is undertreated because the parents do not administer adequate doses of analgesic medication for the child's body weight or fail to encourage them to use active and independent nondrug therapies, children become increasingly distressed during headache attacks and increasingly anxious about their headache problem. On the other hand, when children's headache pain is continually overtreated with potent medication, they may develop a dependency on a certain product. Inevitably, these children will sometimes develop headache attacks when the medication is not available; they then become extremely distressed and frightened. Their strong conviction that the headache will be lessened only by one medication counteracts the potential benefits of all other interventions they receive. These children may become increasingly preoccupied by fear of future attacks and begin to avoid situations where they may not have easy access to their parents and the medication they have grown to depend on.

Parents' uncertainties about medication use also contribute to their inconsistency in responding to children's headache attacks. Parents encourage children to rest and sleep during some attacks, but administer medication during others, or else persuade children to resume activities without medication. While parents' decisions may be based on the presumed pain level, children usually receive contradictory messages about how to manage headache. They do not know the rationale underlying the alternative approaches and may become progressively distressed during headache attacks because they expect continued or increasing pain, rather than adequate pain control.

Usually families do not follow a predictable treatment plan for children during their headache attacks. Mothers, fathers, and other family care

providers may respond differently at different times, with one adult allowing children to stay at home until they are better and another encouraging
them to "tough it out" and continue their activities. In part, the inconsistency is due to the changing circumstances wherein children develop headache—at school, at home, at a party, at a friend's home, or during sports. In
part, the inconsistency is due to caregivers' own schedules and emotions.
They may be busy at the time, frustrated that the child has developed another headache, angry that treatments have failed, annoyed that the attack
will disrupt a scheduled trip, or simply too tired to respond patiently.

Children typically are accustomed to consistent responses when they
experience pain caused by injury. Parents appraise the injury, provide reassurance, cleanse and bandage the injury (as needed), and treat the pain,
often encouraging children to use simple nondrug pain control strategies.
Typically, the management of such acute pain is similar, regardless of where
children are and who is present. The consistency conveys reassurance, understanding, and certainty about the cause and treatment. Children learn the
rationale underlying their parents' behaviors and learn how to cope independently with many of the aches and pains of their daily activities.

When adult care providers do not respond consistently to frequent headache attacks, children become more distressed, uncertain, fearful, and focused on the pain sensations. When care providers do not consistently administer analgesics for strong headaches and do not teach children effective
nondrug strategies, children may learn to expect increasing pain before they
can obtain any relief. They become distressed by the pain and by the inter-
ruptions to their planned activities. Vulnerable because they lack a plan of
action, they become increasing dependent on adults for emotional support
and physical comfort during headache attacks.

Parents' behaviors (as well as those of care providers, teachers, coaches,
and instructors) shape how children respond during headache attacks. Parents may reinforce headache-related disability when they allow children to
stay home from school, encourage them to withdraw from potentially stressful sports or social situations, and relieve them from routine family responsibilities, without helping children to address the underlying causes for headache attacks. Children whose headaches are triggered by their high
expectations for achievement feel relieved of some of the pressure to excel
(either self-imposed or imposed by parents and coaches). Some children
may begin to complain about a headache at the first sign of any muscle
tightness, so that they have a legitimate excuse if their performance fails to
meet their standards. Others, whose headaches are triggered by anxiety about
coping in particular situations (gym class, social interactions at lunch, or
team games), begin to develop more frequent headaches in association with

those situations. They initially miss a few classes, lunches, or games on an intermittent basis because of headache attacks, but then avoid these situations on a more consistent basis.

Other children may adopt increasingly obvious distress behaviors to prove that they have a disabling headache. Some may learn that they receive more support from all adult caregivers when the pain is strong or when they are visibly distressed. These children may gradually develop a set of exaggerated pain behaviors (e.g., atypical quietness, rubbing their heads, or crying) or may determine a particular time period they need for recovery whenever they have a headache, regardless of its strength or duration. The pattern of overt distress behaviors and the length of disability children experience become fixed. Children are not deliberately feigning distress; their disability behaviors become conditioned from the responses of caregivers. The secondary gains associated with increased attention, special privileges, reduced expectations for performance, and avoidance of unpleasant situations can prolong and intensify headache-related disability.

Case study: disability behaviors and failure to resolve stress. Donna S., a 14-year-old girl, had experienced daily stomachaches and monthly headache attacks for 2 years. Mrs. S. reported that Donna's headache attacks were probably related to her menarche (and would coincide with her menstrual periods when they began) since they occurred regularly on a 28-day cycle. Donna was quite disabled by headache throughout a 4-day period; Mrs. S. left work to comfort her and read to her while she stayed in bed.

At the end of the assessment, the therapist informed Mrs. S. that the apparent regularity of Donna's headache attacks was quite unusual and that she suspected that behavioral factors, not hormonal factors, were responsible. She emphasized that we had not yet seen any child whose headache attacks were triggered so regularly unless there were family cues associated with onset. Although Mrs. S. had mentioned several times during the assessment that the headache attacks were very predictable, she adamantly denied that anyone in the family provided cues to Donna that a headache was imminent. However, about 20 minutes later, when we were booking the next appointment, Mrs. S. checked her appointment book and said that she couldn't make the proposed date because Donna would be sick. She had noted the dates in advance so she could adjust her work hours accordingly.

The therapist had also emphasized to Mrs. S. that the length of Donna's headache suggested that behavioral factors were prolonging her disability. Donna had described that her headache lasted approximately 12 hours and occurred on the second day of the 4-day period, but that she felt somewhat unwell the day before the headache and then for the 2 days following it. During this time, Mrs. S. sat on Donna's bed and they talked and spent quiet time together. Donna was the younger of two daughters; her older sister was an outspoken, independent 15-year-old whose opinions contrasted sharply with those of her mother. Mrs. S. described Donna as more like her—how she spoke, how she dressed, how she wore her hair. Mrs. S. acknowledged that she looked forward to their time together during Donna's headaches because soon Donna would be too busy with her friends and she would lose her little girl. Although we are synthesizing the information on behavioral factors in a concise manner, the relevant facts were mentioned in a relatively disparate manner throughout a lengthy interview.

Mrs. S. had an enmeshed relationship with her daughter. Donna was extremely sensitive to her mother's opinion. She did not simply parrot her mother's values; she adopted them outwardly while suppressing her own feelings and individuality. Mrs. S. had initially encouraged Donna to need her during headache attacks, and subsequently to need the headache attacks and the 4-day recovery period. Mrs. S.'s reinforcement of Donna's headache and disability was subtle, unintentional, and gradual. Some of her protective behaviors would have been appropriate to relieve acute injury-related pain, but were maladaptive for recurrent headache. Although Mrs. S. did not believe that she, even unintentionally, had contributed to Donna's disability, she agreed to change her responses to encourage Donna to use more independent nondrug pain control strategies and to return to school earlier. (Behavioral management is described in Chapter 6; the approach used in our program is described in Chapter 8.)

The therapist met with Donna and Mrs. S. weekly. She worked with Donna to help her to identify her feelings and express her own opinions. She worked with Mrs. S. to allow Donna more freedom in selecting her clothes, her hairstyle, etc. The therapist also helped them both to substitute some fun activities that they could share regularly instead of primarily having the headache recovery period as their shared time. At Donna's next headache (still on a 28-day cycle), they followed the therapist's recommendations; Donna reported that the headache was milder and shorter than usual, and that she only missed a day and a half of school. Her next headache occurred 42 days later and lasted only a few hours.

The therapist was surprised by the remarkable improvements within a relatively short time frame. Our clinical experience indicates that a long-term pattern of "learned disability" coupled with emotional factors (i.e., an enmeshed relationship, suppression of emotions) usually requires a longer intervention program. In this case, Mrs. S.'s willingness to almost immediately change her behaviors during her daughter's headache attacks and to overtly lessen her control over Donna's personal choices was critical to the rapid improvement.

Donna's school absences were an indirect consequence of her "learned disability." However, school absences have a different meaning for many children with headache.

Parental behaviors in response to repeated headache attacks. When parents believe that the headaches are caused by an undiagnosed medical condition, typically continuing to seek additional medical and health consultations, their exclusive focus on identifying the elusive medical problem prevents them from addressing the more relevant causes. In addition, many parents are preoccupied by a search for the responsible environmental triggers and deny the possibility of stress-related headache triggers (as discussed above in the section "Beliefs about Headache Etiology").

Stress related to school (either the academic work or peer interactions) is a common headache trigger. When headache prevents these children from attending school, they are removed from the source of stress. If they fail to recognize the source of stress or adequately resolve it, then headache attacks are gradually reinforced by the temporary periods of stress relief they provide. Children should withdraw from planned school, sports, and social activities during some headache attacks, and parents should adjust their expectations accordingly. However, there is a delicate balance between supporting children's recovery and rewarding their withdrawal from stressful activities. Parents should recognize that children's headache attacks may increase as children rely on headache to temporarily relieve stress. Over time, a relatively minor amount of stress will trigger a headache.

In our opinion, the key factor maintaining the syndrome of repeated headache attacks is parents' failure to help children fully resolve the stress they experience. Parents may need to help children to recognize potential stress-inducing situations, particularly if children deny that they feel anxious. As described previously, most children's continuing stress is associated with normal childhood activities and not with a major life event. The common sources of stress we have identified are listed in Table III. Many of these circumstances may seem unimportant from an adult perspective, but they are very important to children. When parents are unable to acknowledge the importance of these stressors, children cannot obtain the help they need to cope with these situations so as to relieve the stress they experience. The stress continues, and headache problems persist.

To minimize stress and anxiety, children need to develop age-appropriate coping strategies. Generally they do not require intensive counseling; instead, they need to learn practical and versatile problem-solving approaches that they can apply to stressful family, school, sports, or social situations. When parents do not help children to cope positively in these situations,

Table III
Common sources of stress for children with recurrent headache

Social Relationships with Peers
  Difficulty making and/or keeping friends
  Difficulty coping with teasing and/or criticism
  Feelings of discomfort and inadequacy in many social situations

School
  Difficulty in understanding class work
  Difficulty in completing assignments on time
  Difficulty in competing in gymnastics or school sports
  Dissatisfaction with grades due to high expectations for achievement
  Poor relationships with classmates or teachers

Sports and Leisure Activities
  Excessive number of supervised activities
  Dissatisfaction with performance due to high expectations for achievement
  Primarily competitive, not relaxing activities
  Poor relationships with team-mates or coaches

Family
  Conflict regarding child's increasing need for independence
  Conflict among siblings
  Discord among immediate or extended family members
  Enmeshed relationship with parent

children become increasingly anxious and more vulnerable to subsequent headache attacks.

EMOTIONAL FACTORS

Situation-specific stress is the primary cause of headache for children. As shown in Table III, many potential sources of stress are associated with children's social, school, and leisure activities, and with family relationships. Most children experience some of these types of situation-specific stress, but most cope well so that the situations become progressively less stressful. Many children with headache do not cope well; they do not effectively resolve the stress they experience. Their anxiety persists or increases as they continue to encounter certain situations.

Some children are very anxious about their acceptance by peers; they feel as if they are always on the fringe and never really part of a social gathering. These children may become increasingly anxious about what to wear, how they look, and what they do in front of their peers, so that once-pleasurable events become a source of major stress. Other children have difficulty making or keeping friends, so that they feel very uncomfortable in new situations. Some children are upset by their classmates' teasing comments because they do not know what to say to lessen the teasing without being subject to further ridicule. Adolescents may be overly concerned about belonging to a particular social group or being included in popular activities.

School stressors typically include children's anxiety about their work load, their grades, and their relationships with their peers. Children may have difficulty in comprehending the material presented in class (due to learning or attention problems), may fall behind in completing assignments (because of poor organization skills and competing time demands), and may have trouble with situations where they are asked to perform in front of others (e.g., public speaking or gymnastics). Children become increasing anxious when they believe they cannot manage the work required. Often, they are unable to figure out why they are experiencing problems and how to resolve them. Some children have such high expectations for achievement that they are continually dissatisfied by their academic performance, irrespective of how well they do. These children experience higher than normal stress in all testing situations and may become increasingly anxious as academic demands increase. Others may experience difficulties with teachers or classmates, feeling stressed when they are in particular classes or when they must work with certain class members.

Anxiety related to sports and leisure activities is a common source of stress for children. Some children are simply too busy with numerous recreational activities. They are over-enrolled in competitive and coached activities, so that they lack time to just relax independently and enjoy their own creative pursuits. Most importantly, they lack opportunities to set and achieve their own personal goals, without continuous evaluation and suggestions for improvement. Hockey, piano, swimming, tennis, and riding lessons can all become sources of stress, especially when children hold extremely high expectations for their performance, occasionally subtly encouraged by well-meaning, but over-zealous parents and teachers. Other children may feel increasing demands to perform well to impress their parents, to justify the cost and time involved, or to satisfy their coach's expectations. These children consistently suppress or deny any stress related to their activities, but may begin to develop headache as a result.

Some children experience headache due to familial stress. A few children may develop headache as a result of a significant change within the family, such as the birth or adoption of a child, marital tension and discord, the death or sickness of a family member, or financial and job difficulties for parents. However, most children with headache related to familial stress simply experience difficulties in their relationships with parents or siblings. Some children may feel that their siblings have unfair advantages—fewer family responsibilities, more attention, and more privileges. As a result, sibling conflicts increase, as does parent-child discord. Some children are unable to express their opinions freely, particularly when their opinions differ from those of their parents. Parents may try to make children conform to their standards (about how they should look, how they should act, and what they should believe), creating more distress for all family members. A few parents exert excessive demands on children, with some becoming enmeshed in an overly dependent and close relationship with their children while others adopt a stronger authoritative role, enforcing increasingly rigid rules in an effort to maintain control.

In addition to anxiety related to situation-specific stress, several emotional factors may influence children's recurrent headache, as listed in Table IV. When parents do not understand their child's diagnosis, they become anxious and frightened that he or she may have an underlying medical condition. Despite reassurance to the contrary, some parents are concerned that their child has a malignant tumor. Even when a doctor assures them that the headaches are not life-threatening, many parents and almost all children remain anxious about likelihood of increasing pain and disability.

Some children, particularly those who receive inadequate pain control during headache attacks, become progressively distressed at headache onset. Parents are equally distressed that their children are suffering. When parents are unable to provide consistent pain relief, they become increasingly frustrated and some children interpret that they, rather than their headaches, are the source of frustration. As headache attacks continue, families also become frustrated by the constant and unpredictable disruptions to their lives. Parents often miss work and cancel planned social activities to care for children, while siblings are upset that they have to be quiet and that life again revolves around their brother (or sister) with headache. Some parents eventually become angry at the health care system because no one has been able to help their children and stop the headache attacks.

Table IV
Emotional factors for children with recurrent headache

Situation-specific stress
Emotional suppression or denial
Anxiety re. high expectations for achievement
Fear re. an undiagnosed condition
Fear re. life-threatening potential
Fear re. the likelihood of increasing pain and disability
Distress during headache attacks
Frustration re. the unpredictability of headache attacks
Frustration re. the interruption of activities for child and family
Anger toward health care providers for failing to cure the pain

Anxiety and depressive disorders may predispose children to develop headache, but in these cases the headache typically does not take the form of recurrent migraine and tension-type headache. Instead, these children develop chronic daily headache, as described in Chapter 9.

INTERPRETING DATA FROM CLINICAL POPULATIONS

Conclusions based on data accrued through the study of clinical referrals may be limited due to a selection bias. Children with a pain problem who seek treatment at specialized centers may be very different from those who do not seek treatment. Thus, conclusions regarding etiology or treatment may not be generalizable to all children with the problem. While we recognize the potential limitations of clinic-generated data, we believe that our conclusions about the causes and contributing factors of headache are applicable for the majority of children with recurrent migraine and tension-type headache.

Children in our research studies were recruited from the community and pain clinic. Children treated in our clinic were referred by family physicians, pediatricians, and neurologists, or were enrolled directly by parents. In all studies, we compared demographics and headache features for children whose families declined to participate to those who entered the study to ensure that the groups were comparable. The catchment area for all studies and for our pain clinic was the wide region of South Western Ontario, including both urban and rural areas. The ethnic distribution of our headache population reflected the ethnic diversity of the population. Children's access to the pain clinic was not limited by financial constraints as our clinical services were provided at no cost to the participants as part of our research program. In fact, families would not have anticipated therapy costs because the province of Ontario provides health care coverage to all residents. Thus, we believe that the information on headache accrued through our research program and pain clinic is accurate and generalizable for children with recurrent migraine or tension-type headache.

SUMMARY

Despite widely held beliefs that many environmental and physical stimuli (e.g., foods, weather conditions, and activities) can trigger headache attacks, the evidence base for these presumed headache triggers is negligible. The results of clinical studies in which children have monitored their daily activities have not revealed any specific environmental triggers. Instead, these studies indicate that stress—particularly a child's inability to fully resolve a stressful situation—is the major cause underlying the suspected diverse environmental triggers. In particular, situation-specific stress (involving social situations, school, sports, and family) is a common trigger for headache attacks. Our research indicates that the continued failure to resolve stress initiates a cascade of cognitive, behavioral, and emotional factors that subsequently maintain this pain syndrome.

Multiple factors are relevant in the etiology of recurrent migraine and tension-type headache. Hereditary factors may predispose children to develop headache, but other factors trigger headache attacks, increase pain, prolong disability, or maintain the cycle of repeated attacks. Cognitive factors are parents' and children's understanding and beliefs about headache. Behavioral factors encompass their specific actions during headache attacks and also their wider behaviors in response to the repeated attacks. Emotional factors include situation-specific stress that can trigger headache and the subsequent anxieties, fears, and frustrations that children and families experience. There is a dynamic interplay among these factors. Parents' beliefs guide their behaviors toward their children and shape their children's emotional responses to the pain problem. Parents generally hold inaccurate beliefs about headache etiology, effective therapies, and the role of environmental versus stress triggers. Consequently, they fail to consistently administer analgesics for strong headaches and to teach children effective nondrug strategies. Parents unintentionally may reinforce headache-related disability when they allow children to withdraw from potentially stressful situations, without helping children to address the underlying causes for headache attacks.

Typically, several factors are evident for all children with recurrent headache, but the extent to which they represent a trigger, the primary underlying cause, or a secondary contributing factor varies among children. Thus, we must ascertain which factors are relevant for which children so we can select the most appropriate drug or nondrug therapy for each child. With this approach, the emphasis of treatment shifts from an exclusively headache-centered focus to a more child-centered focus.

REFERENCES

Andrasik F, Burke EJ, Ahansio V, Rosenblum EL. Child, parent, and physician reports of a child's headache pain: relationships prior to and following treatment. *Headache* 1985; 421–425.

Andrasik F, Blake DD, McCarran MS. A biobehavioral analysis of pediatric headache. In: Krasnegor NA, Arasteh JD, Cataldo MF (Eds). *Child Health Behavior: A Behavioral Pediatrics Perspective*. New York: Wiley Interscience, 1986, pp 394–434.

Andrasik F, Kabela E, Quinn S, et al. Psychological functioning of children who have recurrent migraine. *Pain* 1988; 34:43–52.

Barlow CF. Precipitating factors of the migraine attack. In: Barlow CF (Ed). *Headaches and Migraine in Childhood,* Clinics in Developmental Medicine, Vol. 91. Philadelphia: J.B. Lippincott, 1984, pp 30–45.

Bener A, Uduman SA, Qassimi EM, et al. Genetic and environmental factors associated with migraine in schoolchildren. *Headache* 2000; 40:152–157.

Bijttebier P, Vertommen H. Antecedents, concomitants, and consequences of pediatric headache: confirmatory construct validation of two parent-report scales. *J Behav Med* 1999; 22:437–456.

Bille B. Migraine in school children: a study of the incidence, and short-term prognosis, and a clinical, psychological and encephalographic comparison between children with migraine and matched controls. *Acta Paediatr Suppl* 1962; 51:1–151.

Blanchard EB, Andrasik F, Evans DD, et al. Behavioral treatment of 250 chronic headache patients: a clinical replication series. *Behav Ther* 1985; 16:308–327.

Brown JK. Migraine and migraine equivalents in children. *Dev Med Child Neurol* 1977; 19:683–692.

Budd KS, Kedesdy JH. Investigation of environmental factors in pediatric headache. *Headache* 1989; 29:569–573.

Budd KS, Workman DE, Lemsky CM, Quick DM. The children's headache assessment scale (CHAS): factor structure and psychometric properties. *J Behav Med* 1994; 17:159–179.

Congdon PJ, Forsythe WI. Migraine in childhood: a study of 300 children. *Dev Med Child Neurol* 1979; 21:209–216.

Cooper PJ, Bawden HN, Camfield PR, Camfield CS. Anxiety and life events in childhood migraine. *Pediatrics* 1987; 79:999–1004.

Cunningham SJ, McGrath PJ, Ferguson HB, et al. Personality and behavioural characteristics in pediatric migraine. *Headache* 1987; 27(1):16–20.

Dalton K, Dalton ME. Food intake before migraine attacks in children. *J R Coll Gen Pract* 1979; 29:662–665.

Egger J, Carter CM, Wilson J, Turner MW, Soothill JF. Is migraine food allergy? A double-blind controlled trial of oligoantigenic diet treatment. *Lancet* 1983; 2:865–869.

Egger J, Carter CM, Graham PJ, Gumley D, Soothill JF. Controlled trial of oligoantigenic treatment in the hyperkinetic syndrome. *Lancet* 1985; 1:540–545.

Fenichel GM. Migraine in children. In: Moss AJ (Ed). *Pediatrics Update: Reviews for Physicians*. New York: Elsevier, 1981, pp 25–41.

Forsythe WI, Redmond A. Two controlled trials of tyramine in children with migraine. *Dev Med Child Neurol* 1974; 16:794–799.

Griffiths JD, Martin PR. Clinical- versus home-based treatment formats for children with chronic headache. *Br J Health Psychol* 1996; 1:151–166.

Hockaday JM. Headache in children. *Br J Hosp Med* 1982; 27:383–4, 386.

Hoelscher TJ, Lichstein KL. Behavioral assessment and treatment of child migraine: implications for clinical research and practice. *Headache* 1984; 24:94–103.

Jackson DN. *The Basic Personality Inventory.* London, Ontario: Research Psychologists Press, 1976.

Joffe R, Bakal DA, Kaganov J. A self-observation study of headache symptoms in children. *Headache* 1983; 23:20–25.

Kowal A, Pritchard D. Psychological characteristics of children who suffer from headache: a research note. *J Child Psychol Psychiatry* 1990; 31(4):637–649.

Labbé EE, Ward CH. Electromyographic biofeedback with mental imagery and home practice in the treatment of children with muscle-contraction headache. *Dev Behav Pediat* 1990; 11:65–68.

Labbé EE, Williamson DA, Southard DR. Reliability and validity of children's reports of migraine headache symptoms. *J Psychopathol Behav Assess* 1985; 7(4):375–383.

Langeveld JH, Koot HM, Passchier J. Do experienced stress and trait negative affectivity moderate the relationship between headache and quality of life in adolescents? *J Pediat Psychol* 1999; 24:1–11.

Larsson B, Melin L. The psychological treatment of recurrent headache in adolescents—short-term outcome and its prediction. *Headache* 1988; 28:187–194.

Larsson B, Melin L, Doberl A. Recurrent tension headache in adolescents treated with self-help relaxation training and a muscle relaxant drug. *Headache* 1990; 30:665–671.

Lee LH, Olness KN. Clinical and demographic characteristics of migraine in urban children. *Headache* 1997; 37:269–276.

Leviton A, Slack WV, Masek B, Bana D, Graham JR. A computerized behavioral assessment for children with headaches. *Headache* 1984; 24:182–185.

Lewis DW, Middlebrook MT, Mehallick L, et al. Pediatric headaches: what do the children want? *Headache* 1996; 36:224–230.

Macdonald A, Forsythe I, Wall C. Dietary treatment of migraine. In: Lanzi G, Balottin U, Cernibori A (Eds). *Headache in Children and Adolescents*. Amsterdam: Elsevier, 1989, pp 333–338.

Maratos J, Wilkinson M. Migraine in children: a medical and psychiatric study. *Cephalalgia* 1982; 2:179–187.

McGrath ML, Masek BJ. Behavioral treatment of headache. In: Schechter NL, Berde CB, Yaster M (Eds). *Pain in Infants, Children, and Adolescents*. Baltimore: Williams & Wilkins, 1993, pp 555–560.

McGrath PA. The multidimensional assessment and management of recurrent pain syndromes in children and adolescents. *Behav Res Ther* 1987; 25:251–262.

McGrath PA. *Pain in Children: Nature, Assessment and Treatment*. New York: Guilford Publications, 1990.

McGrath PA, Hinton GG, Boone JE. Management of recurrent headaches in children. *Abstracts: 7th World Congress on Pain*. Seattle: IASP Press, 1993, p 51.

McGrath PJ, Humphreys P, Goodman JT, et al. Relaxation prophylaxis for childhood migraine: a randomized placebo-controlled trial. *Dev Med Child Neurol* 1988; 30:626–631.

Metsahonkala L, Sillanpaa M, Tuominen J. Social environment and headache. *Headache* 1998; 38:222–228.

Osterhaus SO, Passchier J, Helm-Hylkema H, et al. Effects of behavioral psychophysiological treatment on schoolchildren with migraine in a nonclinical setting: predictors and process variables. *J Pediatr Psychol* 1993; 18:697–715.

Passchier J, Orlebeke JF. Headaches and stress in schoolchildren: an epidemiological study. *Cephalalgia* 1985; 5:167–176.

Price DD. *Psychological Mechanisms of Pain and Analgesia*. Seattle: IASP Press, 1999.

Richter IL, McGrath PJ, Humphreys PJ, et al. Cognitive and relaxation treatment of paediatric migraine. *Pain* 1986; 25:195–203.

Rigg CA. Migraine in children and adolescents. *Acta Paediatr Scand* 1975 (Suppl); 256:19–24.

Ross DM, Ross SA. *Childhood Pain: Current Issues, Research and Management*. Baltimore: Urban and Schwarzenberg, 1988.

Rothner AD. Headaches in children: a review. *Headache* 1978; 18:169–175.

Shinnar S, D'Souza BJ. The diagnosis and management of headaches in childhood. *Pediatr Clin North Am* 1982; 29:79–94.

Vahlquist B. Migraine in children. *Int Arch Allergy* 1955; 7:348–355.

Vahlquist B, Hackzell G. Migraine of early onset: a study of thirty one cases in which the disease first appeared between one and four years of age. *Acta Paediatr (Uppsala)* 1949; 38:622–636.

Waranch HR, Keenan DM. Behavioral treatment of children with recurrent headaches. *J Behav Ther Exp Psychiatry* 1985; 16:31–38.

Correspondence to: Patricia A. McGrath, PhD, Pain Innovations, Inc., 38 Hampton Crescent, London, Ontario, Canada N6H 2N8. Fax: 519-471-8529; email: pamcgrat@julian.wo.ca. Effective 1 July 2001: Department of Anesthesiology, School of Medicine, University of Utah, Salt Lake City, UT 84108, USA.

The Child with Headache: Diagnosis and Treatment.
Progress in Pain Research and Management, Vol. 19,
edited by Patricia A. McGrath and Loretta M. Hillier,
IASP Press, Seattle, © 2001.

5

Drug Therapies for Childhood Headache

Simon D. Levin

*Department of Paediatrics, University of Western Ontario,
London, Ontario, Canada*

This chapter will discuss pharmacological treatment of headache as defined by the Headache Classification Committee of the International Headache Society (1988), recognizing that some authorities consider that pediatric headache requires modification from this adult classification (Gladstein et al. 1997; Winner et al. 1997). There have been significant advances in the drug treatment of headaches in childhood. However, few randomized controlled trials (RCTs) have evaluated drug therapy in children; the vast majority of such trials have been conducted to study the new triptans in adult migraine patients. Children, usually adolescents, have been incorporated into these adult studies, and successful treatment in adults has been extrapolated to the pediatric population.

Nonpharmacological management of headache, as described in Chapters 6–8, is very important. Although few studies have compared psychological and pharmacological treatment of pediatric migraine, psychological treatments may be more effective (Sartory et al. 1998). Other treatments such as acupuncture (Hu 1998; Gao et al. 1999) and spinal manipulation (Nelson et al. 1998) also deserve consideration.

MIGRAINE

BIOLOGICAL BASIS

The pathophysiology of migraine is unknown; the pathogenesis is multifactorial and genetically complex. Concordance rates for migraine in monozygotic twins indicate that 50% of the etiology is genetically based. Familial hemiplegic migraine, a rare subtype, has a strong genetic basis with autosomal dominant inheritance. Three different gene loci have been isolated on chromosomes 19p, 1q21–23, and 1q31. Cases linked to chromosome 19p are associated with mutations of a brain-expressed calcium channel subunit, which has a number of complicated interactions, making the further elucidation of pathophysiology difficult (Gardner 1999). However, such evidence raises the possibility that migraine is a "channelopathy," i.e., a disorder of ion channel regulation.

An episode of classic migraine with aura has two phases: an initial vasoconstriction of cerebral vessels that manifests clinically as an aura (although the oligemia lasts longer than the clinical aura), followed by cerebral and meningeal vessel dilatation that correlates with pain. Research on the trigeminovascular system, serotonin (5-hydroxytryptamine, 5-HT), serotonin receptors, and substance P has provided clues (Solomon 1995) about the pathogenesis of pain in migraine. Unlike the typical pain following nociceptive stimuli, such as trauma, in which the pain is based on neural pathways with activation of nociceptors, migraine appears to have a neural and vascular basis, leading to the hypothesis of a trigeminovascular disorder. It would not be unreasonable to suppose that typical neural pain mechanisms play a role in migraine or that such mechanisms constitute a final common pathway for the pain experienced in migraine, which would explain the effectiveness of common analgesics.

Markowitz and colleagues have proposed that the pain in migraine is produced by an inflammatory response in cerebral and dural blood vessels caused by the release of neuropeptides such as substance P, calcitonin gene-related peptide (CGRP), and neurokinin A from trigeminal nerve efferents innervating these vessels (Markowitz et al. 1988; Hamel 1999). The neurogenic inflammatory response was proposed to cause vasodilatation and plasma extravasation through vessel walls, with stimulation of trigeminal nerve efferents causing pain transmitted via the trigeminal ganglion and trigeminal nucleus to the thalamus and to the cortex. Recent data throw doubt on this mechanism, however; double-blind trials of a potent inhibitor of neurogenic plasma extravasation without vasoconstrictor effect failed to abort acute migraine attacks (Roon et al. 2000). Another mechanism of vasodilatation may involve nitric oxide formation. Histamine activates cerebral endothelial histamine receptors, causing nitric oxide formation in vascular endothelium and thereby inducing vasodilatation (Lassen et al. 1995). Headache relief has been achieved by administering a nitric oxide synthase inhibitor, L-NG-methylarginine HCl (Lassen et al. 1998).

The serotonin concentration in cerebrospinal fluid falls significantly during migraine attacks (Scheife and Hills 1980). The actions of serotonin are mediated by its receptors. There are seven groups of serotonin receptors (5-HT_1–5-HT_7). Within each group are subgroups (designated by subscript uppercase letters when their function is known, e.g., 5-HT$_{1A}$, 5-HT$_{1B}$, 5-HT$_{1D}$, 5-HT$_{1E}$, 5-HT$_{1F}$, and by lowercase letters when their function is unknown). 5-HT$_1$ receptors are expressed throughout the peripheral and central nervous system (CNS) and have been implicated in depression, anxiety, movement disorders, and regulation of food intake. They may play a role in aborting migraine attacks, possibly by modulating neurotransmitter release from the trigeminovascular system. Triptan antimigraine agents are serotonergic agonists that act selectively by causing vasoconstriction through 5-HT$_{1B}$ receptors that are expressed in human intracranial extracerebral arteries and by inhibiting nociceptive transmission through an action at 5-HT$_{1D}$ receptors on peripheral trigeminal sensory nerve terminals in the meninges and on central terminals in brainstem sensory nuclei (Hargreaves and Shepheard 1999). Sumatriptan, a 5-HT$_{1B/1D/1F}$ agonist, potently inhibits the neurogenic inflammatory response caused by activation of the trigeminovascular system. Newer triptans also act on 5-HT$_{1B/1D}$ sites centrally and attenuate the pain response.

In contrast, some drugs that *prevent* migraine and are thought to act by preventing vasoconstriction of meningeal and other CNS vessels (pizotifen, methysergide, cyproheptidine, and amitriptyline) have an antagonistic effect on HT$_{2B}$ receptor sites (Hamel 1999).

The past 10 years have seen a dramatic improvement in the scientific evaluation of the efficacy of migraine treatment, particularly with the introduction of sumatriptan, the first of the 5-HT$_{1B/1D}$ agonists or triptans. Goadsby (1999) presents a detailed discussion of trial methodology and therapeutic goals, including objective measurement of pain and time to relief of symptoms. The management of migraine can be conveniently divided into the treatment of the acute attack and prophylaxis.

MANAGEMENT OF ACUTE MIGRAINE ATTACKS

Analgesics. Medication should be given as soon as possible after the headache (or aura) starts (Table I). The oral route may not be possible if there is vomiting, and other routes (rectal, intranasal, intravenous) of administration should be tried.

Analgesic-antipyretic drugs (Insel 1990) are used in migraine, but their mechanism of action is not specific. In animal models, these drugs are particularly effective when inflammation has sensitized pain receptors. This sensitization is caused by prostaglandins, which lower the threshold of polymodal nociceptors of C fibers (Perl 1976), and these drugs act by inhibiting the enzyme cyclooxygenase and thus reducing prostaglandin synthesis. These drugs include acetaminophen, apirin, and nonsteroidal anti-inflammatory drugs (NSAIDs). Aspirin has been associated with the development of Reye's syndrome in children less than 12 years old and should not be used in this age group (Lanzi et al. 1996). Acetaminophen at oral doses of 15–20 mg/kg (Welborn 1997) up to every 4 hours has been the mainstay of treatment in all age groups. Rectal absorption is variable; doses of up to 45 mg/kg may be required (Graf and Riback 1995). Ibuprofen, an NSAID, is an alternative; the recommended dose for 2–12-year-olds is 5 to 10 mg every 8 hours. Ibuprofen is more effective than acetaminophen in migraine (Hamalainen et al. 1997) and is available as a suspension. In clinical practice, however, acetaminophen is generally used for younger children because of concern for rare, as yet unrecognized risks of ibuprofen use (McCullough 1998), while either drug can be used for older children. Naproxen, another NSAID, has been useful in the treatment of menstrual migraine (Pryse-Phillips et al. 1997) and could be tried in adolescent patients (Graf and Riback 1995). Recent data derived from three double-blind, randomized, placebo-controlled, single-dose trials showed that a nonprescription (over-the-counter) combination of acetaminophen, aspirin, and caffeine is effective both in menstrual migraine and migraine not associated with menses (Silberstein et al. 1999). This combination may be worth consideration in adolescent females. If these analgesics do not provide adequate pain relief, opioids should be used, either codeine orally or morphine intravenously (i.v.) or intramuscularly (i.m.) (see Table I for suggested dosage). Proprietary combinations of acetaminophen and codeine are available that may be convenient to use. Dosing guidelines are the same as for individual drugs. No particular efficacy has been demonstrated.

Ergot derivatives. Ergotamine, a derivative of the tetracyclic compound 6-methylergoline, and its semisynthetic derivative dihydroergotamine have varied, complex actions, some of which are unrelated and even mutually antagonistic. These drugs cause peripheral vasoconstriction, depression of brainstem vasomotor centers, and peripheral adrenergic blockade. The mechanism of action in migraine was thought to be cranial vessel vasoconstriction, but this hypothesis is now disputed (Rall 1990). In animal models, ergotamine and dihydroergotamine (DHE) can block plasma extravasation into the dura mater caused by electrical stimulation of the trigeminal nerve (Markowitz 1988). Ergotamine is effective in relieving migraine in adult patients, although it is neither a sedative nor an analgesic, but it is ineffective in childhood migraine (Welborn 1997). It is difficult to titrate the appropriate dose, it is nauseating at high doses, and ensuring that it is taken at the onset of a migraine attack may be difficult. Intravenous DHE has been used successfully in children as young as 6 years of age with prolonged migraine episodes not responding to conventional treatment. A nasal spray is

Table I
Analgesics used in acute treatment of migraine in children

Drug	Dosage	Comments
NSAIDs		
Acetaminophen	15–20 mg/kg p.o./p.r. q4h p.r.n.	
Aspirin	500–625 mg p.o. q4h p.r.n. (>12 yr)	Avoid in children <12 yr.
Ibuprofen	5–10 mg/kg p.o. q6h p.r.n.; ≥12 yr: 200 mg/dose	
Naproxen sodium	5–7 mg/kg q8h–q12h p.o. p.r.n. (>2 yr)	
Opioids		
Codeine; morphine	1 mg/kg p.o. q6h; 0.1–0.15 mg/kg i.v. or i.m. as single dose	
Ergot Derivatives		
Dihydroergotamine (DHE)	0.1–0.25 mg i.v./s.c./i.m. (may repeat q20 min up to 3 times) plus metoclopramide 0.2 mg/kg 30 min prior to DHE (max. 20 mg)	Not approved by HPB for use in children. Useful in severe prolonged migraine attacks. Use i.v. in emergency room.
Ergotamine	2 mg p.o. initially, then 1 mg at 30-min intervals (max. 6 mg/ attack; 12 mg/week)	Use in adolescents at beginning of attack; no adequate trials in children. Do not use more than 2 days/week to avoid rebound headaches.
Sumatriptan	50 mg (<50 kg), 100 mg (>50 kg) p.o.; 0.06 mg/kg (max. 6 mg) s.c.; 5 mg intranasally	Use not well established in children. No HPB approval for children.

Source: Adapted from Worthington (1999).
Abbreviations: HPB = Health Protection Branch, Health Canada; i.m. = intramuscularly; i.v. = intravenously; NSAIDs = nonsteroidal anti-inflammatory drugs; p.o. = orally; p.r. = rectally; p.r.n. = as needed; q4h = every 4 hours; s.c. = subcutaneously.

available for adults, but data are lacking on its efficacy in children (Linder 1994; Worthington 1999); continuous i.v. infusion has been used successfully in adults (Ford and Ford 1997). Adolescents can be taught to administer DHE subcutaneously (s.c.) for severe migraine attacks (Graf and Riback 1995).

Serotonin receptor agonists. Sumatriptan, a 5-HT$_{1B/1D}$ agonist approved for use in adults (Pryse-Phillips et al. 1997), has shown dose-related efficacy in large multicenter studies (Moschiano et al. 1997; Pfaffenrath et al. 1998). Subcutaneous administration (6 mg) in adults has been effective, with good tolerability if contraindications are taken into account (Gobel 1999); a second 6-mg s.c. dose is effective when given for recurrent migraine headache 1–24 hours later (Cull et al. 1997). Trials in children have yielded conflicting results, with one controlled, randomized trial of oral sumatriptan showing no greater efficacy than placebo (Hamalainen et al. 1997). Two open-label trials have shown that s.c. sumatriptan is effective. Side effects included injection site reactions, dizziness and drowsiness, and brief, mild chest or neck dysesthesia with a sensation of tingling or pressure; one child had transient confusion lasting 2 hours (Linder 1994; MacDonald 1994). Intranasal sumatriptan is effective in adults (Moore et al. 1997; Ryan et al. 1997) and children, with complete headache relief in 9 of 14 children (Ueberall and Wenzel 1999). Migraine-associated symptoms are also significantly reduced by sumatriptan (Ueberall and Wenzel 1999). Zolmitriptan (Schoenen and Sawyer 1997; Zagami 1997; Mauskop et al. 1999; Tepper et al. 1999; Tuchman et al. 1999) is effective in children as young as 12 (Solomon et al. 1997), with an optimal dose of 2.5 mg (Rapoport et al. 1997). Other triptans include naratriptan (Klassen et al. 1997; Mathew et al. 1997; Bomhof et al. 1998), rizatriptan (Kramer et al. 1998; Teall et al. 1998), avitriptan (Cutler et al. 1998), and eletriptan. It is unclear whether these drugs will have significant therapeutic advantages over sumatriptan.

Antiemetics. Antiemetics are a fundamentally important part of the acute management of migraine because nausea and vomiting frequently accompany migraines. Antiemetics should be given at the onset of symptoms, even in mild cases of migraine, when nausea is a frequent accompaniment of the attack (Table II). In most cases dimenhydrinate is used because it is available over the counter. In cases failing to respond to dimenhydrinate, metoclopramide or prochlorperazine can be used. These drugs infrequently cause idiosyncratic acute dystonic reactions. In adults, prochlorperazine also causes akathisia (restlessness) (Drotts and Vinson 1999).

Chlorpromazine (CPZ) is often used as a stand-alone medication to abort severe migraine attacks. In an uncontrolled clinical trial of 100 adult patients given 1 mg/kg CPZ, pain and nausea or emesis were completely relieved in 96 patients. Eighteen patients suffered hypotension as a side effect, with all but one responding to noninvasive therapy (Iserson 1983). In a prospective, randomized, double-blind, controlled trial, i.m. CPZ 1 mg/kg relieved migraine sufficiently for 9 of 19 patients to return to normal activity, compared to 4 of 17 patients given placebo, although the difference did not reach statistical significance (McEwen et al. 1987). In a prospective, randomized, double-blind study of adult patients, i.v. chlorpromazine was compared with metoclopramide, each drug being given in a dose of 0.1 mg/kg. Both drugs were effective in providing pain relief with similar minor side effects (Cameron 1995).

Guidelines for the management of an acute migraine attack in children. There are no published protocols relating severity of migraine (rated using pain scales) to treatment. The following suggestions are the outcome of personal practice over 15 years.

Mild attacks of migraine (affecting the ability of children to participate in school and/or extracurricular activities but not incapacitating) can be managed with mild analgesic medication (acetaminophen, NSAIDs such as ibuprofen, aspirin in those older than 12 years, or codeine) and an antiemetic such as dimenhydrinate or prochlorperazine (Table I).

Moderately severe attacks (preventing participation in school and extracurricular activities and affecting activities of daily living at home) are most appropriately managed with an opiate (preferably codeine) as well as an antiemetic. Increasingly, sumatriptan is also being used; intranasal administration is most convenient (Table I).

Severe (incapacitating) attacks can be managed using the protocol diagrammed in Fig. 1.

An i.v. infusion of normal saline must be established and the patient given 10 mL/kg before medications are administered (see Table I for doses). Vital signs must be monitored every 10 minutes while giving chlorpromazine, and patients should remain supine for 2 hours after receiving treatment.

Other treatments for severe migraine include i.m. sumatriptan, which is as effective as i.v. chlorpromazine in adults (Kelly et al. 1997). Ergotamine may be useful in adolescents. In adults, i.m. dihydroergotamine with hydroxyzine has been as effective as meperidine and hydroxyzine, with a reduced incidence of dizziness (Carleton 1998).

Table II
Antiemetics used in the acute treatment of migraine

Drug	Dosage	Comments
Dimenhydrinate	1–1.5 mg/kg p.o./p.r. q6h	
Metoclopramide	1–2 mg/kg p.o. (max. 10 mg) or 0.1–0.5 mg/kg i.v. (max. 10 mg)	Can cause acute dystonic reaction. Use i.v. in emergency room (adolescents).
Domperidone	0.3–0.6 mg/kg p.o.	
Chlorpromazine	1 mg/kg p.o./i.m. (max. 25 mg) q8h; 0.1 mg/kg i.v. q10–15 min (max 30 mg). Slow push over 5 min (max. 7.5 mg). Repeat at 15-min intervals for a total of 3 doses.	Hypotension with i.v. use (pretreat with i.v. normal saline).
Prochlorperazine	2.5–5 mg p.o./p.r. b.i.d. (up to 0.1 mg/kg in younger children); 10 mg i.v.	Can cause acute dystonic reaction. Use i.v. in emergency room (adolescents).

Source: Adapted from Worthington (1999).
Abbreviations: b.i.d. = twice a day; other abbreviations as in Table I.

PROPHYLAXIS

Children whose migraines are frequent enough to interfere with their normal lifestyle should receive prophylactic medication (Tables III, IV). The indications have not been defined, either for starting prophylactic medication or for length of treatment. In adults the standard of care is to use prophylactic drugs if patients have three or more migraine headaches per month. My clinical practice has been to use prophylaxis in children who have more than one migraine headache per month. For those with frequent migraine headaches, occurring weekly or more often, I have continued prophylaxis for approximately 2 months and then weaned patients from the medication. Longer courses of prophylaxis for up to 1 year are appropriate if migraines occur relatively infrequently (in cases where headaches are disabling and acute treatment is not effective). Treatment is repeated if the migraines recur.

Document vital signs including blood pressure and temperature before treatment
Check vital signs every 30 minutes with pain assessment
Check vital signs every 10 minutes while chlorpromazine is infusing
Pretreat with normal saline 10 mL/kg before giving chlorpromazine
Patients receiving phenothiazines to remain supine for 2 hours

METOCLOPRAMIDE
0.5 mg/kg i.v.
Maximum 10 mg

↓ If no relief in 30–60 min

CHLORPROMAZINE
0.1 mg/kg given by slow i.v. push over 5 minutes
Maximum 7.5 mg/dose
If no relief: may repeat q 15 min for a total of 3 doses

↓ If no relief 30 min after maximum dose

Re-administer dose of metoclopramide
DIHYDROERGOTAMINE
0.5–1.0 mg infused i.v. over 2–3 minutes
If no relief: may repeat 0.5 mg i.v. 30–60 minutes after initial dose

Fig. 1. Emergency room treatment for migraine in patients aged 10 years and above. Based on the protocol at Montreal Children's Hospital (H. Eisman, personal communication, 2000).

In general, medications are started in low doses and increased gradually (Graf and Ribeck 1995). Welborn (1997) recommends treatment for a few months followed by weaning from the medication and taking "drug holidays." Varying degrees of scientific evidence support the use of various drugs. Evidence is best for metoprolol, divalproex, amitriptyline, atenolol, flunarizine, and naproxen (Becker 1999). Data in children are scarce, and management is mostly derived from adult data. In a review of drug efficacy, Ramadan et al. (1997) ranked clinical trials of various drugs from +5 to –5 and derived an average scientific score (Table III). As an example of the difficulty of assessing true efficacy, metoprolol has a much higher scientific score than propranolol, even though many more trials have been conducted with propranolol. This may only reflect the fact that trials with propranolol, conducted earlier, were less rigorous than those with metoprolol; both drugs may in fact be effective.

Beta-blockers. Propranolol, timolol, and metoprolol (Andersson et al. 1983) are effective for the prophylaxis of migraine (Tfelt-Hansen 1986), but the mechanism of this effect is not known, and these drugs are not useful in the treatment of acute attacks (Bannerjee and Findley 1991; Fuller and Guiloff

Table III
Quality of the scientific evidence supporting
the use of some drugs commonly used as
migraine prophylactics

Drug	No. of Trials†	Score‡
Metoprolol	3	4.3
Divalproex	4	3.8
Amitriptyline	3	2.3
Atenolol	3	2.3
Flunarizine	6	2.2
Naproxen	6	2.2
Propranolol	18	1.4
Methysergide	3	1.3
Pizotifen	10	1.1
Verapamil	4	1.0
Fluoxetine	2	0.0

Source: Adapted from Ramadan (1997).
† Randomized, double-blind, placebo-controlled trials.
‡ Average of the ratings for the individual studies. A high-quality study showing evidence for a prophylactic effect would be rated +5, and a high-quality study showing no prophylactic effect would be rated –5. (See Ramadan 1997; Becker 1999.)

Table IV
Drugs used in the prophylaxis of childhood migraine

Drug	Dosage	Comments
Beta-Blockers		
Propranolol	1–3 mg/kg/day as b.i.d. dose	Side effects: fatigue, bradycardia, hypotension, depression. Contra-indications: asthma, heart block, bradyarrhythmias, diabetes, congestive heart failure. Avoid abrupt withdrawal.
Tricyclic Antidepressants		
Amitriptyline	0.2–2.0 mg/kg/day as t.i.d. dose	Side effects: weight gain, drowsiness, anticholinergic effects. Contra-indications: cardiac disease.
Serotonin Antagonists		
Pizotifen	0.5 mg t.i.d. (may use 0.5–1.5 mg/kg as t.i.d. dose)	Side effects: sedation, weight gain. Start small dose at night and increase at weekly intervals to t.i.d. dose.
Methysergide	2–6 mg/day	Side effect: retroperitoneal fibrosis. Discontinue for 1 month every 3–6 months. Use in adolescents only.
Calcium Channel Blockers		
Flunarizine	5 mg/day	Side effects: bradycardia, hypotension, weight gain, drowsiness. Contra-indications: depression, extrapyramidal disorders.
Antihistamines		
Cyproheptadine	Age 2–6 yr: 2 mg q8–12h (max. 12 mg/ day). Age 7–14 yr: 4 mg q8–12h (max. 16 mg/day)	Side effects: drowsiness.
NSAIDs		
Naproxen sodium	275–550 mg b.i.d.	Side effects: gastrointestinal. Useful for menstrual migraine. Use no more than 1 week per month.
Antiepileptic Drugs		
Valproate	10–50 mg/kg/day as b.i.d. dose	Side effects: hepatotoxicity, thrombocytopenia. Start at low dose and increase at weekly intervals.
Gabapentin	300–400 mg t.i.d.	Start at 100 mg t.i.d. and increase daily by 100 mg t.i.d. to maximum dose.

Source: Adapted from Worthington (1999).
Abbreviations: b.i.d. = twice a day; t.i.d. = three times a day; other abbreviations as in Table I.

1991). The relevance of β-adrenergic blockade in migraine prophylaxis has been questioned (Edmeads 1988). Propranolol is commonly used in children if there are no contraindications such as asthma, congestive heart failure, atrioventricular conduction defects, or diabetes (Welborn 1997). Efficacy was demonstrated in one study (Ludvigsson 1974), but not in two others (Forsythe et al. 1984; Olness et al. 1987). Suggested starting dose is 1 mg/kg/day in two divided doses, gradually increasing to 3 mg/kg/day if needed.

Serotonin antagonists. Pizotifen, a serotonin antagonist, did not reduce the frequency and duration of migraine attacks, but was well tolerated in a double-blind, placebo-controlled crossover trial (Gilles et al. 1986) and was effective in a study of abdominal migraine (Symon and Russell 1995).

Tricyclic antidepressants. Amitriptyline is useful in adolescents with migraine who also have depression or muscle contraction headaches (Sorge et al. 1982). Trazodone significantly reduces the frequency and severity of migraines (Battistella et al. 1993).

Antihistamines. Cyproheptadine, an antihistamine and $5\text{-}HT_2$ antagonist, is commonly used in migraine prophylaxis, but there are no published controlled studies (Welborn 1997).

Calcium channel blockers. Flunarizine at doses of 5 mg/day significantly reduces the frequency and severity of migraine headaches in children (Sorge and Marano 1985; Sorge et al. 1988). In adults, predictive factors for a good response are family history and high intensity of pain; negative factors are frequent attacks and a history of analgesic abuse (Lucetti et al. 1998).

NSAIDs. Naproxen may be useful in the prophylaxis of menstrual migraine in adolescents (Graf and Riback 1995).

Antiepileptic drugs. Valproate was effective in 60% of adult patients with migraine resistant to conventional prophylactic treatment (Ghose and Niven 1998) and in 66% of adults with migraine without aura (Kaniecki 1997), being as effective as propranolol. Since valproate is widely used as an antiepileptic drug in children, it may be worth using in children with migraine. Lamotrigine, a glutamate antagonist that works by blocking voltage-sensitive sodium channels, can prevent migraine aura and reduce the frequency of migraine headache in adults (Lampl et al. 1999). Primarily an antiepileptic drug that is extensively used in children, lamotrigine may be worth consideration in migraine prophylaxis. Preliminary studies in adults suggest that neurontin is useful in migraine prophylaxis (Mathew and Lucker 1996), even in cases resistant to other therapies (Nicolodi and Sicuteri 1997). In a case report, an adult female had intractable facial pain and migraine despite treatment with amitriptyline, propranolol, and carbamazepine; gabapentin completely controlled her symptoms for 12 months (Schachter and Carrazana 1997).

Other. High-dose riboflavin (vitamin B_2; 400 mg/day) has shown efficacy in a randomized trial compared with placebo, with 59% of adult patients demonstrating at least a 50% reduction in headache frequency (Schoenen et al. 1998).

Guidelines for prophylaxis. There is no relationship between severity of migraine headaches and type of prophylaxis to be used. Propranolol and pizotifen are the most frequently used drugs in the prophylaxis of migraine. Despite data indicating that other drugs are more effective, at least in adults (Table III), these two drugs continue to be the most widely used because of their long history of apparent efficacy in children. Until direct comparisons are made between these drugs and others in children, it is unlikely that physicians will change their prescriptions. The considerable placebo effect seen in migraine may be an explanation for the apparent success of these drugs. My experience suggests that both drugs are "effective." Because of the high prevalence of reversible airways disease (asthma) in the childhood population, propranolol must be used cautiously. If propranolol and pizotifen are ineffective, amitriptyline and flunarizine would be the next drugs of choice in children; a careful review suggests that these drugs should be used more often (Becker 1999). If none of these drugs are effective, an anticonvulsant such as divalproex or gabapentin would be worth trying. Anxiety about possible hepatotoxicity is a disincentive to the use of valproate. Cyproheptadine is rarely used, and the side effects of methysergide essentially preclude its use in children, although it is occasionally used in adolescents with migraine resistant to all other treatment.

Given increasing data and growing confidence in the use of serotonin receptor agonists, Cleland (1997) has suggested that these drugs be used for acute attacks that occur less frequently than four times a month and that pizotifen be reserved for patients having four or more attacks a month. In Cleland's study, prophylactic pizotifen did not improve migraine control significantly over oral sumatriptan given at the time of migraine attacks.

TENSION-TYPE HEADACHE

PATHOPHYSIOLOGY

The pathophysiology of acute and chronic tension-type headaches is very poorly understood. A number of studies have failed to demonstrate associations with substance P, neuropeptide Y, vasoactive intestinal peptide (Ashina et al. 1999), serotonin (Bendtsen et al. 1997; Bendtsen and Mellerup 1998), or with plasma lactate and pyruvate levels (Okada et al. 1998). Debate continues as to whether pericranial muscle tenderness is a primary source of pain in tension-type headache associated with a local, reversible sensitization of nociceptors in pericranial muscles (Jensen 1996). The failure of botulinum toxin to reduce pain in tension-type headache suggests that peripheral mechanisms such as increased muscle tenderness play only a minor role in its pathogenesis (Rollnik et al. 2000).

MANAGEMENT

Behavioral, psychological, and other complementary/alternative therapies (Vernon et al. 1999) have been used successfully in tension-type headache. While psychological treatment is felt to be superior to drug therapy in tension-type headache, recent studies have demonstrated efficacy of drug therapy in adults. A recent review demonstrates that only antidepressants have been extensively studied and that they are useful (Redillas and Solomon 2000). Amitriptyline is effective in chronic but not episodic tension-type headache (Cerbo 1998). Acetaminophen and ketoprofen produced worthwhile effect in 61% and 70% of bouts of episodic tension-type headache, respectively—a significant difference from placebo, which produced significant effects in 36% of episodes (Steiner and Lange 1998). Other studies have compared the efficacy of ketoprofen with that of ibuprofen (van Gerven et al. 1996) and acetaminophen (Dahlof and Jacobs 1996). Ketorolac is an NSAID with minimal anti-inflammatory activity at analgesic doses. It is superior both to placebo and to meperidine when given i.m. in adults for acute exacerbations of tension-type headaches (Harden et al. 1998). Data are lacking on its use in children.

Guidelines for management of tension-type headache. We lack good data in children to determine the most appropriate analgesic to use. Acetaminophen remains the most commonly used analgesic, with increasing use of ibuprofen in recent years. It is routine practice to give one of these analgesics for tension-type headache. Amitriptyline may be also useful. Anecdotal observation suggests that tension-type headaches that do not respond to these simple analgesics also fail to respond to more aggressive analgesic treatment and are more appropriately treated by nonpharmacological means, including the identification and resolution of emotional stressors. Indeed, failure to respond to analgesic medication may be a characteristic feature of tension-type headaches.

Cluster headache. This incapacitating form of headache is rarely seen in children. A 12-year-old girl with classical clinical features responded completely to antihistamines, initially astemizole and subsequently, loratadine (Neubauer et al. 1997). Topiramate, a relatively new anticonvulsant with multiple actions, has been used successfully in its treatment in adults (Wheeler and Carrazana 1999). The safety profile for topiramate as an adjunct treatment in childhood epilepsy is now well established and it could be tried in children on an emergency release basis. In adults, lithium, which has been widely used, was found to be ineffective in the prophylaxis of cluster headache (Steiner et al. 1997).

Headache associated with substances and their withdrawal. A recent retrospective study found that children on daily analgesics did suffer analgesic rebound headaches. Discontinuation of analgesics and concomitant treatment with amitriptyline proved effective (Vasconcellos et al. 1998). Some children may have *worsening* of their headaches in association with use of analgesics (acetaminophen, ibuprofen, and codeine); abrupt withdrawal of the medication may stop their headaches (Symon 1998).

Other types of headache. Headache has been reported in association with disorders of the cranium, neck, eyes, ears, nose, sinuses, teeth, and other facial or cranial structures. The underlying cause should be treated. Acetaminophen, aspirin, NSAIDs, or codeine may be useful.

SUMMARY

Despite decades of intense interest in headache, substantial areas of ignorance remain. The pathophysiology of migraine is only partially known, and we have almost no knowledge of the underlying biological mechanisms involved in tension-type headache. These two headache types constitute the vast majority of headaches seen in children.

The advent of the 5-HT agonists (triptans) approximately 12 years ago led to a significant change in the quality of studies on drug efficacy, particularly in migraine but also in the management of other headaches. While most effort has been directed toward headache in adults, there have been significant improvements in drug studies of children with pain, for example in the use of ibuprofen. Further prospective, double-blind, randomized, controlled studies are needed on the management of headaches in children.

REFERENCES

Ahlin JH. Pediatric dental treatment for children with headache. *J Gen Orthodont* 1999; 10(1):23–24.

Andersson PG, Dahl S, Hansen JH, et al. Prophylactic treatment of classical and non-classical migraine with metoprolol: a comparison with placebo. *Cephalalgia* 1983; 3(4):207–212.

Ashina M, Bendtsen L, Jensen R, Ekman R, Olesen J. Plasma levels of substance P, neuropeptide Y, and vasoactive intestinal polypeptide in patients with chronic tension-type headaches. *Pain* 1999; 83(3):541–547.

Bannerjee M, Findley L. Propranolol in the treatment of acute migraine attacks. *Cephalalgia* 1991; 11(4):193–196.

Battistella PA, Ruffilli R, Cernetti R. A placebo-controlled crossover trial using trazodone in pediatric migraine. *Headache* 1993; 33:36–39.

Becker WJ. Evidence based migraine prophylactic drug therapy. *Can J Neurol Sci* 1999; 26(Suppl 3):S27–S32.

Bendtsen L, Mellerup ET. The platelet serotonin transporter in primary headaches. *Eur J Neurol* 1998; 5(3):277–282.

Bendtsen L, Jensen R, Hindberg I, Gammeltoft S. Serotonin metabolism in chronic tension-type headache. *Cephalalgia* 1997; 17(8):843–848.

Bomhof MA, Heywood J, Pradalier A, et al. Tolerability and efficacy of naratriptan tablets with long-term treatment (6 months). Naratriptan Long-Term Study Group. *Cephalalgia* 1998; 18(1):33–37.

Cameron JD, Lane PL, Speechley M. Intravenous chlorpromazine vs intravenous metoclopramide in acute migraine headache. *Acad Emerg Med* 1995; 2(7):597–602.

Carleton SC, Shesser RF, Pietrzak MP, et al. Double-blind, multicenter trial to compare the efficacy of intramuscular dihdroergotamine plus hydroxyzine versus intramuscular meperidine plus hydroxyzine for the emergency department treatment of acute migraine headache. *Ann Emerg Med* 1998; 32(2):129–138.

Cerbo R, Barbanti P, Fabbrini G, Pascali MP. Amitriptyline is effective in chronic but not episodic tension-type headache: pathogenetic implications. *Headache* 1998; 38(6):453–457.

Cleland PG, Barnes D, Elrington GM, Loizou LA, Rawes GD. Studies to assess if pizotifen prophylaxis improves migraine beyond the benefit offered by acute sumatriptan alone. *Eur Neurol* 1997; 38(1):31–38.

Cull RE, Price WH, Dunbar A. The efficacy of subcutaneous sumatriptan in the treatment of recurrence of migraine headaches. *J Neurol Neurosurg Psychiatr* 1997; 62(5):490–495.

Cutler NR, Salazar DE, Jhee SS, et al. Pharmacokinetics and pharmacodynamics of avitriptan in patients with migraine after oral dosing. *Headache* 1998; 38(6):446–452.

Dahlof CG, Jacobs LD. Ketoprofen, paracetamol and placebo in the treatment of episodic tension-type headache. *Cephalalgia* 1996; 16(2):117–123.

Drotts DL, Vinson DR. Prochlorperazine induces akathisia in emergency patients. *Ann Emerg Med* 1999; 34(4 Pt 1):469–475.

Edmeads JG. Migraine. *CMAJ* 1988; 138:107–113.

Fuller GN, Guiloff RJ. Propranolol in acute migraine: a controlled study. *Cephalalgia* 1991; 10(5):229–233.

Ford RG, Ford KT. Continuous intravenous dihydroergotamine in the treatment of intractable headache. *Headache* 1997; 37(3):129–136.

Forsythe WI, Gilles D, Sills MA. Propranolol (Inderal) in the treatment of childhood migraine. *Dev Med Child Neurol* 1984; 26:737–741.

Gao S, Zhao D, Xie Y. A comparative study on the treatment of migraine headache with combined distant and local acupuncture points versus conventional drug therapy. *Am J Acupunct* 1999; 27(1-2):27–30.

Gardner K. The genetic basis of migraine: how much do we know? *Can J Neurol Sci* 1999; 26(Suppl 3):S37–S43.

Ghose K, Niven B. Prophylactic sodium valproate therapy in patients with drug resistant migraine. *Methods Find Exp Clin Pharmacol* 1998; 20(4):353–359.

Gilles D, Sills M, Forsythe I. Pizotifen (Sandomigran) in childhood migraine. A double- blind controlled trial. *Eur Neurol* 1986; 25(1):32–35.

Gladstein J, Holden EW, Winner P, Linder S. Chronic daily headache in children and adolescents: current status and recommendations for the future. Pediatric Committee of the American Association for the Study of Headache. *Headache* 1997; 37(10):626–629.

Goadsby PJ. The scientific basis of medication choice in symptomatic migraine treatment. *Can J Neurol Sci* 1999; 26(Suppl 3):S20–S26.

Gobel H, Heinze A, Stolze H, Heinze-Kuhn K, Lindner V. Open-labeled long-term study of the efficacy, safety and tolerability of subcutaneous sumatriptan in acute migraine treatment. *Cephalalgia* 1999; 19(7):676–683.

Graf WD, Riback PS. Pharmacologic treatment of recurrent pediatric headache. *Pediatr Ann* 1995; 24:477–484.

Hamalainen ML, Hoppu K, Valkeila E, Santavuori P. Ibuprofen or acetaminophen for the acute treatment of migraine in children: a double-blind, randomized, placebo-controlled, cross-over study. *Neurology* 1997; 48(1):103–107.

Hamel E. The biology of serotonin receptors: focus on migraine pathophysiology and treatment. *Can J Neurol Sci* 1999; 26(Suppl 3):S2–S6.

Harden RN, Rogers D, Fink K, Gracely RH. Controlled trial of ketorolac in tension-type headaches. *Neurology* 1998; 50(2):507–509.

Hargreaves RJ, Shepheard SL. Pathophysiology of migraine—new insights. *Can J Neurol Sci* 1999; 26(Suppl 3):S12–S19.

Headache Classification Committee of the International Headache Society. Classification and diagnostic criteria for headache disorders, cranial neuralgias and facial pain. *Cephalalgia* 1988; 8(Suppl 7):1–96.

Hu J. Acupuncture treatment of migraine in Germany. *J Tradit Chin Med* 1998; 18(2):99–101.

Iserson KV. Parenteral chlorpromazine treatment of migraine. *Ann Emerg Med* 1983; 12(12):756–758.

Insel PA. Analgesic-antipyretics and anti-inflammatory agents: drugs employed in the treatment of rheumatoid arthritis and gout. In: Gilman AG, Rall TW, Nies AS, Taylor P (Eds). *Goodman and Gilman's The Pharmacological Basis of Therapeutics*. New York: Pergamon Press, 1990, pp 638–681.

Jensen R. Mechanisms of spontaneous tension-type headaches: an analysis of tenderness, pain thresholds and EMG. *Pain* 1996; 64(2):251–256.

Kaniecki RG. A comparison of divalproex with propranolol and placebo for the prophylaxis of migraine without aura. *Arch Neurol* 1997; 54(9):1141–1145.

Kelly AM, Ardagh M, Curry C, D'Antonio J, Zebic S. Intravenous chlorpromazine versus intramuscular sumatriptan for acute migraine. *J Accident Emerg Med* 1997; 14(4):209–211.

Klassen A, Elkind A, Asgharnejad M, Webster C, Laurenza A. Naratriptan is effective and well tolerated in the acute treatment of migraine. Results of a double-blind, placebo-controlled, parallel-group study. Naratriptan S2WA3001 Study Group. *Headache* 1997; 37(10):640–645.

Kramer MS, Matzura-Wolfe D, Polis A. A placebo-controlled crossover study of rizatriptan in the treatment of multiple migraine attacks. Rizatriptan Multiple Attack Study. *Neurology* 1998; 51(3):773–781.

Lampl C, Buzath A, Klinger D, Neumann K. Lamotrigine in the prophylactic treatment of migraine aura—a pilot study. *Cephalalgia* 1999; 19(1):58–63.

Lanzi G, Balottin U, Zambrino CA. Guidelines and recommendations for the treatment of migraine in paediatric and adolescent patients. *Funct Neurol* 1996; 11:269–275.

Lassen LH, Thomsen LL, Olesen J. Histamine induces migraine via the H1-receptor. Support for the NO hypothesis of migraine. *Neuroreport* 1995; 31(6):1475–1479.

Lassen LH, Ashina M, Christiansen I. Nitric oxide synthase inhibition: a new principle in the treatment of migraine attacks. *Cephalalgia* 1998; 18(1):27–32.

Linder S. Treatment of childhood headache with dihydroergotamine mesylate. *Headache* 1994; 34:578–580.

Lucetti C, Nuti A, Pavese N. Flunarizine in migraine prophylaxis: predictive factors for a positive response. *Cephalalgia* 1998; 18(6):349–352.

Ludvigsson J. Propranolol used in prophylaxis of migraine in children. *Acta Neurol Scand* 1974; 50:109–115.

MacDonald JT. Treatment of juvenile migraine with subcutaneous sumatriptan. *Headache* 1994; 34:581–582.

Markowitz S, Saito K, Moskowitz MA. Neurogenically mediated plasma extravasation in dura mater: effect of ergot alkaloids. *Cephalalgia* 1988; 8:83–91.

Mathew NT, Lucker C. Gabapentin in migraine prophylaxis: a preliminary open label study. *Neurology* 1996; 46:A169.

Mathew NT, Asgharnejad M, Peykamian M, Laurenza A. Naratriptan is effective and well-tolerated in the acute treatment of migraine. Results of a double-blind, placebo-controlled, crossover study. The Naratriptan S2WA3003 Study Group. *Neurology* 1997; 49(6):1485–1490.

Mauskop A, Farkkila M, Hering-Hanit R, Rapoport A, Warner J. Zolmitriptan is effective for the treatment of persistent and recurrent migraine headache. *Curr Med Res Opin* 1999; 15(4):282–289.

McCullough HN. Acetaminophen and ibuprofen in the management of fever and mild to moderate pain in children. *J Paediatr Child Health* 1998; 3(4).

McEwen JI, O'Connor JM, Dinsdale HB. Treatment of migraine with intramuscular chlorpromazine. *Ann Emerg Med* 1997; 16(7):758–763.

Moore KH, Hussey EK, Shaw S, et al. Safety, tolerability and pharmacokinetics of sumatriptan in healthy subjects following ascending single intranasal doses and multiple intranasal doses. *Cephalalgia* 1997; 17(4):541–550.

Moschiano F, D'Amico D, Grazzi L, Leone M, Bussone G. Sumatriptan in the acute treatment of migraine without aura: efficacy of 50 mg dose. *Headache* 1997; 37(7):421–423.

Nelson CF, Bronfort G, Evans R. The efficacy of spinal manipulation, amitriptyline and the combination of both therapies for the prophylaxis of migraine headache. *J Manipulative Physiol Ther* 1998; 21(8):511–519.

Neubauer D, Kuhar M, Ravnik IM. Antihistamine responsive cluster headache in a teenaged girl. *Headache* 1997; 37(5):296–298.

Nicolodi M, Sicuteri F. A NMDA modulator, gabapentin, clearly facilitated resolution of chronic migraine. *Pharmacol Res* 1997; 35(Suppl):64.

Okada H, Araga S, Takeshima T, Nakashima K. Plasma lactate and pyruvic acid levels in migraine and tension-type headache. *Headache* 1998; 38(1):39–42.

Olness K, MacDonald JT, Uden DL. Comparison of self-hypnosis and propranolol in the treatment of juvenile classic migraine. *Pediatrics* 1987; 79:593–597.

Perl ER. Sensitization of nociceptors and its relation to sensation. In: Bonica JJ, Albe-Fessard D (Eds). *Proceedings of the First World Congress on Pain,* Advances in Pain Research and Therapy, Vol. 1. New York: Raven Press, 1976, pp 17–34.

Pfaffenrath V, Cunin G, Sjonell G, Prendergast S. Efficacy and safety of sumatriptan tablets (25 mg, 50 mg, and 100 mg) in the acute treatment of migraine: defining the optimum doses of oral sumatriptan. *Headache* 1998; 38(3):184–190.

Pryse-Phillips WEM, Dodick DW, Edmeads JG. Guidelines for the diagnosis and management of migraine in clinical practice. *CMAJ* 1997; 156:1273–1287.

Rall TW. Oxytocin, prostaglandins, ergot alkaloids and other drugs; tocolytic agents. In: Gilman A, Rall TW, Nies AS, Taylor P (Eds). *Goodman and Gilman's The Pharmacological Basis of Therapeutics.* New York: Pergamon Press, 1990, pp 933–953.

Ramadan NM, Schultz LL. Gilkey SJ. Migraine prophylactic drugs: proof of efficacy, utilization and cost. *Cephalalgia* 1997; 17:73–80.

Rapoport AM, Ramadan NM, Adelman JU, et al. Optimizing the dose of zolmitriptan (Zomig, 311C90) for the acute treatment of migraine. A multicenter, double-blind placebo-controlled, dose range-finding study. The 017 Clinical Trial Study Group. *Neurology* 1997; 49(5):1210–1218.

Redillas C, Solomon S. Prophylactic pharmacologic treatment of chronic daily headache. *Headache* 2000; 40(2):83–102.

Rollnik JD, Tanneberger O, Schubert M, Schneider U. Treatment of tension-type headache with botulinum toxin type A: a double-blind, placebo-controlled study. *Headache* 2000; 40(4):300–305.

Roon KI, Olesen J, Diener HC, et al. No acute antimigraine efficacy of CP-122,288, a highly potent inhibitor of neurogenic inflammation: results of two randomized, double-blind, placebo-controlled clinical trials. *Ann Neurol* 2000; 47(2):238–241.

Ryan R, Elkind A, Baker CC, DeBussey S, Asgharnejad M. Sumatriptan nasal spray for the acute treatment of migraine. Results of two clinical studies. *Neurology* 1997; 49(5):1225–1230.

Sartory G, Muller B, Metsch J, Pothmann R. A comparison of psychological and pharmacological treatment of pediatric migraine. *Behav Res Ther* 1998; 36(12):1155–1170.

Schachter SC, Carrazana EJ. Treatment of facial pain with gabapentin: case reports. *J Epilepsy* 1997; 10(3):148–150.

Scheife RT, Hills JR. Migraine headache: signs and symptoms, biochemistry and current therapy. *Am J Hosp Pharm* 1980; 37:365–374.

Schoenen J, Sawyer J. Zolmitriptan (Zomig, 311C90), a novel dual central and peripheral 5HT$_{1B/1D}$ agonist: an overview of efficacy. *Cephalalgia* 1997; 17(Suppl 18):28–40.

Schoenen J, Jacquy J, Lenaerts M. Effectiveness of high-dose riboflavin in migraine prophylaxis. A randomized controlled trial. *Neurology* 1998; 50(2):466–470.

Silberstein SD, Armellino JJ, Hoffman HD, et al. Treatment of menstruation-associated migraine with the nonprescription combination of acetaminophen, aspirin and caffeine: results from three randomized, placebo-controlled studies. *Clin Ther* 1999; 21(3):475–491.

Solomon GD. The pharmacology of medications used in treating headache. *Semin Pediatr Neurol* 1995; 2(2):165–177.

Solomon GD, Cady RK, Klapper JA. Clinical efficacy and tolerability of 2.5 mg zolmitriptan for the acute treatment of migraine. The 042 Clinical Trial Study Group. *Neurology* 1997; 49(5):1219–1225.

Sorge F, Marano E. Flunarizine v. placebo in childhood migraine. A double-blind study. *Cephalalgia* 1985; 5(Suppl 2):145–148.

Sorge F, Barone P, Steardo L. Amitriptyline as a prophylactic for migraine in children. *Acta Neurologica* 1982; 37:362–367.

Sorge F, De Simone R, Marano E, et al. Flunarizine in the prophylaxis of childhood migraine: a double-blind, placebo controlled crossover study. *Cephalalgia* 1988; 8:1–6.

Steiner TJ, Hering R, Couturier EG, Davies PT, Whitmarsh TE. Double-blind placebo-controlled trial of lithium in episodic cluster headache. *Cephalalgia* 1997; 17(6):673–675.

Steiner TJ, Lange R. Ketoprofen (25 mg) in the symptomatic treatment of episodic tension-type headache: double-blind placebo-controlled comparison with acetaminophen (1000 mg). *Cephalalgia* 1998; 18(1):38–43.

Symon DNK, Russell G. Double blind placebo controlled trial of pizotifen syrup in the treatment of abdominal migraine. *Arch Dis Child* 1995; 72:48–50.

Symon DN. Twelve cases of analgesic headache. *Arch Dis Child* 1988; 78(6):555–556.

Teall J, Tuchman M, Cutler N, et al. Rizatriptan (MAXALT) for the acute treatment of migraine and migraine recurrence. A placebo-controlled, outpatient study. Rizatriptan 022 study group. *Headache* 1998; 38(4):281–287.

Tepper SJ, Donnan GA, Dowson AJ, et al. A long-term study to maximise migraine relief with zolmitriptan. *Curr Med Res Opin* 1999; 15(4):254–271.

Tfelt-Hansen P. Efficacy of beta-blockers in migraine: a critical review. *Cephalalgia* 1986; 6(Suppl 5):15–24.

Tuchman M, Edvinsson L, Geraud G. Zolmitriptan provides consistent migraine relief when used in the long-term. *Curr Med Res Opin* 1999; 15(4):272–281.

Ueberall MA, Wenzel D. Intranasal sumatriptan for the acute treatment of migraine in children. *Neurology* 1999; 52(7):1507–1510.

van Gerven JM, Schoemaker RC, Jacobs LD. Self-medication of a single headache episode with ketoprofen, ibuprofen or placebo, home-monitored with an electronic patient diary. *Br J Clin Pharmacol* 1996; 42(4):475–481.

Vasconcellos E, Pina-Garza JE, Millan EJ, Warner JS. Analgesic rebound headache in children and adolescents. *J Child Neurol* 1998; 13(9):443–447.

Vernon H, McDermaid CS, Hagino C. Systemic review of randomized clinical trials of complementary/alternative therapies in the treatment of tension-type and cervicogenic headache. *Complement Ther Med* 1999; 7(3):142–155.

Welborn CA. Pediatric migraine. *Emerg Med Clin North Am* 1997; 15:625–636.

Winner P, Wasiewski W, Gladstein J, et al. For the pediatric headache subcommittee of the American Association for the Study of Headache. Multicenter prospective evaluation of proposed pediatric migraine revisions to the IHS criteria. *Headache* 1997; 37:545–548.

Wheeler SD, Carrazana EJ. Topiramate treated cluster headache. *Neurology* 1999; 53(1):234–236.

Worthington I. Pediatric migraine: how to detect and treat this "hidden" disorder. *Pharm Pract* 1999; 15:48–57.

Zagami AS. 311C90: long-term efficacy and tolerability profile for the acute treatment of migraine. International 311C90 Long-Term Study Group. *Neurology* 1997; 48(Suppl 3):S25–S28.

Correspondence to: Simon D. Levin, MD, FRCP, Department of Paediatrics, Children's Hospital of Western Ontario, 800 Commissioners Road East, London, Ontario, Canada N6C 2V5. Tel: 519-685-8332; Fax: 519-685-8350; email: slevin@julian.uwo.ca.

The Child with Headache: Diagnosis and Treatment.
Progress in Pain Research and Management, Vol. 19,
edited by Patricia A. McGrath and Loretta M. Hillier,
IASP Press, Seattle, © 2000.

6

Nondrug Therapies for Childhood Headache

Patricia A. McGrath,[a,b] Diane Stewart,[a] and Andrea L. Koster[c]

[a]Pain Innovations Inc., London, Ontario, Canada; [b]Department of Pediatrics, Faculty of Medicine, and [c]Department of Psychology, Faculty of Social Sciences, University of Western Ontario, London, Ontario, Canada

An extensive array of nondrug therapies are available to treat children's headache, including counseling, guided imagery, hypnosis, biofeedback, behavioral management, acupuncture, massage, chiropractic manipulation, homeopathic remedies, naturopathic approaches, and herbal medicines. Many such therapies share a common "child-centered" focus, addressing the unique causative and contributing factors for each child's headache. Nondrug therapies are generally regarded as safe, with few contraindications for use in otherwise healthy children. However, they should not be regarded as equally effective. The evidence base supporting their efficacy varies widely from "unknown" (i.e., they have not yet been studied), to "promising" (anecdotal reports suggest possible effectiveness for certain children), to "strong and compelling" (consistent positive results have been obtained in several well-designed studies).

To investigate the efficacy of nondrug therapies for childhood headache, we conducted searches for alternative and complementary medicine, neurology, headache, pediatrics, and psychology on electronic databases (MEDLINE, EMBASE, CISCOM, Healthstar, Psychlit, AltHealth, and the Social Science Citation Index), on respective Internet sites, and on study registries (Cochrane, National Institutes of Health, and DARE). We completed a manual search of recent (1998–2000) books, journals (pediatric neurology, headache, alternative and complementary therapies), conference proceedings, reference lists, and bibliographies of retrieved sources. We contacted the Center for Complementary and Alternative Medicine (National Institutes of Health), international centers conducting pediatric research, and the International Pediatric Chiropractic Association. We reviewed all pediatric studies including meta-analysis, randomized trials, cohort studies, case-control studies, and case series for children and adolescents. We adopted these broad inclusion criteria to reduce selection bias against complementary therapies, in which there might be fewer controlled trials.

COGNITIVE THERAPY

Cognitive therapy, focused on modifying an individual's beliefs, expectations, and coping abilities, is an intrinsic component of all headache treatment. Health care providers educate families about the circumstances that cause headache, often counseling them about how they can alter those circumstances (e.g., through lifestyle management, diet, sleep, and exercise). In addition, children may learn specialized stress management techniques as part of a treatment program. The goal of cognitive therapy in headache management is to help families to understand the effects of their behaviors and to change them so as to lessen headache attacks and minimize headache-related disability. In some programs, therapists teach children how to use cognitive pain control methods such as attention and distraction, guided imagery, and hypnosis to lessen the pain during headache attacks.

Strong and consistent evidence supports the use of cognitive therapies for treating children's headache, as summarized in Table I, which shows the primary type of studies that have been conducted to evaluate each therapy and the consistency of their findings. This format is similar to the approach followed in developing evidence-based practice guidelines for pain relief (American Pain Society 1999). The strength of evidence supporting efficacy increases progressively according to the type of study: case reports, well-

Table I
Cognitive therapy: evidence base for treating children's headache

Therapy	Primary Type of Evidence		Consistency of Evidence	
	Cohort Study	Randomized Trial	Positive Results	Inconsistent Results
Counseling (individual)*	✓	✓	✓	
Counseling (group)*		✓		✓
Stress management*		✓	✓	
Attention and distraction*		✓	✓	
Guided imagery*	✓	✓	✓	
Hypnosis		✓	✓	

* Therapy evaluated as part of multimodal treatment program.

designed nonexperimental studies (e.g., descriptive design), well-designed quasi-experimental studies (e.g., nonrandomized, controlled studies, single-group pre-post studies, and cohort designs), at least one well-designed controlled randomized trial, and a meta-analysis of multiple well-designed controlled trials. (In pre-post studies, children are not randomized into treatment and nontreatment groups. All children within the group receive a certain intervention; their headache activity is compared for equivalent periods before and after treatment.) As shown by the asterisks in Table I, most cognitive therapies have been evaluated within the context of a broader multimodal treatment program rather than studied as single interventions.

COUNSELING

Counseling for pain management encompasses a wide range of approaches, from basic patient education at consultation to formal psychotherapy for children and families (for a review of counseling approaches in pain management, see Gatchel and Turk 1996). Thus, children who are diagnosed with headache should receive some general counseling about the cause and recommended treatment. In addition, health care providers may help families to identify the specific triggers for children's headache attacks and may provide practical recommendations on lifestyle management to ensure that children have healthy diets, adequate sleep, and regular physical exercise.

Individual counseling is a major component of specialized headache treatment programs (as described in Chapter 8). Therapists teach children how to use various pain control techniques (e.g., cognitive, behavioral, or physical) to lessen pain during headache attacks, and guide them to recognize the particular circumstances that trigger attacks. Many programs include formal training sessions in stress management, problem solving, and relaxation exercises. Stress management training involves helping children to recognize sources of stress in their lives and to manage those situations more effectively. Situation-specific stress associated with social situations, school, sports, and family is a common trigger for headache attacks (as described in Chapter 4). Therapists assist parents and children to evaluate these situations, to identify the specific aspects that cause children anxiety, and to develop more effective coping responses (for review of coping skills interventions for children, see Forman 1993).

Therapists often use problem-solving exercises to teach children how to generate several solutions to problems they encounter in their daily activities. They guide children to imagine the consequences of each solution and choose the one that best addresses the situation. By assisting parents and children to change their behaviors so as to minimize headache-related disability, therapists incorporate principles of behavioral management into the counseling program. As indicated in Table I, cohort and randomized controlled trials provide consistent evidence for efficacy of multimodal programs for treating children's headache (Werder and Sargent 1984; Richter et al. 1986; Larsson et al. 1987a,b; Helm-Hylkema et al. 1990; McGrath 1990; Smith et al. 1991; McGrath et al. 1992; Osterhaus et al. 1993; Sartory et al. 1998). Children generally experience significant reductions in headache frequency, with some studies reporting concurrent reductions in headache intensity.

ATTENTION AND DISTRACTION

Attention and distraction are simple and effective pain control methods. They provide children with some independent tools to use during headache attacks—either to relieve mild pain or to complement the medication needed to relieve strong pain (Ross and Ross 1988; McGrath 1990). When children intently attend to something else, they can lessen the pain's intensity and unpleasantness. Distraction is often incorrectly perceived as a simple diversionary tactic; the implication is that the pain is still there but that the child is momentarily focused elsewhere. However, when children's attention is fully absorbed in some engaging topic or activity, distraction can reduce the neuronal responses to a noxious stimulus. Children are not simply ignoring their pain, but are actively reducing it.

The essential feature for achieving pain relief is the child's ability to fully concentrate on something other than their headache. Therefore, the choice of distraction is crucial and varies according to children's ages and interests. Young children usually need to be actively involved with their parents or peers, while older children and adolescents can distract themselves more independently. Children should work with their parents or a therapist to choose distracting activities that they can practically incorporate into their lives. Skills in active concentration on something other than pain are a versatile tool for use in the diverse settings in which children may develop headache. Even a brief distraction may prevent a headache from intensifying. The efficacy of attention and distraction for relieving children's headache has been evaluated only as part of a broader cognitive-behavioral program (McGrath et al. 1993).

Human brain imaging has revealed possible mechanisms for the attentional modulation of pain (Bushnell et al. 1999; 2000; Peyron et al. 1999). Studies have shown that subjects experience less pain from noxious heat pulses when their attention is focused on a visual or auditory stimulus.

When attention is thus directed away from the painful stimulus, pain-evoked activity in the primary somatosensory cortex is reduced significantly.

GUIDED IMAGERY

Guided imagery helps children to concentrate fully on an imaginary experience or situation, just as if it were occurring in the present moment. Children are guided to vividly describe the colors, sounds, tastes, and tactile qualities of the situation. Guided imagery can be considered a specific method of distraction and attention as well as a way to induce physiological changes to relax the body.

Children generally have rich imaginations, and thus guided imagery can be a very effective pain control tool. Ross and Ross (1988) reported how seven children with migraine used imagery spontaneously and successfully. In most instances, children incorporated relaxation techniques with their imagery, as shown by this 11-year-old boy:

> I lie down and then I let myself go all over like I'm the laundry bag emptied on the bed, you know? Like all over. Then I start right at the beginning of the game (baseball) against (rival school) and it's not just a shut-out, it's like a real massacre, the whole nine innings we do everything great and I hit a homer (Ross and Ross 1988, p. 283).

Guided imagery is generally used for treating headache in combination with other cognitive and behavioral therapies (Werder and Sargent 1984; Smith et al. 1991; McGrath et al. 1993). It is a valuable tool for helping children to relax and use distraction. Although the manner in which imagery lessens pain is not yet understood, its efficacy depends on children's ability to absorb themselves in their imagination. Thus, the physiological mechanisms may be very similar to those responsible for the attentional modulation of pain.

HYPNOSIS

The earliest descriptions of hypnosis in children are included in the writings of Franz Mesmer (1734–1815), who reported how "magnetism," a healing force transmitted by iron rods, had helped several children and adolescents (Bloch 1980). Although the scientific community eventually discredited Mesmer's findings, the power of patients' imagination and their response to suggestion gradually emerged as aspects worthy of scientific study. James Braid (1795–1860), the English surgeon who first described the process of "hypnosis," theorized that the hypnotist directs vital forces within the patient's body to produce dramatic changes. Such theories contributed to an evolving scientific study of hypnosis, which has become an accepted tool in modern psychology, psychiatry, and dentistry.

Hypnosis usually begins with an induction procedure in which a child's full attention is focused gradually on the therapist's suggestions. The induction procedure typically includes progressive muscle relaxation for adolescents and guided imagery for children. Young children are guided into a hypnotic state as they vividly imagine their favorite television shows, movies, books, or cartoon characters (Olness and Gardner 1978; Gardner and Olness 1981; Hilgard and LeBaron 1984; LeBaron and Zeltzer 1996; Olness and Kohen 1996; Hall 1999). As they imagine an activity, scene or character, children gradually receive suggestions for relaxation, reduced anxiety, increased control, and reduced pain. The therapist provides consistent, positive suggestions, rather than authoritative commands, placing the emphasis on the child's own natural abilities: "Notice that your head feels lighter, and the heaviness and pain are starting to lessen. It seems as if the headache doesn't hurt as much as before. You are doing well at turning down the pain switch."

During a hypnotic state, individuals become extremely susceptible to suggestions, including suggestions for pain relief. Children become so involved in thoughts or ideas that they dissociate from a "reality orientation" (LeBaron and Zeltzer 1996). Hypnosis enables children to redirect their attention from the painful sensation or to reinterpret the sensation as something more pleasant and less aversive or bothersome (Kuttner 1993; Olness and Kohen 1996). Like adults, children differ in their ability to be hypnotized; the ability to use one's imagination is the key component in determining hypnotic susceptibility. Susceptibility rises rapidly from the age of 4–5 years to reach a maximum at 8–12 years (London and Cooper 1969). Scores then decrease gradually with age, although some individuals remain highly susceptible throughout their lives.

Although hypnosis has been used successfully as a component of cognitive-behavioral programs for treating migraine headache in children (Olness and MacDonald 1981; Kapelis 1984; Waranch and Keenan 1985; Smith et al. 1991), its efficacy as a single psychological intervention has been evaluated in only one study. Olness and colleagues (1987) conducted a randomized drug trial where 28 children (aged 6–12 years) with classic migraine received either placebo or propranolol for a 3-month period and then crossed over to the other group for 3 months. After this crossover period, all children used self-hypnosis techniques for the next 3 months instead of drug therapy. Headache frequency decreased significantly to an average of 5.8 headaches per month in the 3-month self-hypnosis period, compared to 13.1

headaches per month while on placebo and 14.9 headaches per month on propranolol.

Two current theories about hypnosis are contradictory. According to the traditional viewpoint, hypnosis produces an altered state of consciousness, often referred to as a *trance state* (Hilgard 1973; Hilgard and Hilgard 1983), that differs from waking or sleeping. In contrast, the *alternative theory of hypnosis* (a term coined by Barber in 1963) disputes the trance state and claims that hypnotized individuals simply follow the hypnotist's suggestions because they think they should (Spanos 1986). They are not fakers or malingerers, but are behaving in accordance with their attitudes and beliefs about how hypnosis should change them.

Recent research supports aspects of both the traditional and alternative theories. Studies using advanced imaging techniques indicate that multiple psychological and neurophysiological factors are involved, including some that mediate production of a hypnotic state, some that interrelate hypnotic state with suggestions for analgesia, and some that interrelate hypnotic suggestions with changes in pain experience and behavior (for review, see Price 1999). Several research findings have special clinical relevance. The different components responsible for hypnotic analgesia (i.e., reductions in pain affect due to changes in the meaning of sensations and the context in which they occur, reductions in pain intensity due to mechanisms that divert pain from conscious awareness after nociceptive signals have reached higher cortical centers, and inhibition of pain signals at the spinal level) may vary in different individuals. Hypnotic susceptibility may not be the limiting factor in deciding who could benefit from hypnosis. Reductions in pain affect are unrelated to hypnotic susceptibility, and these reductions are greater and more prevalent than reductions in pain intensity. Price (1999) concludes that hypnotic approaches should include suggestions for reducing both intensity and affective dimensions of pain, so as to optimize an individual's ability to diminish the experience of pain.

TEACHING COGNITIVE PAIN CONTROL METHODS TO CHILDREN

Children can easily learn several cognitive methods for reducing pain and distress during headache attacks. As they acquire confidence in using a few basic methods, they seem to naturally adapt them to fit their personality or invent new, equally effective methods. A therapist guides them throughout this process, as outlined in Table II. Children should be interested in learning some independent pain control methods. They seem more adept than adults at using nondrug therapies, presumably because they are usually

Table II
Teaching cognitive pain control methods to children

Qualities of Child and Therapist
Interest and motivation (for child)
Belief in the approach (for therapist)
Positive rapport between child and therapist
Comfortable teaching situation
Components of Process
Provide rationale for using pain control method (familiar examples)
Select age-appropriate distractor or image
Practice attention or guided imagery
Assess child's ability to absorb him/herself fully
Guide child in deep breathing and relaxing when practicing the method
Teach child how to regain a relaxed state if interrupted
Evaluate effectiveness during a headache attack
Refine methods as necessary to optimize effectiveness
Gradually increase the number of methods until the child has a versatile repertoire

less biased than adults about their potential efficacy. However, because adults teach children how to use these methods, the biases of adults (either parents or health care providers) can weaken treatment efficacy. Therefore, it is essential to consider not only a child's capabilities and needs, but also the attitudes, beliefs and motivations of the relevant adults. Parents must support children's efforts to use cognitive pain control methods during headache attacks (as described in Chapter 8).

The therapist explains the rationale for cognitive pain control therapies using familiar examples from children's lives. Children easily understand a practical analogy: they often do not hear their parents calling them because they are busy watching television or playing a game. In essence, they selectively tune out noises that are not relevant to what they are doing. At this point in the session, the therapist usually asks children to listen to the hum of the ventilation system. Children acknowledge that the sound has been present throughout the session, but that they have not really been listening to it. The therapist explains that they can learn to tune out their headache pain in a similar manner.

A listening analogy is also useful in teaching young children how to use a pain control method during a headache attack:

> Imagine that you and I are watching a movie in a theatre. Two people come in and sit in front of us. They are eating a jumbo box of popcorn and candies in crinkly plastic wrappers. They are making a lot of noise with their crunching and unwrapping. What if I told you not to pay attention to the

noise that they are making, but to concentrate only on the movie? (McGrath 1990, p. 204).

Most children respond that if they tried too hard to block out the sounds of the people eating they would probably pay more attention to them than if they simply forgot about them and concentrated on watching the movie. The therapist uses this example to teach children that they should not constantly monitor how well their pain control method is working; they should simply use it when they have a headache and then evaluate its efficacy with the therapist later.

Most children should learn simpler methods such as attention and distraction before trying guided imagery and hypnosis. Although the simpler methods are easier for children to learn, therapists must consider carefully the age, interests, and situations in which children develop headache in order to select an appropriate distraction method that will allow them to concentrate fully on something other than the headache. The same activity or image will not be consistently effective for all children; complete concentration is the critical component for pain reduction, not the particular method used to achieve it.

The therapist should allow children to practice a method in the session, and should summarize the method in writing so that children can follow the steps at home. After children have mastered the method in the session, the therapist reminds them that they will naturally become more relaxed as they use the method and may encourage them to use deep breathing to regain this relaxed feeling in case something interrupts them when they are using the method during a headache. Children should monitor both headache activity and their use of pain control methods between sessions, so that the therapist will be able to evaluate and, if necessary, strengthen or refine the method. The therapist encourages children to personalize the method and to develop new methods based on the same principles, so that they eventually learn an extensive repertoire to use in the different situations in which they develop headache. (For a review of cognitive pain control methods used for children, see Ross and Ross 1988.)

BEHAVIOR THERAPY

Behavior therapy is a common component of headache treatment. The primary objectives are to modify any behaviors that may trigger attacks, increase pain, or prolong disability. Behavior therapy is often used in combination with cognitive therapy. Behavioral methods are targeted either for children or for the adults who respond to them when they experience headache. At the initial consultation, health care providers may assess whether children's behaviors or those of key adults (parents, teachers, or coaches) are influencing the pattern and severity of headache attacks. They recommend changes that will improve pain control and lessen disability. (For a review of behavior management techniques in pain treatment, see Keefe and Lefebre 1994.)

Alternatively, psychologists and therapists counsel families about the impact of their behaviors and assist families to make changes using operant conditioning programs. In addition, they may teach children specific behavioral methods to lessen pain during headache, such as relaxation and biofeedback. Consistently strong evidence supports the efficacy of behavior therapy for treating children's headache, as summarized in Table III.

RELAXATION TRAINING

Relaxation training is the most common behavioral method used to treat children's headache. Therapists train children how to achieve a state of mental and physical relaxation with techniques they can use independently when they are stressed or develop a headache. Therapists may teach children guided imagery, hypnosis, deep breathing, or progressive relaxation exercises. Children learn to breathe very deeply and regularly as therapists breathe with them or count to a slow rhythm. As children continue to breathe in this manner, the therapist asks them to notice how much more relaxed they feel, especially in their shoulders, neck, and head. Children practice this exercise at home so that they can use it without the therapist's coaching.

Progressive muscle relaxation (PMR) training involves the systematic tightening and relaxing of various body regions and muscle groups. Many

Table III
Behavior therapy: evidence base for treating children's headache

Therapy	Primary Type of Evidence			Consistency of Evidence	
	Case Report	Cohort Study	Randomized Trial	Positive Results	Inconsistent Results
Relaxation		✓	✓	✓	
Biofeedback		✓	✓	✓	
Biofeedback and relaxation		✓	✓	✓	
Operant conditioning	✓	✓	✓	✓	
Biofeedback and relaxation*			✓	✓	
Operant conditioning*			✓	✓	

* Therapy evaluated as part of multimodal treatment program.

of the training procedures used for children are variants of the technique developed for adults by Jacobson (1938), in which adults can eventually recognize and control even slight muscle contractions. Children begin with an easy task such as making a tight fist, holding it for a few seconds, and then relaxing it and wiggling their fingers. The therapist guides children to feel the difference between the tense and relaxed states. The objective is to enable children to recognize when their bodies are physically stressed and to be able to relax the tense region. In clinic sessions, children use the same tightening-relaxing process in progressively more difficult regions (e.g., arms, shoulders, and neck) and in some cases, to more specific areas of the face, jaw, and forehead. Sessions can be taped so that children can practice these exercises at home.

Autogenic relaxation training generally involves guiding children to imagine and subsequently experience specific sensations of warmth or heaviness. As an example, Labbé (1995) informed children that learning to warm their hands would improve their headaches. Children were guided to imagine their hands becoming warm as well as to relax.

The efficacy of relaxation training (primarily PMR training) as a single therapy for children's headache has been evaluated in many studies (Labbé and Williamson 1984; Fentress et al. 1986; Larsson and Melin 1986, 1988; Richter et al. 1986; Emmen and Paschier 1987; Larsson et al. 1987a,b, 1990; McGrath et al. 1988; Wisniewski et al. 1988; Passchier et al. 1990; Engel 1992; Engel et al. 1992; Labbé 1995; Larsson and Carlsson 1996; Bussone et al. 1998; Kröner-Herwig et al. 1998). Typically, children receive several (5–10) 1-hour training sessions, scheduled weekly. In some studies, children are asked to practice relaxation exercises regularly between sessions. They record how often they use relaxation and monitor headache activity on daily diaries.

All studies cited previously, except that of Passchier et al. (1990), demonstrated that children who received relaxation therapy experienced significantly fewer headache attacks in comparison to control groups (i.e., an information control, self-monitoring control, or waiting-list control). The studies reporting positive results differ in several ways from Passchier et al.'s study, in which children received PMR in large groups from relatively inexperienced instructors (physical education teachers who received a brief training program). The placebo control condition included a series of physical concentration exercises (balancing on a wooden beam or concentrating before shooting basketball penalties). Although children in both groups (PMR and placebo) experienced significant reductions in headache frequency, the PMR group was not superior to the placebo. The authors concluded that a large-group format did not enable children to receive optimal benefits from relaxation exercises. Also, the training sessions were comparatively short and decreased progressively to 10 minutes in length.

For optimal headache prevention, children should use relaxation exercises in the everyday situations in which they develop headaches (Andrasik et al. 1986). In our clinic, children also use relaxation exercises during headaches to lessen their intensity. It is not yet known exactly how these therapies work to prevent headaches. They may reduce sympathetic arousal, help to manage the physiological responses associated with headache, reduce stress, and enhance feelings of self-efficacy or control (Holroyd et al. 1984; Arena and Blanchard 1996; Schwartz 1998).

BIOFEEDBACK

Biofeedback is a technique for transforming the electrical activity of the body into easily observable signals. Biofeedback is especially useful for children, who often need immediate and direct feedback about the state of their bodies to remain motivated when they are learning to relax. Two types of biofeedback are used regularly with children: skin temperature biofeedback and electromyographic biofeedback (EMG). In skin temperature biofeedback, a temperature thermistor is attached to a child's finger, while for EMG biofeedback, surface electrodes are attached to the skin or to specific muscle groups. The child's skin temperature or the electrical signals from the electrodes are amplified and the signals displayed. Children either watch these signals on a video screen or listen to sounds projected through a speaker. When they tense their muscles, they can see busy zigzag patterns on the screen (of high amplitude and high frequency) or hear loud or continuous sounds (beeps or static noise). As they learn to relax and control their bodies, they lessen the busyness of the pattern or lower the noise level. Thus, biofeedback is a concrete tool that assists children to first distinguish between relaxed and tense states and then learn how to achieve relaxed states on their own. As such, it is particularly appropriate for use with children whose headache is caused or exacerbated by physiological changes associated with a stressed or tense state.

The components of a training process for using biofeedback with children are outlined in Table IV. The therapist explains the rationale for using a relaxation-based pain control method and describes the biofeedback equipment. When possible, children should be asked whether they prefer an audio or visual feedback format. The therapist selects the region or muscle group for electrode placement. Although the frontalis muscle is often used, many children with headache learn to relax with electrodes placed in distal sites. In our clinic, the therapist may select the area between the thumb and forefinger so children can easily see where the electrode is. It is also easier for children to tense and relax their fists in comparison to their frontalis muscles.

The therapist talks with children to gauge their creativity (for mental imagery) and to determine how they relax normally at home. He or she then suggests a relaxation technique that builds on personal strengths. As in cognitive pain control training, the therapist is positive and emphasizes children's progressive success at small steps. Once children have visualized or heard the difference between tense and relaxed body states, the biofeedback may be turned off so that children can fully focus on relaxing rather than on both relaxing and monitoring the signal. Some children report that the signals make it more difficult to concentrate on relaxing; instead, they are monitoring how well they are relaxing. Once children are beginning to relax, the signal is turned on again so that they can use the feedback to relax more deeply. After guiding children to use a relaxation technique, therapists should allow children to quietly use the technique and relax, without providing constant coaching. Therapists should document the EMG levels as children relax to determine which techniques are most efficient for them and to monitor their progress over sessions. Children practice exercises at home and should use them during headache attacks. (For a brief "how to" guide for clinicians interested in using biofeedback for other types of pain control, see Arena and Blanchard 1996.)

Biofeedback is widely used to treat children's headache (Ross and Ross 1988; Duckro and Cantwell-Simmons 1989; Hermann et al. 1995; Schwartz 1998). As shown in Table III, biofeedback has been evaluated in both cohort

Table IV
Components of biofeedback-assisted relaxation training

Provide rationale for using relaxation as a pain control method (use familiar examples)
Explain equipment and allow children to choose display format (audio or visual)
Seat children in comfortable reclining chair
Select body site and apply EMG surface electrodes
Adjust monitor so that children can observe amplified signals at rest
Ask children to tighten body site and observe increased signal
Select mental imagery, deep breathing, or progressive muscle relaxation
Guide children to use technique with an emphasis on relaxing without trying too hard
Allow them to immerse themselves and relax without constantly talking to them
Intermittently ask children to observe that the signals are decreasing
If children are having difficulty, select another technique
Record levels before and after each session (or technique)
Assign a feasible practice schedule for children to follow at home
Ask children to use the technique during periods of stress or during headache
Evaluate efficacy by asking the child to use a headache diary

studies (Burke and Andrasik 1989; Grazzi et al. 1990; Hermann et al. 1997) and randomized controlled trials (Labbé and Williamson 1984; Fentress et al. 1986; Guarnieri and Blanchard 1990; Labbé 1995; Allen and Shriver 1997; Bussone et al. 1998; Kröner-Herwig et al. 1998). Children typically receive 8–12 1-hour training sessions, scheduled weekly; they are instructed to practice the relaxation component (without the biofeedback equipment) at home between sessions. Children record headache activity on daily diaries; they generally experience significantly fewer headache attacks after biofeedback therapy.

Four studies have directly compared the efficacy of biofeedback-assisted relaxation training versus relaxation training alone (not simply a relaxation placebo); all studies demonstrate equivalent reductions in headache frequency immediately following treatment (Fentress et al. 1986; Labbé 1995; Kröner-Herwig et al. 1998; Sartory et al. 1998). Several studies have evaluated multimodal cognitive-behavioral programs that include biofeedback (Werder and Sargent 1984; Waranch and Keenan 1985; Mehegan et al. 1987; Womack et al. 1988; Helm-Hylkema et al. 1990; Allen and McKeen 1991; McGrath et al. 1993; Allen and Shriver 1997). These studies demonstrated that children have significantly fewer headache attacks after the multimodal treatment, with some studies showing less general headache activity (a composite score that varies widely among studies; calculations typically include some measure of pain intensity, headache frequency, and headache duration, as described in Chapter 2).

In summary, strong evidence supports the efficacy of biofeedback-assisted relaxation for treating children's headache. The vast majority of children enjoy using biofeedback, easily learn to monitor their physical states, and eventually improve their ability to relax in the situations that cause headache. However, biofeedback is contraindicated for children who have extremely high performance expectations. These children usually try so hard during training sessions that biofeedback increases their stress and tension.

OPERANT CONDITIONING AND BEHAVIORAL MANAGEMENT

Therapists use behavioral management techniques to identify an individual's maladaptive behaviors, to determine how they are reinforced, and to structure a program to eliminate them. The behavioral approach is based on operant learning theory, in which an individual's behaviors are determined by the responses of other people in the environment. The behaviors that generate positive outcomes will continue to occur, while those that have negative outcomes will decrease. The behaviors of adults and children who experience pain are inevitably shaped by the reactions of significant others in their environment. Certain overt behaviors, such as seeking reassurance or withdrawing from activities, may be rewarded by increased attention, empathy, and comfort, or by reduced performance expectations. These positive outcomes, whether explicitly or implicitly communicated, will encourage children to repeat the behaviors that elicited the favorable responses. Children with headache may develop many conditioned maladaptive behaviors. (The common behavioral factors for children with headache are described in Chapter 4.)

Thus, some aspect of behavioral management is frequently included in multimodal programs for treating children's headache. The goals are to lessen the specific behaviors that trigger headache attacks, exacerbate pain, or prolong disability, while concomitantly increasing healthy behaviors. Therapists identify all of a child's pain and disability behaviors (verbal and nonverbal), evaluate the response of the adults who care for them (explicit and implicit), and then modify the responses of children and adults accordingly. Typically therapists initially target only one or two behaviors so as not to overwhelm families. For example, when children use a pain control method during a headache, parents can reward children for using the method rather than focusing on the pain complaint. Other behaviors are added after the child has clearly modified previous behaviors.

The selection of behaviors and rewards is critical to the success of the program. Therapists design a reward system that will effectively motivate families. Young children may earn stickers or points to be applied toward a treat; adolescents may earn points toward a special purchase, increased social activities, or greater independence. Both parents and children must agree to follow the program consistently, with rewards contingent on the child's fulfilling the well-defined behavioral criteria. The child (and parents) must be able to achieve the positive behavioral criteria.

Although two case studies report that operant conditioning successfully decreased headache complaints for a 6-year-old-girl with migraine and an adolescent with chronic daily headache (Yen and McIntire 1971; Ramsden et al. 1983), no compelling evidence supports its use as a single therapy. Instead, consistent and strong evidence supports the benefits of a behavioral management approach as a component in a multimodal program for treating children's headache.

COGNITIVE-BEHAVIORAL AND MULTIMODAL THERAPY

As cited in the previous sections on cognitive and behavioral therapies, most cognitive and behavioral methods for controlling children's headaches are used in combination, rather than independently. In fact, the term *cognitive-behavioral* is gradually evolving as the most appropriate description of comprehensive treatment programs. While the specific cognitive, behavioral, physical, and pharmacological components may vary, these programs generally combine a wide range of treatment strategies and techniques. However, multimodal programs need not include every possible approach; rather, they can carefully integrate the tools necessary to relieve children's pain, lessen the frequency of headache attacks, and decrease headache-related disability. Specific methods should be selected on the basis of the unique causative and contributing factors for each child, as described in Chapter 8.

Given the multifactorial etiology of recurrent migraine and tension-type headache, multimodal programs provide an effective treatment approach for many children. Therapists can choose the most appropriate combination of therapies to address the responsible cognitive, behavioral, emotional, and familial factors in accordance with a child's age, interests, and abilities. As reviewed in the previous sections, evidence consistently supports the efficacy of these programs for treating children's headache.

INDIVIDUAL VERSUS GROUP THERAPY

Recent attention has focused on delivering therapies to children with headache more cost-effectively than in an individual therapist-administered format. Alternative approaches include group therapy sessions, home-based self-help treatments, and a tiered treatment approach. Studies of cognitive-behavioral therapy delivered in a group format yield inconsistent results. The group format may be differentially effective depending on the treatment components, type of headache, setting, and age of children. For example, Larsson and Melin (1986) conducted a randomized trial to evaluate the efficacy of a clinic-based group format for adolescents; the treatment consisted of relaxation training exercises. The treatment significantly reduced headache activity in 82% of the adolescents in comparison to a waiting-list control group and an information-only control group. In contrast, Barry and von Baeyer (1997) reported that the group format failed to reduce headache activity in children aged 7–12 years; their treatment consisted mainly of cognitive therapy.

Larsson et al. (1987a) demonstrated the efficacy of a school-based group treatment format (self-help relaxation training) for relieving headache in adolescents. In a subsequent review of data obtained in three previous studies, Larsson and Melin (1988) concluded that headache activity improved more for participants with tension-type headache than for those with migraine headache (data from 108 adolescents, aged 16–18 years). Osterhaus and colleagues (1993) also reported that a combined group and individual cognitive-behavioral treatment reduced migraine attacks for 32 children (aged 12–19 years).

The home-based self-help format effectively reduces headache activity when children learn biofeedback (Burke and Andrasik 1989; Guarnieri and Blanchard 1990), relaxation (Larsson et al. 1987b; Larsson and Melin 1989), and cognitive-behavioral skills (McGrath et al. 1992; Griffiths and Martin 1996). McGrath and colleagues (1992) conducted a randomized trial to compare 8-week therapist-administered, self-administered, and control treatments for 87 adolescents, aged 11–18 years. The self-administered treatment included a written manual and cassette tapes with instructions on different coping and relaxation exercises; the therapist contacted participants weekly to answer any questions and discuss homework assignments. The therapist- and self-administered treatments were equally effective in reducing headache activity in comparison to the control group, but the self-administered treatment was substantially more cost-effective. Griffiths and Martin (1996) evaluated a clinic-based group format and a home-based format for 42 children, aged 10–12 years. The clinic format consisted of eight 90-minute treatment sessions, scheduled weekly. Treatment components included education, progressive muscle relaxation, cognitive coping skills, and autogenic relaxation training. The home-based format included the same treatment components, but children attended only three clinic sessions (weeks 1, 4, and 8); they received the contents of the other sessions in a manual at home. Both treatment formats resulted in significant decreases in children's headache index scores in comparison to a control group and seemed equally efficacious.

A tiered treatment approach has components of both the clinic- and home-based formats. At diagnosis, parents receive information about the common causes and contributing factors for children's headache, guidelines for how to manage pain during headache attacks and lessen disability, and suggestions for identifying and modifying situation-specific stress (as described in Chapter 7). Families implement these suggestions at home with minimal continuing contact with their primary health care providers. Many children improve with this practical and cost-effective intervention, while those who require more specialized assistance from a therapist are referred to more intensive, clinic-based programs.

PHYSICAL TECHNIQUES

Physical techniques include thermal stimulation, visual modulation, transcutaneous nerve stimulation (TENS), acupuncture, massage, and chiropractic or osteopathic manipulation. Although each technique has been used to treat headache in children, almost no studies have been conducted to objectively evaluate their efficacy. Instead, physical techniques are recommended primarily on the basis of clinical experience and anecdotal information, as summarized in Table V.

THERMAL STIMULATION

Many parents apply warm or cool compresses to the painful area when children have headache. Children report that they feel more comfortable and that their pain is lessened. However, there is only anecdotal evidence that thermal stimulation (either warming or cooling) is effective. Many children also use analgesic medication, remove themselves from a stressful situation, and rest in a comfortable setting. Thus, at present, thermal stimulation should be considered only as an adjunctive therapy that may benefit some children.

VISUAL MODULATION

Parents often report that their children's headache attacks can be triggered by certain light conditions, such as bright sunlight or the flickering of fluorescent lights. Good and colleagues (1991) evaluated a visual modulation therapy to prevent children from developing headache from fluorescent school lights. Children were randomized to wear either red- or blue-tinted

Table V
Physical and complementary therapy: evidence base
for treating children's headache*

Therapy	Type of Evidence			
	Anecdotal	Case Report	Cohort Study	Randomized Trial
Thermal	✓			
Visual				✓†
TENS		✓†		
Acupuncture				✓†
Massage	✓			
Chiropractic manipulation	✓	✓†		
Osteopathic medicine			✓†	
Homeopathy	✓			
Naturopathy	✓			
Dietary			✓	✓

* The evidence for all listed therapies is only suggestive, due to an insufficient number of trials.
† Therapy evaluated in only one study.

glasses 8 hours a day for about 5 months; the red-tinted glasses filtered approximately 80% of the short-wave 50-Hz flicker. Both groups of children improved initially, but children in the red group had significantly fewer headache attacks at 4 months. However, the study results are inconclusive due to the small sample ($N = 20$), the differential dropout rate (0 and 4 for the red and blue groups, respectively), and the difference in headache frequency at baseline (6.2 and 2.7 attacks per month for the red and blue groups, respectively).

TRANSCUTANEOUS ELECTRICAL NERVE STIMULATION

Transcutaneous electrical nerve stimulation (TENS) consists of a mild electric current administered to electrodes placed on the skin. Many stimulators are available commercially; they generally consist of small battery-operated units, with electrodes attached to flexible wires. The frequency and intensity of pulses can be varied. Pain is usually reduced during stimulation and for a variable time period afterwards, depending on the type of pain and the intensity and frequency of stimulation. The analgesia evoked by TENS has been attributed to a combination of peripheral and central mechanisms (for review, see Woolf and Thompson 1994). High-frequency, low-amplitude pulses selectively activate large-diameter, low-threshold (Aβ) afferents and inhibit second-order nociceptive transmission (Garrison and Foreman 1994). Acupuncture-like TENS (low-frequency, high-amplitude pulses) may activate an endogenous endorphin-mediated analgesia system (Sjölund and Eriksson 1979).

The evidence supporting the use of TENS in treating headache is based primarily on studies with adults (for review, see Vernon et al. 1999). We identified one trial where TENS was used to treat children's headaches, but it was uncontrolled and included insufficient information about how TENS was used and how pain relief was evaluated (Lapeer 1986). Thus, little evidence supports the use of TENS for treating children's headache.

ACUPUNCTURE

Traditional acupuncture is part of an ancient Chinese theory of medicine in which all diseases and pains are attributed to an imbalance in the vital energy, called *Ch'i* or *Qi*, which is thought to flow along channels ("meridians"); health is said to depend on the balance of polar forces called *Yin* and *Yang* within the system. Located on the energy channels are 365 classical acupuncture points, each with a defined therapeutic effect, that can be stimulated by the insertion of thin needles or by the application of heat, laser light, finger pressure, or low-frequency, high-intensity electrical pulses to balance the energy flow. Headache might result from a deficiency or an excess in the energy flow within meridians that pass through the head (Kaptchuk 2000). The location, pain characteristics, and associated symptoms of various types of headache reveal the pattern of energy imbalance and guide the practitioner to treat specific points to restore the body to a proper state of balance. Herbal medicines, diet, and massage may complement acupuncture sessions to promote healing. (For a review of the concepts and theory underlying the traditional practice of acupuncture, see Takagi 1982.)

In contrast, modern medical descriptions of acupuncture mechanisms focus on the neuropharmacology and neurophysiology of acupuncture treatment. Analgesia evoked by acupuncture involves multiple mechanisms at local, segmental, and supraspinal levels (for review, see Chapman and Gunn 1994). Many modern acupuncturists follow a hybrid model, combining traditional concepts with current knowledge of neurophysiology and pain trigger points (Helms 1998).

Although acupuncture is used with children, its efficacy for relieving migraine and tension-type headache has been studied almost exclusively in adults. Melchart and colleagues (1999) conducted a systematic review of randomized, controlled trials and concluded that while most trials comparing true and sham acupuncture for recurrent headache showed a positive trend in favor of true acupuncture, the quality and amount of evidence was not fully convincing. Only one randomized, controlled trial has been conducted with children (Pintov et al. 1997). In this study, 22 children with migraine (aged 7–15 years) received either true acupuncture (subdermal electrical stimulation according to traditional Chinese medicine) or placebo acupuncture (superficial electrical stimulation in the stratum corneum at the same sites). After 10 weeks of treatment (15-minute sessions), children in the true acupuncture group had significantly fewer and milder headaches in comparison to children in the placebo acupuncture group. These improvements paralleled an increase in panopioid activity in blood plasma and an increase in β-endorphin levels for children in the true acupuncture group. The authors concluded that acupuncture might be effective for treating children with migraine headache, but that larger trials were needed to unequivocally demonstrate its efficacy.

MASSAGE

Massage therapy includes several methods for manipulating muscles and other soft tissues of the body to prevent or alleviate pain and discomfort. The primary physiological effect is regulation of muscle tone through reflex and mechanical actions (Lee et al. 1990). Although the analgesic mechanisms are unknown, massage stimulates pressure receptors, induces physical and mental relaxation, and may improve circulation and reduce tissue swelling. Pain relief may result from activation of both peripheral and central inhibitory mechanisms. (For review of various manipulative techniques, see Goats 1994; Haldeman 1994.)

Many parents naturally massage the painful area when young children have a headache. Children report that the gentle rubbing eases their pain and increases their comfort. However, there is only anecdotal evidence that parent-provided massage relieves headache. Similarly, only anecdotal evidence has shown that therapeutic massage can lessen headache for some children (observations from our clinical practice). We were unable to identify any published descriptive reports or research studies documenting the efficacy of massage for treating children's headache.

CHIROPRACTIC MANIPULATION

Chiropractic treatment involves manual techniques to restore the normal alignment and mobility of the vertebrae, including manipulating and mobilizing the joint. According to chiropractic practitioners, misalignment of the spinal vertebrae ("subluxations") and mechanical impediment of associated structures either cause or contribute to disease, depending upon the theoretical orientation of the practitioner (Kaptchuk and Eisenberg 1998). Headache is attributed to abnormalities in the cervical spine/craniovertebral region, such as misalignment of the vertebrae, impingement and/or irritation of nerves or blood vessels, and myofascial dysfunction (Kidd and Nelson 1993). Chiropractic treatment is used for both migraine and tension-type headaches. Headache treatment may also include soft tissue therapy, trigger point therapy, massage, and counseling to prevent exacerbations of subluxations (through better posture or sleep position and stretching exercises).

However, strong evidence is lacking to support the efficacy of chiropractic manipulation for treating headache. Two systematic reviews evaluated the efficacy of manipulation and mobilization of the cervical spine in the treatment of adult headache and concluded that its efficacy could not be determined due to an insufficient number of well-designed studies (Hurwitz et al. 1996; Vernon et al. 1999).

Children receive chiropractic treatment for various health problems including headache (Verhoef and Papadopoulos 1999). However, its efficacy in children has not been evaluated. We were able to locate only one case report describing its efficacy as adjunctive therapy for a 13-year-old girl, who was diagnosed with chronic tension headache secondary to moderate thoracic segmental dysfunction and mild-to-moderate myofibrosis in the cervical and thoracic regions (Hewitt 1994). Chiropractic treatment has potential adverse effects, including temporary discomfort, pain, fatigue, and vascular accidents (Senstad et al. 1997). However, no information has been documented on the prevalence of side effects and risks of chiropractic treatment for children's headache.

OSTEOPATHIC MEDICINE AND VISCERAL MANIPULATION THERAPY

Osteopathic medicine is predicated on the "whole person" concept—the functional and biomechanical structures, psychological and life stressors, and general homeostatic mechanisms (for review of osteopathic techniques, see Kuchera and Kuchera 1994; DiGiovanna and Schiowitz 1997). The therapy is based on the premise that structure and function are interrelated. A structural problem in the musculoskeletal system (muscles, bones, ligaments, organs, or fascia) impairs the functioning of associated organs and tissues. Physical manipulation treats the underlying structural dysfunction so that the body is able to repair itself and thereby restore optimal function. The choice of osteopathic manipulative treatment (the nature and site of stimulation) depends on the particular somatic dysfunction. Depending on the structural examination and diagnosis, manipulation therapy may include techniques to correct compensatory, adaptive, postural, and habitual factors. Therapy often includes counseling to address other contributing factors, including postural changes, stress reduction, exercise, and nutrition. Although osteopathic manipulation is used to treat children's headaches, its efficacy has not been evaluated in controlled trials (for a review of strategies in the diagnosis and treatment of adult headache, see Gallagher 1998).

Cranial sacral therapy and visceral manipulation therapy are specialized forms of osteopathic manipulation therapy. These techniques are described as gentle and non-invasive, with a very low risk-to-benefit ratio. Cranial sacral therapy focuses on the movement of the cranial bones and the rhythm of the cerebrospinal fluid. It is hypothesized that a restriction in the movement of the bones disturbs the normal cranial rhythm of the cerebrospinal fluid, causing or contributing to headache. Treatment involves gentle, manual pressure applied to the head to either reduce or remove the restrictions, thus restoring flow and balance (Upledger and Vredevoogd 1983). In contrast, visceral manipulation therapy focuses on fixations in soft tissues. It is hypothesized that a healthy organ or viscus in good health has physiological motion. The motion of the viscera is interdependent because of the serous membranes that envelop all organs and living tissues. Any restriction, fixation, or adhesion to another surface creates functional impairment. During treatment, a therapist assesses the site of restriction and applies minimal pressure to primary and successive areas of soft tissue contracture and fixation. This manipulation technique is intended to release restrictions in order to increase the mobility and motility of the soft tissues (Barral and Mercier 1988).

No studies have been published on the efficacy of cranial sacral and visceral manipulation therapy for treating children's headache. However, we conducted a cohort study evaluating visceral manipulation therapy for relieving headache in 50 children with traumatic brain injury (Lunn et al. 1997). All children experienced at least a 50% reduction in headache frequency, with many parents reporting concurrent changes in children's irritability level and ability to concentrate, along with other changes in behavior or temperament.

HOMEOPATHY

Homeopathy is a system of therapy developed by Samuel Hahnemann based on the "law of similia," likes are cured by likes, which holds that a medicinal substance that in large doses can evoke certain symptoms in healthy individuals may be effective in treating illnesses with similar symptoms (Lockie and Geddes 1995). Homeopathic medicine uses various plants, minerals, or animal products in infinitesimal doses to stimulate the sick person's natural defenses. "Homoios" in Greek means *similar* and "pathos" means *disease* or *suffering*. Symptoms reflect the organism's efforts to re-establish homeostasis or balance. Thus, extremely dilute doses of substances that in large doses can provoke such symptoms should complement a person's natural defenses (Bellavite and Signorini 1995).

The homeopathic remedies used to treat headache are selected according to the individual's overall symptoms (headache features and emotional factors), rather than according to conventional headache diagnostic criteria (Lockie and Geddes 1995). Homeopathic treatment may also include other management strategies, including diet manipulation, lifestyle changes, and relaxation training. Ernst (1999) conducted a systematic review of randomized, controlled trials to assess the efficacy of homeopathic remedies for treating headache. Although the evidence did not support the superiority of homeopathic remedies in comparison to placebo, the number of well-designed trials was insufficient to define its efficacy for adults. Children have been included in some adult trials (Brigo and Serpelloni 1991), but no scientific evidence has specifically demonstrated the efficacy of homeopathic medicine for treating children's headache.

NATUROPATHIC MEDICINE

Naturopathic medicine is a distinct profession of primary health care, emphasizing prevention, treatment of the whole person, and the promotion of optimal health through the use of therapeutic methods and modalities that encourage an individual's natural healing process (for review see Murray and Pizzorno 1998). Naturopathic physicians use physiological, psychological, and mechanical methods as well as natural medicines, naturally processed foods, herbs, and natural remedies. A major principle is to "do no harm." Thus, the emphasis is on using methods and medicinal substances that minimize the risk of harmful side effects, avoiding, when possible, the harmful suppression of symptoms, and respecting an individual's healing process, using the least force necessary to diagnose and treat illness. Although no controlled trials have evaluated the efficacy of an exclusive naturopathic approach for treating children's headache, several of the therapies used in naturopathy have been studied. In addition, some trials have evaluated dietary interventions and herbal remedies.

Dietary restrictions are based on the belief that certain foods (e.g., dairy products, carbonated beverages) trigger or exacerbate migraine headache in susceptible individuals. Although there is much anecdotal support for eliminating supposed food triggers from children's diets, scientific support is scarce. Studies in which children have been placed on restrictive diets, rotation diets, or elimination diets (in which all suspected triggers are eliminated from the diet and reintroduced one at a time) have yielded primarily negative results (Forsythe and Redmond 1974; Congdon and Forsythe 1979; Salfield et al. 1987).

Only two studies report high success rates. Egger and colleagues (1983) conducted a cohort study in which 88 children (aged 3–16 years) were placed on an oligoantigenic diet (restricted to very few types of food). Almost all children (93%) improved with the diet, and 90% relapsed when food triggers were reintroduced. In a second phase, 40 of the children who relapsed entered a randomized trial where they received either food triggers or placebos for a week and the alternate items for a second week. Children had more headache attacks in response to the food triggers. However, the 1-week evaluation period was too short to establish accurate changes in headache frequency, and the data were not statistically evaluated. MacDonald and colleagues (1989) evaluated an elimination diet in 60 children with migraine; 46 children improved and entered a challenge phase where foods were reintroduced. Although headache increased for some children in this phase, most children did not comply with the study protocol. Thus, the positive findings from these two studies fail to provide compelling evidence that elimination diets are effective for treating children's headache.

Several herbal medicines are used to treat headache, including feverfew, valerian, passionflower, cayenne and willow. However, only feverfew has been evaluated for treating migraine in adults. Vogler and colleagues (1998) conducted a systematic review of the randomized, controlled trials evaluating feverfew in migraine prophylaxis and concluded that feverfew may be effective, but that the evidence is not compelling due to an insufficient number of well-designed studies. No trials have evaluated the effectiveness of feverfew for treating children's headache.

SUMMARY

Many nondrug therapies can modify the factors that trigger headache attacks, increase pain, and prolong disability in children. Nondrug therapies are frequently used in combination within a broad multimodal treatment program. A multimodal approach is ideally suited for a child-centered treatment because the specific components (i.e., stress management, hypnosis for pain control, or biofeedback-assisted relaxation training) can vary according to the primary factors responsible for the headache attacks and the unique needs of children and families.

Strong and consistent evidence supports the efficacy of most cognitive and behavioral therapies for relieving children's headache. In particular, the large number of well-designed studies on behavioral therapies enables investigators to conduct systematic and meta-analytic reviews to further demonstrate their efficacy (Duckro and Cantwell-Simmons 1989; Hermann et al. 1995; Holden et al. 1999). Cognitive and behavioral therapies provide children with some practical and versatile pain control tools that they can use independently in the different situations in which they develop headache. Also, counseling helps children to understand the causes and change any behaviors that contribute to their headache problem.

As yet, few controlled trials have been conducted to evaluate the efficacy of physical therapies. The evidence supporting their efficacy derives primarily from anecdotal and case reports; the inadequacy of the published information makes it impossible to summarize whether findings are consistently positive. Little pediatric research has been conducted on many of the therapies regarded as complementary to traditional medical approaches, despite increasing interest in their safety and efficacy; further studies are needed to determine their efficacy in treating children's headache.

In summary, nondrug therapies are an intrinsic component of headache treatment, even when children are receiving drug therapy. Drugs relieve the pain of headache attacks, but do not mitigate the factors responsible for repeated attacks. We consider that an integrated, flexible approach combining cognitive, behavioral, and physical methods is more effective than drug therapy alone for alleviating headache. Moreover, children can incorporate many nondrug therapies practically into their daily activities. These methods enable children to improve their independent control during headache attacks and to modify their lives to prevent additional attacks and prolonged disability.

REFERENCES

Allen KD, McKeen LR. Home-based multicomponent treatment of pediatric migraine. *Headache* 1991; 31:467–472.

Allen KD, Shriver MD. Enhanced performance feedback to strengthen biofeedback treatment outcome with childhood migraine. *Headache* 1997; 37:169–173.

American Pain Society. *Guideline for the Management of Acute and Chronic pain in Sickle Cell Disease.* Glenview, IL: American Pain Society, 1999.

Andrasik F, Blake DD, McCarran MS. A biobehavioral analysis of pediatric headache. In: Krasnegor NA, Arasteh JD, Cataldo MF (Eds). *Child Health Behavior: A Behavioral Pediatrics Perspective.* New York: Wiley Interscience, 1986, pp 394–434.

Arena JG, Blanchard EB. Biofeedback and relaxation therapy for chronic pain disorders. In: Gatchel RJ, Turk DC (Eds). *Psychological Approaches to Pain Management.* New York: Guilford Press, 1996, pp 179–220.

Barber TX. The effects of "hypnosis" on pain. *Psychosom Med* 1963; 25:303–333.

Barral J-P, Mercier P. *Visceral Manipulation.* Seattle: Eastland Press, 1988.

Barry J, von Baeyer CL. Brief cognitive-behavioral group treatment for children's headache. *Clin J Pain* 1997; 13:215–220.

Bellavite P, Signorini A. *Homeopathy: A Frontier in Medical Science.* Berkeley, CA: North Atlantic, 1995.

Bloch GJ. *Mesmerism: A Translation of the Original Medical and Scientific Writings of F.A. Mesmer, M.D.* Los Altos, CA: William Kaufmann, 1980.

Brigo B, Serpelloni G. Homeopathic treatment of migraines: a randomized double-blind controlled study of sixty cases. *Berlin J Res Homeopathy* 1991; 1:98–106.

Burke EJ, Andrasik F. Home- vs. clinical-based biofeedback treatment for pediatric migraine: results of treatment through one-year follow-up. *Headache* 1989; 29:434–440.

Bushnell MC, Duncan GH, Hofbauer RK, et al. Pain perception: is there a role for primary somatosensory cortex? *Proc Natl Acad Sci USA* 1999; 96:7705–7709.

Bushnell MC, Duncan GH, Ha B, Chen J-I, Olausson H. Non-invasive brain imaging during experimental and clinical pain. In: Devor M, Rowbotham MC, Wiesenfeld-Hallin Z (Eds). *Proceedings of the 9th World Congress on Pain,* Progress in Pain Research and Management, Vol. 16. Seattle: IASP Press, 2000, pp 485–495.

Bussone G, Grazzi L, D'Amico D, Leone M, Andrasik F. Biofeedback-assisted relaxation training for young adolescents with tension-type headache: a controlled study. *Cephalalgia* 1998; 18:463–467.

Chapman CR, Gunn CC. Acupuncture. In: Wall PD, Melzack R (Eds). *Textbook of Pain.* Edinburgh: Churchill Livingstone, 1994, pp 1805–1821.

Congdon PJ, Forsythe WI. Migraine in childhood: a study of 300 children. *Develop Med Child Neurol* 1979; 21:209–216.

DiGiovanna EL, Schiowitz S (Eds). *An Osteopathic Approach to Diagnosis and Treatment.* Philadelphia, PA: Lippincott, 1997.

Duckro PN, Cantwell-Simmons E. A review of studies evaluating biofeedback and relaxation training in the management of pediatric headache. *Headache* 1989; 29:428–433.

Egger J, Carter CM, Wilson J, Turner MW, Soothill JF. Is migraine food allergy? A double-blind controlled trial of oligoantigenic diet treatment. *Lancet* 1983; 2:865–869.

Emmen HH, Passchier J. Treatment of headache among children by progressive relaxation. *Cephalalgia* 1987; 7(Suppl 6):387–389.

Engel JM. Relaxation training: a self-help approach for children with headaches. *Am J Occup Ther* 1992; 46(7):591–596.

Engel JM, Rapoff MA, Rogot Pressman A. Long-term follow-up of relaxation training for pediatric headache disorders. *Headache* 1992; 32:152–156.

Ernst E. Homeopathic prophylaxis of headaches and migraine? A systematic review. *J Pain Symptom Manage* 1999; 18:353–357.

Fentress DW, Masek BJ, Mehegan JE, Benson H. Biofeedback and relaxation-response training in the treatment of pediatric migraine. *Dev Med Child Neurol* 1986; 28:139–146.

Forman SG. *Coping Skills Interventions for Children and Adolescents.* San Francisco: Jossey-Bass Publishers, 1993.

Forsythe WI, Redmond A. Two controlled trials of tyramine in children with migraine. *Dev Med Child Neurol* 1974; 16:794–799.

Gallagher RM. Current strategies in the diagnosis and treatment of headache. *J Am Osteopath Assoc* 1998; 98(Suppl):S1–S20.

Gardner GG, Olness K. *Hypnosis and Hypnotherapy in Children.* New York: Grune and Stratton, 1981.

Garrison DW, Foreman RD. Decreased activity of spontaneous and noxiously evoked dorsal horn cells during transcutaneous electrical nerve stimulation (TENS). *Pain* 1994; 58:309–315.

Gatchel RJ, Turk DC (Eds). *Psychological Approaches to Pain Management.* New York: Guilford Press, 1996.

Goats GC. Massage—the scientific basis of an ancient art. Part 1. The techniques. *Br J Sports Med* 1994; 28:149–152.

Good PA, Taylor RH, Mortimer MJ. The use of tinted glasses in childhood migraine. *Headache* 1991; 31:533–536.

Grazzi L, Leone M, Frediani F, Bussone G. A therapeutic alternative for tension headache in children: treatment and 1-year follow-up results. *Biofeedback Self Regul* 1990; 15:1–6.

Griffiths JD, Martin PR. Clinical-versus home-based treatment formats for children with chronic headache. *Br J Health Psychol* 1996; 1:151–166.

Guarnieri P, Blanchard EB. Evaluation of home-based thermal biofeedback treatment of pediatric migraine headache. *Biofeedback Self Regul* 1990; 15(2):179–184.

Haldeman S. Manipulation and massage for the relief of back pain. In: Wall PD, Melzack R (Eds). *Textbook of Pain.* Edinburgh: Churchill Livingstone, 1994, pp 1251–1262.

Hall H. Hypnosis and pediatrics. In: Tennes R (Ed). *Medical Hypnosis: An Introduction and Clinical Guide.* New York: Churchill Livingstone, 1999, pp 79–93.

Helm-Hylkema HVD, Orlebeke JF, Enting LA, Thussen JHH, Van Ree J. Effects of behaviour therapy on migraine and plasma β-endorphin in young migraine patients. *Psychoneuroendocrinology* 1990; 15(1):39–45.

Helms JM. An overview of medical acupuncture. *Alt Ther Health Med* 1998; 4:35–45.

Hermann C, Kim M, Blanchard EB. Behavioral and prophylactic pharmacological intervention studies of pediatric migraine: an exploratory meta-analysis. *Pain* 1995; 60:239–256.

Hermann C, Blanchard EB, Flor H. Biofeedback treatment for pediatric migraine: prediction of treatment outcome. *J Consult Clin Psychol* 1997; 65:611–616.

Hewitt EG. Chiropractic care of a 13-year-old with headache and neck pain: a case report. *J Can Chiropract Assoc* 1994; 38:160–162.

Hilgard ER. A neodissociation interpretation of pain reduction in hypnosis. *Psychol Rev* 1973; 80(5):396–411.

Hilgard ER, Hilgard JR. *Hypnosis in the Relief of Pain.* Los Altos, CA: William Kaufmann, 1983.

Hilgard JR, LeBaron S. *Hypnotherapy of Pain in Children with Cancer.* Los Altos, CA: William Kaufman, 1984.

Holden EW, Deichmann MM, Levy JD. Empirically supported treatments in pediatric psychology: recurrent pediatric headache. *J Pediatr Psychol* 1999; 24:91–109.

Holroyd KA, Penzien DB, Hursey KG, et al. Change mechanisms in EMG biofeedback training: cognitive changes underlying improvements in tension headache. *J Consult Clin Psychol* 1984; 52:1039–1053.

Hurwitz EL, Aker PD, Adams AH, Meeker WC, Shekelle PG. Manipulation and mobilization of the cervical spine. *Spine* 1996; 21:1746–1760.

Jacobson E. *Progressive Relaxation.* Chicago: University of Chicago Press, 1938.

Kapelis L. Hypnosis in a behaviour therapy framework for the treatment of migraine in children. *Aust J Clin Exper Hypnosis* 1984; 12:123–126.

Kaptchuk TJ. *The Web That Has No Weaver: Understanding Chinese Medicine,* 2nd ed. Chicago: Contemporary Books, 2000.

Kaptchuk TJ, Eisenberg DM. Chiropractic: origins, controversies, and contributions. *Arch Intern Med* 1998; 158:2215–2224.

Keefe FJ, Lefebre JC. Behaviour therapy. In: Wall PD, Melzack R (Eds). *Textbook of Pain.* Edinburgh: Churchill Livingstone, 1994, pp 1367–1380.

Kidd RF, Nelson R. Musculoskeletal dysfunction of the neck in migraine and tension headache. *Headache* 1993; 33:566–569.

Kröner-Herwig B, Mohn U, Pothmann R. Comparison of biofeedback and relaxation in the treatment of pediatric headache and the influence of parent involvement on outcome. *Appl Psychophysiol Biofeedback* 1998; 23:143–157.

Kuchera ML, Kuchera WA. *Osteopathic Considerations in Systemic Dysfunction.* Columbus, OH: Greyden Press, 1994.

Kuttner L. Hypnotic interventions for children in pain. In: Schechter NL, Berde CB, Yaster M (Eds). *Pain in Infants, Children, and Adolescents.* Baltimore: Williams & Wilkins, 1993, pp 229–236.

Labbé EE. Treatment of childhood migraine with autogenic training and skin temperature biofeedback: a component analysis. *Headache* 1995; 35:10–13.

Labbé EE, Williamson DA. Treatment of childhood migraine using autogenic feedback training. *J Consult Clin Psychol* 1984; 52:968–976.

Lapeer GL. High-intensity transcutaneous nerve stimulation at the Hoku acupuncture point for relief of muscular headache pain. Literature review and clinical trial. *Cranio* 1986; 4:164–171.

Larsson B, Carlsson J. A school-based, nurse-administered relaxation training for children with chronic tension-type headache. *J Pediatr Psychol* 1996; 21:603–614.

Larsson B, Melin L. Chronic headaches in adolescents: treatment in a school setting with relaxation training as compared with information-contact and self-registration. *Pain* 1986; 25:325–336.

Larsson B, Melin L. The psychological treatment of recurrent headache in adolescents—short-term outcome and its prediction. *Headache* 1988; 28:187–194.

Larsson B, Melin L. Follow-up on behavioral treatment of recurrent headache in adolescents. *Headache* 1989; 29:250–254.

Larsson B, Melin L, Lamminen M, Ullstedt F. A school-based treatment of chronic headaches in adolescents. *J Pediatr Psychol* 1987a; 12(4):553–566.

Larsson B, Daleflod B, Hakansson L, Melin L. Therapist-assisted versus self-help relaxation treatment of chronic headaches in adolescents: a school-based intervention. *J Child Psychol Psychiatry* 1987b; 28:127–136.

Larsson B, Melin L, Doberl A. Recurrent tension headache in adolescents treated with self-help relaxation training and a muscle relaxant drug. *Headache* 1990; 30:665–671.

LeBaron S, Zeltzer LK. Children in pain. In: Barber J (Ed). *Hypnosis and Suggestion in the Treatment of Pain.* New York: Norton, 1996, pp 305–340.

Lee MHM, Itoh M, Yang GW, Eason AL. Physical therapy and rehabilitation medicine. In: Bonica JJ (Ed). *The Management of Pain.* Philadelphia: Lea and Febiger, 1990, pp 1769–1788.

Lockie A, Geddes N. *The Complete Guide to Homeopathy.* Montreal: R.D. Press, 1995.

London P, Cooper LM. Norms of hypnotic susceptibility in children. *Develop Psychol* 1969; 1(2):113–124.

Lunn D, Boniface S, McGrath PA, Seifert CE. Visceral manipulation therapy and cognitive-behavioral therapy for children with post-traumatic headache. *Pain Res Manage* 1997; 2(1):64.

Macdonald A, Forsythe I, Wall C. Dietary treatment of migraine. In: Lanzi G, Balottin U, Cernibori A (Eds). *Headache in Children and Adolescents.* Amsterdam: Elsevier, 1989, pp 333–338.

McGrath PA. *Pain in Children: Nature, Assessment and Treatment.* New York: Guilford Publications, 1990.

McGrath PA, Hinton GG, Boone JE. Management of recurrent headaches in children. *Abstracts: 7th World Congress on Pain.* Seattle: IASP Press, 1993, p 151.

McGrath PJ, Humphreys P, Goodman JT, et al. Relaxation prophylaxis for childhood migraine: a randomized placebo-controlled trial. *Dev Med Child Neurol* 1988; 30:626–631.

McGrath PJ, Humphreys P, Keene D, et al. The efficacy and efficiency of a self-administered treatment for adolescent migraine. *Pain* 1992; 49:321–324.

Mehegan JE, Masek BJ, Harrison RH, Russo DC, Leviton A. A multicomponent behavioral treatment for pediatric headache. *Clin J Pain* 1987; 2:191–196.

Melchart D, Linde K, Fischer P, et al. Acupuncture for recurrent headaches: a systematic review of randomized controlled trials. *Cephalalgia* 1999; 19:779–786.

Murray M, Pizzorno J. *The Encyclopedia of Natural Medicine.* Rocklin, CA: Prima Publications, 1991.

Olness K, Gardner GG. Some guidelines for uses of hypnotherapy in pediatrics. *Pediatrics* 1978; 62:228–233.

Olness K, Kohen DP. *Hypnosis and Hypnotherapy with Children.* New York: Guilford Press, 1996.

Olness K, MacDonald J. Self-hypnosis and biofeedback in the management of juvenile migraine. *J Dev Behav Pediat* 1981; 2:168–170.

Olness K, MacDonald JT, Uden DL. Comparison of self-hypnosis and propranolol in the treatment of juvenile classic migraine. *Pediatrics* 1987; 79(4):593–597.

Osterhaus SO, Passchier J, Helm-Hylkema H, et al. Effects of behavioral psychophysiological treatment on schoolchildren with migraine in a nonclinical setting: predictors and process variables. *J Pediatr Psychol* 1993; 18:697–715.

Passchier J, van den Bree MB, Emmen HH, et al. Relaxation training in school classes does not reduce headache complaints. *Headache* 1990; 30:660–664.

Peyron R, Garcia-Larrea L, Gregoire MC, et al. Haemodynamic brain responses to acute pain in humans: sensory and attentional networks. *Brain* 1999; 122(Pt 9):1765–1780.

Pintov S, Lahat E, Alstein M, Vogel Z, Barg J. Acupuncture and the opioid system: implications in management of migraine. *Pediat Neurol* 1997; 17:129–133.

Price DD. *Psychological Mechanisms of Pain and Analgesia.* Progress in Pain Research and Management, Vol. 15. Seattle: IASP Press, 1999.

Ramsden R, Friedman B, Williamson D. Treatment of childhood headache reports with contingency management procedures. *J Clin Child Psychol* 1983; 12:202–206.

Richter IL, McGrath PJ, Humphreys PJ, et al. Cognitive and relaxation treatment of paediatric migraine. *Pain* 1986; 25:195–203.

Ross DM, Ross SA. *Childhood Pain: Current Issues, Research, and Management*. Baltimore: Urban and Schwarzenberg, 1988.

Salfield SA, Wardley BL, Houlsby WT, et al. Controlled study of exclusion of dietary vasoactive amines in migraine. *Arch Dis Child* 1987; 62:458–460.

Sartory G, Müller B, Metsch J, Pothmann R. A comparison of psychological and pharmacological treatment of pediatric migraine. *Behav Res Ther* 1998; 36:1155–1170.

Schwartz A. Headache: selected issues and considerations in evaluation and treatment. In: Schwartz MS (Ed). *Biofeedback: A Practitioner's Guide*. New York: Guilford Press, 1998, pp 313–407.

Senstad O, Leboeuf-Yde C, Borchgrevink C. Frequency and characteristics of side effects of spinal manipulative therapy. *Spine* 1997; 22:435–440.

Sjölund BH, Eriksson MBE. The influence of naloxone on analgesia produced by peripheral conditioning stimulation. *Brain Res* 1979; 173:295–301.

Smith MC, Womack WM, Chen ACN. Anxiety and depression in the behavioral treatment of headache in children and adolescents. *Int J Adolescent Med Health* 1991; 5(1):17–35.

Spanos NP. Hypnotic behavior: a social-psychological interpretation of amnesia, analgesia, and "trance logic." *Behav Brain Sci* 1986; 9:440–467.

Takagi H. Critical review of pain relieving procedures including acupuncture. In: Yoshida H (Ed). *Neuropeptides*. Advances in Pharmacology and Therapeutics, Series II: CNS Pharmacology, Vol. 1. Elmsford, NY: Pergamon Press, 1982, pp 79–92.

Upledger JE, Vredevoogd JD. *Craniosacral Therapy*. Chicago: Eastland Press, 1983.

Verhoef MJ, Papadopoulos C. Survey of Canadian chiropractors' involvement in the treatment of patients under the age of 18. *J Can Chiropract Assoc* 1999; 43:50–57.

Vernon H, McDermaid CS, Hagino C. Systematic review of randomized clinical trials of complementary/alternative therapies in the treatment of tension-type and cervicogenic headache. *Complementary Therapies Med* 1999, 7:142–155.

Vogler BK, Pittler MH, Ernst E. Feverfew as a preventive treatment for migraine: a systematic review. *Cephalalgia* 1998; 18:704–708.

Waranch HR, Keenan DM. Behavioral treatment of children with recurrent headaches. *J Behav Ther Exp Psychiatry* 1985; 16:31–38.

Werder DS, Sargent JD. A study of childhood headache using biofeedback as a treatment alternative. *Headache* 1984; 24:122–126.

Wisniewski JJ, Genshaft JL, Mulick JA, Coury DL, Hammer D. Relaxation therapy and compliance in the treatment of adolescent headache. *Headache* 1988; 28:612–617.

Womack WM, Smith MS, Chen ACN. Behavioral management of childhood headache: a pilot study and case history report. *Pain* 1988; 32:279–283.

Woolf CJ, Thompson JW. Stimulation-induced analgesia: transcutaneous electrical nerve stimulation (TENS) and vibration. In: Wall PD, Melzack R (Eds). *Textbook of Pain*. Edinburgh: Churchill Livingstone, 1994, pp 1191–1208.

Yen S, McIntire RW. Operant therapy for constant headache complaints: a simple response-cost approach. *Psychol Rep* 1971; 28:267–270.

Correspondence to: Patricia A. McGrath, PhD, Pain Innovations, Inc., 38 Hampton Crescent, London, Ontario, Canada N6H 2N8. Fax: 519-471-8529; email: pamcgrat@julian.wo.ca. Effective 1 July 2001: Department of Anesthesiology, School of Medicine, University of Utah, Salt Lake City, UT 84108, USA.

The Child with Headache: Diagnosis and Treatment.
Progress in Pain Research and Management, Vol. 19,
edited by Patricia A. McGrath and Loretta M. Hillier,
IASP Press, Seattle, © 2001.

7

Treating Recurrent Headache: An Effective Strategy for Primary Care Providers

Patricia A. McGrath[a,b] and Loretta M. Hillier[a]

[a]*Pain Innovations Inc., London, Ontario, Canada;* [b]*Department of Pediatrics, Faculty of Medicine, University of Western Ontario, London, Ontario, Canada*

Recurrent migraine and tension-type headaches are a prevalent pain problem in otherwise healthy children and adolescents. The headache is not a symptom of an underlying disease or disorder; instead, recurrent headache *is* the disorder. Analgesic drugs can relieve the pain of individual headache attacks, but drug therapy alone does not alleviate the cycle of repeated attacks. Effective treatment of this syndrome requires a multimodal approach with cognitive-behavioral therapy in addition to abortive drug therapy. The treatment regimen is based on modifying both the factors that trigger attacks and conditions that exacerbate pain and disability.

Although some children require a specialized multi-session treatment program, others benefit from a brief educational intervention where primary care providers explain the syndrome and guide parents to recognize and modify causative factors. This chapter describes the educational intervention we designed based on the common factors that trigger headache and cause disability for children.

RATIONALE FOR AN EDUCATIONAL INTERVENTION

We have conducted pain assessments, developed treatment plans, and evaluated various therapies for more than 1500 children and adolescents with recurrent headache. The results of our studies have confirmed our clinical impression about the common causes of recurrent headache and have shown that other causes are unique to individual children. While certain cognitive,

behavioral, and emotional factors seemed relevant for all children with recurrent headache, the extent to which they were primary causes or secondary contributing factors varied among children (as described in Chapter 4).
Thus, we designed a cognitive-behavioral treatment program to address the
common causative factors for most children, but also to target any unique
causes for individual children (McGrath 1990).

We considered that a multi-strategy approach would be necessary to
modify the different factors that initiated headache attacks, increased the
painfulness or duration of headache, and prolonged disability for children.
We integrated educational and counseling components with biofeedback-
assisted relaxation training, behavioral management guidelines, practical
stress-identification and problem-solving training, and basic nondrug pain
control strategies in order to address the primary contributing factors.
Through trial and error, we concluded that therapists required approximately
six working sessions to deliver all treatment components to children. At the
end of the program, parents and children had accurate information about
recurrent headache, children used a versatile repertoire of pain control techniques during a headache attack, and parents could help children to recognize and resolve the stressful situations that previously had triggered headache attacks. Children had significantly fewer and milder headaches after
participating in this program; these reductions in headache activity were
maintained at 12-month follow-up for 90% of the children.

Because our preliminary evaluation was an unblinded clinical trial, we
conducted a blinded randomized controlled trial with 287 children aged 5 to
16 years to more rigorously evaluate the efficacy of our multi-strategy treatment program (McGrath 1990; McGrath et al. 1993). Children with recurrent
migraine or tension-type headache (according to a neurologist's diagnosis)
were randomized into one of three treatment conditions: the structured cognitive-behavioral program, a waiting-list control (to control for spontaneous
remission of headache over the study time period), and a feedback group (to
control for the effects of simply providing information about recurrent headache). All children first participated in a comprehensive pain assessment, as
described in detail below, but were randomized to treatment groups before
the results were interpreted. One month after initial assessment, a therapist
provided general information about recurrent headache to the parents of
children assigned to the cognitive-behavioral and feedback groups (but not
to parents of children assigned to the waiting-list control).

In this 90-minute feedback session, the therapist informed parents that
their children had recurrent pain syndrome, a common (and treatable) pain
problem affecting many otherwise healthy and pain-free children. She used
diagrams to briefly explain the presumed mechanisms for migraine and

tension-type headache, but emphasized that much of the information on the pathophysiology of headache had been extrapolated from adult studies and that research on children's pain problems was still relatively new. She then provided general information about the common precipitating and maintaining factors, stating that we had learned about some of these factors from treating children with headache referred to our clinic. She did not specify which factors were relevant for each child. (Chapter 4 covers the causative and contributing factors in detail.)

Instead, the therapist described the role of stress in triggering headache attacks and the contributing impact of inconsistent parental responses, secondary gains (where headache may allow the child to avoid unpleasant situations), decreased expectations for performance (at school or in sports), increased attention or special privileges, and conditioned environmental pain triggers. She explained that environmental triggers (e.g., hot weather) were often just a "red herring"; instead, anxiety about performing to an unrealistically high standard might be to blame. In addition, an inability to identify and resolve stressful issues, finding it difficult to relax, general anxiety about events, depression, an apparent maturity beyond their chronological age, difficulty in recognizing and expressing emotions, and somatization of emotional distress were relevant emotional factors for some children.

The therapist also described some of the possible familial factors contributing to headache and disability, including positive family history of headache, high parental expectations for children's performance, children's exclusive dependence on parental reassurance and on passive methods of pain control during headache, few or no independent coping strategies, a continuous search for external and environmental causes with little attention to internal factors, overprotective parents, and (in some single-parent families) treatment of a child as an adult spouse who is expected to provide emotional support to the parent.

At the end of this feedback session, children received their next appointment date from the clinic secretary—either in 2 weeks for children in the program group or in 3 months for children in the feedback-only group. The latter date was the endpoint for treatment evaluation; at that time all children were reassessed by a research assistant who was blinded about the specific treatment children had received. As expected, headache frequency and pain intensity were significantly reduced for children who received the cognitive-behavioral program. Surprisingly, however, many children who received only feedback about recurrent headache also experienced significant improvement in comparison to children in the waiting-list control group.

We had included a feedback-only treatment group in the randomized controlled trial because of our clinical impressions as we explored various treatments for children with headache. Many parents seemed to benefit from an explanation of headache and of relevant factors according to the model shown in Fig. 1. We wondered whether some children, probably those who had experienced the problem for less than a year or who had infrequent or mild attacks, might only need practical information about the syndrome. With some understanding of their child's headache triggers and of the exacerbating factors, and simple pain management strategies, many parents should be able to help their child make the changes necessary to lessen attacks and reduce headache pain and disability. We believed that some, but not necessarily all, children with headache would still require additional assistance from a therapist. Our objective was to better match treatment to the individual child in a cost- and time-effective manner.

Thus, after we completed the controlled trial, we explored whether we could assign children to the shorter feedback intervention on the basis of their pain assessment results—specifically, children with relatively recent onset of headache (up to 12–18 months) or a mild problem (no more than one attack per month or mild headache pain), or who did not have many or longstanding causative factors. Our initial results demonstrated a high success rate, especially when therapists provided explicit information about the child's primary causative factors and specific treatment recommendations. We developed a four-step educational intervention, based on the results of our feedback-only intervention. We believe that this program, described in detail below, is valid from both a theoretical and empirical perspective. Moreover, this straightforward treatment strategy could be implemented at the level of the primary care provider and not only at specialized pain centers.

A BASIC EDUCATIONAL INTERVENTION FOR CHILDREN'S HEADACHE

STEP 1: INITIAL CONSULTATION AND HEADACHE ASSESSMENT

Pain assessment is an integral component of treating children with headache. The clinical interview should provide accurate information about specific pain features—headache location, frequency, length, pain quality, pain severity, syndrome duration, the nature and extent of accompanying symptoms, and disability level. (Our recommended measures are described in Chapter 2.)

At the initial consultation, parents should complete a brief intake form while they are waiting to see the physician, providing a concise history of the headache problem and of potential contributing factors. Such parent-completed documentation facilitates the clinical interview, enabling physicians to obtain pertinent facts quickly and to use the interview with parents

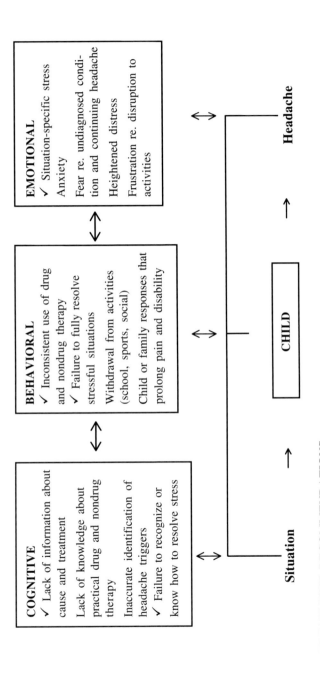

Fig. 1. A model depicting the common situational factors that can cause or exacerbate recurrent headache. The cognitive, behavioral, and emotional factors listed in the boxes were identified in our research and clinical program as the main factors that trigger headache, increase pain, or prolong headache-related disability.

for more in-depth questioning about the most relevant issues. The parent intake form (provided in Appendix 2) is also a useful item to include in children's medical records and is invaluable for evidence-based monitoring of treatment efficacy.

When possible (depending on the nature of the clinical practice), the child should be interviewed separately as part of the medical examination during the initial consultation. Otherwise, children's descriptions of their headache may be influenced by their parent's responses. Children seem to recall the sensory features of their headache more easily when they remember a specific headache, such as their last one. They also remember more accurately what they were doing, whom they were with, what they did to relieve their headache, and how long it lasted. After they describe a particular headache, it seems easier for them to make comparative judgments as to whether all their headaches follow that same pattern or if not, how they differ. To shorten the time required for the medical examination, another member of the practice could interview children before they see the physician, providing a completed interview form for the physician to review. The Children's Headache Interview (provided in Appendix 1) is an essential component of our pain program; it may be shortened for use in a more diverse clinical practice.

The results of the medical examination and assessment interviews provide the information needed to diagnose headache type and to recognize which of the common causes for recurrent headache are relevant for a child. Physicians can then provide explicit feedback to parents about some of the underlying causes, the true headache triggers, and specific treatment recommendations for lessening pain during headache attacks and for decreasing the number of attacks. Physicians and primary care providers who have treated children regularly may be able to identify some of the unique causative factors for a particular child. Generally, however, a more comprehensive pain assessment is necessary to identify these unique factors, as described in Chapter 8. Such assessments are typically conducted in pain or headache clinics because they require specially trained interviewers and longer appointments than are typically available in diverse clinical practices.

STEP 2: DIAGNOSTIC INFORMATION

As shown in Table I, an unequivocal diagnosis is the first component of the feedback intervention for children with recurrent headache. In our clinical experience, parents often are confused by their child's initial headache diagnosis—accepting that the physician did not find anything wrong, but often believing that something is wrong with their child that might be found with more intensive tests. Thus, the emphasis of the traditional diagnosis can be somewhat negative—"a failure to find something" rather than a positive confirmation of an understandable and therefore treatable condition. We believe it is essential to provide parents and children with a confident, positive diagnosis of the headache type—migraine, tension-type, or mixed—with an emphasis on our improved understanding of this common recurrent pain problem.

Most parents benefit from written information about recurrent headache that incorporates the key points summarized in Table I. When feasible, physicians should supplement their verbal diagnostic information and treatment recommendations with printed information. Concise fact sheets are a practical way to share information about children's headache with both parents (as typically only one parent attends the initial consultation) and with any other family caregivers. Our general information on recurrent headache and its causes is presented in Table II, which health care providers can modify to meet the needs of their clinical practice; our parent information sheet is provided in Appendix 3.

Parents should be informed that recurrent headache is a common problem affecting many healthy children. It probably differs from any other pain that their child has experienced as it has no single cause (unlike most types of acute pain caused by disease or trauma). Because it has several causes, no single treatment will immediately solve the problem. In addition, two children might experience apparently similar headaches (i.e., of the same location, intensity, and frequency), but each child's pain may have very different causes. With our improved understanding of childhood headache, the emphasis in treatment has shifted from an exclusively headache-centered focus to a more child-centered approach. Thus, the consultation should

Table I
Components of feedback intervention

Diagnostic Information
    Positive confirmation of recurrent migraine or tension-type headache
    Common pain problem for children and adolescents
    Multifactorial etiology, unlike acute pain

Treatment Information
    Unlike acute pain, a multimodal approach
    Targeted at all causes and contributing factors
    Drug or nondrug therapy effective for relief of headache pain
    Nondrug therapy effective for treating causes

Explicit Recommendations
    Over-the-counter analgesics and nondrug methods to use during headache
    Guidelines on how to identify stressors through prospective monitoring
    Guidance on how to modify causes and contributing factors for the child
    Guidance for parents on how to minimize disability behaviors

---

Table II
The causes of recurrent headache: information for parents

Migraine and tension-type headache are an extremely common problem for otherwise healthy children and adolescents.

Although we are still learning how the physiological mechanisms may differ for the two types of headache, extensive research in the past 15 years has taught us a great deal about what causes headache and about the most effective treatments for children.

Recurrent headache is very different than other types of pain children experience. Rather than a single cause, there are usually several. The longer children have suffered from repeated headache attacks, the more causes can be found.

Although we suspected that migraines in children, like adults, could be caused by certain foods, weather conditions, or activities, we have learned that this is not true for the majority of children.

Instead, headaches are caused by many factors—some factors affect all children, and some are unique for an individual child. Our assessment helps us to find the specific causes for each child's headache.

The most common cause is stress associated with normal childhood activities, especially related to schoolwork, sports participation, or peer relationships. Often children do not recognize that they are stressed and are unable to fully deal with their stress and anxiety, which eventually trigger a headache.

include a neurological examination and an assessment of whether any of the common factors that cause headache in children apply to the patient, so that the physician can provide child-centered, rather than headache-centered, treatment recommendations.

STEP 3: TREATMENT INFORMATION FOR PARENTS

Some parents appreciate a brief explanation of headache pathophysiology, especially if their child has experienced an aura or consistently suffers from nausea and vomiting. However, most parents seem more interested in what factors trigger the headache episodes. The pain model shown in Fig. 1 provides a framework for providing feedback to parents about common causative factors and headache triggers. In this model, we have listed the most common factors that we have observed. Physicians could check the relevant factors for each child or alternatively, they could complete a more individualized form. In our clinic, we use a form listing only the headings and then write any relevant factor under the appropriate heading (cognitive, behavioral, and emotional) as we explain it to parents. We use examples from parents' and children's responses during the pain assessment to show why we consider a factor relevant. After describing these factors, the therapist outlines a treatment plan (see Table III).

Again, the emphasis is on the multifactorial etiology of headache and thus a multimodal treatment approach is recommended, in direct contrast to

Table III
Treatment recommendations: fact sheet for parents

Our treatment goals are to reduce your child's pain during a headache and to change the factors that trigger headache.

When headache pain is mild, your child should be able to lessen it with distraction, for example, by taking a short break to stretch and move his/her shoulders and neck, by resting for a few minutes, or by changing activities. Distraction is a simple but powerful tool that can help to end the headache or prevent it from becoming stronger.

When headache pain is moderate-to-strong, your child should use one of the products available to block pain rather than try to tough it out. [Recommend either a particular product based on your clinical preference or the product the family currently uses for other types of pain control.] You probably already use some of the NSAIDs (nonsteroidal anti-inflammatory drugs) that are sold on an over-the-counter basis for pain relief. Many can be safely used for children; just make sure you administer the recommended dose according to your child's weight.

Be consistent when your child has a headache. Show your concern, but try to emphasize following the treatment plan to relieve pain so that your child can resume normal activities. Assess the pain level, help your child to choose a nondrug method (even when you are also administering medication), and praise him/her for following the plan.

The day after the headache, take a few minutes to talk with your child about what was happening at school, in sports, or with friends. You may recognize what was upsetting, even though your child did not think that anything was the matter. If the situation is still causing some anxiety, then help your child to understand that his or her feelings may have caused the headache and that there are ways to fix the problem so it will not cause another headache. Teaching your child some practical ways to deal with this situation will help him/her learn how to truly lessen stress.

All pain control during headache is really symptom control. You and your child must deal with the underlying causes to prevent future headache attacks.

the "single cause and single treatment" approach normally adequate for relieving acute pain. Parents and children should understand that each causative factor must be treated and that the most effective treatment includes education, basic drug and nondrug pain management techniques, and resolution of the stressful situations that provoke headache. Thus, the primary treatment objectives in the feedback intervention are to: (1) educate parents and children about recurrent migraine and tension-type headache; (2) inform them about common headache triggers; (3) provide explicit recommendations for managing pain and preventing disability; and (4) offer guidance to parents and children about how to identify and resolve situation-specific stress in order to lessen headache attacks.

Some parents have difficulty in accepting that stress is a cause, especially if they see their child suffering from disabling headaches which they believe are directly related to environmental causes. These attitudes can constitute a huge obstacle for those treating their children. Although as clinicians we may not agree with the parents, we should avoid challenging their beliefs while delaying the child's treatment. Thus, in our practice we emphasize honestly that while we have not yet seen a child whose headaches are consistently triggered by certain foods, weather conditions, and so on, we are willing to consider that their child might be the first one. However, at the same time, we would be remiss if we did not also treat the factors identified in the assessment that seem to be contributing to the repeated headache attacks and causing disability. Our intention is to switch the primary emphasis for families from looking for environmental stimuli to dealing with other (and probably the only) relevant factors. Through prospective monitoring we will be able to ascertain the possible role of environmental stimuli, but treatment should not be postponed while we continue to investigate. Also, parents should not be encouraged to focus exclusively on the physical environment as the main cause for children's headache.

Some parents prefer to attribute headache to environmental causes because they view these external causes as independent and beyond their control, while they perceive that stress reflects some failure for their child or their family. These parents need additional reassurance that stress is a part of life and that many children need assistance in coping with difficult situations at some time in their life. While some children easily recognize their anxiety about a situation and seek assistance, thus lessening their anxiety, other children attempt to struggle on their own without recognizing that they are anxious or knowing the source of their anxiety. Headache (or stomachache) is often the first sign that these children are experiencing stress.

Other parents have difficulty accepting that their children are stressed by activities that should be enjoyable, especially those that parents view as special opportunities. Hockey, horseback riding, skating, gymnastics, soccer, baseball, ballet, tennis, and swimming can be stressful as well as relaxing. Stress may be related to performance expectations, competitive pressures, peer interactions or coach–team interactions, or may simply be due to an extremely busy schedule with many demanding extramural activities. These activities may be costly for parents, put pressure on demanding family schedules, and have a special status for children. Children may be reluctant to admit that these activities are stressful because of the cost, time, or privileged status, and many children simply do not recognize that they are stressful.

For these children, stress identification and management are major components of headache treatment. Some parents will be able to use the information from the feedback intervention and work with children so that they can develop the problem-solving skills needed to cope with these situations. Other parents may require additional assistance from pain therapists or psychologists. Parents must understand that children's headaches will continue as long as the unresolved stress continues. If children have long-standing problems in resolving stress, then the process of stress identification and resolution will take time, and headaches will decrease gradually. However, in the interim, parents can still help to lessen pain and disability by following other treatment recommendations, as summarized in the text in Table III from a fact sheet for parents.

Although analgesics effectively lessen pain and can shorten a headache, many parents do not administer medication when it would be appropriate. Some parents are concerned that children may become addicted to analgesics, but most parents seem unsure about what to use and when to use it. They may medicate children inconsistently, administer less than the recommended therapeutic dose, and lose confidence in a product quickly without having allowed a sufficient time period for it to work. While pain medication may not be needed for all headache attacks, parents should be able to administer analgesics confidently. For most children, analgesics should be used for strong pain, and nondrug methods for mild pain. Parents and children need to decide jointly which method is most appropriate for moderate pain; this decision should be based on which method is more effective in a particular situation. Children may need medication to block the pain so that they can continue their regular activities, or they may find that simple nondrug techniques are effective.

Parents should leave the appointment with a concrete plan for what to do when their child develops a headache, as described in Table III. In most instances, this plan should include an immediate pain intervention for children and a subsequent discussion with children about what triggered the headache and how that situation could be changed. We recommend that an analgesic be administered before the pain becomes too strong, and that children also use a nondrug pain control method. Children should use the analgesics that their family typically uses for symptomatic pain relief; doses for children should be based on children's weight, rather than their age. In their initial assessment interview, most children report that they have used some nondrug pain control methods—usually distraction or rest/sleep—and that they can lessen the pain or completely relieve the headache. The combined consultation and feedback appointment allows insufficient time to teach children additional pain control methods, so the methods they have previously used with success should be incorporated into the recommendations for treating headache. (Please see Chapter 6 for a review of nondrug therapies and see Chapter 8 for an in-depth description of how to teach children simple pain control methods.)

Generally, parents should discuss the probable headache trigger within a couple of days of the headache episode. But when children are very young or very distressed, their parents may help them to deal with their nervousness by focusing on the causes without focusing on the link between their nervousness and headache onset. Parents can guide their children to set more realistic expectations about their performance, modify stressful schedules, set a schedule for completing school assignments, or learn what to say to their classmates when they are teased. As children gain confidence and competency in handling life stressors, they should have fewer headache attacks. But they will probably still get an occasional headache; parents can then discuss the link between stressful situations and headache so that children can gradually learn how to independently identify their headache triggers. We emphasize that all pain control during headache is really symptom control; parents and children must deal with the underlying causes to prevent future headache attacks.

STEP 4: PROSPECTIVE MONITORING AND FOLLOW-UP APPOINTMENT

Many methods are available for monitoring headache activity in children, as reviewed in Chapter 2. Prospective records can provide objective information about headache triggers, pain characteristics, and treatment effectiveness. For the feedback intervention, children complete a pain calendar for the period between the initial consultation and their follow-up appointment (usually 1 month) and submit a headache log for each headache that they experience. We ask children to complete these forms independently as we wish to obtain information from their own perspective rather than from their parents'. We may also ask parents to independently monitor their children's headaches.

The pain calendar is a blank monthly calendar. Our pediatric headache patients receive a calendar with their name on it and printed instructions. We ask children to post the calendar on their refrigerator or beside their bed, and mark the days when they have a headache (young children may use stickers). If children report at the initial consultation that they have several headaches a week, we ask them to mark the days that they do *not* have a headache (to begin to switch their focus to pain-free days). Children should mark the calendar at the same time each day, usually before they go to bed. Children also complete a headache log for every headache. Children receive a colored file folder with the calendar sheet, several headache logs, and a copy of the printed guidelines on headache that we provide to parents. We encourage children to mark a calendar or headache log with "I forgot" when they did not complete the form within a day, rather than to try to remember what happened.

A follow-up appointment should be scheduled in 2 to 6 weeks (depending on headache frequency). Sufficient time should be allowed between appointments to allow parents and children to follow treatment recommendations, so that the physician can assess any improvement in frequency or intensity of headache. During this period, children should prospectively monitor headache onset, pain intensity, and the interventions used and their effectiveness. Children and their parents should also attempt to determine the cause for any headaches that develop and generate solutions to prevent a similar headache attack.

At the follow-up visit, the physician or other primary care provider can review the completed headache records to identify relevant contributing factors. As an example, a headache record for Andy, a 10-year-old boy with tension-type headache, is shown in Fig. 2.

Headache Log

Name: ___*Andy*___

COMPLETE A SEPARATE SHEET FOR EACH HEADACHE THAT YOU HAVE FROM NOW UNTIL YOUR NEXT APPOINTMENT

1. Day ___*Saturday*___ Date ___*May 16*___

    When (what time) did it start? ___*2:30*___ am/***pm***

2. What were you doing when you started to get the pain?

    ___*playing computer games with my friend*___

3. How were you feeling emotionally? ___*sort of angry*___

4. At its strongest, how much did it hurt? (draw a circle around the best words)

    very mild   mild   ***medium/moderate***   strong   very strong

5. At its strongest, how much did it bother you? (draw a circle around the best words)

    not at all   a little   ***between a little and a lot***   a lot   very much

6. What did you do to stop the headache? When (what time) did you do this?

    How much did it help?

    (If you took medication, please write down what you took and how much.)

    What I tried: Time   How much did it help?

    took (decongestant) 1 dose   ___*3:00*___   not at all   a little   a lot   ***it took it away***

    lay down, had a rest   ___*3:15*___   not at all   a little   ***a lot***   it took it away

7. What time did the headache end? ___*3:30–3:45*___

8. What were you doing when it ended? ___*resting on my bed*___

9. What do you think caused this headache? ___*the computer games—the lights*___

Fig. 2. A headache log completed by a 10-year-old boy with recurrent headache.

As shown, Andy's headache began when he was playing a computer game with his friend. He thought that the fast-moving lights in the games caused the headache. However, Andy noted that he felt "sort of angry" at the time. When the therapist asked, "Why were you angry?" he described his friend as very competitive and said that he had been taunting him as they played. When he got the headache, his friend had to go home. As they talked about the situation, the therapist suggested that his headache was probably triggered more by anger and frustration about his friend's attitude toward winning the computer game than by the computer lights. Usually when children attribute a headache to environmental stimuli (i.e., weather, foods, or as in this instance, computer games), it is clear that children encounter those stimuli many times each week without developing a headache. The therapist can explain this to children and guide them to look for other aspects of the situation. She suggested to Andy: "I'm wondering whether the headache started because you were feeling upset and mad because of what your friend was saying and doing. Feeling mad was a sign that there was a problem there for you that needed to be solved. But you didn't say anything to him, and you ended up having a headache that got worse."

Headache logs can provide an objective record of the temporal pattern for children's headache (e.g., specific days, times, or in association with certain activities), as well as any patterns related to children's level of physical and mental activity, their social interactions, and their emotional state. These records provide a solid framework for working with children and their parents to better understand the causes and to select the most appropriate intervention for different headache attacks. For example, once Andy's friend left, his mother gave him a decongestant because his parents thought that many of his headaches were triggered by allergies. The therapist used the information on medication (from several logs) to guide Andy's parents that decongestants were not appropriate for all his headaches. Discussing the common themes emerging from several headache logs, Andy's mother said that her son sometimes complained about not getting along with the other children on his sports team. Andy suppressed his feelings when he was with these children, but complained later to his mother. Although his mother had listened empathetically, she had not helped him with some specific things he could do or say when the other children bothered him. Andy needed this type of concrete assistance to cope in many social situations.

Although Andy felt that decongestants immediately relieved his pain, he still chose to lie down and rest for many headaches. The therapist worked with Andy (using the interventions listed on his logs) to select different pain control methods based on what was causing his headache. For example, for the headache in Fig. 2, the therapist encouraged Andy to think about what else he could have done, other than take the decongestant and remove himself from the situation. Andy responded that he could have asked his friend if they could switch activities, and perhaps watch a movie or ride their bikes. The therapist supported his suggestions and asked that he try one of these alternative methods the next time. Andy's headache logs enabled the therapist to address many tangible issues effectively with him and his parents.

Headache records can be used to evaluate the child's (and the family's) ability to manage the headaches using the pain control recommendations provided at the previous appointment, and determine whether parents are able to help children recognize and resolve causative factors or whether the family requires further assistance from pain therapists or psychologists. In a pain management program (as described in Chapter 8), therapists work with children and parents to help them identify headache triggers and resolve stressful situations before they cause a headache. Objective documentation is an essential component of all headache interventions, as demonstrated in the following case study.

CASE STUDY—FEEDBACK INTERVENTION

Trevor, an 8-year-old boy, had developed monthly headaches shortly before his seventh birthday. His family physician had referred Trevor to a pediatric neurologist for diagnosis (migraine) and management (naproxen and anti-emetics). Trevor's parents subsequently requested a referral to our clinic so that he could learn some nondrug methods of pain control to complement his drug therapy. Trevor's headache was localized behind both his eyes and lasted approximately 2 hours. His pain varied in strength from 5 to 9 on the 0–10 Colored Analogue Scale (described in Chapter 2). His headache had atypical qualities in that he described the pain as sharp, aching, and stinging. He was consistently lethargic, felt nauseous, and usually vomited during a headache episode.

Trevor was a sensitive, affectionate child, who was the younger of two children. He was in Grade 2 in a regular school program and had an above-average level of achievement. Although his teachers had not expressed any concerns about his academic performance or his relationships with classmates, his mother indicated that he was sometimes anxious about doing well in school. Both Trevor and his mother identified numerous stressors related to headache onset (i.e., hockey, special occasions, peer relationships, fatigue, and skiing).

At the initial consultation the therapist concluded that anxiety (primarily about his athletic and academic performance) was the main cause for his recurrent headache. His pain was exacerbated by distress due to his inability to independently control the pain. The therapist began the feedback intervention, presenting the material described previously on recurrent headache. She recommended that Trevor use some practical nondrug strategies in addition to medication. Initially he should use medication for every headache, but as he became more comfortable with some simple distraction techniques (e.g., physical and mental relaxation), he should try to use these strategies instead of medication for mild to moderate headache. She helped him to compose a short list of activities to do during a headache.

The therapist recommended that Trevor's mother encourage him to independently manage his pain. Her encouragement should help his pain and lessen his distress in feeling that he had no control and that he would inevitably become sick. Trevor's mother should ask him: "What do you think you could do to stop this headache?" and then encourage him to decide whether he needed to take his medication or to select a distraction method from his list. At his follow-up appointment, the therapist reviewed the headache logs with Trevor. She then discussed how Trevor's mother could help him to lessen his generalized anxiety about sports and school, by identifying specifically what was happening to make him feel anxious and then to think about the best ways to deal with the situation and resolve the problem.

Trevor's mother was very insightful about the factors that were triggering his headaches and was certain that she could work with Trevor and follow the treatment guidelines. She used the headache logs to help him to recognize the relationship between stress and his headaches, to resolve this stress, and to manage his headaches with a combination of medication and active nondrug strategies. The therapist contacted Trevor's mother a month later and learned that his headaches were shorter. He was also able to resume his regular activities during a headache rather than spend time in bed. At our last contact, Trevor had not experienced a headache within 6 months.

THE NEED FOR SPECIALIZED PAIN MANAGEMENT

Although we have seen remarkable reductions in headache frequency and pain intensity at the follow-up appointment, most children will need some continued assistance from parents as they encounter new situations that cause anxiety. Some parents can independently work with children and follow the physician's treatment recommendations. Other parents will need additional support to stop searching for external triggers, to understand the true triggers, to consistently encourage children to cope with stressful situations, and to minimize profound disability for children. These parents require special assistance from physicians, pain specialists, or psychologists. Some physicians may provide the required counseling through their practice or in conjunction with a group practice, but generally children and their parents should be referred to pain specialists who can provide an intensive multimodal pain management program that addresses their needs.

In our clinical experience, the children who do not benefit from the feedback intervention have a longstanding history of headache or of multiple somatic complaints. Their parents are convinced of an as-yet undiagnosed medical problem and demand additional tests, or steadfastly attribute headache solely to environmental factors and are interested only in pharmacological therapy. The children may be so significantly disabled by headache that they have not attended school or other activities for a lengthy period, and they may have longstanding anxiety or depression. As yet, we lack a reliable method for differentiating at the initial consultation children who will benefit from feedback intervention from those who require a multimodal pain management program or who require psychological or psychiatric therapy. The prospective records of headache activity, combined with the intake information at the consultation, enable primary care providers to critically appraise how well children and parents have followed treatment recommendations. At present, this follow-up appraisal has proven to be our best method for ascertaining which families require additional assistance and which services are likely to be most appropriate for children. In some instances, the feedback intervention provides parents with the necessary framework for understanding the multifactorial etiology of headache and for accepting that their children require further specialized assistance.

TREATMENT DILEMMAS

While treating childhood headache is often challenging due to the multiple child, parent, and life issues that contribute to the syndrome, three situations are exceptionally challenging. These include children who complain of headache, but do not experience headache as frequently as they complain; children who are excessively and continuously disabled by headache, even though the attacks are infrequent; and children who have multiple learned headache triggers. The feedback intervention may be an adequate treatment for these children, if the parents are able to accept the diagnostic information about the true causative factors.

WHEN IS A HEADACHE REALLY JUST A PAIN COMPLAINT?

Most children who seek treatment for headache suffer discrete episodes of moderate to strong pain. However, some children complain of pain when they do not have a headache. They may report pain when they experience normal somatic sensations because they are overly concerned about their health. Some children's pain complaints gradually increase because they have received special attention and support during headache attacks or because previous attacks enabled them to avoid unpleasant and stressful situations. Perhaps expectations for their performance in school, sports, or social activities are reduced when they have a headache. These secondary gains, as well as strong behavioral and emotional factors, can occasionally maintain a child's headache complaints in the absence of headache (McGrath and Hillier 1996).

For example, Anne, an 11-year-old-girl, was referred to the clinic for management of intermittent moderately strong headaches that lasted only about 5 minutes. Her first headache occurred a year earlier after she hit her head in a bicycle accident. The headache lasted for a week and she suffered from nausea and vomiting throughout that period. All medical tests were normal, but subsequently she began experiencing short headache attacks.

The assessment revealed that Anne's initial head injury and hospitalization had been very distressing for her. She was afraid that she would be punished because she did not have permission to go bike riding and did not wear a helmet. Since then, headache would develop after minor bumps during play. As a result of her anxiety about her previous injury, whenever she bumped her head she was excessively concerned about it and labeled it as a major problem and headache. Anne needed assistance from a therapist to learn the difference between a true headache and this minor head pain— specifically, how her complaints were related to mild traumas that were the normal and relatively benign injuries of childhood.

Moreover, the severe anxiety associated with Anne's injury, and from the nausea and vomiting accompanying her first headache, were intensified when her medical examinations did not find any abnormalities. Anne and her parents feared that an undiagnosed medical problem was the cause. Any pain in her head—even those attributed to normal bumps—concerned the family. Thus, her headache complaints reflected her anxious attention to normal somatic sensations. In the follow-up appointment, a month after the consultation and general feedback, the therapist taught Anne that she could manage these pains independently through distraction with other activities. Anne did not require an individualized treatment program and was discharged. She had not experienced any additional headaches at follow-up 5 months later.

WHEN CHILDREN ARE EXCESSIVELY DISABLED

Frequently we receive an urgent request to assist children with headache because they have been unable to attend school for several weeks. Children with disabling headache may have different diagnoses (migraine, tension-type, or chronic daily headache), but their complaints share some common features. First, these children's apparent disability far exceeds their reported pain level, headache frequency, and headache duration. The children and their families report that "staying at home" is the only treatment that prevents headache or prevents headache exacerbation. When children are asked to rate the painfulness of common injuries they have experienced (e.g., a cut hand, scraped knee, having orthodontic braces tightened, or having stitches) as well as their usual headache, they often rate the headache as relatively low in comparison to other pains. They and their parents also may report that they no longer get many headaches because they are avoiding the causes by staying at home; in essence, they are headache free but extremely disabled.

Second, children do what they want when they are at home, often remaining physically and socially active with their peers—but outside of school. Even when children report almost constant pain, they are selectively disabled and choose what they can and cannot do. Third, at least one parent fully supports the child's attitudes that he or she should stay home. Often this parent feels disappointed with the health care system because the family had previously been told to send the child to school even though he or she still complained of headache. The parent believes that health care providers did not believe the child and did not understand the severity of the problem. These parents subtly encourage children's disability as tangible proof that the headache is a major problem. In some families, mothers leave jobs outside of the home to remain with children and home-school them. If health care providers are able to convince parents to reintegrate children into school, the parents are waiting for the first complaint of headache to justify that they were right and that the child should not be in school.

Fourth, parents place demands on health care providers to cure the headache problem before they will address the disability problem. A futile cycle ensues, with health care providers attempting to restore normal functioning and parents refusing to cooperate until the headache is relieved. Fifth, the longer children have been disabled by headache, the more learned triggers they have developed and the more secondary gains they have received. Finally, the longer children are disabled, the greater their risk for emotional difficulties and psychological problems.

Children with severe disability constitute a unique clinical challenge. Gradually we have learned to immediately identify the problem to families as two-fold—a headache problem and a disability problem. Usually disability is the more serious problem. Thus, treatment should immediately focus on both aspects—we must deal with the headache problem, but concurrently we must deal with the increasing disability. Treatment for the disability should not be postponed until the headache is completely relieved.

Some parents have difficulty accepting that children's disability should be directly treated, believing instead that it is truly a byproduct of the headache. We spend additional time at the consultation explaining that initially children's efforts to avoid activities that seemed to trigger or intensify headache were appropriate protective behaviors. However, their continued avoidance of these activities and their parents' protective stance after the headache has been diagnosed are inappropriate and encourage disability. For some parents, we use the example of a child's broken arm or sprained ankle to describe how protecting the area while it is healing is appropriate, but that continuing to allow children to guard the area and avoid using it normally is inappropriate. Even if parents are anxious that the child might injure the arm or ankle again, they quickly understand that the child should not continue to overprotect it when it has healed. We find the broken arm analogy very useful with children because most children have known someone who has broken a bone and required a cast for a limited time.

Almost all children who have a major disability problem related to headache require additional treatment beyond the feedback intervention. They need assistance to re-enter school, cope with stressful situations, and resume their responsibilities. Parents need to support a treatment plan that generally includes a strict behavioral management program and counseling to help children address the underlying emotional factors that made them vulnerable for disability.

MULTIPLE LEARNED TRIGGERS

Children's headaches develop in specific circumstances and in a particular environment. Parents naturally look for potential headache triggers in those circumstances and may initially suspect certain foods, weather conditions, or activities. Parents have reported each of the 18 headache triggers listed in Table IV. Most parents endorse only a few triggers and acknowledge that they do not consistently trigger headache, but only in certain circumstances. Most parents believe that their children's worrying can cause headache, even if there are other causes too. However, some parents and children endorse many items, excluding worrying, and insist that they always

Table IV
Suggested triggers for children's headache

Soda	Loud noises
Cheese	Car trips
Chocolate	Sports
Hot weather	Crowds
Humid weather	Feeling tired
Bright sun	Feeling excited
School tests	Feeling worried
Math	Feeling hungry
Menstrual periods	Too much physical activity

cause headache. Over time, parents often blame certain foods that they then eliminate from their children's diets, and identify some situations that they then avoid. In discussing these "possible triggers," parents usually cite examples of how their children developed headache when they reintroduced the suspected food or situation.

However, parents cannot reintroduce suspected triggers in a blinded manner. They and their children are waiting, often anxiously, for the effect. The anxiety may be the real trigger for a subsequent headache. It is extremely difficult to identify headache triggers without prospective monitoring of multiple aspects of the circumstances. For example, parents may believe that the motion or noise from children on the school bus causes a morning headache for children. When the parents drive their children to school, the headache complaints lessen or stop. The parents understandably believe the bus was the trigger, but other aspects of the situation remain uninvestigated, such as who sits next to their child and whether other children tease their child. Those aspects may be the more relevant triggers. The higher the number of reported headache triggers, the more likely are the relevant triggers to be denied. Also, our clinical impression is that parents' endorsement of multiple triggers often coincides with a reluctance to accept that there is no underlying medical condition. Moreover, these parents seem to believe that only a pharmacological or physical intervention can prevent headache attacks.

We recommend an individualized cognitive-behavioral program for these children, so that we can work with parents to objectively and thoroughly evaluate all possible triggers, and work with children to lessen pain. (The program is described in Chapter 8.) However, many parents decline further treatment because they do not believe that this educational approach, combined with analgesic therapy, would be more effective than simply avoiding the multiple external triggers.

SUMMARY

Recurrent migraine and tension-type headache is a prevalent pain problem for otherwise healthy children and adolescents. Effective treatment of this syndrome requires a multimodal approach with cognitive-behavioral therapy in addition to abortive drug therapy. The treatment regimen is based on modifying the factors that trigger attacks and those that exacerbate pain and disability. Although some children require a specialized multi-session treatment program, other children benefit from a brief feedback intervention.

The emphasis of this intervention is on the fact that headache, with its multifactorial etiology, necessitates a multimodal treatment approach, in direct contrast to the "single cause and single treatment" approach normally adequate for relieving acute pain. Parents and children should understand that each causative factor must be treated and that the most effective treatment includes education, basic drug and nondrug pain management techniques, and resolution of the stressful situations that provoke headache. In the first consultation, primary care providers can teach parents and children about the common headache triggers for recurrent migraine and tension-type headache and make explicit recommendations for managing pain and preventing disability. At the follow-up appointment, the primary care provider can review the prospective records of headache activity to identify relevant contributing factors, evaluate children's (and their family's) ability to manage the headaches using the pain control recommendations provided at the previous appointment, and guide parents to identify and resolve situation-specific stress to lessen children's headache attacks.

When feasible, physicians should supplement their verbal diagnostic information and treatment recommendations with printed information. Parents should leave the appointment with a concrete plan for what to do when their child develops a headache, as described in Table III. In most instances, this plan should include an immediate pain intervention for children and a subsequent discussion with children about what triggered the headache and how that situation could be changed. This brief feedback intervention can significantly lessen headache attacks, decrease pain, and minimize disability for children with recurrent migraine and tension-type headache.

REFERENCES

McGrath PA. *Pain in Children: Nature, Assessment and Treatment*. New York: Guilford Publications, 1990.

McGrath PA, Hillier LM. Controlling children's pain. In: Gatchel R, Turk D (Eds). *Psychological Treatment for Pain: A Practitioner's Handbook*. New York: Guilford Press, 1996, pp 331–370.

McGrath PA, Hinton GG, Boone JE. Management of recurrent headaches in children. *Abstracts: 7th World Congress on Pain*. Seattle: IASP, 1993, p 51.

Correspondence to: Patricia A. McGrath, PhD, Pain Innovations, Inc., 38 Hampton Crescent, London, Ontario, Canada N6H 2N8. Fax: 519-471-8529; email: pamcgrat@julian.uwo.ca. Effective 1 July 2001: Department of Anesthesiology, School of Medicine, University of Utah, Salt Lake City, UT 84108, USA.

The Child with Headache: Diagnosis and Treatment.
Progress in Pain Research and Management, Vol. 19,
edited by Patricia A. McGrath and Loretta M. Hillier,
IASP Press, Seattle, © 2001.

8

A Cognitive-Behavioral Program for Treating Recurrent Headache

Loretta M. Hillier[a] and Patricia A. McGrath[a,b]

[a]Pain Innovations Inc., London, Ontario, Canada; [b]Department of Pediatrics, Faculty of Medicine, University of Western Ontario, London, Ontario, Canada

The effective treatment of recurrent migraine and tension-type headache requires a multimodal approach. The treatment regimen we recommend for children is based on modifying the multiple factors that trigger attacks, exacerbate pain, prolong disability, and maintain the cycle of repeat headache attacks. All children benefit from a brief educational intervention, where primary care providers explain the syndrome and describe the common causative factors (as described in Chapter 7). However, some children also require individualized multisession treatment programs in which therapists teach children how to lessen pain during headache attacks and guide families to identify and modify relevant causative and contributing factors. This chapter describes the cognitive-behavioral treatment program designed in our clinic for children with recurrent headache.

RATIONALE FOR A CHILD-CENTERED PROGRAM

As emphasized throughout this volume, recurrent migraine and tension-type headache share a multifactorial etiology. While certain cognitive, behavioral, and emotional factors are relevant for all children with recurrent headache, the extent to which they are primary causes or secondary contributing factors varies among children (as described in Chapter 4). Thus, we designed a cognitive-behavioral program to address the common causative factors for most children, while also targeting any unique causes for individual children (McGrath 1990; McGrath et al. 1993).

A multistrategy approach is necessary to modify the different factors that initiated headache attacks, increased the painfulness or duration of headache, and prolonged disability in children. Our original program included a pain assessment (structured interviews, standardized questionnaires, and prospective monitoring of headache activity), a feedback session a month later (to review the results of the pain assessment), and six therapy sessions scheduled every other week (McGrath 1990). In these sessions, a therapist would educate parents and children about recurrent headache, teach children a versatile repertoire of pain control strategies, including biofeedback-assisted relaxation training, counsel parents and children how to recognize and effectively resolve the stressful situations that could trigger headache attacks, and guide parents in behavioral management techniques to minimize headache-related disability. The efficacy of this cognitive-behavioral program for treating headache in children aged 5–16 years was evaluated in a randomized controlled trial (McGrath et al. 1993). As described in Chapter 4, headache frequency and pain intensity were significantly reduced for children who received the program.

In order to objectively evaluate the program, the therapists adhered to a structured protocol in which children received the same treatment components (e.g., relaxation training, problem-solving assistance) in the same order according to the session number. However, many children seemed to achieve their treatment goals before the sixth session, suggesting that the program could be shortened for most children. In clinical practice, the treatment components could be delivered more efficiently based on an individual child's progress within each session, rather than adhering to the six-session regimen. Also, in our clinical judgment, not all children require every treatment component included within the full program. Instead, the specific treatment components should be individualized for children, based on the specific causative and contributing factors identified through the pain assessment.

Since the completion of this study, we have progressively refined our program delivery to make it more efficient. Our cognitive-behavioral approach is the same, but the results of a child's pain assessment now guide our selection of the specific components and shape the emphasis of individual programs. We have learned that this child-centered focus enables us to reduce headache attacks, improve pain control, and lessen headache disability for most children in only three or four therapy sessions. At the end of the program, parents and children have accurate information about recurrent headache, children can use a versatile repertoire of pain control methods during a headache attack, and parents can help children to recognize and resolve the stressful situations that previously had triggered headache attacks.

AN INDIVIDUALIZED COGNITIVE-BEHAVIORAL PROGRAM

The general framework for an individualized cognitive-behavioral program is outlined in Table I. Although this program is based on the common factors that contribute to recurrent headache, the primary emphasis and specific treatment components (e.g., the type of nondrug pain control method, the inclusion of a behavioral contingency program to encourage children to attend school, and the use of biofeedback) may vary depending on the results of the pain assessment and in consideration of a child's sex, age, and cognitive level. The extent to which cognitive, behavioral, emotional, and familial factors are the primary causes for recurrent pain will determine the unique composition of the treatment. Individualized programs are potentially the optimal and most practical interventions because they match treatments to the particular needs of each child.

PAIN ASSESSMENT

A comprehensive pain assessment is the foundation of a child-centered program for treating recurrent headache. The assessment provides the therapist with a concise history of the headache problem, a descriptive profile of the current headache characteristics (i.e., location, intensity, quality, temporal

Table I
Cognitive-behavioral treatment program

Pain Assessment (~ 90-minute consultation)
    Conduct clinical interviews (parent and child)
    Administer Children's Headache Interview (child)
    Administer headache history (parent-completed form)
    Provide calendar and headache logs (prospective monitoring of headache activity)
    Provide initial diagnosis and general treatment information

Feedback Appointment (~ 60-minute consultation)
    Complete headache model, with explicit treatment recommendations
    Review headache logs
    Provide assessment results (parents and children individually)
    Provide specific treatment recommendations for managing headache attacks

Therapy Sessions (2–4 sessions, ~ 60 minutes)
    Formulate explicit treatment objectives (child)
    Review headache logs and use information in session
    Teach pain-reducing strategies to use during headache attacks (child)
    Teach stress-identification and stress-management techniques (child and parent)
    Provide guidelines (and if needed, behavioral program) to minimize disability behaviors

Outcome Evaluation
    Document progress in achieving treatment objectives
    Provide discharge information (and as appropriate, follow-up plans)

---

pattern, and duration), and an evaluation of the usual causative and contributing cognitive, behavioral, and emotional factors. This information enables a therapist to confirm a diagnosis of recurrent migraine or tension-type headache and provide appropriate treatment recommendations. We require the results of a neurological examination (described in Chapter 3) before we schedule children for a pain assessment.

Parents often are unsure what to expect at a pain assessment, not knowing how it may differ from previous medical consultations and examinations. When we first started our headache program, some parents were disappointed at the assessment when they learned that their children would only be interviewed and would not receive an additional brain scan or physical examination. Thus, we now send a letter to parents outlining the assessment process when we confirm a child's appointment, as shown in Table II. The therapist begins the assessment by reviewing this information with the accompanying parent, explaining the rationale underlying our broad assessment approach. The therapist describes the multifactorial etiology of recurrent headache using the model shown in Chapter 4, emphasizing our focus on determining which factors trigger attacks, increase pain, cause disability, and maintain the cycle of repeat attacks.

It is important to establish a trusting partnership with parents and children at the assessment so that they feel comfortable enough to reveal accurate personal information about the headache problem and its impact on their lives. We believe that the best approach for establishing a positive therapeutic relationship is to explain that while we know much about the causes of headache in children, we need to work together to discover the

Table II
Referral information for parents

Recurrent migraine and tension-type headaches are common problems for many otherwise healthy and pain-free children.

Usually, there are several causes for the recurrent headache attacks. Even though children may have similar headache attacks, the causes can be different.

In order to determine the causes for your child, we will conduct a comprehensive pain assessment in addition to the neurological examination your child has already received.

The pain assessment lasts approximately one and a half hours. The therapist will interview you and your child to obtain a detailed pain history.

The therapist will then interpret the results of the assessment to determine the causes of your child's headaches. You will receive feedback about these causes and our recommendations for a treatment plan at a second appointment.

relevant causes for this child. The therapist then explains that our interviews are conducted separately, so that children are not unduly influenced by listening to their parents' responses.

The therapist conducts the Children's Headache Interview (CHI), a semi-structured interview that includes questions about headache characteristics, situational factors that can cause or exacerbate headaches, children's and their family's responses to headaches, and potential sources of stress for children. (The CHI is provided in Appendix 1.) Children then receive a colored file folder with a pain calendar and several headache logs so that they can prospectively monitor headache activity for 1 month. Children mark the days on the calendar when they have a headache. When children report several headaches each week, we ask them to mark the days that they do *not* have a headache (to begin to switch their focus to pain-free days). Children also monitor headache activity for 2 weeks to 1 month (depending on headache frequency), as shown in Fig. 1.

While children are being interviewed, their parents complete a brief intake form that provides a concise summary of the child's headache history. (Our parent intake form is provided in Appendix 2.) The therapist reviews the intake form with parents to confirm the child's headache history, parents' understanding of headache etiology, children's pain and disability behaviors, parental responses, the type and efficacy of interventions used (especially parents' criteria for when to medicate), and the impact of the headache problem on the child's and family's lives. After discussing headache-specific information, the therapist asks the parents to describe the child's personality and temperament and to compare and contrast the child with his or her siblings. The therapist is interested in learning whether children generally express themselves openly or suppress their feelings, lead or follow, enjoy social or solitary activities, hold high expectations for their achievement, or worry more often or more intensely than other children, and how they resolve typical childhood conflicts and problems. The therapist reminds parents that stress is a common headache trigger, but that the stressful situations are usually routine school, sports, and leisure activities or interactions with teachers, coaches, peers, or family members. The therapist discusses probable stress triggers that were revealed during the interview with the child or when reviewing the parent intake form.

At the end of this interview, the therapist informs parents whether the assessment results are consistent with a diagnosis of recurrent migraine or tension-type headache. If so, the therapist reviews the parent information sheet on recurrent headache, providing general recommendations for treating headache attacks. (Parent information is described in Chapter 7, and the information sheet is provided in Appendix 3.) When parents have demonstrated an understanding of the probable causative factors, especially the need to help children to resolve anxiety associated with school, sports, etc., and if children have relatively few causes and have not developed maladaptive disability behaviors, the therapist may recommend that children receive the brief educational treatment detailed in Chapter 7. When children have a long-standing headache problem with a complex set of causes and contributing factors and when parents are unable to understand the interplay of factors that trigger headache attacks, increase pain, and prolong disability, the therapist recommends that children enroll in the headache treatment program.

The therapist must review the prospective records of children's headache activity before completing the pain assessment report and individualized treatment plan. However, at the end of the assessment appointment, the

Headache Log

Name: __*Tom*__

COMPLETE A SEPARATE SHEET FOR EACH HEADACHE THAT YOU HAVE FROM NOW UNTIL YOUR NEXT APPOINTMENT

1. Day ____*Tuesday*____   Date __*June 17*__

    When (what time) did it start? ____*6:00*____ am/***pm***

2. What were you doing when you started to get the pain? __*Just finished supper*__

3. How were you feeling emotionally? __*Good*__

4. At its strongest, how much did it hurt? (Use the Colored Analogue Scale) __*4.5*__

5. At its strongest, how much did it bother you? (draw a circle around the best words)

    not at all   a little   ***between a little and a lot***   a lot   very much

6. Which face shows me how you felt deep down inside when you had this headache? Use the Facial Scale) __*C (0.37)*__

7. What did you do to stop the headache? When (what time) did you do this? How much did it help?

    (If you took medication, please write down what you took and how much.)

    What I tried: __*Relaxation tape and lay down on couch*__

    Time: __*6:20*__

    How much did it help?   not at all   a little   a lot   ***it took it away***

8. What time did the headache end? __*6:27*__

9. What did you do then? ____*Went outside to play*____

10. What do you think caused this headache? ___*Maybe something I had to eat*___

Fig. 1. A headache log completed by a 12-year-old boy.

therapist reviews the information obtained during the interviews and summarizes the probable responsible factors and treatment emphasis, as shown in Fig. 2. This preliminary pain profile is extremely valuable in specialized clinics where psychologists supervise different levels of professional trainees as they learn how to conduct pain assessments, prepare reports, and treat children, as it provides a succinct summary for a supervisor to examine after reviewing the child's assessment results.

EVALUATION OF CAUSES AND CONTRIBUTING FACTORS

Complex and dynamic interactions occur among cognitive, behavioral, and emotional factors, as reviewed in Chapter 4. The therapist must appraise all factors to determine their relevance as a cause or contributing factor for a particular child. No simple formula can be used to match certain responses during the interviews with certain factors. Instead, this information is derived

Pain Profile Working Sheet for Assessment Report

Name: **Allison**

Severity of Headache Problem (mild, moderate, severe; provide brief rationale): *severe—daily headaches, rated at 8/10; exacerbations linked to stressful situations.*

Primary Responsible Factors (rank order): *(1) Possible emotional distress, as yet unspecified. Perhaps related to generalized anxiety, school or peer relationships. (2) Stress related to her excessively high expectations for her academic performance set by herself and her parents. (3) Inability to identify and resolve stressors.*

Secondary Responsible Factors: *(1) Anxiety and worry experienced by her and her parents regarding her headaches and their prognosis; expectations that her headaches will be disabling and protracted. (2) Focus on environmental pain triggers that prevents her from identifying and resolving stressors.*

Queries for Feedback Session: *Special attention from parents during pain episodes? Is lack of insight into relationship between stress and her headaches a factor? What happened during Grade 10 to her grades?*

Probable Treatment Emphasis: *(1) Evaluate whether underlying emotional distress is responsible for her headaches. (2) Assist her to identify and truly resolve stressors. (3) Teach her practical pain management strategies to increase her control over her pain in order to reduce her feelings of helplessness during pain episodes. (4) Educate her and her parents about recurrent headaches, and the relationship between stress and headaches.*

Fig. 2. Pain profile working sheet for assessment report completed for a 16-year-old girl.

from careful consideration of all the assessment material—interviews, intake forms, and headache logs. For some children, the evaluation of responsible factors is a continual process throughout a treatment program. Families initially may be reluctant to disclose information about marital problems, mental health conditions, financial difficulties, or substance abuse until they feel that a trusting and supportive therapeutic relationship has been established.

COGNITIVE FACTORS

Generally parents and their children hold inaccurate beliefs about headache etiology, effective drug and nondrug therapies, and the role of environmental versus stress triggers. Information about these beliefs is easily accessible during the interviews when the therapist asks open-ended questions: "What causes the headache problem? What drugs relieve pain? Which nondrug methods does 'Ashley' know? What can you do to prevent repeat attacks?" Parents usually are candid in answering these questions. They indicate when they believe that headaches are hereditary, with attacks triggered by environmental stimuli. The checklist of triggers in Table III provides a valuable summary of "presumed headache triggers." As shown, a mother noted that only environmental (or hormonal) triggers provoked headache attacks for her 12-year-old daughter; she was certain that there were no emotional triggers. However, the therapist concluded from other information in the interview and prospective monitoring of headache activity that emotional factors were primarily responsible for the child's headaches.

Although some parents report that their children's worries can trigger headache attacks, many indicate that emotional factors are not relevant. Parents may not recognize continuing sources of stress, or they may deny that the stress is sufficiently strong to provoke headache attacks. During the interview, these parents consistently report that their children are not unduly stressed. However, children's stress is often evident when they describe their feelings about their school and social activities to the therapist. For example, Kristen, a 9-year-old girl, had experienced weekly headaches for 3 years. Her mother explained that while she did not know the specific cause of her headaches, she was confident that they were not related to stress, especially stress associated with school. Kristen enjoyed school and earned excellent grades. However, when the therapist interviewed Kristen about a typical school week, she learned that the girl spent many hours completing her homework and often felt panicked. Kristen would not hand in work until she judged that it was perfect. Moreover, she was so concerned about completing special assignments in advance of the due date that she often canceled social activities to do schoolwork. Kristen admitted becoming very upset when she did not get perfect grades on tests. Prospective monitoring of Kristen's school activities, her feelings, and her headache onset confirmed that her unrealistically high expectations for achievement in all her schoolwork were the primary causes of her headache attacks.

Parents readily admit when they are concerned that children's headaches are symptomatic of an undiagnosed medical condition. They also express their fears that headaches will persist throughout their children's lives, perhaps with increasing disability. Both parents and children indicate their beliefs, expectations, and fears throughout the interview. For example, when asked: "Do you think that you will get rid of your headaches someday?" a child responded: "I will always have headaches. My mother has headaches too."

Table III
Parent intake form: questions about headache etiology

Many different foods, environmental factors, and emotional factors can cause headaches. Do any of these regularly cause your child's headaches?

	Yes	No	Don't Know
Drinking pop?	[ ]	[ ]	✓
Eating cheese?	[ ]	[ ]	✓
Eating chocolate?	[ ]	[ ]	✓
Hot weather?	✓	[ ]	[ ]
High humidity?	✓	[ ]	[ ]
Bright sun?	[ ]	[ ]	✓
Feeling excited?	[ ]	✓	[ ]
Feeling hungry?	[ ]	✓	[ ]
Feeling tired?	[ ]	✓	[ ]
Feeling sad?	[ ]	✓	[ ]
Feeling worried about schoolwork?	[ ]	✓	[ ]
Feeling worried about getting schoolwork done on time?	[ ]	✓	[ ]
Feeling worried about grades?	[ ]	✓	[ ]
Feeling worried about how friends think of him/her?	[ ]	✓	[ ]
Feeling worried about doing well in sports?	[ ]	✓	[ ]
Feeling worried about the family?	[ ]	✓	[ ]
Being really physically active?	*Worsens if pain present*		
Her menstrual periods? (girls only)	[ ]	[ ]	✓

Anything else? Specify:
Maybe trips.
She has not started menstruating yet, but I feel that hormones are playing a part.
What do you think is the number one cause of your child's headaches?
Storms (actually the day before when the weather is changing)

Similarly, parents and children readily indicate which methods do and do not relieve pain during headache attacks. The therapist reviews the information about medication use on the intake form and discusses why parents believe that some methods are effective and others are not. The semi-structured format enables the therapist to ask relevant follow-up questions about the drugs tried and how they were used. Parents may have concluded that certain medications are ineffective after only one trial, even though they failed to administer an appropriate analgesic medication in an adequate dose or at the recommended dosing interval. For example, Daniel, a 14-year-old boy, had about two headaches a week for several years. His mother's responses on the intake form revealed her opinion that four medications were equally effective (Table IV; generic names have been substituted for the brand names reported). Yet the medications were quite different—two strengths of acetaminophen; acetaminophen plus codeine; and butalbital, acetaminophen, and caffeine (Fioricet; Novartis Pharmaceuticals). Daniel's family believed that the medication was effective when it helped him to sleep because he was headache-free after a few hours' sleep. He used most of the medications interchangeably, with no clear rationale for using a different dose or potency. Daniel's mother indicated that she would like more information on how to use pain medications; approximately 90% of all parents respond "yes" to this question.

Table IV
Parent intake form: medication use

How often does your child take medication when he/she has pain?

Never   Rarely   *Sometimes*   Usually   Always

Is your child allowed to take pain medication on his/her own?   Yes _✓_ No___

If not, when does he/she ask you for medication?

When (if ever) do you give your child medication for pain without him/her asking?
Encourage it when he is in obvious distress

List the medications that your child has tried and indicate how well each worked:

Medication	Dosage	Amount of Pain Relief			
Acetaminophen	*325 mg*	None	Slight	*Moderate*	Complete
Acetaminophen	*500 mg*	None	Slight	*Moderate*	Complete
Acetaminophen plus codeine	*?*	None	Slight	*Moderate*	Complete
*Fioricet**	*?*	None	Slight	*Moderate*	Complete

Which medications does your child use now?   *Above, except Fioricet*

Would you like more information about how to use pain medications for your child?   Yes _✓_   No ___

* Butalbital plus acetaminophen plus caffeine.

Some parents may over-rely on certain medications without carefully evaluating whether they are primarily responsible for relieving pain, or may administer certain products when children feel the first twinge of pain, rather than waiting to see whether the pain intensifies. Conversely, some parents may not consistently use medication because of unfounded concerns about drug addiction or dependency; the therapist may notice a discrepancy between their responses that medication relieves children's headache and the fact that they do not use it. Parents' responses about pain control are usually straightforward, and therapists can quickly ascertain when they do not know how to use medication, how to help children use nondrug pain control methods, and how to select different methods depending on headache severity or on the circumstances in which headaches develop (e.g., at school or at home). Children's responses are similarly straightforward; they readily describe what they can do and how well different methods work. Children will explain why they use different methods; they may use nondrug methods at home, but not at school, because they do not know how to incorporate simple methods into their daily routine. They may admit that they depend on relatively ineffective methods, simply "because doing something is better than doing nothing at all."

BEHAVIORAL FACTORS

The therapist must assess whether parents' or children's behaviors during headache attacks are inadvertently increasing children's distress, pain, and disability. The CHI and parental interview provide general information about how parents respond when children first complain about a headache and about how they relieve the pain. However, prospective monitoring often reveals subtle discrepancies between what parents do and what they *think* they do. Parents may believe and report that they act consistently, but often the headache logs demonstrate that there is no consistent plan that all care providers follow at all times. Drug and nondrug methods are used without understanding when particular methods would be appropriate. Sometimes parents advise children to withdraw from activities and rest, while at other times encouraging them to continue what they are doing. Thus, we ask children to monitor headache activity and their behaviors for a month so that the therapist can accurately appraise the extent to which behavioral factors are contributing to the headache problem.

The information obtained on the headache logs and CHI provide excellent teaching tools for working with families to modify contributing factors. As an example, a boy's responses on the CHI about what he did when he had a headache clearly indicated that he adopted a passive approach and believed that most interventions provided no pain relief, as shown in Table V. The therapist used this information to show his parents that he was not using any practical methods that could lessen pain. She taught the boy that each method might work, depending on the circumstances in which he developed a headache. With his family's encouragement, he tried different methods and more objectively evaluated their effectiveness on his headache logs.

When parents provide special attention to children when they have a headache, protect them from stressful situations, relieve them from their normal workload (i.e., school, home, sports, and social activities), encourage passive methods of pain control, *and* fail to address the underlying causes for headache attacks, their behaviors contribute directly to the cycle of recurrent headache. The therapist interprets information from the interviews and headache logs to determine whether this pattern of behaviors is present. As an example, Jack, a 7-year-old boy, had experienced recurrent headache attacks for 2 years. Although his headaches were usually mild, his mother always administered acetaminophen and sent him to bed. His mother, Mrs. J., reported that she suffered from severe migraine attacks and always needed strong medication to relieve her pain. Mrs. J. described Jack as a perfectionist who became very upset when things did not go as planned. Nevertheless,

Table V
Children's Headache Interview: behaviors during headache attacks

I'm going to ask you whether you do any of these things, how often and whether they help to get rid of your headaches. Do you ever . . .

Rest or sleep? *Always   Mild to complete relief*

Put warm/cold cloths on your head? *Never*

Rub or massage the painful area? *Rarely   No relief*

Try to ignore the pain and keep doing what you were doing? *Sometimes   No relief*

Do something physically active to get rid of your headache, for example, ride your bike, go for a walk, get some exercise? *Sometimes   No relief*

Stop physical activities and sports? *A lot   No relief*

Do anything socially active to get rid of your headache, for example, play with/hang out with your friends, invite a friend over, call a friend? *Never*

Stop playing/socializing with your friends? *A lot   No relief*

Try to keep your mind busy, for example by playing computer games, reading, coloring, or writing? *Never*

Try to figure out what caused the headache? *Never*

Think or imagine pleasant or good things to keep your mind off the headache and to relax? *Never*

Take medicine? *Rarely   No relief*

Do you do anything else that I haven't mentioned? (Specify) *Nothing* she believed that humidity, heat, and noise were the main causes for his headache attacks. Mrs. J. noted these environmental factors as the triggers on Jack's headache logs, even though he was also experiencing stress at those times. She did not help him to resolve the stress, but encouraged him to remove himself from the situation and rest. Mrs. J was unintentionally teaching Jack to be disabled.

In order to evaluate whether such family responses are reinforcing children's disability, the therapist first evaluates whether children's sick time (length of time and extent of physical limitations) is proportional to headache severity (pain intensity, headache length, and accompanying nausea). Some children are very disabled for a certain time period, regardless of headache severity. If so, their parents or primary care providers usually are reinforcing this disability. They may have directly taught children that they should stop all activities and rest. If parents have not recognized relevant stress triggers, they may have more subtly encouraged children's disability by allowing children to avoid stressful situations at the first hint of a headache.

As described in Chapter 4, the major trigger for recurrent headache attacks is children's anxiety about some aspect of their lives. The therapist can identify the source of anxiety for most children from their responses on the CHI. Since parents' responses during their interviews clearly reveal whether they recognize the "stressors" in children's lives, the therapist can quickly ascertain whether they are assisting children to resolve the stress and thereby prevent new headache attacks. When parents ignore underlying anxiety and report that environmental stimuli cause the headache, they usually attempt to minimize children's exposure to the supposed triggers. The resulting "avoidance behaviors" may be inappropriate because the suspected triggers were not confirmed, because the behaviors adversely impact children (e.g., limiting physical activities, imposing restrictive diets), or because the family is avoiding addressing the true causes. When parents report that some undiagnosed medical condition is responsible for children's headaches, they continually seek additional medical consultations and diagnostic investigations. Their exclusive focus on finding a medical cause prevents them from addressing the real causes.

EMOTIONAL FACTORS

As described in Chapter 4, situation-specific stress associated with children's normal social, school, and leisure activities and with family relationships is the primary cause of recurrent headache. The therapist can identify the source of stress for most children from their responses on the CHI, as they converse about what children do during the week and how they feel about various aspects of their life. In this part of the interview, the therapist begins with general inquiries, followed by more explicit questions to capture children's feelings about their activities. For example, after asking children where they attend school and what grade they are in, the therapist probes gently about the school and what it is like to be a student, leading to more specific questions about children's subjects, their grades, homework, classmates, and teachers. School-related stress may be an important cause for headache, even when headache attacks do not prevent children from attending school. Although some children with school-related stress will develop headache attacks fairly regularly during certain periods (e.g., during a difficult class, in gym class, or during the recess or lunch period when they should be interacting with peers), many develop headache after school or on weekends. The temporal pattern of headache onset is relevant, but it is not sufficient to reveal underlying sources of stress. Instead, the therapist interprets the temporal pattern in accordance with the interview data on children's feelings and subsequently confirms the presence and type of situation-specific stress with the headache logs.

School stress usually is related to peer relationships (difficulty in making or keeping friends, in dealing with teasing or criticism, and in coping when peer pressures compete with family values, and generalized feelings of discomfort and inadequacy) or to the satisfactory completion of schoolwork (difficulty in understanding the material presented verbally, in completing assignments on time, in competing on tests or in physical activities, and in accepting less-than-perfect evaluations).

Anxiety related to sports and leisure activities is a common source of stress for children. Often, the therapist notes a close temporal link between the activity and headache onset. In many instances, children report that the activity is fun. The therapist guides children to talk about specific events and interactions (e.g., a competition, a certain practice session, the coach's behaviors toward different children, and parents' reactions to the child's performance). Children may gradually reveal that the activity used to be fun, but is no longer enjoyable. The say that they feel pressured to perform, and that they do not want to disappoint their teammates, parents, or coach. They may feel a general discomfort, but are unsure why, especially if their parents regard the activity as a special luxury. Some children may be stressed by an overly busy schedule, rather than by one particular activity. These children are frequently enrolled in so many supervised and structured activities that they lack time to relax and independently plan what they would like to do. In contrast, other children are stressed by a schedule where they have limited physical activity and lack the natural stress reduction that exercise can provide.

Some children experience headache due to familial stress. Although headache onset may coincide with significant family stressors (e.g., divorce, illness, and job loss), the temporal pattern is less revealing for the majority of children, whose headache attacks occur in a seemingly unpredictable manner. However, as the therapist reviews children's headache logs, a subtle pattern emerges of headache onset linked to family activities (or activities with certain family members), sibling disagreements, conflicts with a parent over a child's increasing need for independence, or periods of discord among extended family members.

In addition to situation-specific stress, the therapist evaluates whether other emotional factors are relevant. Essentially, the therapist interprets the information from the interviews to determine the extent to which parents and children are anxious about the etiology of the headache problem and its prognosis. As described above, most parents will readily express their fears about an undiagnosed medical condition, continuing headache attacks, and increasing disability. They are equally candid in describing their child's emotional reactions to the headache attacks and the impact of the episodes on the entire family. The therapist relies on parent and child information to assess children's general emotional temperament—whether they are anxious, have high expectations for achievement, and tend to suppress or deny their true feelings. In the CHI, the therapist uses concrete problems that children routinely encounter to determine whether they recognize their feelings and to assess their problem-solving ability.

During the assessment, the therapist may identify major and long-standing emotional problems for children that suggest mood disorders, anxiety disorders, and somatoform disorders. In these instances, the headache attacks appear to be symptoms of those disorders rather than recurrent migraine or tension-type headache. We have seen adolescents who have features of several mental health disorders, but who do not fully satisfy the DSM-IV criteria for a specific disorder (Diagnostic and Statistical Manual of Mental Disorders 1994). (Although we are documenting their pain profiles, we have not yet compiled a sufficient number for an accurate descriptive study.)

At the end of the pain assessment, the therapist reviews the features of recurrent headache and provides general treatment recommendations. Although the session may have revealed some of the probable causes, parents are informed that the therapist must carefully review the information obtained in the assessment and children's headache logs before completing an assessment report and developing a specific treatment plan. The therapist schedules a feedback appointment in 2–6 weeks, depending on headache frequency, to obtain a representative record of headache activity.

FEEDBACK APPOINTMENT

The components of the feedback appointment are outlined in Table I. The therapist first reviews the headache calendar and logs to determine whether attacks are linked to specific situations or emotional states. He or she also notes how children and parents treated each attack to assess whether they followed the pain control recommendations provided at the previous appointment, and confirms whether or not the pattern of headache activity, stressful situations, and child and parent behaviors is consistent with the causes and contributing factors identified in the pain assessment.

The therapist meets individually with parents, first inquiring generally about children's recent headache attacks and providing an opportunity for parents to ask questions before presenting the specific assessment results. With this approach, the therapist can assess whether parents are beginning to recognize causative factors and were able to follow treatment recommendations. Most parents ask about potential triggers that they have just noticed and want to know how they could respond in a way that can help children relieve pain without inadvertently prolonging their disability. Many parents spontaneously describe new insights they have acquired since the pain assessment. The therapist then describes the factors responsible for children's recurrent headache, using the model introduced previously during the assessment (as shown in Fig. 3). The therapist completes the model before the feedback appointment and, if necessary, revises the list of contributing factors after reviewing the headache logs. The therapist describes each factor, using concrete examples from the assessment interviews or headache logs. For example, Lily, a 10-year-old girl, had experienced about two moderately strong headaches each week for 3 years. As shown in Fig. 3, several cognitive, behavioral, and emotional factors contributed to her headaches. However, the therapist believed that Lily's extremely high expectations for her performance were the primary cause. She used examples from the CHI to show that Lily worried regularly about how well she would complete school assignments and that she subsequently developed headaches. In fact, Lily had even worried about how to complete her headache log. The therapist commented to Mrs. L. that the logs were very unusual—Lily had carefully printed all information, with capital letters precisely twice the size of lower-case letters (as if she had used a ruler to measure letter size), that she had used appropriate punctuation, and corrected spelling errors. Lily had used stickers on her headache calendar to show her pain-free days; each sticker was carefully centered in the middle of the relevant day. Lily's headache records quickly confirmed her perfectionistic tendencies and enabled Mrs. L. to describe other examples of overly conscientious behaviors.

Factors Involved in Lily's Pain: Summary Sheet

Cognitive Factors

Lack of understanding of the causes of headache and the best treatments

✓Expectations for continuing pain, vomiting, and disability

✓Lack of knowledge about drug and nondrug therapies for pain control

Failure to recognize or know how to resolve stress

Behavioral Factors

High behavioral distress

Withdrawal from all activities

Strong secondary gains from temporary stress reduction

✓Lack of active and independent methods of pain control

✓Inconsistent parental responses (support to frustration)

Failure to resolve stress

Positive family history of headaches

Emotional Factors

✓Anticipatory anxiety related to nausea and vomiting

✓Situation-specific stress related to unrealistic expectations for her academic performance

✓Stress related to developing new peer relationships

✓Anxiety in new situations

✓Increasing anxiety because of her failure to resolve stressful issues effectively

⇕   ⇕   ⇕

Lily

STRESSFUL   HEADACHE
SITUATION

Treatment Recommendations:

1. Assist Lily to develop more realistic expectations for her performance.
2. Assist Lily (and her parents) to effectively identify and resolve stressful problems, particularly her anxiety about making new friends.
3. Teach Lily and her parents about pain systems, recurrent headache, and true headache triggers.
4. Teach Lily simple and practical stress reducing strategies to reduce her pain thereby increasing her independent control over her pain.
5. Assist Lily's parents to respond to Lily's pain complaints in a consistent manner that encourages her to be active and independent.

Fig. 3. Headache model depicting the causative and contributing factors for a 10-year-old girl with recurrent headache. Check marks denote the primary factors.

Reviewing each factor with parents, the therapist makes a clinical judgment as to whether it is primary or secondary. The therapist defines primary factors as causative, emphasizing to parents that the treatment plan must address those factors to truly alleviate children's recurrent headache (as denoted by the check marks in Fig. 3). Secondary factors contribute to children's pain, distress, and headache disability. While these factors should also be addressed in a treatment program, they are not primarily responsible. We make this distinction to emphasize to families which of the multiple factors should be the main focus of their child's cognitive-behavioral program.

The therapist may inform parents that children are likely to develop, or may already have, a disability problem in addition to a headache problem. Parents usually consider that any disability is a direct consequence of the headache attacks, so they often do not recognize that children have developed an independent behavioral problem (e.g., children miss school for a prolonged period even for mild headache attacks). In these situations, the therapist clearly explains that the treatment program should focus both on the headache problem and on the emerging disability problem. Otherwise, parents will continue to reinforce children's disability behaviors while they wait for the therapist "to fix the headaches."

After discussing all factors, the therapist recommends whether children should participate in a treatment program designed to help families to achieve specific treatment objectives, as listed for Lily at the bottom of Fig. 3. The therapist presents each objective separately so that parents can understand how it will address one or more of the listed causative factors. Parents reported that it was easier to understand the rationale for the treatment when the objectives were presented individually so that they could discuss each item thoroughly before proceeding to the next. Depending on their preference, therapists either write down each objective as they describe it to parents or cover the lower part of the model until they are ready to introduce the next objective.

The goal of the feedback appointment is to provide our best interpretation of the causes and contributing factors for children's recurrent headache. When parents do not accept our conclusions and recommendations, we generally do not argue about who is right. Instead, we attempt to shift the focus to addressing those factors that the therapist and parent both agree are contributing in some way to the child's headache problem. With this approach, we hope to convince parents that it would be useful to enroll children in the program and give it a chance to help them—even if they think it may only help in a minor way. (Our integrated research and clinical program does not receive fees for enrolling children in a treatment program.)

However, when parents insist that children's headaches are caused only by environmental triggers, we confront them as tactfully as possible with the fact that we have not yet (over a period of 17 years in which we have assessed children with headache) identified any child whose headache attacks were provoked by environmental factors independent of other, more salient, factors. We emphasize the negative, albeit unintentional, repercussions of focusing exclusively on these factors, including that children will probably develop "learned" environmental triggers, that headache attacks will continue because the family is not addressing the underlying causes, and that children will learn to use pain as a reason for avoiding stressful situations.

After providing feedback to parents, the therapist invites children to join them and reviews the main findings in straightforward and age-appropriate language. Using the child's own terminology (from the assessment interviews), following the pain model, and including examples from the headache logs, the therapist briefly explains that there are several reasons why children are developing headache, emphasizing a few of the causes. Generally, this approach benefits parents: they are able to listen to the feedback information again in simpler language, they do not have to contribute to the discussion, and they can observe how readily children accept the findings. Children typically are interested, understand the link between their feelings and their headache, and volunteer new examples of how some stressful situations cause or exacerbate headache. (The therapist does not reveal any confidential information that children provided during the assessment.) The therapist meets with adolescents individually at the feedback session, describing the assessment results and treatment recommendations and emphasizing the multifactorial etiology and the need for a multimodal treatment targeted at each of the responsible factors. The therapist then outlines the treatment program (two to four sessions at 2-week intervals, where the therapist and child or adolescent will work together to achieve specific treatment goals), and concludes the session by asking children or adolescents if they would like to participate in this program.

After obtaining appropriate consent, the therapist prepares a report to summarize the results of the pain assessment and feedback session for the referring physician or health care provider, as shown in the following pain assessment report.

PAIN ASSESSMENT REPORT

Kendra, an 8-year-old girl, was referred to the pain clinic for assessment and management. The purposes of the assessment were to evaluate the sensory characteristics of her headaches, to identify the primary and secondary factors responsible, to determine whether her headaches were characteristic of recurrent headache, and to recommend appropriate treatment. The assessment included structured interviews with Kendra and her mother (Mrs. K.), and standardized pain questionnaires were used.

HEADACHE CHARACTERISTICS

Onset: Gradual onset, 5 years ago.
Frequency: Approximately two headaches per week.
Location: Unilateral; left or right eye and temporal region.
Length: Approximately 2 hours.
Intensity: Described as a "strong" pain; numerical rating usually 8 (on the 0–10 Colored Analogue Scale).
Quality: "Pushing" and aching.
Accompanying symptoms: Nausea, lethargy, photophobia, and phonophobia.
Seasonal/temporal variation: Headache attacks usually begin at school.
Pain control: Lacks effective methods. For mild headaches, she puts her head down on her desk for a few minutes. For severe headaches, she sleeps, and intermittently uses acetaminophen.
Perceived control: None.
Level of disability: Moderate; she misses class time and is bedridden at least twice a week.
Triggers: Exclusive focus on external factors: various foods and drinks, weather (humidity, bright sun, change of weather, low or high barometric pressure).
Other pains: No other recurrent pains.
Family history of pain: Strong positive history. Mrs. K. suffers from debilitating migraines; Mr. K. has chronic back pain.

HEADACHE HISTORY

Kendra has had occasional headaches since she was 3 years old. During the past 2 years, they have increased in frequency and length, increasing her disability. Kendra reports that severe headaches are preceded by a visual aura. She is nauseous during many headaches.

There is a strong history of chronic pain within the family. Mrs. K. has a long-standing history of frequent, debilitating migraine headache. She has tried various medications, but all have been ineffective. Mr. K. is on long-term disability due to a work-related accident; he has severe chronic back pain.

RELEVANT PERSONAL HISTORY

Family: There is some family stress. Kendra lives at home with her parents and brother Scott (11 years). Kendra reported that she and Scott fight continually and that she does not like to play with him. Mr. K. requires much assistance; he is at home most of the time and Kendra perceives that he is constantly nagging her about helping around the house. Mrs. K. commented that he teases Kendra, but mainly to remind her to complete her chores and homework.

School: There is moderate stress at school. Kendra is in the third grade and has average grades. She is frequently disruptive in class and freely admits that she does not like to work, but prefers to socialize with her classmates. Her teachers informed Mrs. K. that they are constantly reminding her to listen to them and that she frequently disturbs other children. (A previous assessment conducted by a school psychologist indicates that she does not have a learning disability.)

Activities: There is moderate to high stress in her peer relationships. Kendra enjoys swimming lessons and karate lessons regularly, where she receives individual coaching. She has a history of disruptive behaviors in sports and activities that require teamwork.

Personality: Kendra presents as a happy, personable, and very talkative child. While she readily discusses her life, she tends to deny all typical problems children encounter and any specific problems related to her activities and relationships. In the interview, she demonstrated poor problem-solving ability. Mrs. K. reported that Kendra attempts to solve her problems independently, but she usually needs her mother's assistance. When her mother helps her, Kendra usually spends most of the time justifying her actions and opinions.

CONCLUSIONS

Kendra has a moderate pain and disability problem. The results of the assessment indicate that Kendra's headaches are typical of recurrent headache. Although several factors are maintaining her headaches, they may be precipitated primarily by underlying emotional distress, possibly caused by anxiety or low self-esteem. This distress is reflected in her difficulty in maintaining peer relationships and in resolving conflicts with classmates and teammates. Mr. K.'s pain and disability cause significant family stress. Mrs. K.'s belief that Kendra's headaches are caused only by environmental triggers and her tendency to deny the existence of any familial or school-related stress prevent her from helping Kendra to resolve the true headache triggers. Moreover, Mrs. K.'s own migraine-related disability provides a salient role model for headache disability and suffering.

Therefore, we recommended a cognitive-behavioral treatment program in which a therapist would assist Mrs. K. and Kendra in identifying and resolving the true headache triggers and in developing more effective stress management and problem-solving skills, especially regarding peer relationships. The therapist would further evaluate the role of emotional distress in maintaining her headaches and would provide counseling as needed. The therapist would teach Kendra some active and independent pain control methods and would help Mrs. K. to differentiate her own headaches from Kendra's so that she can respond to her daughter's pain complaints in a manner that encourages her to relieve her headache and minimize disability.

FEEDBACK APPOINTMENT

Mrs. K. and Kendra received feedback about the assessment results and our recommendations for treatment. Although Mrs. K. strongly believed that barometric pressure was the primary cause of Kendra's headaches, she accepted that some attacks might be stress-related and enrolled Kendra in our program. Kendra's headaches and disability improved significantly throughout the program, with headache frequency reduced to one mild attack per month.

THERAPY SESSIONS

Generally two to four therapy sessions are needed to achieve the treatment objectives. These sessions usually last 1 hour and are scheduled every 2 weeks. Children record their headache attacks throughout this period, so that the therapist can monitor headache activity, the interventions used, and the extent of disability, and determine treatment efficacy. The therapist meets with parents individually during part of each session, but usually spends the majority of time with children. In the first session, the therapist briefly reviews the key findings from the pain assessment and explains the general plan for the program. Children are encouraged to ask questions about headache triggers, drug and nondrug therapies, and the circumstances in which they get headaches. Many children ask what happens in their bodies to produce a headache. The therapist answers all questions, using simple analogies and diagrams as needed to illustrate pain mechanisms.

The therapist then helps children think about their own treatment goals—what is most important to them. The therapist guides children to choose one overall goal and the smaller steps needed to achieve that goal. Children list their goals on a blank treatment plan, usually printed on brightly colored art paper, as shown in Fig. 4. These are goals for Lily, the 10-year-old-girl whose causative factors are listed in the headache model in Fig. 3. Young children are encouraged to name their treatment plan; "Get well plan" and "My get rid of headaches plan" are popular choices. The therapist uses these forms throughout the program to mark when children have achieved a particular goal. We have noticed that children are more motivated when they think about their own goals and refer to them throughout the program than when we independently present the goals.

As time permits, the therapist continues the session by reviewing the headache logs with children to begin teaching them about what caused the headache and to discuss how similar attacks could be prevented. The therapist continues these teaching reviews in subsequent sessions and uses the most appropriate cognitive and behavioral methods to achieve children's treatment goals, building progressively from session to session. The contents of

Get Rid of Headaches Plan for Lily

MAIN GOAL: *To have fewer headaches and to be able to make them hurt less*

Goal 1:   ***To learn how pain works***
                We have pain gates
                What I think, feel, and do can increase and decrease pain

Goal 2:   ***To learn about headaches***
                There are different kinds of headaches
                Headaches vary in strength and cause, therefore treatment varies
                We can have control over headache pain

Goal 3:   ***To figure out what causes my headaches***
                Unsolved problems can lead to headaches
                What are my problems?
                What is it about school, making friends that makes me anxious?
                How can I solve my problems?

Goal 4:   ***To resolve headache causes***
                Change pain behaviors
                Use problem-solving skills
                Talk about my feelings

Goal 5:   ***To learn ways to make pain hurt less***
                Change what I think, feel, and do
                Use my pain control list
                Learn how medication works and how to use it

Fig. 4. Treatment goals for a 10-year-old girl.

each session are paced according to children's understanding and mastery of specific skills (e.g., pain control methods, stress identification, and problem-solving techniques). Although the overall treatment objectives are the same for all children (i.e., to lessen pain and modify causative factors), the emphasis of each therapy session will vary depending on the primary factors responsible for the headaches and the unique needs of each child and family. Thus, the components of the therapy sessions are described according to primary causative factors rather than according to session number.

BELIEFS ABOUT HEADACHE ETIOLOGY, PAIN CONTROL, AND STRESS

Generally, parents and children hold inaccurate beliefs about headache etiology, effective drug and nondrug therapies, and the role of environmental versus stress triggers. Erroneous beliefs are usually secondary contributing factors, but the therapist must address them early in the treatment program because parents' understanding about recurrent headache guides their behaviors when children develop headache and shapes children's emotional responses to the pain problem. Although parents receive accurate information about migraine and tension-type headache at the assessment and feedback appointment, the therapist continues to teach parents about triggers and effective therapies in subsequent sessions.

The therapist briefly reviews children's headache activity with parents, selecting one or two headache logs for discussion. The therapist asks for more details about the circumstances surrounding the attack. Parents usually describe why they responded in a particular manner, especially if they have deviated from the treatment recommendations. We follow the same format as described previously when we interpret the results of the headache logs to identify causative factors. The therapist guides parents to identify the probable triggers and discusses how parents might intervene so that those situations will no longer provoke attacks. Similarly, the therapist guides parents to identify and consider changing any behaviors that contributed to children's pain, distress, or disability.

The therapist uses the same educational approach with children, using concrete examples from headache logs to discuss headache activity and to evaluate what has been happening in school and at home. The therapist explains why some situations and emotions can provoke headache. The identification of stress triggers is an important component of every session; children should eventually recognize the true triggers without guidance. The therapist also explains that the way that children (and their parents) behaved influenced their pain, distress, and disability. The therapist then guides children to think about different behaviors that might lessen the impact of the headache. Since most children do not know any practical active pain control methods, the therapist begins to teach children a few nondrug methods.

NONDRUG PAIN CONTROL METHODS

The therapist teaches all children four specific pain control methods: attention and distraction, guided imagery, hypnotic-like suggestions for analgesia, and progressive muscle relaxation (incorporating biofeedback as needed). The approach that has proven most beneficial in our clinic has been to teach children a few standardized methods, and then to encourage them to personalize these methods or to design new methods with their parents (for younger children) or independently (for adolescents). The therapist recommends that they use these methods during headaches to complement analgesic medications, or alternatively, as the main pain control method for mild headache attacks. The therapist helps children to practice these methods during sessions and encourages children to use them during headache attacks. Children review the headache logs to evaluate which methods work best for them. Some children may require a structured behavioral management program, where they earn points for using these methods.

Attention and distraction. Most children already know that when they are truly interested and fully focused on some activity, that they can become oblivious to their surroundings. The therapist emphasizes children's ability to reduce pain by being able to control their minds (in much the same way that they are learning to control their bodies through relaxation). The most important feature is that they must concentrate fully on "something else"— an event, a distracting situation, or an activity. Their full concentration is the critical component for pain reduction, not the particular method they use to achieve it. The therapist helps children to compose a list of activities for use at home and school, as shown for an 8-year-old girl in Table VI. Children should have as much choice as possible about which pain control strategies they use. The more enjoyable the method, the more motivated children will be to use it. Although some methods temporarily pull children away from schoolwork or a sport, the therapist emphasizes that children need to "actively" relax their mind for a few minutes so that they can then resume their previous activities. The therapist explains that the method helps them to enjoy their regular activities, not avoid them.

Guided imagery. The therapist guides children to imagine a previous experience, a special event, or a fantasy; this guided imagery enables them to relax and selectively tune out pain. Children are encouraged to actively

Table VI
A 10-year-old girl's pain control list

Change what I think—think positively:
   "I can do this. I can make it better myself"
   "I can control my pain"
   "Remember what I learned"
   "I should relax"

Change how I feel:
   Stay calm
   Don't panic

Change what I do—relax:
   At home:
      Lie down (rest or sleep)
      Use an ice pack
      Take medicine, plus do something else on my list
      Do fun things:
         Watch television
         Look at picture books or magazines
         Color
         Draw
         Play cards
         Go outside
         Play with friends
         Talk to Mom or Dad
   At school:
      Take a break
      Put my head down on the desk
      Go to the washroom
      Get a drink
      Rub my forehead

immerse themselves in the image—the colors, sounds, and feelings they experience—rather than passively describe a scene. The therapist guides children initially by asking questions such as, "Remember being at the beach, think about what it was like and what you were doing. Imagine that you are there right now. How hot is the sun? Are there a lot of people there? Tell me what you are doing? Is the water cold?" While adults would tend to imagine tranquil scenes, children often choose relaxing sporting and social activities. Children can learn to use imagery independently to lessen pain and stress.

Hypnotic-like suggestions for analgesia. Use of hypnotic-like suggestions for analgesia is a more abstract cognitive method that children learn after they are able to use guided imagery. The term "hypnotic-like" refers to the fact that the suggestions are similar to those used to induce analgesia under hypnosis, but children do not receive a standard induction procedure. Instead, the therapist builds on the skills children have mastered when they learned to tune out pain by selectively concentrating their attention else-where. Children previously needed an activity or image to enable them to concentrate away from the pain. The therapist teaches them that they may be able to tune out pain without needing the distraction or the imagery. Chil-dren have usually experienced some tingling or numbness sensations, either because of a lack of circulation while sitting or sleeping or because of a local anesthetic. They also know that sleeping usually relieves their head-ache. Children thus can readily accept that they will not feel pain as strongly when different parts of their bodies "fall asleep." They gradually learn that they can make a body region "go to sleep." The therapist initially uses imagery to teach children. For example, a young child might begin by imag-ining a television character with special powers. The therapist works with the child's imagination and creativity, suggesting that he or she has special powers to block pain, and provides consistent positive suggestions, such as: "Notice that your head now feels sleepy so when I touch you on the fore-head, it feels lighter than before. It seems as if you don't feel the hurt as much as before. You are learning how to turn down the pain switch." The therapist often uses the analogy of a dimmer switch, rather than an on-off switch, so that children can be successful in progressively reducing pain strength. With practice, many children can learn to turn the pain switch down when they have a headache.

Relaxation and biofeedback. Relaxation techniques provide an excel-lent physical intervention that children can use independently. The therapist introduces progressive muscle relaxation to demonstrate the difference be-tween a relaxed and tense body state. Children quickly understand that any type of pain can be intensified when muscles are tightened and stressed. Since fear and anxiety creates some body tension, children need to recog-nize when they are tense and then learn to relax physically. Children are usually motivated about how to control their bodies because they want to change the physical states that increase pain during headache attacks. With progressive relaxation, the therapist coaches children first to breathe deeply and regularly, and then progressively to tighten and relax different body regions, starting with easy areas (e.g., toes or fists) and gradually moving toward the shoulder, neck, and forehead regions. The relaxation session is audiotaped so that children can practice at home.

Biofeedback is an excellent tool for teaching children how their bodies react involuntarily to pain- and anxiety-arousing situations. Biofeedback is particularly useful for adolescents who do not believe in an association between headache attacks and their emotional reactions to stress. Although initially they may believe that certain situations are not stressful, signals from a biofeedback unit enable them to see or hear how their body responds to discussing these triggers with the therapist (often with increased surface muscle activity). They realize that the situation is provoking a physical response. The therapist teaches children and adolescents to lower these amplified signals, using deep breathing, progressive muscle relaxation, guided imagery, or hypnosis.

As the therapist assists children to more effectively resolve stressful issues, biofeedback is also a valuable tool to teach children that the situations no longer exert the same negative arousal. However, we do not use biofeedback regularly for children who have unrealistically high expectations for their performance; such children often feel more stress during training sessions because they want to achieve unrealistic reductions in the amplified signals. Instead, we may use biofeedback once to illustrate how their high expectations can easily cause frustration.

Children learn to incorporate several methods into a flexible repertoire of pain-control strategies. The emphasis is placed on the manner in which they are reducing pain, rather than on the "magical" properties of any one method. Children should not develop a false reliance on a particular method; instead, they should learn the principles of pain management, so that they will naturally evolve their own methods. (Nondrug methods are reviewed in detail in Chapter 6.)

PARENT AND CHILD BEHAVIORS

Many parents respond to children's pain complaints in a manner that inadvertently increases distress, pain, and disability. When parents seek further medical tests, attribute headaches solely to environmental triggers, and fail to identify and resolve relevant stress triggers, they contribute directly to the cycle of repeat attacks. Parents receive guidelines for consistent headache management at the assessment, and the therapist works with parents and children throughout the sessions to modify these behaviors. In particular, the therapist works with families to encourage them to follow a predictable headache management plan (as described in Chapter 7). The therapist uses children's headache logs to learn specifically what children did during headache attacks and how parents responded. The therapist then guides parents to respond more consistently to children's pain complaints in a manner that promotes children's independent coping and encourages them to continue their regular activities, particularly attending school.

The focus of children's sessions is to progressively increase their consistent use of a headache management plan, which includes more active pain control methods and more effective stress management techniques. The therapist uses basic behavioral management principles (encouragement and praise) when reviewing children's records of what happened during headache attacks. The therapist counsels children to identify and resolve causative stress triggers (as described in the next section on emotional factors). The therapist teaches children that their pain control lists are essential "prescriptions" and guides them to select an appropriate method based on headache severity, causative factors, and resulting disability. Children may need both analgesic medication and sleep to relieve severe pain, but for moderate pain they may only need medication and may be able to continue their daily activities. Nondrug methods generally relieve mild pain.

As necessary, the therapist counsels children about the enormous negative impact of constantly avoiding certain sports, social activities, or school. Children gradually learn that the avoidance increases disability rather than decreasing pain. The therapist uses concrete analogies with young children to distinguish protective behaviors from disability behaviors. For example: "Suppose that you broke your arm when you were playing with your friends and that you had a cast on for a couple of months so that the bone would heal. The cast was removed and the doctor says that your arm is healed. But when you get home from his office, you are afraid that you might hurt it again. You start holding your arm in a special way and you stop playing with your friends and doing some of the other things that you did before you broke it. Instead, you keep it safe and protected as if it was still in the cast and broken. Would this be good to do?" Almost all children immediately answer that it would be inappropriate. The therapist uses this example to explain that protective behavior (like wearing a cast) was appropriate when the bone was healing, but becomes disability behavior when the bone has healed. In the same way, some behaviors are protective when parents are trying to understand why children are developing headache, but become disabling when we understand the headaches. The therapist encourages children to use pain control methods and to resume activities as quickly as possible after, *or even during*, headache attacks in order to lessen disability. With young children, the therapist focuses on helping children to "unlearn" bad habits.

Significant disability that includes prolonged recovery periods independent of headache severity, limited physical or social activities for fear of headache attacks, and excessive school absences is reinforced by protective parents. Thus, the therapist also explains the distinction between protective and disabling behaviors to parents, emphasizing that parents' behaviors were appropriate early on in the cycle of repeat attacks, but are now inappropriate. As needed, the therapist emphasizes that children are developing (or already have) a separate disability problem as well as a pain problem. In order to relieve the disability, parents must lessen the secondary gains associated with headache complaints such as increased attention, special privileges, reduced expectations for performance, and avoidance of unpleasant or stressful situations. Therapists use this adult approach when discussing disability behaviors with adolescents.

The focus of parents' sessions is to progressively increase their support of children's more independent pain control during headache attacks, to advise them on how to assist children to resolve the stress triggers responsible for the headaches documented on the logs, and to teach them how to minimize any maladaptive behaviors that contribute to increased pain or repeat attacks. When children report a headache, the therapist guides parents to acknowledge the pain but simultaneously encourage active and independent pain management. For example, parents might respond: "I'm sorry. Let's get your pain control list," and help children to select an appropriate method. Parents learn that our emphasis is on helping children to manage their pain independently and to understand the causes for their headaches. Children monitor headache activity themselves; they design and use pain control lists, and ultimately they evaluate the efficacy of the treatment. The therapist advises parents about how to assist their children in a manner that is not directive, but which supports their children's treatment decisions and their attempts to identify and resolve causative factors. Parents' behaviors should enhance positive coping and minimize disability.

Some parents need extra help in changing their behaviors, especially if children are excessively distressed during headache attacks or are extremely disabled by headache. The therapist may then provide additional written guidelines for what parents should say and do. The therapist lessens the pressure on parents by informing young children (in front of their parents) that their parents have rules or a headache plan that they too must follow, emphasizing that they are the therapist's rules and that the parents (just like the children) have some homework. When appropriate, the therapist prepares similar guidelines for classroom teachers and caregivers to enable them to respond consistently to children during all headache attacks. As an example, the therapist added the following rule to Lily's guidelines: "Do not let Lily's headaches prevent her from doing her chores, schoolwork, going to her music lessons, or playing with her friends. When she is stressed or overwhelmed, help her to figure out how to complete her work or join the activity so that she is not as overwhelmed by it."

The therapist also evaluates whether parents are receiving any secondary gains from children's disability. For example, parents with a similar pain problem may believe that their limitations regarding work, physical, and social situations are beyond their control because their disability is a direct and unavoidable consequence of their pain. These parents unintentionally model disability. Some of these parents actively reinforce their children's withdrawal from schoolwork and household responsibilities. They seem to need their children to be similarly disabled, as though this would prove that their own pain problem is debilitating. In these instances, the therapist assists parents to understand that children's disability is different than their own, and attempts to gain their support in following our treatment recommendations. Other parents may benefit from time off work to "nurse" young children or enjoy sharing special activities with children while they are recovering from headache. These parents also unintentionally reinforce children's disability. The therapist assists them to substitute more positive responses—shifting the emphasis from sickness to recovery, from dependence to independence, and from passive suffering to the healthy resumption of activities, suggesting some activities that parents can share with children.

Structured behavioral management programs are designed for those children who do not follow the therapist's recommendations to use active pain control methods during headache attacks and for those families who continue to reinforce children's disability behaviors. The therapist targets the specific behaviors (of both children and parents) that exacerbate children's pain and disability. The therapist selects the most maladaptive behaviors and outlines a series of progressive steps that families can follow so as to eventually change those behaviors. Only one maladaptive behavior at a time is targeted for reduction, with other behaviors added after children (or parents) have consistently modified their previous behaviors. A reward system is designed that will motivate children (and parents) to achieve positive behavioral criteria. Stickers, points to be applied toward a treat, special time with parents, increased social activities with peers, or increased independence in decision-making are effective rewards. Both parents and children must agree to follow the program consistently, with rewards contingent on the child's fulfilling well-defined behavioral criteria, such as using a method from the pain control list, staying in school, identifying the real headache trigger, and using problem-solving techniques to reduce stress.

Behavioral programs are ideally suited for parents who need a therapist's support "at home" when they are trying to follow treatment recommendations, such as responding in a certain way when children first complain about a headache or refraining from picking up children at school. This support seems most effective when a behavioral contract, containing clear information about what should happen throughout the program to eventually reduce headache and disability, is signed by parents and children.

EMOTIONAL FACTORS

Families typically are anxious and fearful as they search for the cause of children's headache. Much of their anxiety, fear, and frustration with the health care system (when their experience has been many consultations and no definitive answers) is lessened from the information they receive at the assessment and feedback appointments. Typically, families continue to have some anxiety until they notice some tangible improvements in children— their outlook about the headache problem, the frequency and severity of headache attacks, and the extent of their disability. Family anxieties and fears progressively lessen throughout the course of the program. The therapist assists parents to express any underlying fears and uses the headache review section of each session to allay their concerns, using concrete examples from children's own lives when possible. All parents are asked to sign a consent form enabling us to use the information we gain in treating their children in our educational, clinical, and research programs. When therapists need to use an example, they are thus able to tap a rich resource of real-life scenarios without identifying children or families.

Many potential sources of situation-specific stress are associated with children's normal social, school, and leisure activities (as described in Chapter 4). Each session begins with a pain update and review of headache logs, in which the therapist helps children to identify possible headache triggers, describing first the general importance of these triggers for other children as a neutral way of introducing their importance to children in the program. This approach is particularly important for children who are hesitant to admit that they are stressed and for adolescents who are embarrassed or perceive that they have failed in certain situations. Children are then encouraged to discuss whether the same situations exist for them. The therapist helps them to understand that it is normal to experience discomfort or stress from those situations, suggesting why those situations might produce anxiety and guiding children to consider alternative solutions or behaviors in those situations—solutions that might more effectively lessen stress.

The therapist introduces problem-solving techniques to children in the first session, guiding children to identify a problem they have encountered since the feedback appointment and teaches them to follow 10 steps: (1) honestly think about how they feel; (2) identify the real problem; (3) determine whose problem it really is; (4) figure out what they want to happen; (5) stop and think about different solutions; (6) think about what will happen for each solution; (7) figure out which solutions may be good ideas and which are bad ideas; (8) throw out the bad ideas and keep the good ones; (9) try one of the good ideas; (10) think about what happened— was the problem solved and did they feel better? Problem solving is usually a major component of each session because many children need assistance from the therapist and their parents if they have developed a pattern of denying stressful situations.

The therapist teaches children to recognize, discuss, and develop effective problem-solving and stress management techniques. As mentioned previously, the therapist can use biofeedback to show them how stress affects the body. The therapist attaches the surface electrodes and then converses with children about what has happened in their lives since the last appointment. The therapist deliberately introduces stress-inducing topics into the conversation. Although children initially may not admit that certain situations provoked stress, they often exhibit much higher electrical activity when they talk about those situations. The therapist helps children to understand that they must address the situation so that they do not remain distressed. In homework assignments, children demonstrate their ability to think about practical solutions to the routine stressful situations they experience. Parents learn how to assist children in following their 10-step program. Parents gradually acquire more insight as to the probable stress triggers and often request assistance in responding to the stressful situations that have developed for their children.

Parents often seek assistance in helping children to set more realistic expectations for their performance. Parents typically want children to strive to do their best, but while some parents equate doing your best with being the best, most do not. In fact, many parents readily identify children's high expectations for achievement as a source of stress, but they do not know how to change them. They may have adopted a pattern of dismissing children's expectations, rather than helping children to change them. Or, they may have failed to recognize the steadily increasing strain on children as they try to "excel in all that they do" as the demands (schoolwork, sports, household responsibilities, and part-time jobs) have progressively increased.

The longer children have held unrealistically high expectations for their performance or the longer they have had perfectionistic tendencies, the more time will be required for them to truly change how they evaluate their performance. The therapist may follow these children monthly for a few sessions after the more intensive phase of the pain management program, to help them and their parents as they continue to address the ongoing situations that provoke children's dissatisfaction with their performance. Some children with perfectionistic tendencies will attempt to please the therapist by stating that they are no longer bothered by less-than-perfect grades. But this is not true, and their suppressed disappointment builds until they develop a headache. Therapists need to work with these children and their parents by focusing on the specific circumstances that disappoint children and helping children to learn how to distinguish between doing their best and being the best.

OUTCOME EVALUATION

At the end of each session, the therapist reviews children's progress, checking off any treatment objectives that have been achieved and adding new ones. As children gain new insights into causes and contributing factors, they frequently wish to update their goals and may add some specific goals about solving continuing problems. In the first two sessions, the therapist generally leads the discussion about whether any treatment goals have been achieved and then refers to the goal sheet to emphasize what children should focus on during the period until their next appointment. Gradually, the therapist shifts the responsibility for evaluating progress to children, guiding them only as necessary. As described previously, the treatment emphasis throughout all sessions is for parents and children to apply the principles of pain control, stress identification, and problem resolution they have learned to new situations that naturally arise within the family, in children's peer and social groups, in the school environment, and during sports and leisure activities.

Children have completed their overall treatment objectives when they are using independent pain control methods as part of a consistent treatment plan and when they and their parents have modified the primary contributing factors that were identified in the pain assessment. The frequency, intensity, and length of headache attacks typically decrease progressively as children achieve these objectives. For example, Lily (whose treatment recommendations are presented in Fig. 3) completed a four-session program. Her headaches decreased significantly from two moderate-to-strong attacks per week to one mild attack per month. She managed these attacks effectively and was no longer disabled. While most children experience concomitant reductions in headache frequency and intensity, some experience only reductions in headache frequency. Nevertheless, all children who achieve their treatment objectives are less distressed and disabled by headache. At the final session, the therapist reviews with both parents and children how and why the headaches have changed since the pain assessment. Before formally discharging them from the program, the therapist emphasizes that children may continue to develop some headaches in response to stressful situations—stress that they either fail to recognize or are unable to resolve. Their headache attacks may temporarily remove them from the source of stress, but they should follow the plan they have learned to control the pain and its source—the stressful situation. At discharge, the therapist informs parents privately about the headache characteristics that signal a different type of headache and may warrant further medical consultation, as detailed in Chapter 3.

Most children are discharged at the third or fourth session, but some may require additional sessions to achieve their treatment goals. The therapist then schedules a follow-up appointment—either a phone consultation or another session 4–6 weeks later—to can confirm whether or not children can continue the treatment plan independently. After the follow-up, the therapist prepares a discharge summary for the family physician, including an objective report of headache improvement and documentation of the progress achieved on all recommendations outlined previously in the pain assessment report.

TREATMENT DILEMMAS

Certain therapy situations are exceptionally challenging. Three common situations include children who complain of headache, but do not experience headache as frequently as they complain; children who are excessively and continually disabled by headache, even though attacks are infrequent; and children who have multiple learned triggers. (These situations were described in Chapter 7.) Two other situations include children for whom the recurrent headache problem serves an important adaptive family function and children whose parents outwardly support the program, but continually undermine treatment efficacy. The cognitive-behavioral program is generally ineffective in these situations. Instead, children and families should be referred for individual and family counseling.

HEADACHE SERVES AN ADAPTIVE ROLE WITHIN THE FAMILY

For some families, children's recurrent headache attacks serve an important role in maintaining family harmony. Their adaptive significance may not be evident until the therapist has developed a positive working relationship with children. The therapist notes that the headache problem diverts the family focus onto the health of the child and away from other problems. For example, a young girl had frequent headache attacks as she was getting ready for bed. At the assessment, the mother reported that she stayed with the child until she fell asleep. However, the therapist learned during the program that the mother slept with her daughter all night, often using her daughter's headaches to avoid sleeping with her husband.

Generally, the signs are more subtle. The therapist notes that the usual behaviors that prolong headache disability are not simply "bad habits" intended to comfort children. Instead, the behaviors seem to be driven by some underlying and unexpressed need to keep children sick or to have a distinctive pain problem. On meeting both parents, the therapist often detects discord in their attitudes about the headache and in their differing perspectives of the disruptive impact on family life. Mothers may quit jobs (that on closer discussion they found dissatisfactory) to care for children. One (or both) parents may use the child's headaches to control the behaviors of siblings or extended family members, or to avoid certain family activities.

If the child's headache problem seems to be satisfying a greater family need, the therapist discusses these conclusions with parents and revises the feedback information about the causative and contributing factors. In almost all cases, the therapist recommends that the family (or parents) receive counseling to address these newly identified factors. Such long-standing issues usually require more specialized family therapy for resolution before children can optimally benefit from a specific headache management program.

PARENTS WHO UNDERMINE TREATMENT EFFICACY

When the therapist describes the causes and contributing factors for children's headaches at the feedback session, some parents express doubts about the role of stress. Most parents agree to enroll children in the program and agree to support the treatment recommendations, but they may only agree outwardly with the therapist. Throughout the program, they consistently subvert the therapist's efforts to help children. Rather than following the treatment plan, they encourage their children's disability and increase their children's reliance on them; moreover, they explicitly deny triggers or minimize their importance. In some instances, parents debrief children as they drive home after a session, explaining how the therapist did not fully understand the situation.

These parents challenge almost every conclusion and interpretation—usually subtly (claiming that the other parent or their family physician questions the therapist's actions). They often announce at the beginning of each session (in a somewhat pleased manner) that children's headache attacks have not yet improved and that the treatment plan does not work. Where it is possible to document concretely how parents are adversely affecting the program, the therapist will confront parents with the evidence. This discussion must be begun very tactfully, while ensuring that parents understand how they are truly undermining the therapeutic process. The therapist then can spend additional time with parents during sessions to help them support their children. Some parents change their behaviors, but others take offense and withdraw children from the program. Some adolescents may experience significant headache improvement regardless of their parents' behaviors, but parent support is an essential component of our treatment program for most children and treatment efficacy is severely compromised when parents work against the therapist.

SUMMARY

This cognitive-behavioral treatment program was designed for children with migraine and tension-type headache to modify the multiple factors that trigger headache attacks, exacerbate pain, prolong disability, and maintain the cycle of repeat headache attacks. A comprehensive pain assessment is the foundation of our child-centered program. The assessment provides a concise history of the headache problem, a descriptive profile of the headache characteristics, and an appraisal of whether the usual causative and contributing factors are relevant for children. The therapist provides feedback to parents and children about the responsible factors and outlines a practical treatment program. In this two-to-four-session program, the therapist assists parents and children to understand the multifactorial etiology of recurrent headache, to follow a practical treatment plan for reducing pain during headache attacks, and to modify the responsible factors so as to lessen headache attacks and headache-related disability.

This program was not designed for children whose headache attacks are caused primarily by major or long-standing emotional problems suggestive of mood disorders, anxiety disorders, and somatoform disorders. However, because many of the same contributing factors may apply, we believe that our program's cognitive-behavioral approach could be an effective component of these children's psychiatric treatment.

REFERENCES

American Psychiatric Association. *Diagnostic and Statistical Manual of Mental Disorders: DSM-IV*, 4th ed. Washington, DC: American Psychiatric Association, 1994.

McGrath PA. *Pain in Children: Nature, Assessment and Treatment*. New York: Guilford Press, 1990.

McGrath PA, Hinton GG, Boone JE. Management of recurrent headache in children. *Abstracts: 7th World Congress on Pain*. Seattle: IASP, 1993, p 151.

Correspondence to: Patricia A. McGrath, PhD, Pain Innovations, Inc., 38 Hampton Crescent, London, Ontario, Canada N6H 2N8. Fax: 519-471-8529; email: pamcgrat@julian.uwo.ca. Effective 1 July 2001: Department of Anesthesiology, School of Medicine, University of Utah, Salt Lake City, UT 84108, USA.

The Child with Headache: Diagnosis and Treatment.
Progress in Pain Research and Management, Vol. 19,
edited by Patricia A. McGrath and Loretta M. Hillier,
IASP Press, Seattle, © 2001

9

Chronic Daily Headache in Children and Adolescents

E. Wayne Holden,[a] Pamela Bachanas,[b]
Kris Kullgren,[b] and Jack Gladstein[c]

[a]ORC Macro, Inc., Atlanta, Georgia, USA; [b]Department of Psychiatry and
Behavioral Sciences, Emory University School of Medicine, Atlanta, Georgia,
USA; [c]Department of Pediatrics, University of Maryland School of Medicine,
Baltimore, Maryland, USA

Chronic daily headache (CDH) is a relatively new diagnostic category that describes a subset of headache sufferers who present with daily or near-daily headache pain in the absence of organic pathology. This category was created to characterize individuals who do not qualify for the diagnosis of episodic tension or migraine headaches, but instead present either initially or later in the course of their headache disorder with chronic daily pain. Clinical experience in specialized, tertiary care headache centers for adults in the 1980s led to the recognition that some of the most difficult headache patients to treat were those who presented with chronic daily pain. Furthermore, much of the initial clinical experience surrounding these cases suggested that intermittent episodic headaches may evolve over time into chronic pain syndromes.

The first description of CDH as a separate diagnostic entity for adults was published in the late 1980s by Mathew and colleagues (1987), describing a chronic recurrent headache that transformed from either episodic migraine or tension-type headache. In subsequent work, symptom patterns were systematically investigated in panels of adult patients (Messinger et al. 1991; Solomon et al. 1992), and specific diagnostic subcategories were proposed (Silberstein et al. 1994). More recently, population-based research has led to estimates of a relatively high point prevalence rate of 5% for CDH among adults (Scher et al. 1998; Castilo et al. 1999). Clinical trials investigating pharmacological and behavioral treatment strategies for CDH in adults have begun to appear in the literature (Holroyd et al. 1995; Peters et al. 1996; Monzon and Lainez 1998).

Much of the early work on CDH, however, did not consider developmental variations that are encountered within pediatric populations. Recurrent headache among children and adolescents is a prevalent condition with wide-ranging diagnostic characteristics that can result in substantial functional disability (Holden et al. 1998a, 1999). The psychosocial context in which children and adolescents are maturing creates a complex environmental scenario for shaping the development and course of any pain-producing condition.

Accurate prevalence rates for pediatric headache have been difficult to determine in population-based studies due to variability in both definitions and sampling frames. The different characteristics of recurrent headache in children in contrast to adults offer significant challenges to current diagnostic and classification systems (Viswanathan et al. 1998). Overall estimates for recurrent pediatric headache range from 2.5% for severe recurrent headache (Newacheck and Taylor 1992) to 5.7% for migraine (Sillanpää and Anttila 1996). Recurrent headache is the most prevalent somatoform disorder in adolescent populations (Essau et al. 1999). Specific information on CDH in children and adolescents is more limited; published prevalence estimates range from 0.2% (Sillanpää et al. 1991) to 0.9% (Abu-Arafeh and Russell 1994), but these rates most likely underestimate the true distribution of CDH within child and adolescent populations.

This chapter will address the current state of knowledge about CDH in children and adolescents. We will review diagnostic criteria, focusing on the applicability of those criteria within pediatric populations. We will briefly discuss the pathophysiology and genetics of CDH, and describe associated disability and coping and potential treatment methods (both behavioral and pharmacological). We will conclude with an overview of the clinical state of the art of the diagnosis and treatment of CDH in children and adolescents and a discussion of important priorities for the future.

CHARACTERISTICS OF CHRONIC DAILY HEADACHE

The publication of clearly operationalized diagnostic criteria for headache syndromes in 1988 by the International Headache Society (Headache Classification Committee 1988) represented a significant advance in the conceptualization and identification of recurrent headache. Chronic tension-type headache was identified as a distinct diagnostic entity. However, the devotion of a single diagnostic category to chronic headache failed to capture the diverse presentations of CDH that were being treated in clinical settings serving adults.

A more differentiated system for diagnosing CDH was proposed several years later (Silberstein et al. 1994). This classification system includes four distinct categories of CDH:

Transformed migraine is characterized by a pre-existing, well-defined migraine headache that blurs across time into chronic daily or near-daily pain that can include a mixture of autonomic and tension-type symptoms. Headache duration is greater than 4 hours per day, and symptoms have progressed with increasing frequency and decreasing severity over at least 3 months. This pattern may represent up to 50% of the cases of CDH in the adult population (Castillo et al. 1999).

Chronic tension-type headache is defined primarily by frequency (e.g., more than 180 episodes per year) and by the relative absence of autonomic nervous system symptoms. Headache pain is pressing or squeezing and bilateral. There is a history of episodic tension-type headache, with a transformation period of at least 3 months Chronic tension-type headache is the second most frequent type of CDH in the general adult population (Castillo et al. 1999).

New daily persistent headache is characterized by an abrupt onset of head pain that continues on a daily basis. Pain episodes last more than 4 hours per day and have been present for more than 1 month. There is no history of episodic migraine or tension-type headache. This type of CDH is relatively rare within the general population (Castillo et al. 1999), but is encountered more frequently within specialized headache treatment centers.

Hemicrania continua is characterized by unilateral pain that is present on a daily basis for at least 1 month. Pain is continuous but fluctuating, is of moderate severity, and lacks precipitating mechanisms. One of the hallmark characteristics of hemicrania continua is a positive response to indomethacin. This type of CDH is extremely rare in both clinical settings and the general population (Silberstein et al. 1994).

The etiology (Spierings et al. 1998), accompanying characteristics (Castillo et al. 1999; Deleu and Hanssens 1999), and treatment (Holroyd et al. 1995; Peters et al. 1996; Monzon and Lainez 1998) of CDH in adults have received substantial attention in the general headache literature over the last few years.

Investigations into the diagnostic characteristics and etiology of CDH in children and adolescents have received much less attention. Gladstein and Holden (1996) evaluated the utility of diagnostic criteria for CDH in patients at a specialty pediatric headache center. They attempted to classify children consecutively presenting with chronic daily headache pain into

Silberstein et al.'s adult criteria (1994), but found themselves unable to accurately classify 45% of the participants. An intensive qualitative investigation of the characteristics of this subgroup of patients indicated that a fifth subcategory of CDH was needed. Gladstein and Holden termed this category "comorbid headache," which described children and adolescents who presented with daily tension-type headache that was accompanied by intermittent and less frequent episodes of well-defined migraine. In these cases, transformation of migraine symptoms had not occurred. The original classification of these cases according to Silberstein et al.'s (1994) criteria and the reclassification with comorbid headache added as a fifth diagnostic category are presented in Fig. 1. These findings suggest that the onset and course of CDH may be directly influenced by developmental stage, with a different expression of symptoms in children and adolescents compared to adults. The results of this study should be qualified by the fact that it was conducted in a referred population. The distribution of diagnostic subtypes of CDH within the general pediatric population remains unknown.

The general characteristics of CDH in children and adolescents are somewhat different from those found in adults. The frequency of occurrence is similar to that of adults and by definition is daily or near-daily. A frequency of five or more days per week is necessary for a case to be included as CDH

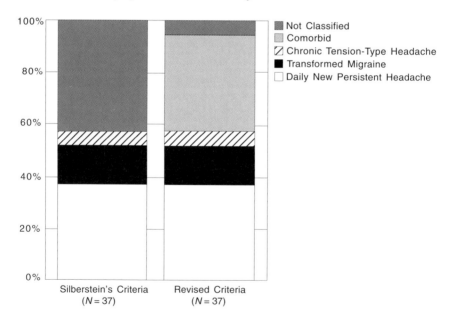

Fig. 1. Classification of 37 children with chronic headache according to the criteria of Silberstein et al. (1994) at left, and the revised criteria of Gladstein and Holden (1996) at right.

in research protocols. Location of pain can be variable, although bifrontal pain appears to be the norm in pediatric populations presenting for services in specialized treatment centers (Gladstein et al. 1993). Duration of pain may vary from relatively brief (e.g., several minutes) in chronic tension-type headache to continuous in new daily persistent headache and hemicrania continua. Severity will vary tremendously depending upon individual coping skills and responses from those in the patient's family and community. Functional disability may be expressed in school absenteeism or poor academic performance, disrupted peer or social activities, and stressful family interactions (Gladstein et al. 1997).

PATHOPHYSIOLOGY AND GENETICS

The pathophysiology of recurrent headaches in pediatric and adult populations is not completely understood. General models of headache etiology propose an inherited predisposition that is triggered by a wide range of biological or psychosocial factors. Once a headache pattern has evolved, the course of the condition is moderated by multiple individual differences ranging across the biopsychosocial spectrum (Martin 1993). Support for this more general model can be found in recent twin studies that have found a significant genetic basis for both migraine and tension-type headaches that is stronger for women than men, with unshared environmental factors moderating phenotypic expression (Honkasalo et al. 1995; Larsson et al. 1995).

On an episode-specific level, both central and peripheral nervous system components are likely to be involved in headaches. Unstable serotonergic pathways and inflammatory neuropeptides have received support as factors involved in initiating and sustaining individual headache episodes (Rapoport and Sheftell 1996). Most of the research in this area has focused on migraine or other episodic headaches in adults, and the results may not be directly generalizable to children and adolescents. For example, Hermann and Blanchard (1998) recently reported that psychophysiological reactivity did not differ between pediatric migraine patients and healthy controls. These authors suggested that analysis of physiological parameters in pediatric populations allows researchers to minimize confounding factors such as chronicity, chronic medication effects, and comorbid headache presentations.

Investigations of the pathophysiology specific to CDH have begun to appear in the literature, although none have specifically addressed the condition in pediatric populations. Pericranial muscle tenderness (Lipchik et al. 1996) and postural, myofascial, and mechanical musculoskeletal abnormalities (Marcus et al. 1999) occur at a higher rate among adult CDH patients.

Furthermore, Jensen et al. (1998) suggested that prolonged muscle contraction in chronic headaches may sensitize the central nervous system to a lower general sensitivity to pain. Changes in local cerebral blood flow in cortical gray matter are similar in adults with transformed migraine and in those with episodic migraine, suggesting that serotonin agonists may be the preferred pharmacotherapeutic strategy as opposed to other prophylactic, abortive, or analgesic agents (Konno et al. 1999).

ASSOCIATED DISABILITY AND COPING PATTERNS

In understanding and describing CDH in children, it is important to consider the developmental progression of their conceptualization of recurrent pain and of their coping strategies. It is generally considered that children's conceptualization of pain, much like their understanding of illness or death, corresponds with Piaget's stages of cognitive development (Thompson and Gustafson 1996). Studies supporting a Piagetian development of pain conceptualization have found that children's understanding of pain moves from the very concrete, perceptually dominated to the more abstract, psychologically dominated (Gaffney 1993). As these changes in cognitive understanding of pain progress, the types of interventions recommended also change. Specifically, distraction and parental support are recommended for preoperational children, activity and cognitive strategies for concrete-operational children, and cognitive-behavioral strategies for formal-operational children (Gaffney 1993). For other views on the development of children's conceptualization of pain, see Ross and Ross (1984).

Martin (1993) proposed a functional model of psychological factors involved in chronic headaches. This model posits that environmental and individual subjective events occurring before, during, and after pain episodes moderate the course and outcomes associated with recurrent headache syndromes. Antecedents and consequences of headaches are included in the model as etiological factors and targets for intervention. Martin (1993) suggests that antecedents to the onset of headache episodes may include predisposing factors, such as a strong family history or a personality style that is more stress reactive, and onset variables, such as head or neck trauma or significant increases in environmental stress. In addition, situational factors (e.g., coping skills and social support) can influence headache pain, and immediate factors (e.g., certain foods or emotional distress) can trigger or exacerbate headache episodes. Particularly important for children and adolescents are the consequences of a painful episode. For example, the ways in which caregivers and family members react to a headache episode can positively or negatively reinforce the occurrence of headaches.

Martin's functional model was originally based on clinical and research experience with adults, and evidence in the adult literature supports the importance of considering antecedents and consequences in recurrent headache syndromes (Martin et al. 1993). Developmental adaptations of this model are applicable to recurrent pediatric headache. In addition, there is some support in the pediatric literature for targeting antecedents and consequences of headache episodes in children to identify factors related to the development and maintenance of recurrent headaches (Holden et al. 1998b; Wall et al. 1998). Martin's conceptual model provides a comprehensive cognitive-behavioral approach for understanding individual psychological, familial, and environmental factors that influence CDH expression and selecting targets for intervention for children, adolescents, and adults.

A conceptual model of pediatric pain developed by McGrath (1990) offers some advantages over Martin's (1993) functional model as a framework for understanding factors influencing recurrent and chronic pain syndromes in children and adolescents. This integrated model posits four types of variables that can influence the relationship between pain sources and pain sensation, including (1) *cognitive factors* such as expectations, perceptions of control, and understanding of the condition resulting in pain; (2) *behavioral factors,* including those directly related to pain expression and more indirect behaviors that provide a buffering effect and enhance coping, such as physical and social activities; (3) *emotional factors* such as anxiety, fear, anger, and depression; and (4) various *demographic, family, and cultural influences.* This bidirectional model, in which each area of functioning can be reciprocally influenced by characteristics of the pain experience, provides a useful framework for clinical assessment, for the development and implementation of treatment protocols, and for interpretation of the results of the literature on recurrent pediatric headache.

Several recent studies have indicated that children and adolescents with CDH have higher rates of functional disability and emotional/behavioral disturbance than do those with migraines or those without headaches. Children with CDH have frequent absences from school, diminished academic performance, and psychosocial comorbidity (Allen et al. 1999), and they seem to miss more school days than do children with migraines (Holden et al. 1994). In addition, children with CDH tend to have social and peer difficulties, including experiencing stress at school, having problems getting along with other children, and being bullied more often (Carlsson et al. 1996; Metsähonkala et al. 1998).

In general, pediatric headache sufferers report more somatic complaints, stress, and psychological symptoms than do children without headaches (Carlsson et al. 1996). Children and adolescents with CDH often have higher rates of psychiatric disorders compared to those with migraines; in a study by Holden et al. (1994), 46% of the group with CDH but only 17% of the group with migraine carried at least one psychiatric diagnosis at intake for services at a pediatric headache clinic. One-half of the diagnoses for the CDH group were in the general category of depression, although somatization and conversion disorders were also represented. In adolescents, some evidence suggests that stress may moderate the effect of headaches on psychological functioning (Langeveld et al. 1999). Pediatric patients with CDH may be misdiagnosed with psychiatric disorders because many general practitioners are not familiar with chronic daily headaches as a diagnostic entity (Holden et al. 1994).

Several studies have suggested that gender differences influence the patterns of emotional and behavioral disturbance in children and adolescents with chronic headaches. Specifically, females more often exhibit internalizing behaviors or symptoms of depression and anxiety, and males tend to exhibit more externalizing behaviors and disruptive disorders (Egger et al. 1998, 1999). Parental response to recurrent headaches also seems to depend upon the gender of the child. For example, Holden and colleagues (1994) found that parents tend to respond more negatively (e.g., exhibiting anger or frustration) to female children with recurrent headache episodes, whereas they tended to respond less negatively to male children with recurrent headaches. Differences in the psychobiological processes underlying the associations between somatic complaints and psychiatric disorders in children and adolescents may account for these gender differences (Egger et al. 1999).

The cross-sectional investigations reviewed above included large-scale population-based investigations and clinical cohort studies. In two cases (Egger at al. 1998, 1999; Metsähonkala et al. 1998), the data were collected as part of large epidemiological studies with representative samples. In these studies, headache measures with uncertain reliability and validity were obtained as part of larger assessment batteries including measures such as the Child and Adolescent Psychiatric Assessment (CAPA) scale, which was developed to assess psychiatric diagnoses and accompanying behavioral/emotional symptoms. These results have greater generalizability to the population of children and adolescents. However, their direct relevance to clinical assessment and intervention with children who experience chronic daily headaches and accompanying disability is limited. The smaller-scale clinical cohort studies (Holden et al. 1994; Carlsson et al. 1996; Langveld et al. 1999) focused on populations that were defined by specific diagnostic criteria, most often the standard criteria used in specialty clinical centers and specific measures of child and adolescent functioning with documented reliability and validity. The results of these studies have greater utility in informing clinical decision making, but may not be as informative in developing normative models of headache etiology due to biased sampling. The results of both large-scale population-based studies and clinical cohort studies are essential for more informed prevention and treatment of recurrent headache in children and adolescents.

INTERVENTIONS FOR CHRONIC DAILY HEADACHE IN CHILDREN AND ADOLESCENTS

Both behavioral and pharmacological interventions are available to treat children and adolescents with CDH. The evidence base for these interventions primarily rests on the results of research with adult samples or with heterogeneous samples of children and adolescents with recurrent headache. Relevant literature in this area will be reviewed to provide a basis for discussing clinical issues.

Nonpharmacological interventions for CDH represent an important line of treatment for children who are affected by these recurrent pain episodes. Typically, behavioral and psychological interventions are the most thoroughly studied, most often utilized, and best understood of the available nonpharmacological interventions for pediatric headache. Of the most common psychological interventions, relaxation, self-hypnosis, biofeedback, and combinations of these treatments are most frequently researched. While many studies describing the efficacy of treatments for recurrent headaches in children have included samples of children with varying clinical presentations such as migraine or tension-type headache, few use the term "chronic daily headache" when describing these children's condition. Thus, the impact of these behavioral and psychological interventions on CDH in children is not clear. However, we will assume that treatments found efficacious for other types of recurrent pediatric headache will also have utility in the treatment of CDH in children and adolescents.

RELAXATION THERAPIES

Relaxation therapies include self-hypnosis, relaxation training, autogenic training (a form of relaxation training that includes a self-monitoring component; Holden et al. 1998a), and guided imagery. The goals behind such therapies in the treatment of pediatric headache are twofold (Holden et al. 1998a). First, training in these techniques allows children to enlist

positive coping strategies that provide a distraction from the painful headache episode. In learning coping skills, children can gain control over their
physical symptoms. Second, relaxation produces numerous physiological
changes such as vasodilation, increased blood volume, and decreased heart
rate, which are incompatible with the vasoconstriction often associated with
headaches. Typically, relaxation therapies involve teaching children devel-
opmentally appropriate guided imagery or progressive muscle relaxation
techniques. Daily practice may have a prophylactic effect, and these techniques can eventually be used as an active coping mechanism at the start of
a headache episode.

In general, the literature on the utility of relaxation techniques in treating the intensity and frequency of pediatric headache has been promising.
Relaxation therapies proved more effective than placebo controls in some
studies (Larsson and Melin 1986; McGrath et al. 1992), but not others
(Emmen and Paschier 1988; McGrath et al. 1988). Additionally, in randomized, controlled interventions, such therapies were more effective than the
waiting-list control condition (Engel et al. 1992) or self-monitoring alone
(Larsson et al. 1987a,b). In studies that followed patients at varying post-
treatment intervals, changes in headache frequency and intensity were maintained consistently (Larsson and Melin 1986; Larsson et al. 1987ab; McGrath
et al. 1988; Wisniewski et al. 1988; Engel et al. 1992; McGrath et al. 1992).

Several studies have shown that relaxation interventions provided in a
school setting can be as effective as those delivered in the clinic (Larsson
and Melin 1986; Larsson et al. 1987a; Emmen and Paschier 1988). These
findings are important because treatment by a school nurse or counselor is
likely to be more cost effective than clinic-based care. In addition, providing the opportunity for coaching in relaxation techniques on a daily basis
may offer specific clinical benefits for the child or adolescent who has a
daily headache pattern.

BIOFEEDBACK

Biofeedback training represents an additional method for helping children and adolescents with CDH to control their pain. Biofeedback usually
involves monitoring physiological reactivity in the frontalis muscle and/or
changes in skin conductance or temperature. Children are trained to recognize and control these sensations to reduce the subjective perception of
pain. Traditional types of biofeedback include EEG biofeedback, muscle
EMG biofeedback, temporal pulse biofeedback, and finger temperature biofeedback. While biofeedback information is usually gathered with complex
computer programs, finger temperature biofeedback can be practiced at home.

As with relaxation, biofeedback is thought to be beneficial because it leads to changes both in the physiological response to headache and in perceptions of self-control over pain.

Biofeedback is an effective treatment for recurrent pediatric headache, both used independently and in combination with other treatments. Specifically, its efficacy has been demonstrated in a migraine study using waiting-list controls (Labbé and Williamson 1984), in studies that lacked controls (Grazzi et al. 1990; Hermann et al. 1997), in a comparison of clinic- versus home-based therapy (Guarnieri and Blanchard 1990), and in multiple baseline studies (Labbé and Williamson 1983; Burke and Andrasik 1989; Allen and McKeen 1991). In general, these studies have shown no differences in outcome regardless of the context (i.e., clinic- vs. home-based) or length of the biofeedback intervention. Treatment gains have been maintained for as long as 2 years post-intervention.

Of studies that have examined biofeedback in combination with other approaches in the treatment of recurrent pediatric headache, most have explored combinations of biofeedback and relaxation. These studies have demonstrated both initial effectiveness of combined treatments and maintenance of gains at follow-up intervals (Olness and MacDonald 1981; Werder and Sargent 1984; Engel and Rapoff 1990; Labbé and Ward 1990; Smith et al. 1991). However, studies comparing biofeedback to relaxation techniques have found conflicting results, with evidence for the superiority of autogenic relaxation to biofeedback (Labbé 1995), equal effectiveness of the treatments (Fentress et al. 1986), and some superiority of biofeedback to relaxation (Kroener-Herwig et al. 1998).

Other behavioral methods of psychological treatment for pediatric headache have been explored, usually in combination with traditional relaxation training and biofeedback interventions. Typically, these additional interventions have included either contingency management or cognitive-behavioral therapies intended to address other factors that might maintain pain-related behaviors and associated disability (Holden et al. 1998a). Specifically, studies using contingency management in addition to biofeedback or relaxation training have found declines in headache activity (Kapelis 1984; Warnach and Keenan 1985; Mehegan et al. 1987; van der Helm-Hylkema et al. 1990), with results maintained for up to 33 months post-intervention. Cognitive-behavioral interventions that address the thought patterns that may maintain pain-related behaviors and pain perceptions have shown some promise when combined with biofeedback, with gains maintained for as long as 22 months post-intervention (Richter et al. 1986). One study showed that using parent-mediated strategies to manage children's pain behavior in addition to biofeedback results in significantly greater reductions in headache frequency compared to biofeedback alone (Allen and Shriver 1998).

PHARMACOLOGICAL INTERVENTIONS

Similar to the behavioral and psychological interventions, specific data are scarce on the efficacy of pharmacological interventions for pediatric CDH. However, several medications have proven effective for controlling pediatric headaches. This section briefly describes typical protocols followed for drug management of recurrent pediatric headaches in clinical settings. More detailed information on pharmacological interventions for childhood headache can be found in Chapter 5.

Acute headaches in children and adolescents are frequently treated with analgesics or abortive medications. Over-the-counter analgesics such as ibuprofen and acetaminophen are often effective in treating acute episodes. Abortive medications have a vasoconstrictive effect that interrupts the pathophysiological sequence of vasospasm and dilation. Combined medications with sedative, vasoconstrictive, and analgesic components, such as acetaminophen/isometheptene and acetaminophen/butalbital, may also be effective for acute headache episodes. Acute migraine episodes are often treated with serotonin agonists such as sumatriptan. For children and adolescents with intractable acute migraine episodes, dihydroergotamine (DHE) is frequently given. Due to potential side effects, this medication should be administered in an emergency room or inpatient setting.

Children and adolescents who experience recurrent or chronic headaches should be considered for prophylactic medications. Holden et al. (1998) recommend that children and adolescents be considered for prophylaxis only if they exhibit significant functional disability (e.g., if they miss more than 3 days of school per month or experience social isolation or family discord due to their headaches) and experience severe episodes. Several medications are used for prophylaxis in children and adolescents with recurrent or chronic headaches, including antidepressants, β-blockers, calcium channel blockers, and antihistamines (see Chapter 5 for details). The tricyclic antidepressant amitriptyline is an effective prophylactic treatment for chronic tension headaches in adults (Jensen et al. 1998) and may be beneficial in pediatric and adolescent patients.

Chronic headache sufferers may become habituated to the over-the-counter analgesic medications. Chronic use of such medications may cause analgesic rebound headaches when the child is withdrawn from them (Vasconcellos et al. 1998). Children and adolescents with rebound headaches need to be withdrawn from daily analgesics and provided with alternative relief (e.g., a prophylactic medication such as amitriptyline and other pain relievers such as sumatriptan) (Vasconcellos et al. 1998).

In general, pharmacological interventions for chronic headache have been investigated less thoroughly in children and adolescents than in adults. Moreover, few studies in the pediatric literature have compared the efficacy of behavioral and psychological interventions to pharmacological treatments. In a recent meta-analysis of the treatment outcome literature, Hermann and colleagues (1995) reported greater efficacy for psychological interventions than for pharmacological therapies in pediatric migraine. In addition, two pediatric studies have directly compared the efficacy of behavioral interventions to pharmacotherapy, and both found the behavioral therapies more effective than medication in treating recurrent headaches (Olness et al. 1987b; Larsson et al. 1990). These data, combined with the multiple studies reported above, provide conclusive evidence that relaxation techniques such as self-hypnosis are a well-established and efficacious treatment for recurrent pediatric migraine and tension headaches. Strong evidence also supports the use of biofeedback in treating pediatric migraines. Research with adults has indicated that a combination of psychological and pharmacological treatments may be more effective than either approach alone (Holroyd et al. 1995). Further research is needed with pediatric populations before definitive conclusions can be drawn about the efficacy of combined behavioral and pharmacological interventions with CDH in children and adolescents.

STATE-OF-THE-ART DIAGNOSIS AND TREATMENT

For patients with CDH, a skilled and careful history is the first step to insuring an accurate diagnosis and effective plan of action. Serious medical conditions must be ruled out. History of infections, sinus disease, trauma, hypertension, cerebrospinal pressure abnormalities, and ocular disorders should be recorded, and suspicion of factitious disorders or somatization should be noted (Gladstein et al. 1997). Dietary, sleep, and medication histories may help pinpoint aggravating factors. Family history of headache and psychiatric disease will help to clarify the diagnosis. Clinicians should also explore coping mechanisms and assess disability, primarily by measuring absences or early dismissal from school, visits to school nurses for medication, a drop in grades, and inability to participate in after-school activities. A thorough physical examination should be conducted to convince both the practitioner and the patient of benign etiology before proceeding with a treatment plan.

Patients with suspicious histories or abnormal physical findings need a more extensive medical evaluation. For patients with growth delay or pubertal delay or arrest, endocrine parameters should be evaluated. Where dermatological examination indicates a neurocutaneous disorder, brain imaging is recommended. Sinus tenderness or painful, limited jaw opening may warrant dental investigation. Most patients with CDH whose headaches have progressed from acute to chronic are imaged, unlike patients with new daily persistent headache, where chronic headache was present from the onset. Studies of young children with recurrent headache show that in the absence of abnormalities on physical examination or suspicious histories for increased intracranial pressure, brain imaging yields negative results (Chu and Shinnar 1992). Most patients do not need further imaging; similarly, EEGs are unhelpful in the vast majority of cases (Daly and Markland 1990).

Psychological assessment is an important component of the initial evaluation of children and adolescents with CDH. General behavior rating scales such as the Child Behavior Checklist (Achenbach and Edelbrock 1991) can be useful in evaluating internalizing or externalizing symptoms. The presence of substantial psychiatric symptoms or a previously diagnosed mental health disorder may warrant a more intensive evaluation of behavioral and emotional functioning. Useful measures are available for assessing the pain experience (Holden et al. 1998), coping (Walker et al. 1997), functional disability (Walker and Greene 1991) and parental reactions (Wall et al. 1998).

Martin's (1993) functional model provides a conceptual framework for identifying antecedents and consequences that may be implicated in the genesis and maintenance of CDH. Interviews with parents and children and direct observation of parent-child interactions within the office setting can provide information for completing a full functional assessment. In many cases, it is important to initiate a diagnostic headache diary to evaluate the severity and quality of pain and to ascertain both antecedents and consequences in the natural environment. We have found it useful to ask the child or adolescent to rate the severity of pain at multiple points each day and to note subjective experiences as well as others' reactions. Obtaining this information over a 1–2-week period can assist greatly in clarifying diagnostic status and can serve as a baseline for measuring changes as a result of intervention (Holden et al. 1998). We strongly advocate the continued use of headache diaries during treatment episodes to obtain systematic outcome data on changes in severity and in specific symptoms.

We have found that approaches that include pharmacological interventions to break the daily headache pattern and relieve symptoms along with a behavioral intervention offering relaxation training and other approaches to enhance coping skills can be effective in treating the child or adolescent with CDH. However, in our clinical experience the treatment course may be lengthy, and each case may require frequent reassessment and treatment adjustment. A rational approach based on careful consideration of headache type, functional disability, and the presence or absence of medication overuse will assure relief of symptoms. Assessment of the patient's ability to adhere to behavioral interventions such as relaxation training will help to optimize outcome. Patient preference should also be considered in designing and implementing a treatment plan.

Diagnostic subtypes of CDH in children and adolescents offer different challenges in the clinical setting. For example, we have found new daily persistent headache and transformed migraine or the comorbid pattern complicated by analgesic abuse to be the most difficult forms of CDH to effectively treat. These more recalcitrant patterns may require inpatient hospitalization for administration of intravenous DHE combined with intensive observation and interviewing to identify psychological or behavioral factors that may be contributing to the CDH pattern. Intensive follow-up on an outpatient basis, including daily or near-daily telephone contact, is frequently required in these cases. Functional disability that affects achievement or attendance at school may require a case management approach, including the clinician's active participation in school-based conferences. The school can be a particularly important setting for antecedents and consequences that strongly influence headache patterns.

A team approach is important when treating children and adolescents with CDH. These complex cases require both medical and behavioral expertise for accurate assessment and effective management. Patients often present with histories complicated by unsuccessful treatment attempts by poorly informed health care personnel who have exacerbated their headaches through misdiagnosis and inappropriate treatment plans. Such mismanagement occurs with both pharmacological and nonpharmacological approaches that may be useful for episodic headaches, but too often are applied indiscriminately to those presenting with CDH. Teams combining behavioral and medical expertise can be useful in disentangling the factors that are implicated in CDH patterns and make effective clinical decisions at critical junctures in the treatment process.

CASE ILLUSTRATIONS

The two case descriptions that follow illustrate our approach to diagnosing and managing children and adolescents with chronic daily headache.

The first case is a 14-year-old male who for the past year had experienced daily or near-daily headaches lasting for several hours. He had previously experienced severe headaches approximately once a month from the age of seven. His previous intermittent headaches, which were not preceded by an aura, were characterized by bifrontal pounding pain with accompanying nausea, vomiting, dizziness, pallor, and a need to sleep. The boy experienced both photophobia and sonophobia during these headache episodes. Both his mother and maternal grandmother had a history of migraines. The boy's primary care physician had diagnosed him with migraine without aura and had treated him primarily with analgesics and occasionally with abortive medications. Over the past year, the frequency of his headaches had increased markedly, but the severity of symptoms had abated. In the past, it was not uncommon for him to have to lie down for 6–8 hours with a cold compress during headache episodes. At the time of referral, he no longer needed to lie down during an episode, and could continue to function despite mild photophobia and sonophobia. As the boy's symptoms had transformed over the last year, his physician had prescribed naproxen sodium on an episodic basis. By the time of the boy's referral to the pediatric headache clinic, an analgesic abuse pattern had emerged and he was taking the medication daily.

This teenager was the oldest of three siblings in a high-achieving, intact two-parent family. He was the president of his class at a suburban high school and played lacrosse. His performance in school was above-average to excellent, and his parents reported that he placed a lot of pressure on himself to succeed and that he internalized the stress that he experienced. No other significant behavioral or emotional symptoms were present.

We diagnosed the boy with transformed migraine, and recommended a treatment regimen consisting of pharmacotherapy and a cognitive-behavioral stress and pain management approach. The family agreed to pursue a pharmacotherapy regimen as they believed that the headache pattern was purely medical in nature. The boy was started on amitriptyline at gradually increasing doses, and he improved significantly on a dose of 30 mg nightly. Once his headaches had decreased to one episode every 2 weeks, daily use of naproxen sodium was discontinued. After 4 months of treatment, the dose of amitriptyline was gradually phased out. He continues to do well, with episodic migraines approximately once every 2 months controlled by intranasal sumatriptan.

The second case is a 16-year-old girl with sudden onset of daily headaches following a viral syndrome approximately 2 months prior to referral. There was no previous history of headache, either for the patient or other family members. Bifrontal, squeezing pain was continually present without accompanying autonomic nervous system symptoms. The severity of the girl's pain varied, and her functional disability was quite high. She had missed 10 days of school over the past 2 months, and the headaches were curtailing her ability to participate in activities with peers outside school. She was an honors student, but her grades had dropped due to school absences and her concern about the etiology of her headaches. Physical examination was normal and psychiatric history was negative, although the girl presented as moderately depressed at the time of referral. She lived at home with her mother.

We diagnosed the patient with new daily persistent headache and asked her to immediately start to keep a daily headache diary so as to monitor her symptoms. She attended outpatient sessions weekly where her self-monitoring was reviewed, and she learned a self-hypnosis procedure that she practiced twice a day. In addition, she used a cognitive-behavioral problem-solving approach to identify antecedents to symptom fluctuation and bolster her coping skills. Over 4 weeks of treatment, her pain intensity decreased significantly and she began to experience symptom-free intervals each day. Her school absenteeism also decreased significantly. At that point, she was placed on a low dose of amitryptiline. She continued with weekly outpatient sessions to further develop cognitive-behavioral approaches to her headache pain and accompanying depressive symptoms. Headache pain completely disappeared after 10 weeks of treatment and her amitriptyline was gradually tapered. As her symptoms abated, her school performance returned to previous levels and she was able to increase her involvement in activities with peers. She was functioning in the normal range on measures of depression 3 months following the initiation of treatment.

CONCLUSIONS AND FUTURE DIRECTIONS

The study of CDH in children and adolescents is in its nascent stages. CDH has been recognized as an important and relatively prevalent diagnostic entity in pediatric populations. Classification schemes developed for adults have been applied to children and adolescents, and developmental variations in expression of CDH have been recognized. Pharmacological and behavioral treatments, whose evidence base primarily rests on data collected with adults or with children and adolescents who display various forms of recurrent headache, sometimes including CDH, are being used with increasing frequency in clinical settings. It is likely that even more attention will be given to CDH in children and adolescents in the future.

However, scientific investigations are needed to further develop the evidence base for work in the area of CDH with children and adolescents. Basic epidemiological research is essential to help us to understand not only the prevalence, but also age-specific incidence rates and developmental factors that influence the emergence and maintenance of this condition. Adding to our scarce information about the specific pathophysiology and genetic underpinnings of CDH will assist researchers in developing strategies for identifying children and adolescents at risk and designing early interventions to alter the course and development of CDH. Clinical trials that focus specifically on the efficacy of pharmacological, behavioral, or combined approaches to treatment are needed to provide a more systematic basis for selecting appropriate interventions. If CDH is indeed different from other forms of headache in children and adolescents, then therapeutic, prophylactic, and behavioral trials could guide us in offering an evidence-based approach to the treatment of this sometimes debilitating condition. Further understanding of the mechanisms underlying pediatric CDH should translate into more precise and earlier identification of cases and the wide-scale provision of effective and cost-efficient treatment strategies.

REFERENCES

Abu-Arafeh I, Russell G. Prevalence of headache and migraine in schoolchildren. *BMJ* 1994; 34:508–514.

Achenbach TM, Edelbrock C. *Manual for the Child Behavior Checklist.* Burlington, VT: Department of Psychiatry, University of Vermont, 1991.

Allen KD, McKeen LR. Home-based multicomponent treatment of pediatric migraine. *Headache* 1991; 31:467–472.

Allen K, Shriver M. Role of parent-mediated pain behavior management strategies in biofeedback treatment of childhood migraines. *Behav Ther* 1998; 29:477–490.

Allen K, Mathews J, Shriver M. Children and recurrent headaches: assessment and treatment implications for school psychologists. *School Psychol Rev* 1999; 28:266–279.

Burke EJ, Andrasik F. Home- vs. clinical-based biofeedback treatment for pediatric migraine: results of treatment through one-year follow-up. *Headache* 1989; 29:434–440.

Carlsson J, Larsson B, Mark A. Psychosocial functioning in schoolchildren with recurrent headaches. *Headache* 1996; 36:77–82.

Castillo J, Munoz P, Guitera V, Pascual J. Epidemiology of chronic daily headache in the general population. *Headache* 1999; 39:190–196.

Chu ML, Shinnar S. Headaches in children younger than seven years of age. *Arch Neurol* 1992; 49:79–82.

Daly DD, Markland OM. Focal brain lesion. In: Daly DD, Pedley TA (Eds). *Current Practice of Clinical Electroencephalography.* New York: Raven Press, 1990.

Deleu D, Hanssens Y. Primary chronic daily headache: clinical and pharmacological aspects. A clinic-based study in Oman. *Headache* 1999; 39:432–436.

Egger H, Angold A, Costello E. Headaches and psychopathology in children and adolescents. *J Am Acad Child Adolesc Psychiatry* 1998; 37:951–958.

Egger H, Costello J, Erkanli A, Angold A. Somatic complaints and psychopathology in children and adolescents: stomach aches, musculoskeletal pains, and headaches. *J Am Acad Child Adolesc Psychiatry* 1999; 38:852–860.

Emmen HH, Paschier J. Treatment of headache among children by progressive relaxation. *Cephalalgia* 1988; 7:387–389.

Engel JM. Relaxation training: a self-help approach for children with headaches. *Am J Occup Ther* 1992; 46:591–596.

Engel JM, Rapoff MA. Biofeedback-assisted relaxation training for adult and pediatric headache. *Occup Ther J Res* 1990; 10:283–299.

Engel JM, Rapoff MA, Pressman AR. Long-term follow-up of relaxation training for pediatric headache disorders. *Headache* 1992: 32:152–156.

Essau CA, Conradt J, Petermann F. Prevalence, comorbidity and psychosocial impairment of somatoform disorders in adolescents. *Psychol Health Med* 1999; 4:169–180.

Fentress DW, Masek BJ, Mehegan JE, Benson H. Biofeedback and relaxation-response training in the treatment of pediatric migraine. *Dev Med Child Neurol* 1986; 28:139–146.

Gaffney A. Cognitive developmental aspects of pain in school-age children. In: Schechter NL, Berde CB, Yaster M (Eds). *Pain in Infants, Children, and Adolescents.* Baltimore: Williams and Williams, 1993, pp 75–85.

Grazzi L, Leone M, Bussone G. A therapeutic alternative for tension headache in children: treatment and 1-year follow-up results. *Biofeedback Self-Regul* 1990; 15:1–6.

Gladstein J, Holden EW. Chronic daily headache in children and adolescents: a 2 year prospective study. *Headache* 1996; 36:349–351.

Gladstein J, Holden EW, Peralta L, Raven M. Diagnoses and symptom patterns in children presenting to a pediatric headache clinic. *Headache* 1993; 33:497–500.

Gladstein J, Holden EW, Winner P, Linder S. Chronic daily headache in children and adolescents: current status and recommendations for the future. *Headache* 1997; 37:626–629.

Guarnieri P, Blanchard EB. Evaluation of home-based thermal biofeedback treatment of pediatric migraine headache. *Biofeedback Self-Regul* 1990; 15:179–184.

Headache Classification Committee of the International Headache Society. Classification and diagnostic criteria for headache disorders, cranial neuralgias and facial pain. *Cephalalgia* 1988; 8(Suppl 7):1–96.

Hermann C, Blanchard EB. Psychophysiological reactivity in pediatric migraine patients and health controls. *J Psychosom Res* 1998; 44:229–240.

Hermann C, Kim M, Blanchard EB. Behavioral and prophylactic pharmacological intervention studies of pediatric migraine: an exploratory meta-analysis. *Pain* 1995; 60:239–255.

Hermann C, Blanchard EB, Flor H. Biofeedback treatment for pediatric migraine: prediction of treatment outcome. *J Consult Clin Psychol* 1997; 65:611–616.

Holden EW, Gladstein J, Trulsen M, Wall B. Chronic daily headache in children and adolescents. *Headache* 1994; 34:508–514.

Holden EW, Levy J, Deichmann M, Gladstein J. Recurrent pediatric headaches: assessment and intervention. *J Dev Behav Pediatr* 1998a; 19:109–117.

Holden EW, Rawlins C, Gladstein J. Children's coping with recurrent headache. *J Clin Psychol Med Settings* 1998b; 5:147–158.

Holden EW, Deichmann MM, Levy JD. Empirically supported treatments in pediatric psychology: recurrent pediatric headaches. *J Pediatr Psychol* 1999; 24:91–109.

Holroyd KA, France JL, Cordingley GE, et al. Enhancing the effectiveness of relaxation/thermal biofeedback training with propranolol HCL. *J Consult Clin Psychol* 1995; 63:327–330.

Honkasalo ML, Kaprio J, Winter T, et al. Migraine and concomitant symptoms among 8167 adult twin pairs. *Headache* 1995; 35:70–78.

Jensen R, Berndtsen L, Olesen J. Muscular factors are of importance in tension-type headache. *Headache* 1998; 38:10–17.

Kapelis L. Hypnosis in a behavior therapy framework for the treatment of migraine in children. *Aust J Clin Exp Hypnosis* 1984; 12:123–126.

Konno S, Meyer JS, Margishvili GM, Rauch RA, Haque A. Transformed migraine is a cause of chronic daily headaches. *Headache* 1999; 39:95–100.

Kroener-Herwig B, Mohn U, Pothmann R. Comparison of biofeedback and relaxation in the treatment of pediatric headache and the influence of parent involvement on outcome. *Appl Psychophysiol Biofeedback* 1998; 23:143–157.

Labbé EE. Treatment of childhood migraine with autogenic training and skin temperature biofeedback: a component analysis. *Headache* 1995; 35:10–13.

Labbé EE, Ward CH. Electromyographic biofeedback with mental imagery and home practice in the treatment of children with muscle-contraction headache. *J Dev Behav Pediatr* 1990; 11:65–68.

Labbé EE, Williamson DA. Temperature biofeedback in the treatment of children with migraine headaches. *J Pediatr Psychol* 1983; 8:317–326.

Labbé EE, Williamson DA. Treatment of childhood migraine using autogenic feedback training. *J Consult Clin Psychol* 1984; 52:968–976.

Langeveld J, Koot H, Passchier J. Do experienced stress and trait negativity moderate the relationship between headache and quality of life in adolescents? *J Pediatr Psychol* 1999; 24:1–11.

Larsson B, Melin L. Chronic headaches in adolescents: treatment in a school setting with relaxation training as compared with information-contact and self-registration. *Pain* 1986; 25:325–336.

Larsson B, Bille B, Pederson NL. Genetic influence in headaches: a Swedish twin study. *Headache* 1995; 35:513–519.

Larsson B, Daleflod B, Hakansson L, Melin L. Therapist assisted versus self-help relaxation treatment of chronic headaches in adolescents: a school-based intervention. *J Child Psychol Psychiatry Allied Disciplines* 1987a; 28:127–136.

Larsson B, Melin L, Lamminen M, Ullsted F. A school-based treatment of chronic headaches in adolescents. *J Pediatr Psychol* 1987b; 12:553–566.

Larsson B, Melin L, Doberl A. Recurrent tension headache in adolescents treated with self-help relaxation training and a muscle relaxant drug. *Headache* 1990; 30:665–671.

Lipchik GL, Holroyd KA, Christopher R, Kvaal SA. Central and peripheral mechanisms in chronic tension-type headache. *Pain* 1996; 64:467–475.

Marcus DA, Scharff L, Mercer S, Turk DC. Musculoskeletal abnormalities in chronic headache: a controlled comparison of headache diagnostic groups. *Headache* 1999; 39:190–196.

Martin P. *Psychological Management of Chronic Headaches.* New York: Guilford Press, 1993.

Martin P, Milech D, Nathan P. Towards a functional model of chronic headaches: investigation of antecedents and consequences. *Headache* 1993; 33:461–470.

Mathew NT, Reuveni U, Perez F. Transformed or evolutive migraine. *Headache* 1987; 27:102–106.

McGrath PA. *Pain in Children: Nature, Assessment and Treatment.* New York: Guilford Publications, 1990.

McGrath PJ, Humphreys P, Goodman JT, et al. Relaxation prophylaxis for childhood migraine: a randomized placebo-controlled trial. *Dev Med Child Neurol* 1988; 30:626–631.

McGrath PJ, Humphreys P, Keene D, et al. The efficacy and efficiency of a self administered treatment for adolescent migraine. *Pain* 1992; 49:321–324.

Mehegan JE, Masek BJ, Harrison RH, Russo DC, Leviton A. A multicomponent behavioral treatment for pediatric migraine. *Clin J Pain* 1987; 2:191–196.

Messinger HB, Spierings ELH, Vincent AJP. Overlap of migraine and tension-type headache in the International Headache Society classification. *Cephalalgia* 1991; 11:233–237.

Metsähonkala L, Sillanpää M, Tuominen J. Social environment and headache in 8- to 9-year-old children: a follow-up study. *Headache* 1998; 38:222–228.

Monzon MJ, Lainez JM. Chronic daily headache: long-term prognosis following inpatient treatment. *Headache Quarterly* 1998; 9:326–330.

Newacheck PW, Taylor WR. Childhood chronic illness: prevalence, severity, and impact. *Am J Public Health* 1992; 82:364–371.

Olness K, MacDonald J. Self-hypnosis and biofeedback in the management of juvenile migraine. *J Dev Behav Pediatr* 1981; 2:168–170.

Olness K, MacDonald J, Uden DL. Comparison of self-hypnosis and propranolol in the treatment of juvenile classic migraine. *Pediatrics* 1987; 79:593–597.

Peters ML, Turner SM, Blanchard EB. The effects of aerobic exercise on chronic tension type headache. *Headache Quarterly* 1996; 7:300–334.

Rapoport AM, Sheftell FD. *Headache Disorders: A Management Guide for Practitioners.* Philadelphia: W.B. Saunders, 1996.

Richter IL, McGrath PJ, Humphreys PJ. Cognitive and relaxation treatment of pediatric migraine. *Pain* 1986; 25:195–203.

Ross DM, Ross SA. Childhood pain: the school-aged child's viewpoint. *Pain* 1984; 20:179–191.

Scher AI, Stewart WF, Lieberman J, Lipton RB. Prevalence of frequent headache in a population sample. *Headache* 1998; 38:497–506.

Silberstein SD, Lipton RB, Solomon S, Mathew NT. Classification of daily and near-daily headaches: proposed revisions to the IHS criteria. *Headache* 1994; 34:1–7.

Sillanpää M, Anttila P. Increasing prevalence of headache in 7-year-old schoolchildren. *Headache* 1996; 36:466–470.

Sillanpää M, Piekkala P, Kero P. Prevalence of headache at preschool age in an unselected child population. *Cephalagia* 1991; 11:239–242.

Smith MS, Womack WM, Chen ACN. Anxiety and depression in the behavioral treatment of headache in children and adolescent. *Int J Adolesc Med Health* 1991; 5:17–35.

Solomon S, Lipton RB, Newman LC. Evaluation of chronic daily headache—comparison to criteria for chronic tension type headache. *Cephalagia* 1992; 12:365–368.

Spierings ELH, Schroevers M, Honkoop PC, Sorbi M. Development of chronic daily headache: a clinical study. *Headache* 1998; 38:529–533.

Thompson RJ, Gustafson KE. *Adaptation in Chronic Childhood Illness.* Washington, DC: American Psychological Association Press, 1996.

van der Helm-Hylkema H, Orlebeke JF, Enting LA, Thijssen JHH, van Ree J. Effects of behaviour therapy on migraine and plasma beta-endorphin in young migraine patients. *Psychoneuroendocrinology* 1990; 15:39–45.

Vasconcellos E, Pina-Garza JE, Milan EJ, Ernesto J, Warner JS. Analgesic rebound headache in children and adolescents. *J Child Neurol* 1998; 13:443–447.

Viswanathan V, Bridges SJ, Whitehouse W, Newton RW. Childhood headaches: discrete entities or continuum? *Dev Med Child Neurol* 1998; 40:544–550.

Walker LS, Greene JW. The Functional Disability Inventory: measuring a neglected dimension of child health status. *J Pediatr Psychol* 1991; 14:231–243.

Walker LS, Smith CA, Garber J, Van Slyke DA. Development and validation of the Pain Response Inventory for Children. *Psychol Assessment* 1997; 9:392–405.

Wall BA, Holden EW, Gladstein J. Parental response in pediatric headache. *Headache Quarterly* 1998; 9:331–337.

Warnach HR, Keenan DM. Behavioral treatment of children with recurrent headaches. *J Behav Ther Exp Psychiatry* 1985; 16:31–38.

Werder DS, Sargent JD. A study of childhood headache using biofeedback as a treatment alternative. *Headache* 1984; 24:122–126.

Wisniewski JJ, Genshaft JL, Coury DL, Hammer D. Relaxation therapy and compliance in the treatment of adolescent headache. *Headache* 1988; 28:612–617

Correspondence to: E. Wayne Holden, PhD, ORC Macro, Inc., 3 Corporate Square, Suite 370, Atlanta, GA 30329, USA. Tel: 404-321-3211; Fax: 404-321-3688; email: wholden@macroint.com.

The Child with Headache: Diagnosis and Treatment.
Progress in Pain Research and Management, Vol. 19,
edited by Patricia A. McGrath and Loretta M. Hillier,
IASP Press, Seattle, © 2001.

10

Understanding Children's Headache: Current Status and Future Challenges

Patricia A. McGrath

*Pain Innovations Inc., London, Ontario, Canada; and Department of
Pediatrics, Faculty of Medicine, University of Western Ontario,
London, Ontario, Canada*

Unprecedented scientific and clinical attention has focused on the unique pain problems of infants, children, and adolescents during the last two decades. New research has dramatically increased our understanding of how children perceive pain and how we can alleviate their suffering. One of the most exciting advances has been the increasing recognition that children's pain is not simply and directly related to tissue damage. Recognition of the plasticity and complexity of pain in children has profound implications for pain management. We now understand that we cannot completely control a child's pain by gearing our treatment solely to the putative source of tissue damage. Instead, we must also identify the situational factors that can cause or exacerbate a child's pain and target our interventions accordingly. Our treatment emphasis thus should shift from an exclusive disease-centered focus to a more child-centered focus.

A child-centered focus is particularly important in the treatment of headache because most childhood headaches are not caused by an underlying disease or disorder. Recurrent migraine and tension-type headaches typically are caused by cognitive, behavioral, and emotional factors. Some factors are present for all children, but their relevance as a primary cause or a secondary contributing factor varies. Thus, children may have similar headache features (i.e., location, intensity, quality, and frequency of attacks), but very different causal factors. The diagnosis of childhood headache should include an assessment of the relevant factors that trigger headache attacks, intensify pain and distress, prolong headache-related disability, or maintain the cycle of repeated attacks for particular children. An objective appraisal of these factors enables us to select the most appropriate drug and nondrug therapies for each child with headache.

The challenge for the future is to integrate this child-centered approach more efficiently into clinical practice. At present, the main diagnostic and treatment paradigm underlying the treatment of childhood headache remains disease-centered. Diagnostic criteria for headache classification include pain characteristics, accompanying symptoms, and neurological findings. Yet, the criteria for determining the most appropriate treatment for headache also should include information on relevant cognitive, behavioral, and emotional factors, including the presence and nature of situation-specific stress. We need to build from the research of the past two decades and incorporate our knowledge of the plasticity and complexity of children's pain into a multi-factorial model for recurrent headache.

CLINICAL CHALLENGES

Recurrent headache is increasingly being recognized as a major health problem for children and adolescents (McGrath 1990; Vieyra et al. 1991; Williamson et al. 1993; Holden et al. 1994; Labbé 1999; Larsson 1999; McGrath 1999). Effective treatment of migraine and tension-type headache, the most prevalent types affecting otherwise healthy children and adolescents, requires a multimodal approach with cognitive-behavioral therapy in addition to abortive drug therapy. The treatment regimen should be based on modifying the factors that trigger attacks and those that exacerbate pain and disability. Although some children require a specialized treatment program, many children (especially if they have had headaches for only a few months) may benefit from a brief educational intervention. However, few primary health care providers teach parents about the multifactorial etiology of headache and the need for a multimodal treatment approach, in contrast to the more familiar "single cause and single treatment" approach normally adequate for relieving acute pain.

Primary care providers should help parents and children to learn that each causative factor must be treated and that the most effective treatment includes education, basic drug and nondrug pain management techniques, and the resolution of any stressful situations that provoke headache. In the first consultation appointment, primary care providers should teach parents and children about the common headache triggers for recurrent migraine and tension-type headache and make explicit recommendations for managing pain and preventing disability. In most instances, parents should receive written guidelines about which drug to administer, which dose is required, how to use simple nondrug strategies, how to encourage children's recovery, and why they should eventually talk with their child about what may have triggered the headache and how that situation could be changed. Children should monitor any headaches they experience for a limited period and record which methods they used to relieve their pain.

At the follow-up appointment, primary care providers should review prospective records of headache activity to identify relevant contributing factors, evaluate children's (and their family's) ability to manage the headaches using the pain control recommendations provided at the previous appointment, and guide parents to identify and resolve situation-specific stress to lessen children's headache attacks. This brief feedback intervention can significantly lessen headache attacks, decrease pain, and minimize disability for children with recurrent migraine and tension-type headache.

Pain assessment is an integral component of diagnosis and treatment for children with recurrent headaches. Although many behavioral and self-report scales have been validated as pain measures for children, few health care providers use any validated measures or adopt a standardized format for interviewing children about their headache experience. Behavioral scales must be used when children are unable to communicate directly about their headache experience; while these scales provide only an indirect estimate of pain intensity, they directly measure headache-related disability. Several self-report tools can be easily incorporated into a semistructured clinical interview to enable health care providers to objectively document children's headaches—location, frequency, length, pain intensity, pain quality, disability level, and accompanying symptoms. Parents often are asked to monitor children's headache activity between clinical appointments, but they may receive inconsistent information about which headache features to monitor and how to assess them. Parents and children can record easily relevant headache features using simple pain logs and diaries; such documentation can provide a practical and accurate baseline for determining treatment efficacy.

Ordinary clinical care can be regarded as a form of evidence-based practice because health care providers determine the causes for children's headaches, select an intervention from various alternatives, evaluate the effectiveness of the intervention and any side effects, and adjust the treatment as required to maintain a proper balance between effectiveness and side effects. All health care professionals constantly evaluate the effectiveness of their treatments and use this information to guide future decisions about headache management, but they may not document their evaluations in a consistent manner for all children. The increasing trend toward evidence-based health care requires that all clinicians routinely document more objectively and more consistently. We know how to evaluate children's headaches with practical time- and cost-effective methods. The challenge is to put this knowledge into practice. The benefits will be a vastly improved understanding of the causes of children's headaches and an enhanced ability to select the best treatment for each child.

RESEARCH CHALLENGES

As described throughout this volume, we have learned much about the etiology, diagnosis, and treatment of children with headache. However, several key questions remain unanswered. What is the natural history of headache? Can we identify children who are at risk for developing disabling headache? What is the true cost (personal and economic) of childhood headache? Can we individualize treatments so that children receive the drugs or nondrug therapies that would be particularly effective for them? How can we deliver multimodal therapies in a cost-effective manner? Which of the myriad of complementary therapies are effective for treating children's headache?

Epidemiologic studies have reported various lifetime, period, and point prevalence rates for migraine and tension-type headache, using different diagnostic criteria to determine whether children have headache and different methods for sampling different populations. As such, these studies provide diverse cross-sectional "snapshots" of children in particular countries at particular time periods. These snapshots yield valuable data on headache prevalence for children at specific ages and frequently provide rich descriptive data on headache characteristics. However, we cannot understand how headaches may change as children mature solely by combining these disparate snapshots. We do not know the natural history of children's headache. Only a few follow-up studies have been conducted, noting either high spontaneous remission rates or high persistence rates, depending on the study and on the child's age at headache onset. Longitudinal studies are needed to determine the extent to which childhood headaches remit, persist, or change in severity.

Future epidemiologic studies should include a child-centered approach for collecting and analyzing such data, based on our improved understanding of children's headache. Single prevalence estimates of the spontaneous remission rate or estimates of the continuing prevalence rate probably are not meaningful in predicting the course of a child's headache. Instead, studies should determine prevalence rates for relevant subgroups of the population, stratified by socioeconomic status, age, age of onset, sex, headache type, headache severity, and extent of headache-related disability. The natural course of headache may vary according to these factors, and prevalence, remission, and persistence rates should be evaluated accordingly. Estimates obtained in this manner may have more prognostic value for individual children.

Longitudinal case-control and cohort studies are also needed to evaluate other prognostic factors, to determine risk factors, and to identify any high-risk groups that require special intervention to reduce the likelihood that disabling headache will continue into adult life. Despite extensive research on the environmental, familial, and child characteristics associated with migraine and tension-type headache, we do not yet know which factors (other than positive family history) may predispose certain children to develop headache and which factors are the result of living with repeated headache attacks.

Many epidemiologic studies demonstrate that a substantial proportion of children suffer from repeated headache attacks for a prolonged period. Headache causes significant suffering and disability for children, ongoing anxiety for parents, unpredictable disruptions for families, and considerable costs for health care systems. Although extensive efforts have been made to estimate the personal and economic impact of adult headache, only recently has attention focused on the impact of childhood headache. We need to obtain accurate data on the personal burden for children and families and the financial costs to society. Special attention should focus on evaluating the impact over time. Headache has been regarded generally as one of the "benign pains" of childhood, but the benign nature of repeated headache attacks is questionable in light of the sequelae of continued pain throughout adolescence and adulthood. Particularly troubling are the results of our clinical studies indicating that adolescents who have endured recurrent headache for several years may develop numerous emotional problems (McGrath 1990).

Drug therapies for treating children's headache include analgesics, ergot derivatives, serotonin receptor agonists, antiemetics, β-blockers, serotonin antagonists, tricyclic antidepressants, antihistamines, calcium channel blockers, and antiepileptics (as described in Chapter 5). Yet, their efficacy has generally been accepted on the basis of studies with adults rather than demonstrated in controlled trials with children and adolescents. In view of the frequently high spontaneous remission rate for childhood headache, more research should be conducted to determine which drugs are effective for certain types of headache.

The array of nondrug therapies for treating children's headache is similarly extensive. Therapies include counseling, guided imagery, hypnosis, biofeedback, behavioral management, acupuncture, massage, chiropractic manipulation, homeopathic remedies, naturopathic approaches, and herbal medicines (as described in Chapter 6). While the evidence base supporting the efficacy of most cognitive and behavioral therapies is strong, few controlled trials have been conducted to evaluate the efficacy of physical techniques or therapies regarded as complementary to traditional medical approaches. Their empirical support derives primarily from anecdotal reports and case descriptions. However, because children are increasingly using alternative and complementary therapies (Spigelblatt et al. 1994; Ernst 1999), future research efforts must include objective evaluations of these modalities. The lack of evidence about their efficacy does not indicate that these therapies are ineffective, but rather that we lack research in this area. In light of the multiple factors contributing to childhood headache, some of these therapies may prove very beneficial for children.

Nondrug therapies are an intrinsic component of headache treatment, even when children are also receiving drug therapy. Drugs relieve the pain of headache attacks, but for most children they fail to mitigate the factors responsible for repeated attacks. An integrated, flexible approach combining cognitive, behavioral, and physical methods is more effective for alleviating headache. Moreover, children can incorporate many nondrug therapies practically into their daily activities. These methods enable children to improve their independent control during headache attacks and to modify their lives to prevent additional attacks and avoid prolonged disability.

The choice for pain control is not merely "drug" versus "nondrug" therapy; rather, a therapy that mitigates both the causative and contributing factors in pain should be implemented. The major emphasis in future clinical trials should shift from evaluating whether a certain treatment is effective to evaluating for whom it is effective. Many therapies seemingly are equivalent with respect to their overall success rate, measured as the proportion of children who achieve at least a 50% reduction in headache activity. However, closer examination may reveal significant differences among children with respect to their individual responses to treatment. Some children may experience a profound improvement, while others may receive few or no benefits.

Greater effort should be expended on evaluating therapies according to individual children, beginning by identifying which children respond optimally (i.e., immediately or with a major improvement) to particular therapies. Future studies should be designed so as to identify child characteristics that will enable us to better match treatments to individual children, and not only to headache type. Special attention should be given to children who do not seem to improve, regardless of the treatment they receive. Particular research attention should be directed toward children with chronic daily headache, and toward children who suffer mixed trauma-related and tension-type headache, in addition to significant cognitive and physical disabilities, following traumatic brain injury.

We must devote careful consideration to the design of future studies. Regrettably, the findings in many treatment studies may not be generalizable to all children with headache. Common design flaws include small sample sizes combined with multiple outcome measures, so that the study lacks the power to evaluate statistically and clinically meaningful differences among groups. Other studies may have sufficient power to evaluate treatment effects on one outcome measure (e.g., headache frequency), but the investigators conduct multiple analyses on additional outcome measures and on different subgroups of children. Thus, some of their reported findings are substantive, and others exploratory, but the authors may not distinguish between the two levels of support, citing all findings as definitive and equally conclusive. In addition, many studies provide insufficient details about how children assess headache intensity. For example, investigators may state that children used an analogue scale (with appropriate adjectives for the different pain levels), but fail to describe the specific adjectives. In such cases it is impossible for readers to discern whether children were judging pain level according to intensity, affect, disability, or some combination. The failure to describe how children evaluated headache activity thus compromises our interpretation of the treatment effects.

It is difficult to compare treatment results across studies because of many differences in how headache improvement is assessed. Many studies use an index of headache activity, a numerical value combining information on headache frequency, pain intensity, and headache length. However, the headache index is not a uniform measure because the specific calculation varies across studies. Some studies present data separately on the effects of treatment for headache frequency and pain intensity. All future studies should include this information, as well as the particular formula used to determine headache activity. These data are especially important from a clinical perspective. Children may experience significant clinical improvements because their headache attacks lessen (even though pain intensity is unchanged), because their headaches are less painful (even though headache frequency is unchanged), or because they are less distressed and disabled during attacks (even though both pain intensity and headache frequency are unchanged). It is likely that different treatments differentially affect these headache characteristics, but this relevant information is masked when investigators report treatment effectiveness using only a combined headache index.

Efforts to ensure that the diagnostic criteria for headache classification are clinically meaningful and scientifically sound should be extended to other important aspects of headache assessment and treatment. Clinicians and scientists should achieve a consensus about the key outcome measures to use in all therapeutic trials. Moreover, they should consider whether the traditional 50% improvement in headache activity continues to be the best reference point for evaluating therapeutic efficacy. A child-centered improvement in the headache features that are most relevant—headache frequency, intensity, distress, or disability—might constitute a more sensitive and clinically meaningful measure of efficacy.

Given that most centers lack a sufficient patient base of children, multicenter randomized, controlled trials are needed to address important research questions in a timely manner. In view of the increasing pressure on health care systems, research studies should include a cost-benefit analysis. A major challenge for the future is to develop a balanced, coordinated, cohesive, and comprehensive plan for conducting the necessary epidemiologic and therapeutic research. We can meet this challenge by designing careful studies with well-defined objectives, adequate sample size based on appropriate power calculations, an explicit description of the clinically meaningful reduction in headache, the designation of clear primary and secondary outcome measures, and careful selection of the headache-free comparison groups.

Concurrent with our research efforts to improve our understanding of children's headache, to strengthen the evidence base for drug and nondrug therapies, and to better match treatments to the individual child with headache, we must focus on integrating our scientific knowledge into clinical practice. We have at our disposal a repertoire of effective therapies, child-centered multimodal programs, and innovative ideas for implementing treatment guidelines in clinical practice. Optimal treatment for all children begins with the differential diagnosis of headache type and a comprehensive pain assessment to identify the relevant causative and contributing factors. A creative clinical approach will enable health care providers to select the most appropriate therapies to modify the different factors that trigger headache attacks, intensify pain, prolong disability, and maintain the cycle of repeated attacks for each child with headache.

REFERENCES

Ernst E. Homeopathic prophylaxis of headaches and migraine? A systematic review. *J Pain Symptom Manage* 1999; 18:353–357.

Holden EW, Gladstein J, Trulsen M, Wall B. Chronic daily headache in children and adolescents. *Headache* 1994; 34:508–514.

Labbé EE. Commentary: salient aspects of research in pediatric headache and future directions. *J Pediatr Psychol* 1999; 24:113–114.

Larsson B. Recurrent headaches in children and adolescents. In: McGrath PJ, Finley GA (Eds). *Chronic and Recurrent Pain in Children and Adolescents,* Progress in Pain Research and Management, Vol. 13. Seattle: IASP Press, 1999, pp 115–140.

McGrath PA. *Pain in Children: Nature, Assessment and Treatment.* New York: Guilford Publications, 1990.

McGrath PJ. Commentary: headaches in adolescents are a significant problem. *J Pediatr Psychol* 1999; 24:25–27.

Spigelblatt L, Laine-Ammara G, Pless IB, Guyver A. The use of alternative medicine by children. *Pediatrics* 1994; 94:811–814.

Vieyra M, Hoag NL, Masek BJ. Migraine in childhood: developmental aspects of biobehavioral treatment. In: Bush JP, Harkins SW (Eds). *Children in Pain: Clinical and Research Issues from a Developmental Perspective.* New York: Springer-Verlag, 1991, p 373–396.

Williamson DA, Baker JD, Cubic BA. Advances in pediatric headache research. In: Ollendick TH, Prinz RJ (Eds). *Advances in Clinical Child Psychology.* New York: Plenum Press, 1993, pp 275–304.

Correspondence to: Patricia A. McGrath, PhD, Pain Innovations, Inc., 38 Hampton Crescent, London, Ontario, Canada N6H 2N8. Fax: 519-471-8529; email: pamcgrat@julian.wo.ca. Effective 1 July 2001: Department of Anesthesiology, School of Medicine, University of Utah, Salt Lake City, UT 84108, USA.

Appendix 1

Children's Headache Interview

Child: _____ Date: _____ Therapist: _____

We have learned a great deal about what can cause headaches and how we can treat them. There are many different causes and many different treatments, and many children have a few causes for their headaches, not just one. In order to figure out the causes for your headaches, I need to ask you some questions about your headaches and also your life. In that way, I can suggest some treatments that should work well for you.

Recent Headache

1.0 First, let's talk about your last headache. *(Note the specific circumstances.)* When was that?_____

1.1 Where were you when it started? _____

_____

1.2 What were you doing?_____

_____

2.0 Can you show me exactly where it hurt? *(Note whether child has difficulty in localizing the specific area(s), shade outline, and confirm location with child.)*

Difficulty in localizing?   Yes _____ No _____

2.1 Painful area(s):

2.2 Was the pain on just the one side?
Right ____ or left ____ or on both sides? _____

2.3 Did the pain stay in the same place for the whole headache?
Yes ____ or spread? Where did it spread or change to? _____

3.0 How strong was the pain/headache?

_____

3.1 *If the child answered with one of the responses listed below, then check it. Otherwise ...* I'm going to read out some words that describe how strong pain can be. I'd like you to listen to them and pick out the one that best describes how strong your headache was:

(~7 years and younger)	*(~8 years and older)*
a) A little bit	a) Slight
b) A little	b) Mild
c) Medium	c) Moderate
d) A lot	d) Strong
e) A real lot	e) Intense

3.2 Now, I'd like you to use our pain scale to show me how much it hurt.

Administer the Colored Analogue Scale (CAS): This scale is like a ruler. The bottom where it is small and there is hardly any color at all means no pain at all. The top, where it is large, very red, and a long way from the bottom means the most pain. I want you to slide the marker up the scale to show me how much your headache hurt.

Present the scale with the marker at the bottom, the number side facing you.
CAS rating: _____

3.3 Headache pain sometimes changes in strength after it starts. Did your headache start low and get stronger? _____ Or did it start strong? _____

4.0 We've talked a lot about how much it hurts, but it's also important to know what your headache felt like. Some pains are sharp, like needles, and some are dull, like a pushing feeling. What did your headache feel like?

_____

_____

Do any of these words describe how your pain felt?

	Yes	No			Yes	No
4.1 Sharp?	[ ]	[ ]	4.7 Hot?		[ ]	[ ]
4.2 Dull?	[ ]	[ ]	4.8 Burning?		[ ]	[ ]
4.3 Aching?	[ ]	[ ]	4.9 Stinging?		[ ]	[ ]
4.4 Pounding?	[ ]	[ ]	4.10 Tingling?		[ ]	[ ]
4.5 Throbbing?	[ ]	[ ]	4.11 Cutting?		[ ]	[ ]
4.6 Cold?	[ ]	[ ]	4.12 Another word?		_____	

5.0 How much did that headache bother you?

_____

5.1 *If the child answered with one of the responses listed below, then check it. Otherwise, ask if it was:*

    a) a little bit ___   d) a lot ___

    b) a little ___   e) a real lot ___

    c) medium/moderate amount ___

I am going to read some of the words people feel when they have headaches and I wonder if any of these words describe how you felt?

		Yes	No			Yes	No
5.2	Sad	[ ]	[ ]	5.6	Angry	[ ]	[ ]
5.3	Annoyed	[ ]	[ ]	5.7	Frightened	[ ]	[ ]
5.4	Miserable	[ ]	[ ]	5.8	Worried	[ ]	[ ]
5.5	Upset	[ ]	[ ]	5.9	Anxious	[ ]	[ ]

5.10 Now, I'd like you to use the facial scale to show me how much it bothered you.

Administer the Facial Affective Scale (FAS): Now I'm going to show you a series of different faces; some are really happy and some really upset. I want you to choose the face that looks like you felt when you had that headache. Choose the face that looks like how you felt deep down inside, not necessarily the face you showed to the world. *Present the scale with the number side facing you.* FAS rating: _____

Now I'd like to ask you about other things you might have felt when you had this headache. Did you:

		Yes	No	Don't Know
6.0	Have aches in your arms or legs?	[ ]	[ ]	[ ]
6.1	Have aches in your neck or shoulders?	[ ]	[ ]	[ ]
6.2	Feel dizzy?	[ ]	[ ]	[ ]
6.3	Feel that light bothered your eyes?	[ ]	[ ]	[ ]
6.4	See bright lights, dots, flashes out of the corner of your eyes?	[ ]	[ ]	[ ]
6.5	Feel that sound bothered you?	[ ]	[ ]	[ ]
6.6	Feel really tired?	[ ]	[ ]	[ ]
6.7	Feel sick to your stomach?	[ ]	[ ]	[ ]
6.8	Throw up?	[ ]	[ ]	[ ]
6.9	Have a sore throat?	[ ]	[ ]	[ ]
6.10	Feel hot and sweaty?	[ ]	[ ]	[ ]
6.11	Feel your heart beat really fast?	[ ]	[ ]	[ ]
6.12	Have sweaty hands?	[ ]	[ ]	[ ]
6.13	Anything else I haven't mentioned?	[ ]	[ ]	[ ]

Specify: _____

6.14   Did you have any sign or warning signal beforehand that you were going to get a headache?

  No ____   Don't know ____

  Yes ____   (What?) _____

6.15   Sometimes people have a visual aura; that means they see things in their eyes before they get a headache. Did that happen?

  No ____   Don't know ____

  Yes ____   What was it like? _____

7.0 How long did that headache last? _____

7.1 *If the child answered with one of the responses listed below, then check it. Otherwise, ask if it was:*

  a) A few minutes ____   e) 4½ to 6 hours ____

  b) About half an hour ____   f) All day (~12 waking hours) ____

  c) 1 to 2 hours ____   g) Other (specify) _____

  d) 2½ to 4 hours ____

7.2 What did you do to get it to stop?_____

Usual Headache Characteristics

(Note: some children can clearly distinguish between two different types of headache that they may get regularly. If possible, determine the following headache characteristics for both mild and strong headaches so as to be able to accurately evaluate treatment efficacy. Otherwise, obtain information about the usual or most common type of headache.)

8.0 Thanks for telling me about your last headache. Now I'd like to know more about the other headaches you get. Are all your headaches that strong?

  Yes ____ No ____ Don't know ____

8.1 *If no:* Show me on the scale (CAS) how strong they usually are:

_____

8.2 And show me on the scale how little/mild they can be:

_____

8.3 And how strong they can be:

_____

9.0   Which headaches do you get more often, the mild ones _____ or the strong ones _____?

10.0 Are all your headaches in exactly the same place?

  Yes ____ No ____ (where else?) _____ Don't know ____

11.0 How often do you get headaches now?

_____

11.1 *If the child answered with one of the responses listed below, then check it. Otherwise ask:* Do you get your (mild/strong/usual) headaches:
    a) Hardly ever _____
    b) About once or twice a month _____
    c) About once or twice a week _____
    d) Several times a week (3–5 times) _____
    e) Every day _____
    f) Other *(specify)* _____

12.0 Sometimes headaches happen very regularly—the same number every week or month. Do you always have headaches this often?
    Yes _____ No _____

12.1 *If no,* How do they change—what is the least number of headaches you get each week? _____

12.2 And what is the most? _____

Sometimes people get headaches more often at certain times of the year, week, day or even during certain activities. Do you ever get headaches more often at these times?

12.3 Winter, spring, summer, or fall?
    No ___ Yes (when?) _____ Don't know _____

12.4 Mondays through Fridays or weekends?
    No ___ Yes (when?) _____ Don't know _____

12.5 Mornings, afternoons or evenings?
    No ___ Yes (when?) _____ Don't know _____

12.6 When you are doing certain things, like sports or hobbies?
    No ___ Yes (when?) _____ Don't know _____

12.7 Do you have more headaches at school or at home?
    No ___ Yes (when?) _____ Don't know _____

We talked about what your last headache felt like, and now I'd like to know what your usual headaches feel like:

	Yes	No			Yes	No
13.0 Sharp?	[ ]	[ ]	13.6	Hot?	[ ]	[ ]
13.1 Dull?	[ ]	[ ]	13.7	Burning?	[ ]	[ ]
13.2 Aching?	[ ]	[ ]	13.8	Stinging?	[ ]	[ ]
13.3 Pounding?	[ ]	[ ]	13.9	Tingling?	[ ]	[ ]
13.4 Throbbing?	[ ]	[ ]	13.10	Cutting?	[ ]	[ ]
13.5 Cold?	[ ]	[ ]	13.11	Another word?	_____	

14.0 How long do your usual headaches last?
    a) A few minutes _____   e) 4½ to 6 hours _____
    b) About half an hour _____   f) All day (~12 waking hours) _____
    c) 1 to 2 hours _____   g) Other (specify) _____
    d) 2½ to 4 hours _____

14.1 *If child responds that headache is constant, then ask: (Otherwise, go to #15.)*
Do you mean that your headache starts every day when you wake up and open your eyes and lasts until you go to bed?
    Yes _____ No _____

14.2 *If no, then determine when it starts and ends, using the child's schedule as a frame of reference, e.g., starts when brushing teeth/having breakfast/riding the school bus, and ends after school/after dinner/at bedtime.*

_____

_____

14.3 Does your headache come and go throughout the day? _____
Or is it there all the time? _____

14.4 Does it get less painful sometimes during the day? _____
Or is it always the same strength? _____

15.0 How much your headaches usually bother you? _____

_____

15.1 *If the child answered with one of the responses listed below, then check it. Otherwise, ask if it was:*

    a) a little bit _____   d) a lot _____
    b) a little _____   e) a real lot _____
    c) medium/moderate amount _____

Do your headaches usually make you feel:

		Yes	No			Yes	No
15.2	Sad	[ ]	[ ]	15.6	Angry	[ ]	[ ]
15.3	Annoyed	[ ]	[ ]	15.7	Frightened	[ ]	[ ]
15.4	Miserable	[ ]	[ ]	15.8	Worried	[ ]	[ ]
15.5	Upset	[ ]	[ ]	15.9	Anxious	[ ]	[ ]

15.10 Now I'd like you to use the facial scale (FAS) to show me how much your headaches usually bother you: _____

I'd now like to check about some of the other things you might feel when you have your usual headaches. Do you:

		Yes	No	Don't Know
16.0	Have aches in your arms or legs?	[ ]	[ ]	[ ]
16.1	Have aches in your neck or shoulders?	[ ]	[ ]	[ ]
16.2	Feel dizzy?	[ ]	[ ]	[ ]
16.3	Feel that light bothers your eyes?	[ ]	[ ]	[ ]
16.4	See bright lights, dots, flashes out of the corner of your eyes?	[ ]	[ ]	[ ]
16.5	Feel that sound bothers you?	[ ]	[ ]	[ ]
16.6	Feel really tired?	[ ]	[ ]	[ ]
16.7	Feel sick to your stomach?	[ ]	[ ]	[ ]
16.8	Throw up?	[ ]	[ ]	[ ]
16.9	Have a sore throat?	[ ]	[ ]	[ ]
16.10	Feel hot and sweaty?	[ ]	[ ]	[ ]
16.11	Feel your heart beat really fast?	[ ]	[ ]	[ ]
16.12	Have sweaty hands?	[ ]	[ ]	[ ]
16.13	Anything else I haven't mentioned?	[ ]	[ ]	[ ]

Specify: _____

17.0 Do you usually get a warning signal beforehand that your headache is going to start?

     Yes ____ (What?) _____

     No ____ Don't know ____

18.0 Do your headaches ever start in the middle of the night when you are sleeping?

     Never ____ Sometimes ____ Don't know ____

Headache Triggers

19.0 What do you think causes your headaches?

_____

_____

Do any of these also cause your headache? *(omit any items the child mentioned in #19.0)*

		Yes	No	Don't Know
19.1	Drinking pop?	[ ]	[ ]	[ ]
19.2	Eating cheese?	[ ]	[ ]	[ ]
19.3	Eating chocolate?	[ ]	[ ]	[ ]
19.4	Hot weather?	[ ]	[ ]	[ ]
19.5	High humidity?	[ ]	[ ]	[ ]
19.6	Bright sun?	[ ]	[ ]	[ ]

		Yes	No	Don't Know
19.7	Feeling excited?	[ ]	[ ]	[ ]
19.8	Feeling hungry?	[ ]	[ ]	[ ]
19.9	Feeling tired?	[ ]	[ ]	[ ]
19.10	Feeling sad?	[ ]	[ ]	[ ]
19.11	Feeling worried about school?	[ ]	[ ]	[ ]
19.12	Feeling worried about getting your school work done on time?	[ ]	[ ]	[ ]
19.13	Feeling worried about your grades?	[ ]	[ ]	[ ]
19.14	Feeling worried about what your friends think of you?	[ ]	[ ]	[ ]
19.15	Feeling worried about doing well in sports?	[ ]	[ ]	[ ]
19.16	Feeling worried about your family?	[ ]	[ ]	[ ]
19.17	Being really active in sports or gym?	[ ]	[ ]	[ ]
19.18	Menstrual periods *(girls only)*?	[ ]	[ ]	[ ]
19.19	Anything else?	[ ]	[ ]	[ ]

Specify:_____

19.20 There are a lot of causes for headaches. But what do you think is the main reason you usually get headaches?

_____

_____

Pain Control Methods

20.0   There are lots of things people do to get rid of headaches. What do you usually do to get rid of your very small/mild headaches?

_____

_____

20.1   And your strong headaches?

_____

_____

20.2.   How do you manage headaches at home?

_____

_____

20.3   And at school? *(Note any differences)*

_____

Do you ever . . .		Yes/No	**If So, How Often?** **O**nce in a while Sometimes Frequently Always	**How Much Does It Help?** Makes it **Worse** **No** relief **Mild** relief **Moderate** relief **Complete** relief
20.4	Rest or sleep?			
20.5	Put warm/cold cloths on your head?			
20.6	Rub or massage the painful area?			
20.7	Try to ignore the pain and keep doing what you were doing?			
20.8	Do something physically active to get rid of your headache, for example, ride your bike, go for a walk, get some exercise?			
20.9	Stop physical activities and sports?			
20.10	Do something socially active to get rid of your headache, for example, play with or hang out with your friends, invite a friend over, call a friend?			
20.11	Stop playing/socializing with your friends?			
20.12	Try to keep your mind busy, for example by playing computer games, reading, coloring, or writing?			
20.13	Try to figure out what caused the headache?			
20.14	Think or imagine pleasant or good things to keep your mind off the headache and to relax?			
20.15	Take medication?			
20.16 Do you do anything else that I haven't mentioned? Specify: _____				

Now I'd like to ask you about other things that you might also do when you have a headache:

21. Can you show me on this (CAS) scale how strong your headache has to be before you take medication or ask for it?   CAS rating _____

22. Do you think you can stop a headache without using medication?
    No ____ Sometimes ____ Most of the time ____ Always ____

General Impact of Headaches

23.0 Now I'd like to ask you about the effects or impact of these headaches on your life. What is hard about having headaches?

_____

_____

23.1 So are they much of a problem for you?
      A little problem ____ A medium problem ____ A big problem ____

23.2 Do your headaches often interfere with what you are doing?
      Yes ____ No ____ Don't know ____

Have they ever prevented you from:

	No	Sometimes	Many Times
23.3 Playing sports/attending gym class?	[ ]	[ ]	[ ]
23.4 Doing homework?	[ ]	[ ]	[ ]
23.5 Going to parties or movies?	[ ]	[ ]	[ ]
23.6 Doing household chores?	[ ]	[ ]	[ ]
23.7 Playing or socializing with friends?	[ ]	[ ]	[ ]
23.8 Watching television?	[ ]	[ ]	[ ]
23.9 Playing computer games?	[ ]	[ ]	[ ]
23.10 Anything else that I didn't mention already?	[ ]	[ ]	[ ]

Specify: _____

23.11 Have your headaches ever prevented you from attending school?
      Yes ____ No ____

23.12 If so, about how many days of school have you missed
      this week? ____ month? ____ or year? ____

23.13 About how many times have you left school early this month? ____

23.14 *If the child has answered that he/she misses a certain activity frequently, e.g., sports, going to friend's homes, ask:* About how many times have you missed "activity" this month? ____

Headaches can really upset a whole family. I'm going to ask you how people in your family are when you have a headache. Let me know if they are usually especially nice, just a little nicer, the same as when you don't have a headache, or sort of annoyed and frustrated. I'll ask first about your:

24.0 Mom:

Especially nice ____ Little nicer ____The same ____ Annoyed/frustrated___

24.1 Dad:

Especially nice ____ Little nicer ____The same ____ Annoyed/frustrated___

24.2 Brothers:

Especially nice ____ Little nicer ____The same ____ Annoyed/frustrated___

24.3 Sisters:

Especially nice ____ Little nicer ____The same ____ Annoyed/frustrated___

25.0 Does anyone else in your family have headaches too?

　　　　Yes ____ No ____ Don't know ____

25.1 *If yes,* who?_____

26.0 Does anyone in your family have a pain problem? *If yes,* who?

_____

26.1 *If so,* what is it? _____

26.2 *If so,* does the pain really interfere in his/her life (e.g., can he/she work and go out with friends)? _____

27.0 Do you have any other pains that you get a lot? *If yes,* what?

_____

If the child's response suggests another persistent pain problem, obtain information about the usual pain characteristics.

27.1 Where exactly is the pain?_____

27.2 What does it feel like? _____

27.3 How strong is it on this *(CAS)* scale? ____

27.4 How much does it bother you on this *(FAS)* scale? ____

27.5 How often do you get these pains? _____

27.6 How long do they last?_____

27.7 What do you do to stop the pain? _____

27.8 What do you think causes this pain? _____

27.9 Do you have to stop what you were doing when you get this pain?

　　　　Yes ____ No ____

27.10 How long have you had this pain? _____

28.0 Now I'd like to talk more with you about your life so that we can figure out the causes for your headaches and know which treatments would be best for you. First, though, do you think that you will get rid of these headaches someday? _____

28.1 Why or why not? _____

Situational Factors

Information on children's lives and potential sources of continuing stress is more easily obtained in a conversational format guided mainly by children's responses, rather than in a structured format with a predetermined sequence of questions. Thus, this section of the interview lists the basic issues that should be discussed, with suggestions for how to elicit the information as to whether certain social, physical, school, or family situations are contributing to the headache problem.

29.0 **Child's Schedule** *(Assess whether a busy schedule is a source of stress, specifically whether the child has time for him/herself and can manage daily school and recreational activities. Begin by asking about typical schooldays and weekends, determining whether sufficient time is allotted for getting ready in the morning, eating meals, completing homework, participating in sports and hobbies, and keeping up with required practice sessions.)*

Level of stress: None ___ Mild ___ Moderate ___ High ___ Very high ___

Comments: _____

_____

30.0 **School Attitudes** *(Assess whether child generally enjoys school—the atmosphere, subjects, classmates, and teachers. Begin by asking how the child gets to school, noting whether he/she enjoys the bus ride and gets along with children or is uncomfortable. Then, ask about the schoolday to determine the child's attitudes and feelings of acceptance.)*

Level of stress: None ___ Mild ___ Moderate ___ High ___ Very high ___

Comments: _____

_____

30.1 **Schoolwork** *(Assess whether the child is able to understand lessons, has difficulty in one or more subjects, gets acceptable grades, and can complete assigned homework independently. Begin by asking what grade the child is in, how much homework or special projects are typically assigned, how many tests there are, and how easy it is for the child to study and be prepared for class.)*

Level of stress: None ___ Mild ___ Moderate ___ High ___ Very high ___

Comments: _____

_____

30.2 **School Relationships** *(Assess the child's attitudes about friends and classmates, noting whether he/she feels accepted or somewhat apart from other children, may be teased or bullied, enjoys group projects and activities, interacts easily with classmates at recess/free periods, or tends to remain alone.)*

Level of stress: None ___ Mild ___ Moderate ___ High ___ Very high ___

Comments: _____

_____

31.0 **Leisure Activities** *(Assess whether the child has opportunities for relaxation—physical and mental, with some regular exercise, noting the extent to which the child has competitive, organized sports and independent, unsupervised leisure time. Begin by asking the child what he/she does for fun. For competitive activities, inquire about the pressure or demands of the sport, coach's and teammates' attitudes about performing and winning, and the child's own expectations for performing well. Specifically ask how he/she copes with a loss or poor performance. Assess the child's perception of parents' expectations for his/her performance.)*

Level of stress: None ___ Mild ___ Moderate ___ High ___ Very high ___

Comments: _____

_____

32.0 **Social Activities** *(Assess whether the child has an enjoyable social life. Begin by asking what the child does with friends and how often he/she sees them, noting whether the child initiates contact and suggests ideas or simply goes along with the group. Determine whether the child is comfortable regarding his/her appearance, conversational ability with friends.)*

Level of stress: None ___ Mild ___ Moderate ___ High ___ Very high ___

Comments: _____

_____

33.0 Identifying and Resolving Stress *(Assess the extent to which the child denies or recognizes typical problems and sources of stress associated with daily activities. Begin by asking about some of the situations he/she described in response to previous questions, noting whether he/she identifies the problem, recognizes the resulting emotional distress, and responds so as to resolve the stress.)*

Ability to identify and resolve stress:

      Poor ___ Moderate ___ Good ___   Excellent ___

Comments: _____

_____

33.1 General Problem-solving Ability *(Assess the manner in which the child solves life problems. Begin by asking about some of the stressful situations he/she described in response to previous questions, noting whether the child considers different options and the consequences before making a decision. Specifically ask whom the child confides in when he/she has a problem and whether the child is a worrier who keeps things to him/ herself for a while or talks about problems easily as soon as possible. Specifically ask about how children respond to conflicts about values (parents' versus friends' opinions) and for adolescents, ask about conflicts with parents about increasing independence.)*

Ability to problem-solve: Poor___ Moderate___ Good ___ Excellent ___

Comments: _____

_____

34.0   Family *(Assess whether there is any continuing stress within the child's family. Begin by asking about who lives in the house, the child's attitude toward siblings, general work and travel commitments for parents, sharing of household responsibilities, rules and how they are enforced, curfews.)*

Level of stress: None ___ Mild ___ Moderate ___ High ___ Very high ___

Comments: _____

_____

35.0   Child's openness to providing information during the interview:
      Very reluctant ____ Somewhat reluctant ____
      Open ____ Very open ____

36.0   Comments re. child's demeanor:

_____

_____

_____

Appendix 2
Parent Intake Form*

Please complete this intake form so that we have an accurate history of your child's headache problem. The pain therapist will review this information with you. Thank you.

Contact Information

1. Date: _____
2. Person completing form: Mother __ Father __ Other (specify) _____
3. Child's name and nickname: _____
4. Birth date: _____ 5. Age: ____ 6. Sex: ____
7. Address: _____
8. Day phone: _____ Fax: _____
9. Family physician/pediatrician: _____
10. Address: _____
11. Home phone: _____

Headache History

12. About how long has your child had headaches? If possible, list month and year they started: _____

    12.1 Do you remember the first headache? Yes ____ No ____

    12.2 If yes, what happened? _____

13. Did the headaches start gradually, or abruptly? _____

14. Did anything unusual, very new, or stressful (e.g., an accident, birth of a sibling, starting/changing school, a medical condition) happen to your child at about that time that may have triggered the headache?

    Yes ____ No ____ Don't know ____

    14.1 If yes, please describe: _____

    _____

15. Since the headaches first began, have they (circle response):

Become stronger?	Yes	No	Don't know
Occurred more often?	Yes	No	Don't know
Lasted longer?	Yes	No	Don't know
Become more disabling?	Yes	No	Don't know
Changed in any other way?	_____		

    _____

* In our clinic the Parent Intake Form is printed on colored paper so that it may be retrieved easily from children's files.

15.1   When did the headaches become a real problem? _____

_____

15.2   And why? _____

_____

16. How often has your child had headaches during the last month?
    (check one)
    a) Hardly ever? _____
    b) About once or twice a month? _____
    c) About once or twice a week? _____
    d) Several times a week (about 3–5 times)? _____
    e) Every day?_____
    f) Other? (specify) _____

17. Is this the usual frequency? Yes _____ No _____
    17.1 If not, what is the usual frequency? _____

18. Where is your child's pain usually located?
    (Mark the outline if you know the specific area.)

19. Does he/she ever have the headache in another area?
    Yes _____ No _____
    19.1 If yes, where else? _____

20. How strong are your child's headaches usually? (circle one)
    Slight   Mild   Moderate   Strong   Intense

21. Does he/she ever have headaches that are different in strength?
    Yes _____ No _____

    21.1 If yes, how? _____

22. How long do your child's headaches usually last? (check one)
    a) Only a few minutes _____
    b) About half an hour _____

c) 1 to 2 hours ____
d) 2½ hours to 4 hours ____
e) 4½ to 6 hours ____
f) All day (~12 waking hours) ____
g) Other (specify) _____

23. Does he/she ever have headaches that last for a different time period?
Yes ____ No ____
23.1 If yes, how long/short? _____

24. During headache attacks, does your child usually feel:

		Yes	No	Don't Know
24.1	Sad?	[ ]	[ ]	[ ]
24.2	Annoyed?	[ ]	[ ]	[ ]
24.3	Miserable?	[ ]	[ ]	[ ]
24.4	Upset?	[ ]	[ ]	[ ]
24.5	Angry?	[ ]	[ ]	[ ]
24.6	Frightened?	[ ]	[ ]	[ ]
24.7	Worried?	[ ]	[ ]	[ ]
24.8	Anxious?	[ ]	[ ]	[ ]
24.9	Have any other feelings?	[ ]	[ ]	[ ]

Specify: _____

_____

25. During your child's headache attacks, does he/she usually:

		Yes	No	Don't Know
25.1	Have aches in his/her arms or legs?	[ ]	[ ]	[ ]
25.2	Have aches in his/her neck or shoulders?	[ ]	[ ]	[ ]
25.3	Feel dizzy?	[ ]	[ ]	[ ]
25.4	Feel that light bothers his/her eyes?	[ ]	[ ]	[ ]
25.5	See bright lights, dots, flashes out of the corner of eyes?	[ ]	[ ]	[ ]
25.6	Feel that sound bothers him/her?	[ ]	[ ]	[ ]
25.7	Feel really tired?	[ ]	[ ]	[ ]
25.8	Have an upset stomach?	[ ]	[ ]	[ ]
25.9	Throw up?	[ ]	[ ]	[ ]
25.10	Have a sore throat?	[ ]	[ ]	[ ]

	Yes	No	Don't Know
25.11 Feel hot and sweaty?	[ ]	[ ]	[ ]
25.12 Have his/her heart beat really fast?	[ ]	[ ]	[ ]
25.13 Have sweaty hands?	[ ]	[ ]	[ ]
25.14 Have any other complaints?	[ ]	[ ]	[ ]

Specify: _____

_____

26. Does your child ever have a warning signal that a headache will start (e.g., visual aura)?

Yes _____ No _____
26.1   If yes, what? _____

27. Some people get headaches more often at certain times of the year, week, day, or even during certain activities. Does your child ever get headaches more often at these times? (If yes, circle the specific times)

	Yes	No	Don't Know
27.1 Winter, spring, fall or summer?	[ ]	[ ]	[ ]
27.2 Mondays to Fridays or on weekends?	[ ]	[ ]	[ ]
27.3 Mornings, afternoons, or nights?	[ ]	[ ]	[ ]
27.4 While doing certain things like sports?	[ ]	[ ]	[ ]
27.5 At home or at school?	[ ]	[ ]	[ ]

28. What does your child usually do when he/she has a headache?

_____
_____
_____
_____

29. What do you usually do for your child when he/she has a headache?

_____
_____
_____
_____

30. Some children report that different foods or environmental and emotional factors cause headaches. Do any of these regularly cause your child's headaches?

		Yes	No	Don't Know
30.1	Drinking pop?	[ ]	[ ]	[ ]
30.2	Eating cheese?	[ ]	[ ]	[ ]
30.3	Eating chocolate?	[ ]	[ ]	[ ]
30.4	Hot weather?	[ ]	[ ]	[ ]
30.5	High humidity?	[ ]	[ ]	[ ]
30.6	Bright sun?	[ ]	[ ]	[ ]
30.7	Feeling excited?	[ ]	[ ]	[ ]
30.8	Feeling hungry?	[ ]	[ ]	[ ]
30.9	Feeling tired?	[ ]	[ ]	[ ]
30.10	Feeling sad?	[ ]	[ ]	[ ]
30.11	Feeling worried about schoolwork?	[ ]	[ ]	[ ]
30.12	Feeling worried about getting schoolwork done on time?	[ ]	[ ]	[ ]
30.13	Feeling worried about grades?	[ ]	[ ]	[ ]
30.14	Feeling worried about how friends think of him/her?	[ ]	[ ]	[ ]
30.15	Feeling worried about doing well in sports?	[ ]	[ ]	[ ]
30.16	Feeling worried about family?	[ ]	[ ]	[ ]
30.17	Being really physically active?	[ ]	[ ]	[ ]
30.18	Menstrual periods (girls only)?	[ ]	[ ]	[ ]
30.19	Anything else?	[ ]	[ ]	[ ]

Specify: _____

---

31. What do you think is the number one cause of your child's headaches?

_____

_____

32. If any headache attacks were really frightening for you or your child, please describe:

_____

_____

_____

Medication Use

33. How often does your child take medication when he/she has headaches? (circle one)

    Never   Rarely   Sometimes   Usually   Always

34. Is your child allowed to take pain medication on his/her own?

    Yes _____ No _____

    34.1 If not, when does he/she ask you for medication?

    _____

    _____

35. When (if ever) do you give your child medication for headaches without him/her asking? _____

    _____

36. List the medications that your child has tried; indicate how well each worked.

Medication	Dosage	Amount of Pain Relief (circle one)			
_____	_____	None	Slight	Moderate	Complete
_____	_____	None	Slight	Moderate	Complete
_____	_____	None	Slight	Moderate	Complete
_____	_____	None	Slight	Moderate	Complete

37. Which medications does your child use now?

    _____

38. Would you like more information about how to use pain medication for your child?

    Yes _____ No _____

39. What do you think is the best method to relieve your child's headache?

    _____

    _____

    _____

40. What nondrug methods does your child use to relieve his/her headaches?

    _____

    _____

Does your child do any of the following things to relieve pain?
If yes, how often and how much does it help? (Just put the letter or word shown in boldface type in the space.)

Does your child ever . . .	Yes/No	**How Often?** **On**ce in a while **S**ometimes **F**requently **A**lways	**How Much** **Does It Help?** Makes it **Worse** **No** relief **Mild** relief **Moderate** relief **Complete** relief
40.1 Rest or sleep?			
40.2 Put warm/cold cloths on his/her head?			
40.3 Rub or massage the painful area?			
40.4 Try to ignore the pain and keep doing what he/she was doing?			
40.5 Do something physically active to get rid of the headache—for example, ride a bike, go for a walk, get some exercise?			
40.6 Stop physical activities and sports?			
40.7 Do something socially active to get rid of the headache—for example, play with or hang out with friends, invite a friend over, call a friend?			
40.8 Stop playing/socializing with his/her friends?			
40.9 Try to keep his/her mind busy—for example by playing computer games, reading, coloring, or writing?			
40.10 Try to figure out what caused the headache?			
40.11 Think or imagine pleasant or good things to keep his/her mind off the headache and to relax?			
40.12 Do anything else?			
Specify: _____			

41. Do your child's headaches regularly prevent him/her from:

		Yes	No	Don't Know
41.1	Playing sports?	[ ]	[ ]	[ ]
41.2	Doing homework?	[ ]	[ ]	[ ]
41.3	Going to parties or movies?	[ ]	[ ]	[ ]
41.4	Doing household chores?	[ ]	[ ]	[ ]
41.5	Playing or socializing with friends?	[ ]	[ ]	[ ]
41.6	Watching television?	[ ]	[ ]	[ ]
41.7	Playing computer games?	[ ]	[ ]	[ ]

42. How negative is the impact of these headaches on your child's life? (circle one)

Not at all   Slight   Moderate   Major

43. What is the hardest part for him/her?

_____

_____

_____

_____

44. How many school days has your child missed because of headaches:
In the past month? ____
44.1 In the past school year? ____

45. How negative is the impact of your child's headaches on your family's life? (circle one)

Not at all   Slight   Moderate   Major

46. What aspect of the headaches is most problematic for your family's life?

_____

_____

47. Do any other members of your family have headaches? If so, please describe:

_____

_____

48. Does any member of your family have a chronic disease or disability? If so, please describe:

_____

_____

Family/Home Information

49. Child's brothers/sisters (list names and ages):

_____

_____

_____

_____

50. Parent's marital status: Married (or common-law) _____ Separated ___

    Divorced _____ Widowed _____ Single _____

51. List people who live in your home:

_____

_____

52. Employment:

    Mother: _____ Father: _____

53. Is your home: in a city____, small town _____, or in the country ____?

54. Has your child had difficulties with any other family member in the past year? If so, describe: _____

_____

School Information

55. Child's school name: _____

56. Child's grade level: _____

57. School program:
    Regular school program _____
    Language immersion program (Specify language: _____)
    Special education program _____
    Other (specify) _____

58. In general, what is your child's attitude about school (teachers, home-work, and activities with peers)? (circle one)

    Very negative   Negative   Neutral   Positive   Very positive

59. In general, how well does your child do in his/her school work? (circle one)

    Failing   Below average   Average   Above average   Outstanding

60. Does your child generally have high expectations for achieving good grades?

    Yes _____ No _____

61. Has your child's school teacher expressed any concerns about your child's grades, abilities, behavior, or social relationships during the past year? If so, what? _____

_____

62. Has your child had any difficulties with other children (e.g., teasing, bullying) during the past year?

Yes _____ No _____

63. Does your child have any difficulties sleeping or eating?

63.1 If yes, please explain:

_____

_____

_____

64. Is there anything about your child or your child's headaches that you think would be important for us discuss?

_____

_____

_____

_____

_____

_____

_____

Parent Interview

Parents do not receive this part of the form. The therapist completes it during the parent interview.

Prior to reviewing the Parent Intake Form with parents assess what they know about the headaches—what they have already been told about the headaches (type, cause and treatment), and whether they are anxious or fearful about the diagnosis or prognosis.

Parent's Beliefs

Migraine ____ Tension ____ Mixed ____ Other ____

    Single etiology ____ Multiple etiology ____

Willingness to consider multiple etiology:

    Reluctant ____ Neutral ____ Very open ____

Emotional distress:

    Concerned ____ Extremely worried ____ Very frightened ____

    Very anxious ____

When reviewing the form, ask follow-up conversational questions as needed to clarify:

Headache Beliefs and Behaviors

Main causes (environmental, stress, both):

_____

_____

_____

_____

Expectations for the future (continuing attacks and increasing disability):

_____

_____

_____

_____

Consistency between parents and among other caregivers in their behaviors when the child develops headache. (Major inconsistencies are often evident when another family member, especially a parent, is disabled by chronic pain or severe headache. The family member with pain-related disability may consistently reinforce the child's disability while other family members may encourage positive coping.)

_____

_____

Consistency in child's headache attacks (severity, duration, disability), depending on location and parent present:

_____

_____

Consistency of pain control plan (drugs and nondrug methods; criteria for use):

_____

Presence of family members who may be pain models (who, how):

_____

_____

Child and Sources of Situation-specific Stress
Child's personality (outgoing, talkative, quiet, shy):

_____

_____

Child's reaction to performing poorly (grades, sports, games with friends):

_____

_____

Child's expectations for achieving (school, sports, social activities, hobbies):

_____

_____

Child's reaction to problems (keeps them inside, easily talks about them):

_____

Person the child is most likely to confide in when having a problem:

_____

Kind of problems the child usually has:

_____

_____

Child's ability to resolve problems (independent, confident, positive solutions—use example of a recent problem encountered and what the child did):

_____

_____

Child's attitudes about school and work habits (organized, completes
assignments at last minute, has difficult courses, teachers, classmates, etc.):

_____

_____

Child's attitudes about friends (has a few close friends or groups, usually
feels accepted or somewhat apart):

_____

_____

For adolescents, inquire about any friend groups that parents may not
approve of, how parents respond, and how they determine curfews (problem-
solving approach, authoritarian approach, combination):

_____

_____

For adolescents, inquire about any parent-child clashes regarding increasing
independence and decision-making (note the issues and current resolution):

_____

_____

Child's activities (solitary activities, organized and coached activities—
assess whether the child has unsupervised recreational time to play and
whether he/she has regular physical exercise):

_____

_____

Child's and parents' attitudes about any organized activities (enjoyment and
performance at competitions, practice sessions):

_____

_____

Time demands for children's activities (low to high, handles varied commitments easily or with difficulty):

_____

_____

Although parents may not be comfortable revealing personal details of their marriage, family, and personal problems at the first appointment, try to assess whether there is any underlying stress within the family that could contribute to the headache (illness of family member, marital tension, financial difficulties, conflict with a particular family member):

_____

_____

_____

_____

Assess whether the child has any other recurrent or chronic pains:

_____

_____

_____

_____

Appendix 3

Parent Information Sheet: Migraine and Tension-Type Headache

Recurrent headache is an extremely common problem for otherwise healthy children and adolescents. Although we are still learning how the physiological mechanisms may differ for migraine and tension-type headaches, extensive research in the past 15 years has taught us a great deal about their causes and about the most effective treatments for children.

THE CAUSES

Recurrent headache is very different than other types of pain children experience. It usually has several causes; often, the longer children have suffered from repeated headache attacks, the more causes can be found.

Although at first we suspected that migraines in children, as in adults, would be caused by certain foods, weather conditions, or activities, we have learned that this is not true for the majority of children. Instead, headaches are caused by many factors; some affect all children and some are unique for an individual child. Our assessment helps us to find the specific causes for your child's headaches.

The most common cause is stress associated with normal childhood activities, especially those related to school, sports participation, and peer relationships. Not recognizing that they are stressed, children often are unable to fully resolve their anxiety, which eventually triggers a headache.

TREATMENT RECOMMENDATIONS

Our treatment goals are to reduce your child's pain during headache attacks and to change the factors that trigger them.

When headache pain is mild, your child should be able to lessen it with distraction, for example, by taking a short break to stretch and move the shoulders and neck, by resting for a few minutes, or by changing activities. Distraction is a simple but powerful tool that can help to end the headache or prevent it from becoming stronger.

When headache pain is moderate-to-strong, your child should use one of the products available to block pain rather than try to tough it out. You probably already use some of the nonsteroidal anti-inflammatory drugs (NSAIDs) that are sold over-the-counter for pain relief. Many can be safely used for children—just make sure you administer the recommended doses according to your child's weight. You could try *(recommend a particular product based on your clinical preference).*

Be consistent in how you respond when your child has a headache. Show your concern, but encourage your child to work with you in following our recommended treatment plan, with the aim of resuming normal activities as soon as possible.

1) Assess the pain level *(recommend a practical pain intensity scale such as the Colored Analogue Scale).*

2) Decide whether to use medication based on the intensity of pain.

3) Help your child to choose a nondrug method (even when you are also administering medications).

4) Praise your child for following the treatment plan.

5) The day after the headache, take a few minutes to talk with your child about what was happening at school, in sports, or with friends. You may recognize what upset your child, even though he or she may not think that anything was the matter. If the situation is still causing some anxiety, then help your child to understand that his or her feelings may have caused the headache and that there are ways to fix the problem so that it will not cause another headache. Teaching your child some practical ways to deal with this situation will help him or her learn how to truly lessen stress.

All pain control during headache is really symptom control. You and your child must deal with the underlying causes to prevent headache; we will help you make these changes.

Index

Locators in *italic* refer to figures.
Locators followed by t refer to tables.

A

Abdominal migraine, 9
Abortive medications, 68, 232
Acetaminophen
  for chronic daily headache, 232
  with codeine, 93, 112
  drug combinations, 112, 232
  exacerbating headache, 122
  for migraine, 67–68, 111–112, 115
  for tension headache, 72, 121
Acupuncture, 147–148
Acute headache
  causes of, 60t
  classification, 58
  generalized, 63
  recurrent, 58
Adolescent Pediatric Pain Tool, 38
Adolescents
  aspirin for migraine, 115
  biofeedback training, 209–210
  classic migraine, 5
  ergotamine for migraine, 115
  group therapy, 144–145
  headache evaluation, 62
  tension headache in, 70
Alcohol consumption, in migraine, 69
Alice-in-Wonderland syndrome, 66–67
Amitriptyline
  adverse effects, 69
  for migraine
    with depression or muscle contraction headache, 119
    prophylactic use, 61, 68, 111, 117, 120
    transformed, 236
  for new daily persistent headache, 237
  for rebound headaches, 122, 233
  for tension headache, 72, 121, 232
Analgesics
  for chronic daily headache, 232
  exacerbating headaches, 122
  indications for, 169
  for migraine, 111–112, 113t

rebound headaches from, 122, 232–233
Aneurysm, vs. ophthalmoplegic migraine, 66
Antidepressants
  for headache prophylaxis, 232
  for tension headache, 72, 121
Antiemetics, 67, 114, 115, 115t
  Antiepileptics, 69, 119
Antihistamines
  for cluster headache, 121
  for headache prophylaxis, 232
  for migraine prophylaxis, 119
Anxiety
  athletic performance, 83, 102
  in headache, 82–83, 85–86
  as headache trigger, 179, 195
  in migraine, 16–17
  from sports and leisure activities, 196
  in tension headache, 71
Aspirin, 112, 115
Astemizole, 121
Atenolol, 117
Athletics. *See* Sports
Attention, 132–133, 207, *208*
Aura, in migraine, 64, 65, 110
Autogenic relaxation training, 139
Avitriptan, 114
Avoidance, in headache prevention, 195

B

Barbiturates, 67–68
Basic Personality Inventory, 86
Basilar artery migraine, 66
Behavior therapy, 137–145. *See also*
    Cognitive-behavioral therapy
  biofeedback in. *See* Biofeedback
  evidence based, 138t
  objectives, 137
  operant conditioning in, 142–143
  overview, 137–138
  relaxation. *See* Relaxation training
  reward in, 143, 213
  for stress-related headache, 4
  structured programs, 213
Behavioral factors, in headache, 20, 95–101, 96t

Behavioral pain scales, 30–31
Benign focal epileptiform discharges (BFED), 63g
Beta blockers, 117–119, 232
Biofeedback. *See also* Relaxation training
    for chronic daily headache, 230–232
    clinical trials, 87–88
    efficacy of, 141–142
    electromyographic, 140
    in headache management, 209
    home-based, 145
    for migraine, 69, 231
    with relaxation, 231
    skin temperature, 140
    training process, 140–141, 141t
Braid, James, 133
Brain imaging, 132
Brain mapping, 63
Butalbital, with acetaminophen, 232

C
Caffeine, 69, 112
Calcitonin gene-related peptide (CGRP), 110
Calcium channel blockers
    adverse effects, 68
    for headache prophylaxis, 232
    for migraine prophylaxis, 68, 119
Calendars, in pain assessment, 47, *48,* 170, 187
CAPA (Child and Adolescent Psychiatric Assessment), 228
Caregivers, 97, 98, 195
Carnrick, 68
Case studies
    chronic daily headache, 235–237
    disability behaviors and stress resolution, 98–100
    feedback interventions, 173–174
    headache triggers, 80–82
Cayenne, for headache, 153
Cerebral blood flow, in migraine, 226
CGRP (calcitonin gene-related peptide), 110
CHI (Children's Headache Interview). *See* Children's Headache Interview (CHI)
Child and Adolescent Psychiatric Assessment (CAPA), 228
Child Behavior Checklist, 234
Childhood Comprehensive Pain Questionnaire, 43
Children. *See also* Adolescents; Infants; Preschool children

analgesic dependency, 96
early life headache predictors, 14–15
group therapy efficacy, 144
headache behaviors, 95–98
headache impact on, 22
headache management plan
    consistent use of, 210–211
    development of, 204–206, *205*
    pain assessment in, 29–56
    pain control instruction
    cognitive, 135–137, 136t
    nondrug, 207–210
    pain plasticity in, 243
Children's Headache Assessment Scale, 43
Children's Headache Interview (CHI), 253–266
    accompanying symptoms checklist, 52t
    behavioral factors, 193, 194t
    in cognitive-behavioral therapy, 187, 197
    development of, 43, 84
    in educational interventions, 164
    headache location diagram, *47*
    questions
    disability, 53t
    frequency, 45t
    pain intensity and affect, 46t
    stressor identification, 197
Children's Headache Questionnaire, 43
Chiropractic manipulation
    adverse effects, 150
    basis for, 149
    for headache, 149–150
Chlorpromazine (CPZ), 114, 115
Chronic daily headache, 221–241. *See also* Recurrent headache
    adult vs. pediatric, 224–225
    biofeedback for, 230–232
    case studies, 235–237
    characteristics, 222–225
    classification, 223–224, *224*
    conceptual framework, 234
    diagnosis, 233–235
    as diagnostic category, 221–222
    disability from, 227
    drug therapy, 232–233
    emotional and behavioral disturbances, 227–229
    etiology, 223–224
    interventions for, 229–233
    interview in, 234
    pathophysiology, 225–226
    physical examination, 234

prevalence in children, 222
psychological assessment, 234
relaxation therapy, 229–230
research needs, 238
summary, 237–238
team approach to, 235
terminology, 70
treatment of, 234–235
Chronic nonprogressive headache. *See* Tension headache
Chronic paroxysmal hemicrania, 74
Chronic progressive headache
  causes of, 60t
  classification, 58–59
  differential diagnosis, 70
Clinical trials
  causative factor treatments, 86–88
  design of, 250
  educational interventions, 160–162
  headache measures, 42t
  pain diaries in, 39
  research needs, 250
Cluster headaches, 73, 121–122
Codeine, 112, 115, 122
Cognitive development
  in pain assessment, 32, 34
  in pain conceptualization, 226
Cognitive factors
  in headache etiology, 92–93, 94–95, 190–193
  in pain control, 93–94
  in recurrent headache, 90, 92t, 92–95
Cognitive therapy, 130–137. *See also* Cognitive-behavioral therapy
  adult bias and efficacy in children, 136
  analogy in, 136–137
  attention and distraction, 131–132, 207, *208*
  child instruction in pain control, 135–137, 136t
  counseling, 131–132
  evidence based, 130t, 130–131
  goals of, 130
  group approach in children, 144
  guided imagery, 133, 207–208
  hypnosis, 133–135
Cognitive-behavioral therapy, 183–219.
    See also Behavior therapy; Cognitive therapy
  biofeedback in, 231–232
  child-centered focus, 184
  clinical trials, 87–88
  emotional response to headache, 214–216

feedback appointment, 198, 200–201
framework for, 185t
headache causes and contributing factors, evaluation of, 189–198
individual vs. group, 144
individualized program, 185
informed consent in, 214
nondrug pain control methods, 207–210
outcome evaluation, 216–217
pain assessment in, 185–189, 201–204
pain profiles, 189, *189*
parents
  behaviors of, 212–213
  information for, 186t, 186–187
  interviews, 198
  support for therapy, 218–219
problem-solving techniques, 214–215
rationale for, 183–184
realistic performance expectations, adoption of, 215–216
stress management, 214–215
structured behavioral management, 213
therapy sessions
  beliefs about headache, 206–207
  consistent headache management, 210–211
  description of, 204–206
  goals, 204–205, *205*
  headache management plan, development of, 204–206, *205*
  parent and child behaviors, 210–213
tiered approach, 145
utilization, 137, 143–144
Cohort studies, 247
Cold compresses, 146
Colored Analogue Scale (CAS), 2, 38, *50*, 173, 254
Communication, in pain assessment, 32, 34
Comorbid headache, 224, 225, 235
Complex migraine, 65
Computed tomography (CT), 63
Computer usage, 78
Confusional migraine, 66
Coping strategies, 100–101, 226
Counseling, 131–132
Cranial sacral therapy, 150
Cyclooxygenase (COX) inhibitors, 111
Cyproheptadine
  adverse effects, 69
  for migraine prophylaxis, 61, 68, 111, 119, 120

D

Depression
in migraine, 16–17, 64
in tension headache, 71
Diagnostic and Statistical Manual of
Mental Disorders 1994 (DSM-IV),
197
Diaries, headache. *See* Pain diaries and
logs
Dichloralphenazone, 68
Dihydroergotamine (DHE)
contraindications, 232
for migraine, 112–113, 115, 232
serotonin receptor activation, 61
Dimenhydrinate, 114, 115
Disability
assessment of, 52, 53t
excessive, 177–178, 217
headache-related, 2, 3–4
learned, 97–100, 195
medical consultation and, 22
parental modeling of, 212–213
protective vs. disabling behaviors, 211
reinforcement of, 97–100, 195, 211–
213
stress case studies, 98–100
Distraction, 94, 132–133, 207, *208*
Divalproex, 117, 120
Drug therapy
child reliance on, 93
for chronic daily headache, 232–233
dependence on specific analgesics, 96
habituation to analgesics, 232–233
history in pain assessment, 192, 192t
inconsistent administration of, 193
parent education concerning, 169
parental beliefs and, 93–94
prophylactic, indications for, 232
research needs, 247
DSM-IV (Diagnostic and Statistical
Manual of Mental Disorders 1994),
197

E

Early life factors, 14–15
Electroencephalography (EEG), 63, 67
Eletriptan, 114
Emergency room, migraine treatment in,
116
Emotional factors, in headache, 49, *51,*
101–104, 103t, 195–197, 214–216
Encephalopathy, toxic, 66
Environmental factors
in headache, 21, 78–80, 104, 200–201
in migraine, 14

vs. stress, 167–168
Epidemiologic studies, 9, 10t–11t, 12–
13, 246–247
Epilepsy equivalent, 67
Ergot derivatives, 68, 112–113
Ergotamine, 73, 112, 115
Evidence-based care
behavior therapy, 138t
clinical care as, 245–246
cognitive therapy, 130t, 130–131
Evoked potentials, 63
Exercise
as headache trigger, 78–79
reduced participation from headache, 86
for tension headache, 72

F

Facial Affective Scale (FAS)
administration of, 255
headache pain diaries, *18–20*
in pain assessment, *51*
for pain intensity, 38
Family
adaptive role of headache, 217–218
early life factors in headache, 14–15
in headache prevalence, 23
longitudinal studies, 14–15
migraine risk factors, 14, 64
stress factors, 102–103, 197
Feedback
case studies, 173–174
in cognitive-behavioral therapy, 198,
200–201
goals for, 200
parent interviews, 198
as therapeutic intervention, 160–162,
164, 165t, 167, 180, 245
Feverfew, 153
Flunarizine, 117, 119, 120
Foods
as headache triggers, 78–79, 179
in migraine, 64, 69, 152–153

G

Gabapentin, 119, 120
Gender
chronic daily headache and, 228
headache frequency, 58
headache prevalence, 12, 23
Genetics, 14, 109–110, 225
Group therapy
cognitive-behavioral, 144
efficacy, 144–145
vs. individual therapy, 144–145
Guided imagery, 133, 207–208, 229

H

Hahnemann, Samuel, 151
Headache
  activity, 41, 53, 249
  acute. *See* Acute headache
  acute recurrent, 58
  adaptive role within family, 217–218
  age at onset, 23
  assessment of. *See* Pain assessment
  behavioral disorders and, 20
  characteristics, 2–3, 256–259
  chronic nonprogressive. *See* Tension
    headache
  chronic progressive, 58–59, 60t, 70
  classification, 5–8, 58–60, 109
  cluster, 73, 121–122
  diaries. *See* Pain diaries and logs
  differential diagnosis, 57–76
  disability. *See* Disability
  drug therapy, 109–127
    parental beliefs and, 93–94
    prophylactic, 232
    research needs, 247
  early life factors in, 14–15
  emotion support for, 97
  etiology, 3–5, 92–93, 206
  evaluation of, 62–63
  exertional, 74
  from facial and cranial disorders, 122
  family history in, 23
  financial impact of, 247
  frequency, 2, 57–58
  history, 57–58
  impact on children, 22, 262–263
  intensity and duration, 2
  laboratory tests, 62–63
  logs. *See* Pain diaries and logs
  management of
    beliefs about, 93–94
    child-centered, 153, 184, 243–244
    clinical challenges, 244–246
    evaluation, 53
    outcome measures, 250
    research needs, 246–250
    undertreatment, 93
  measures. *See* Pain assessment
  migraine. *See* Migraine
  mixed syndrome. *See* Mixed headache
    syndrome
  muscle contraction. *See* Tension
    headache
  natural course of, 247
  nondrug therapies, 129–158
    behavioral methods, 137–145
    cognitive methods, 130–137

  cognitive-behavioral approach,
    207–210
  homeopathy, 151–152
  individual vs. group therapy, 144–
    145
  multimodal, 144, 153–154
  naturopathic medicine, 152–153
  physical techniques, 145–151, 146t
  research needs, 247–248
  summary, 153–154
  overview, 1
  pain quality, 50
  pathophysiology, 60–61
  prevalence, 1–2, 9, 10t–11t, 12–13,
    246–247
  psychological factors in, 15–21
  recurrent. *See* Recurrent headache
  risk factors, 13–21
  school absence rates and, 22
  somatic complaints and, 17, 19
  stress and. *See* Stress
  from substance withdrawal, 122
  symptoms, 50–52, 52t
  syndrome duration, 45
  temporal patterns, 58, *59*
  tension-type. *See* Tension headache
  triggers. *See* Triggers
Heat
  compresses, 146
  as headache trigger, 78–79
Hemicrania, 57
  chronic paroxysmal, 74
Hemicrania continua, 74, 223
Hemiplegic migraine, 65
Herbal medicines, 148, 153
Homeopathy, 151–152
5-HT (serotonin receptors), 61, 110–111
Humidity, 78–79
Hypnosis
  child instruction in, 208–209
  for headache management, 133–135,
    208–209
  for migraine, 134–135
  self-induced, for chronic daily
    headache, 229
  suggestion in, 134, 135
  theories of, 135

I

Ibuprofen
  for chronic daily headache, 232
  exacerbating headache, 122
  for migraine, 67, 112
  for tension headache, 72, 121
Imagery, guided, 133, 207–208, 229

Indomethacin
    for headache, 73–74
    for hemicrania continua, 74, 223
Infants, migraine in, 7, 12
Informed consent, 214
International Headache Society (IHS)
    diagnostic criteria, 58, 109, 222
        for migraine, 6t, 6–7
        for tension headache, 8, 8t
Interviews. *See also* Children's Head-
        ache Interview (CHI)
    in chronic daily headache assessment,
        234
    in pain assessment, 39, 41, 44, 164,
        187
    parent intake form questions, 277–280
    questions, 45t, 46t
Isometheptene, 68, 232

K
Ketoprofen, 121
Ketorolac, 121

L
Laboratory tests, 62–63
Lamotrigine, 119
Light, as headache trigger, 78–79
Listening, analogy, 136–137
Lithium, 73, 122
Logs, headache. *See* Pain diaries
Longitudinal studies, 246, 247
Loratadine, 121

M
Macropsia, 66
Magnetic resonance imaging (MRI), 63,
    70
Massage, 148–149
Maternal emotions, 17
Mental disorders, 228
Meperidine, 121
Mesmer, Franz, 133
Methylarginine HCl, 110
Methysergide
    adverse effects, 120
    for cluster headache, 73
    for migraine, 61, 111
Metoclopramide, 114
Metoprolol, 117
Micropsia, 66
Midrin, 68
Migraine
    abdominal, 9
    acupuncture for, 148
    acute, management of, 111–115

in adolescents, 5
age at onset, 12
with aura, 64, 65, 110
biofeedback for, 69, 231
biological basis, 109–111
cerebral blood flow in, 226
characteristics, 2–3
chiropractic for, 149
cyclic, 74
depression in, 64
diagnostic criteria, 5–7, 58
    adult vs. children, 6–7
    age factors, 7
    of International Headache Society,
        6t, 6–7
    time factors, 7
differential diagnosis, 64–67
    Alice-in-Wonderland syndrome,
        66–67
    basilar artery, 66
    common, 65
    common vs. classic, 5
    complex, 65
    confusional, 66
    epilepsy equivalent, 67
    hemiplegic, 65
    ophthalmoplegic, 65–66
    variants, 66
drug therapy
    for acute attacks, 111–115
    analgesics, 67–69, 111–112, 113t,
        115, 232
    antiemetics, 114, 115t
    ergot derivatives, 112–113
    pediatric studies, 233
    prophylactic, 61, 68–69, 111, 116–
        120, 117t, 118t
    serotonin receptor agonists, 113–
        114
emergency room treatment protocols,
    116
environmental factors, 14
episodic, 226, 236
evaluation of, 64–67
as familial disorder, 13–14, 64
familial hemiplegic, 109
foods in, 64, 69, 152–153
frequency of, 58
gender in, 12
genetics, 109–110
history, 57–58
hypnosis for, 134–135
individual vs. group therapy, 144–145
in infants, 7, 12
ion channel regulation, 110

learned triggers, 80–82
management of, 67–69
  guidelines, 114–115
  multimodal, 244
  nonpharmacologic, 69
  prophylaxis guidelines, 120
  protocols for severe attacks, 115, *116*
menstrual, 112
multifactorial etiology, 105
natural history, 12–13
neurovascular hypothesis of, 60–61
pain characteristics, 5
pain pathogenesis, 110
parent information sheets, 281–282
pathogenesis, 60–61
placebo in, 120
prevalence, 9, 10t–11t, 12–13, 23
prognosis, 69
psychological factors, 15–17
remission rates, 12–13
sine hemicrania, 67
situational factors in, 84–86
temporal factors, 64
torticollis in, 66
transformed, 69, 223, 226, 235, 236
triggers for, 64
in twins, 14, 109
vertigo in, 66
vomiting in, 66
in young children, 5, 12
Mixed headache syndrome
  classification, 58, *59,* 60
  incidence, 64
  management, 73
Models
  of pediatric pain, 227
  for recurrent headache, 88–90, *89,* 226–227
Monosodium glutamate, 69
MRI (magnetic resonance imaging), 63, 70
Muscle tenderness, pericranial, 225
Musculoskeletal abnormalities, 225

N
Naproxen
  for menstrual migraine, 112, 119
  for migraine prophylaxis, 117
  for transformed migraine, 236
Naratriptan, 114
Narcotic analgesics, 67–68, 112, 115
Naturopathic medicine, 152–153
Neuroimaging, 70
Neurokinin A, 110

Neurological examination, 62
Neurontin, 119
Neuropeptide Y, 120
Neuropeptides, 110
New daily persistent headache
  case studies, 237
  diagnostic criteria, 223
  treatment difficulties, 235
Nitric oxide synthase inhibitors, 110
Nitrites, 69
Noise, 78
Nonsteroidal anti-inflammatory drugs (NSAIDs)
  for acute migraine attacks, 67–68, 111, 112, 115
  for migraine prophylaxis, 68, 119
  for tension headache, 72
Nystagmus, 66

O
Occipital neuralgia, 73
Operant conditioning, 142–143
Ophthalmoplegic migraine, 65–66
Opioids. *See* Narcotic analgesics
Oral contraceptives, 65
Osteopathic medicine, 150–151
Oxygen therapy, 73

P
Pain
  intensity
    assessment of, 49, *50*
    child terminology for, 34
    rating scales, 35, 36t–37t, 38–39
  perception, 89
  plasticity, 243
Pain assessment, 29–56
  accompanying symptoms, 50–52, 52t
  in adolescents, 62
  calendars, 47, *48*
  child ratings vs. parent ratings, 41
  child-focused, 243
  in children, 29–32
  clinical research, 54
  cognitive development and, 32, 34, 226
  in cognitive-behavioral therapy, 185–189
  in diagnosis and treatment, 53–54, 245
  diaries and logs. *See* Pain diaries and logs
  in feedback intervention, 162, 164
  headache characteristics, 43–53, 202
    activity, defined, 41
    duration, 48–49

Pain assessment: Headache characteristics *(cont.)*
　　frequency, 46–47
　　location, 45–46, *47*
　　natural history, 202
　　headache measures
　　　affect, 49, *51*
　　　behavioral, 30–31
　　　classification, 30
　　　criteria for, 30
　　　pain quality, 50
　　　in pediatric clinical trials, 42t
　　　physiological, 31
　　　psychological, 32, *33*
　　　self-report, 54
　　intensity scales, 35, 36t–37t, 38–39, 49, *50*
　　interpretation of ratings, 34–35
　　interviews. *See* Interviews
　　medication usage, 192
　　pain profiles, 189, *189*
　　personal history, 203
　　questionnaires, 43
　　report contents, 201–204
　　self-report tools, 54
　　syndrome duration, 45
　　treatment evaluation, 53
　　triggers. *See* Triggers
Pain diaries and logs
　　behavioral factors, 193–194
　　in chronic daily headache, 234
　　examples, *18–20, 40, 171, 188*
　　utilization, 39, 41, 170–172
Papilledema, 70
Parent information sheet, 187
Parent intake form, 267–276
　　in cognitive-behavioral therapy, 187
　　headache etiology questions, 191t
　　interview questions, 277–280
　　medication usage questions, 192t
　　utilization, 162, 164
Parents
　　behavior of, and child headaches, 95–98, 100–101, 210–213
　　beliefs of
　　　headache etiology, 92–93
　　　pain control, 93–94
　　　stress, 94–95
　　cognitive-behavioral therapy, 210–213
　　discrepancy with child pain ratings, 41
　　failure to recognize child stress, 100
　　fear about child headaches, 197
　　feedback interviews, 198
　　headache treatment plans, 169

　　inconsistent response to children's headaches, 3–5, 85, 93–94, 96–97, 169, 193
　　interview questions, 277–280
　　modeling of disability, 212–213
　　psychological factors in child headache, 17
　　reinforcement of disability, 97–100, 177–178, 211–213, 218
　　treatment information for, 166–170, 167t, 281–282
　　undermining treatment efficacy, 218–219
Passionflower, 153
Peer relationships
　　chronic daily headache and, 227
　　recurrent headache and, 196
　　stress in, 101–102, 203
Perceptual disorders, in migraine, 66
Performance expectations
　　realistic, 215–216
　　stress-inducing, 97–98, 102, 168, 196
Personality traits, 15–16, 203
Photophobia, 236
Physical techniques, 72, 145–151, 146t
Physiological pain scales, 31
Pizotifen, 111, 119, 120
Placebo effect, 120
Preschool children, 15
Primary care providers, 244–245
Problem solving, 131, 214–215
Prochlorperazine, 114, 115
Progressive muscle relaxation (PMR), 138–140
Propranolol
　　adverse effects, 68, 118
　　for migraine prophylaxis, 68, 117, 118–119, 120
Prostaglandins, 111
Protriptyline, 72
Pseudotumor cerebri, 70
Psychiatric disorders, 228
Psychogenic headache. *See* Tension headache
Psychological factors
　　in chronic daily headache, 226–228
　　evaluation of, 63
　　in headache, 15–21, 82–83
　　in migraine, 15–17
　　pain measures, 32, *33*

Q
Questionnaires
　　Childhood Comprehensive Pain Questionnaire, 43

Children's Headache Questionnaire, 43
for headache diagnosis, 61t

R

Rebound headaches, 122, 232–233
Recurrent headache. *See also* Chronic daily headache
acupuncture for, 148
acute, 58
behavioral factors, 95–101, 96t, 193–195, 194t
biofeedback for, 231
child characteristics, 84–86
clinical population data, 104
clinical trials, 86–88
cognitive factors, 90, 92t, 92–95, 190–193
cognitive-behavioral therapy, 87–88, 183–219
educational interventions
    case studies, 173–174
    clinical trials, 160–162
    diagnostic information, 164–166, 165t
    feedback in, 160–162, 164, 167, 180
    follow-up visits, 171–173
    headache assessment, 162, 164
    medication education, 169
    objectives, 167
    parent intake form, 162, 164
    prospective headache monitoring, 170–173
    rationale, 159–162
    specialized pain management, 174–175
    stress identification and management, 167–169
    time factors, 160
    treatment information for parents, 166–170, 180
    treatment plan, *163*, 180
emotional factors, 101–104, 195–197
etiology, 77–107, 166t, *199*
excessive disability from, 177–178
as major health problem, 244
models, 88–90, *89, 91*, 226–227
multifactorial nature of, 83–88, *91*
multimodal therapy, 160, 180
parent information sheets, 281–282
parental response to, 3, 85, 191
pathophysiology, 225
situational factors in, 85–86, *163*, 195

temporal patterns, 196
treatment strategies, 159–181
triggers, 78–83, 177
vs. somatic pain complaint, 176
Relaxation training. *See also* Biofeedback
autogenic, 139
for chronic daily headache, 229–230
efficacy, 139–140, 230
for headache, 138–140, 209
methods, 138
for migraine, 69
progressive muscle relaxation, 138–140
school vs. clinical settings, 230
Research studies
challenges in, 246–250
cost-benefit analysis, 250
pain assessment, 54
Reward, 143, 213
Reye's syndrome, 112
Riboflavin (vitamin B_2), 119
Rizatriptan, 114

S

School attendance
chronic daily headache and, 227
excessive headache disability and, 177
headache and absence rates, 22
learned disability and, 97, 100
stress and, 97–98, 100, 102
Schools, relaxation therapy in, 230
Schoolwork, as headache trigger, 78
Sedatives, 67
Selective serotonin reuptake inhibitors (SSRIs), 72
Self-help training, 145
Self-hypnosis, 229
Serotonin, 120
Serotonin (5-HT) antagonists, 61, 119
Serotonin receptor agonists, 113–114, 120
Serotonin receptors (5-HT), 61, 110–111
Situational factors
in recurrent headache, 85–86, 101–103
tissue damage and pain, 89
Sleep, 63, 94
Sonophobia, 236
Sports, stress from participation, 83, 97–98, 102, 168, 196
SSRIs (selective serotonin reuptake inhibitors), 72
Steroids, 73

Stress
  anxiety about headache etiology, 197
  cognitive factors in headache, 94
  common sources of, 101t
  coping strategies, 100–101
  familial, 102–103, 197, 203
  in headache etiology, 3–4, 82–83, 85–
      86, 89, *89,* 104–105
  management of, 131, 168–169, 215
  peer relationships, 101–102, 203
  recognition of, 100
  relevance in children, 94–95
  school-related, 100, 102, 190–191,
      196, 203
  situation-specific, 101–103, 105, 131,
      214
  from sports and leisure activities, 83,
      97–98, 102, 168, 196
  in tension headache, 71
  vs. environmental factors, 167–168
Substance P, 110, 120
Suggestion, 134, 135, 208–209
Sumatriptan
  for migraine, 68, 111, 113–114, 115,
      232
  for rebound headaches, 233
  serotonin receptor activation, 61

T
Team care, 235
Temporomandibular joint dysfunction,
    73
TENS (transcutaneous electrical nerve
    stimulation), 147
Tension headache
  in adolescents, 70
  causes of, 60t
  chiropractic for, 149–150
  classification of, 59
  clinical features, 70–71
  daily. *See* Chronic daily headache
  definition of, 58
  diagnostic criteria, 8, 8t
  differential diagnosis, 70–73
  drug therapy, 72, 121
  evaluation of, 62
  management of, 72, 121–122
  multifactorial etiology, 105
  multimodal treatment, 244
  muscle contraction in, 226
  muscle tenderness in, 120–121, 225
  pain characteristics, 5
  parent information sheets, 281–282
  pathogenesis, 70

  pathophysiology, 120–121
  prevalence, 223
  psychological factors, 71–72
  situational factors, 84–86
  symptoms, 71
  terminology, 59, 70
Thermal stimulation, 146
Timolol, 117
Tomography, computed (CT), 63
Topiramate, 121–122
Torticollis, paroxysmal, 66
Trance state, hypnotic, 135
Transcutaneous electrical nerve
    stimulation (TENS), 147
Transformed migraine, 69, 223, 226,
    235, 236
Trazodone, 119
Tricyclic antidepressants, 72, 119
Trigeminal vascular system, 61, 110
Trigger point therapy, 148, 149
Triggers, 78–83
  anxiety and, 179
  case studies, 80–82
  Children's Headache Interview
      questions, 259–260
  emotional and psychological, 82–83
  environmental, 78–80
  learned, 79–82, 177, 178–179, 179t
  for migraine, 64
  multifactorial, 105
  parent intake form questions, 191t
  summary of, 78
Triptans, 111, 113–114
Twins, 14, 109, 225
Tyramine, 69

V
Valerian, 153
Valproate, 119, 120
Vasoactive intestinal peptide, 120
Vasodilatation, 110
Verapamil, 61
Verbal scales, 38–39
Vertigo, paroxysmal, 66
Visceral manipulation therapy, 150–151
Visual Analogue Scale (VAS), *18–20,* 38
Visual modulation therapy, 146–147
Vitamin B$_2$ (riboflavin), 119
Vomiting, 66

W
Willow, for headache, 153
Word Graphic Rating Scale (WGRS),
    38–39